الاستنباط من البحرالعميق

AL- ISTINBÃTU MIN AL BAHRI AL A'MÌQ

DROPS FROM THE DEEP OCEAN

REFLECTIONS ON THE QUR'AN

Adab with Allah ﷻ, the Quran, the Sunnah of Rasulullah ﷺ for a True Hope

with a focus on

- ▶ Contemporary Renderings
- ▶ Psychological Explorations
- ▶ Western Discourses
- ▶ Lexical Analysis

VOLUME 4

Dr. M. Yunus Kumek

Address to the Islamic Religious Scholars & Philosophers

Cover Photo by Y. Kumek, Alexandria, Egypt, January 12, 2019.

Medina Houseʳ
publishing

www.medinahouse.org
170 Manhattan Ave, Po. Box 63
New York 14215
contact@medinahouse.org

Copyright © 2021 by Medina Houseʳ Publishing

ISBN 978-1-950979-24-0

Published in the United States of America.

TABLE OF CONTENTS

VOLUME 4

بِسْمِ اللّٰهِ الرَّحْمٰنِ الرَّحِيمِ[1]

الْحَمْدُ لِلّٰهِ رَبِّ الْعَالَمِينَ[2]

اللّٰهُمَّ صَلِّ عَلَى سَيِّدِنَا وَ حَبِيْبِنَا وَ مَوْلَنَا مُحَمَّدٌ[3]

What is the Qurān?

The Qurān is the ummul kitāb, the main Book. Rasulullah ﷺ is the Ummin nabiyy, the main and pure Prophet ﷺ. Makkah is the ummul Qurā, the main city. The word umm is like a mother. The word umm is the source. The word umm is universal and inclusive.

Style of the Qurān

The Qurān has a unique style. It combines spirituality, legality, ethics, virtue, logic, emotions, psychology and other sciences named and unnamed by humans. It is not a mere legal book. The legal books tend to detach their readers with their technical and cold words. Yet, the Qurān flows so gently with the legal lines between the lines of tafakkur, creation, and stories.

As the Qurān is engaging the person with the overwhelming and bursting A'zamah of Allah ﷻ. Then, a breeze comes with the stories to give respite for the limited humans, for us. In this sense, the motifs of the Qurān is so colorful, dynamic, active, vivid, lively, glowing, sparkling, intense, energetic, operational and effective. Therefore, one can review the life of Rasulullah ﷺ, Sahabah (رضي الله عنهم), Tabeîn, and other pious salaf (رحمت الله عليهم) that once they start the Qurān, they don't want to stop. They don't want to stop the sweet moments with Allah ﷻ.

In this sense, the style of the Qurān is very attractive, engaging, engulfing, absorbing, charming, surrounding, winning, captivating, and pleasing. Therefore, the Qurān refutes the early Arabs' claims about the Qurān being magic/sihr or a powerful poem and the Prophet ﷺ

---

1. In the name of Allah, the Entirely Merciful, the Especially Merciful.
2. [All] praise is [due] to Allah, Lord of the worlds.
3. O Allah, bless our master, our beloved, and Mawlana Muhammed (PBUH).

being the magician/sāhir or a good poet as early Arabs before Islam were experts in language, poetry, and literature. In the Qurān, there is a constant repetition reminding the person that this book is not a magic, a poem, imaginative, whimsical, deceitful, false, or deceptive. Yet, immediately, the first line after the Sûrah Fatiha starts with this very strong statement in Sûrah Baqarah that the Qurān is authentic, precise, strong, true, real, certain, firm, factual, genuine, objective, accurate, and exact.

Qurān is a teacher for all level of learners. As most of the people may not have expertise or their education level and intellectual sophistication can be average, the Qurān can address this general audience initially and primarily with its style. Yet at the same time, the experts of each field receive its true and authentic openings for their disciplines.

Usûl-Methodology

One should remember in any of the renderings of the Qurān that one should primarily consider the initial and primary meanings through the methodology of muffasirûn. In this methodology, the understanding of riwāyah[4], narrations as explained by Rasulullah ﷺ with their sabab-ul-nuzul[5], and early salaf of the sahabah and tabeîn precedes the engagements of dirayah, using other analysis in the contexts of intellect, time and context.

One of the ways of reaching out to the meanings and emphasized themes in the Qurān is to trace and analyze the same word within the ayah, page, Sûrah and/or in the entire Qurān. Especially with the language rules of sarf and nahw, a word with different conjugations and different possible positions in a sentence or few lines can reveal different meanings.

This method is also used in academic articles in social sciences and other scientific engagements. Most of the time, the academic deciding body of editors review the article if there is a recurrent theme. In other words, does the author use the same key concepts in different parts of the article to prove his or her point? The more the author uses different perspectives or approaches to converge to the same theme with some

---

4. Narration.
5. The reason they were sent down { the narrations}.

key words or themes, then the more the article becomes academic, scientific and generalizable leading to a possible theory in that field.

The methodology of using the same key concepts through the entire text establishes harmony, strength, and each piece supporting each other, like the bricks of a building making a very strong and robust concrete that cannot be destroyed. If there is a tiny piece or fault that may not seem to fit, then this can be a source of destruction for a building or a criticism for a text or an article. When a person submits an article to an academic journal, one of the rejection points can be this non-uniformity or conflicting pieces within the text. The Qurān openly states this perspective as:

أَفَلاَ يَتَدَبَّرُونَ الْقُرْآنَ وَلَوْ كَانَ مِنْ عِندِ غَيْرِ اللّهِ لَوَجَدُواْ فِيهِ اخْتِلاَفًا كَثِيرًا6 {النساء/82}

الْحَمْدُ لِلَّهِ الَّذِي أَنزَلَ عَلَى عَبْدِهِ الْكِتَابَ وَلَمْ يَجْعَل لَّهُ عِوَجَا7 {الكهف/1}

The word اخْتِلاَفًا with the meaning of conflicting can have a negative disposition when the case is related with the uniformity of a text which indicates strength, clarity and authenticity of the knowledge.

On the other hand, the word اخْتِلاَفًا with the meaning of change or variation can have a positive disposition when the case is related with the diversity and variety as mentioned:

لَمْ تَرَ أَنَّ اللَّهَ أَنزَلَ مِنَ السَّمَاء مَاء فَأَخْرَجْنَا بِهِ ثَمَرَاتٍ مُّخْتَلِفًا أَلْوَانُهَا وَمِنَ الْجِبَالِ جُدَدٌ بِيضٌ وَحُمْرٌ مُّخْتَلِفٌ أَلْوَانُهَا وَغَرَابِيبُ سُودٌ8 {فاطر/27} وَمِنَ النَّاسِ وَالدَّوَابِّ وَالْأَنْعَامِ مُخْتَلِفٌ أَلْوَانُهُ كَذَلِكَ إِنَّمَا يَخْشَى اللَّهَ مِنْ عِبَادِهِ الْعُلَمَاء إِنَّ اللَّهَ عَزِيزٌ غَفُورٌ9 {فاطر/28}

Similarly, one should review and analyze the relationship between the Sûrah names, numerology, and even the relationship with the letters. There have been studies, books, articles written traditionally trying to

---

6. Then do they not reflect upon the Qura'n? If it had been from [any] other than Allah, they would have found within it much contradiction.
7. [All] praise is [due] to Allah, who has sent down upon his Servant [Muhammed (PBUH)] the Book and has not made therein any deviance.
8. Do you not see that Allah sends down rain from the sky, and we produce thereby fruits of varying colors? And in the mountains are tracts, white and red of varying shades and [some] extremely black.
9. And among people and moving creatures and graving livestock are various colors similarly. Only those fear Allah, from among His servants, who have knowledge. Indeed, Allah is Exalted in Might and Forgiving.

engage different perspectives. Yet, one can always update and re-analyze the Qurān with the context and tools of the time and culture.

For example, the ayah {المؤمنون/52} وَإِنَّ هَذِهِ أُمَّتُكُمْ أُمَّةً وَاحِدَةً وَأَنَا رَبُّكُمْ فَاتَّقُونِ [10] can indicate the necessity of taqwa with Allah ﷻ and accordingly a treatment with all humanity as a result of this taqwa as mentioned وَإِنَّ[11] هَذِهِ أُمَّتُكُمْ أُمَّةً وَاحِدَةً وَأَنَا رَبُّكُمْ فَاتَّقُونِ. This is the requirement of being real believers as the name of the Sûrah is المؤمنون[12]. This taqwa[13] should be there as part of being true believers المؤمنون at all times, as there are 52 weeks in a year and this ayah number is 52. Imān as a mumin necessitates taqwa. Imān necessitates continuity and istiqamah. In this example, one can see relationship with the number of the ayah, the content, and the name of the Sûrah. This example is not one but many in the Qurān.

Now, one can argue that this rendering is subjective. Yet, one should know that this the Book of Allah (ﷻ), Al-Bāqi[14]. There can be infinite true and objective derivations, istinbāt[15], from the Qurān as long as they are not contradictory to the usûl, methodology, deduction of knowledge, the main frames as set by the Qurān, the Sunnah/Hadith and basic frame work as established by the pious salaf.

When analyzing the Qurān, sometimes a clue can be given with a letter, a word or a concept through a mental or emotional engagement of the reader. Then, the reader is set in a very perplexed and curious disposition to trace these meanings in order to derive, make istinbāt with different disciplines of Islamic theology such fiqh[16], tasawwuf[17], logic, and others as well as with the fields of social and natural sciences.

We can review the ayah وَالَّذِينَ يَرْمُونَ أَزْوَاجَهُمْ وَلَمْ يَكُنْ لَهُمْ شُهَدَاءُ إِلَّا أَنفُسُهُمْ فَشَهَادَةُ أَحَدِهِمْ أَرْبَعُ شَهَادَاتٍ بِاللَّهِ إِنَّهُ لَمِنَ الصَّادِقِينَ[18] {النور/6}. This ayah is about the legal rulings of the process about a person who wants to set a case against their spouse for the issues of chastity. The process includes finding four

10. And indeed this, your religion, is one religion, and I am your lord, so fear Me.
11. And indeed this, your religion, is one religion, and I am your lord, so fear Me.
12. The believers.
13. Fear of Allah.
14. The Everlasting.
15. Derivations
16. Islamic Law.
17. Islamic Mysticism.
18. And those who accuse their wives [of adultery] and have no witnesses except themselves- then the witness of one of them [shall be] four testimonies [swearing] by Allah that indeed, he is of the truthful.

witnesses. If they cannot find four witnesses, then this person witnesses and take oath against him or herself four times in front of Allah ﷻ.

Although this is a legal ruling as explicitly stated, one can analyze the possibility of this case. In the case of logic or rationality, these cases are rare or impossible to find in a normal society. Therefore, one can ask then, why this is set as a ruling? One of the answers is that the person is discouraged to engage oneself in these cases to implement or pursue things related exposing the faults of others.

On the other hand, one can analyze the style and preferences of the words in the above ayahs to support this embedded essence and theme. For example, the word يَرْمُونَ[19] is used instead of other words in order to discourage the person from this act. This word can have a negative meaning of slandering others. The person is again reminded the one who is accused is not a criminal but their own wifes. Both the words أَزْوَاجَ[20] and هُمْ[21] signals this affinity of the person who he or she is accusing is not any person but a person that they lived a life together. They shared memories and privacy. The expression وَلَمْ يَكُن لَّهُمْ شُهَدَاء[22] again can remind the person with their intimate ones that there is a privacy that the person should not expose. The part إِلَّا أَنفُسُهُمْ again emphasizes this privacy, affinity and relationship with their spouse.

Then, the ayah continues as فَشَهَادَةُ أَحَدِهِمْ أَرْبَعُ شَهَادَاتٍ بِاللَّهِ إِنَّهُ لَمِنَ الصَّادِقِينَ {النور/6} وَالْخَامِسَةُ أَنَّ لَعْنَتَ اللَّهِ عَلَيْهِ إِن كَانَ مِنَ الْكَاذِبِينَ[23] {النور/7}. Then, one can really ask why should one take witness to Allah ﷻ four times about exposing another person's fault even if it is true? The humans always tend to see wrong and can assume evil for others most of the time. Then, is it logical to make Allah ﷻ witness against oneself in case the person is wrong? Then, after all this, is it logical take the risk of taking the lànah of Allah ﷻ in case the person is wrong?

A sound person can and should always avoid oneself about not even be thinking about accusing others even though it may be right. Therefore, the flow, style and preference of the words are giving this strong message explicitly and implicitly to prevent the person from this type of very evil engagement that destroys the relationships, families and

---

19. They accuse.
20. Wives.
21. Their.
22. And they have no witnesses
23. And the fifth [oath will be] that the curse of Allah be upon him if he should be among the liars.

societies. Therefore, there is a very strong stance in its style to prevent the person even coming close to this type of act. Each selected word, letter, pronoun, number and aggregate meanings show this embodied meaning and theme with its balāqah, SubhanAllah! This is a miracle, mu'jiza[24], humbles the person with a'jz, humility and dumbfoundedness.

This sûrah (Nûr) continues to explain the problematic disposition in relationships. Yet, at the same time, if one follows the ayahs in this sûrah as in their ending motifs such as فَإِنَّ اللَّهَ غَفُورٌ رَّحِيمٌ [25] {النور/5}, وَأَنَّ اللهَ تَوَّابٌ حَكِيمٌ [26] {النور/10}, وَأَنَّ أللهَ رَؤُوفٌ رَّحِيمٌ [27] {النور/20}, وَأُللَّه غَفُورٌ رَّحِيمٌ [28] {النور/22}, فَإِنَّ اللَّهَ مِن بَعْدِ إِكْرَاهِهِنَّ غَفُورٌ رَّحِيمٌ [29] {النور/33}, إِنَّ أللَّه غَفُورٌ رَّحِيمٌ {النور/62} one can realize that Allah ﷻ direct the person to always ask forgiveness in all engagements of wrongdoings.

---

24. Miracle.
25. For indeed, Allah is Forgiving and Merciful.
26. And Allah is Accepting of repentance and Wise.
27. And because Allah is Kind and Merciful.
28. And Allah is Forgiving and Merciful.
29. Then indeed, Allah is [to them], after their compulsion, Forgiving and Merciful.

VOLUME 4

Sûrah 2—al-Baqara

[19–20]

أَوْ كَصَيِّبٍ مِّنَ السَّمَاء فِيهِ ظُلُمَاتٌ وَرَعْدٌ وَبَرْقٌ يَجْعَلُونَ أَصْابِعَهُمْ فِي آذَانِهِم مِّنَ الصَّوَاعِقِ حَذَرَ الْمَوْتِ واللّهُ مُحِيطٌ بِالْكافِرِينَ ³⁰ {البقرة/19} يَكَادُ الْبَرْقُ يَخْطَفُ أَبْصَارَهُمْ كُلَّمَا أَضَاء لَهُم مَّشَوْاْ فِيهِ وَإِذَا أَظْلَمَ عَلَيْهِمْ قَامُواْ وَلَوْ شَاء اللّهُ لَذَهَبَ بِسَمْعِهِمْ وَأَبْصَارِهِمْ إِنَّ اللّه عَلَى كُلِّ شَيْءٍ قَدِيرٌ ³¹ {البقرة/20}

The usûl[32] of fiqh[33] is based on the apparent actions but not what is hidden in people's hearts. Therefore, although there are detailed ahkām[34], the rules of fiqh, about the people of kufr[35] who are openly harming Muslims, there are no ahkām, the rules of fiqh about the people of nifāq[36] who declare themselves as Muslims but yet, they may have other motivational reasons. The ultimate judgment for everyone with their inner and external true stances is made by Allah ﷻ.

We can analyze some of the words and expressions in this ayah. For example, the expression can have complementary meanings that can vividly picture this scene. The word يَكَادُ[37] in the expression can indicate proximity and nearness.

The word الْبَرْقُ[38] can indicate the quickness, rapidity, and swiftness. The word يَخْطَفُ[39] can indicate snatching, grabbing or seizing suddenly and roughly. These three words in their meanings can portray something as an unexpected scary sudden occurrence. May Allah ﷻ protect us, Amîn. As it was explained, constant and sudden changing light intensity

---

30. Or [it is] like a rainstorm from the sky within which is darkness, thunder, and lightning. They put their fingers in their ears against the thunderclaps in dread of death. But Allah is encompassing of the believers.

31. The lightning almost snatches away their sight. Every time it light [the way] for them, they walk therein; but when darkness comes over them, they stand [still]. And if Allah had willed, He could have taken away their hearing and their sights. Indeed Allah is over all things competent.

32. Methodology.

33. Islamic Law.

34. Rules.

35. Disbelief.

36. Hypocrisy.

37. Almost.

38. The lightning.

39. Snatched.

as explained prevents them to benefit from the light similar to the phenomenon of flash blindness [1].It is important to realize that these are smiles, metaphors, or examples to vividly describe the realities and at the same time, to contextualize these cases depending on the time and the person. Therefore, one should not miss the main theme and essence of the messages in these ayahs by taking these examples literally.

The expression كُلَّمَا أَضَاءَ[40] can indicate the opportunistic approach of the munāfiqs. In other words, they try to look for different avenues to utilize for their interest. In the expression[41] كُلَّمَا أَضَاءَ لَهُم, the word لَهُم [42] can emphasize this opportunistic approach. In the example of thunder light, even though there is a very short period of lightning, they try to take advantage of it.

The expression مَّشَوْاْ فِيهِ[43] can show that they cannot walk fast. This figurative expression can imply the problems related with their uncertainty of their values and what they try to achieve in their lives.

When one analyzes the statement كُلَّمَا أَضَاءَ لَهُم مَّشَوْاْ فِيهِ[44], the expression فِيهِ[45] can indicate limited, restricted, narrow, constrained, thin, slim, tight and poor quality and quantity of this light. In other words, restricting the light is not a common phenomenon. Yet, فِيهِ[46] indicates this restriction for these people due to their stance of nifāq[47].

In the expression وَإِذَا أَظْلَمَ[48], the part إِذَا[49] can show the certainty in occurrence. In other words, when we take the meanings of وَإِذَا أَظْلَمَ to the general context and meanings of light and opportunities of moving forward, then the state of أَظْلَمَ[50] can show the certain and real dark states of pessimism or hopelessness in the people of nifāq. Although the people of nifāq can externally seem to be happy and satisfied, the part of إِذَا in the expression وَإِذَا أَظْلَمَ can show these definite states of hopelessness.

---

40. Every time it light [the way].
41. Every time it light [the way] for them.
42. For them
43. They walk therein.
44. Every time it light [the way] for them. They walk therein.
45. Therein.
46. Therein.
47. Hypocrisy.
48. But when darkness comes.
49. When
50. Darkness comes.

In the expression وَإِذَا أَظْلَمَ عَلَيْهِمْ قَامُوا[51], the word قَامُوا[52] can indicate the natural optimistic expectations of humans even in the very bad or pessimistic conditions. Humans with all different difficulties of life can have tendency to be in a spiritual state of expectation, hope or change. Yet, this hope and expectation should be directed to the Real Source of Hopes and Expectations Who is Allah (﷾).

In the expression وَلَوْ شَاءَ الله[53], the part شَاءَ[54] can indicate that in everything, the essence is the Mashiyyah[55] of Allah ﷾. The causes are only simple means. One can see in this example that light turning to darkness in the cases of lightning can be against the means or causality of light. Light generally indicates openings, refreshments or spiritual guidance. Yet, in this case, due to its switching on and off with thunder and lighting, it has the opposite negative effects of blindness. Everything is with the Mashiyyah[56] of Allah ﷾.

When we focus on the part وَلَوْ شَاءَ الله لَذَهَبَ بِسَمْعِهِمْ وَأَبْصَارِهِمْ إِنَّ الله عَلَى[57] كُلِّ شَيْءٍ قَدِيرٌ, the Name of Tha'at[58] of Allah ﷾ as الله mentioned especially in وَلَوْ شَاءَ الله[59] and إِنَّ الله عَلَى كُلِّ شَيْءٍ قَدِيرٌ[60]. This can also support the previous disposition that means are only means for the Mashiyyah of Allah ﷾. The mention of الله explicitly instead of other Names or Attributes can signify to understand this important point.

In the expression وَلَوْ شَاءَ الله لَذَهَبَ بِسَمْعِهِمْ وَأَبْصَارِهِمْ[61], the part بِسَمْعِهِمْ is singular, mufrad[62]. The part أَبْصَارِهِمْ[63] is plural, jam'a[64]. This can indicate that what one can hear can be singular or may not require multiplicity. This can indicate the singularity in the truth of the teachings of the Qurān and Rasulullah ﷺ. On the other hand, what one experiences,

---

51. But when darkness comes over them, they stand [still].
52. They stand {still}.
53. And if Allah had willed.
54. Had willed.
55. Permission of Allah.
56. Permission of Allah.
57. And if Allah had willed, He could have taken away their hearing and their sights. Indeed Allah is over all things competent.
58. The being {Allah himself}.
59. And if Allah had willed
60. Indeed Allah is over all things competent.
61. And if Allah had willed, He could have taken away their hearing and their sights.
62. Singular word.
63. Their sights.
64. Plural word.

sees and engages oneself can have multiplicities as indicated by أَبْصَارِهِمْ [65]
. اللّه اعلم [66]

In the part of the ayah {البقرة/20}قَدِيرٌ[67] the word [68]
قَدِير is a sifat mushabahah[69]. This can indicate that the Qudrah of Allah
is continuous without any beginning, end, and limit. All Attributes
of Tha'at of Allah SWT has Permanent Quality of Allah regardless of
their manifestation in the realms of creation or in the realms of humans
or not. This is detailed in the manual of the creed of Imam Tahawi [2].
When one categorizes the people among believers, kāfir[70] and munāfiqîn[71]
as mentioned in the classical tafāsir[72] [3] through the initial ayahs of
Sûrah Baqarah, there can be some sub-classifications under these
classifications. Among believers, there can be a group inviting others to
imān besides their own identities of imān. There can be a group who can
practice imān without inviting much others but following the inherited
practices from their forefathers.

Among the disbelievers (kuffār), there can be a group inviting
others to kufr[73] besides their own identities of kufr. There can be a group
who can practice kufr without inviting much others but following the
inherited practices of kufr from their forefathers.

Among the munāfiqûn, there can be a group inviting others to nifāq
besides their own identities of nifāq. There can be a group who can
practice nifāq without inviting much others but following the inherited
practices of nifāq from their forefathers.

The following ayah and other ones in the Qurān can indicate these
inherited practices from the forefathers and cultures with the renderings
of مِن قَبْلِكُمْ[74] as in {البقرة/21} [75] وَالَّذِينَ مِن قَبْلِكُمْ لَعَلَّكُمْ تَتَّقُونَ.

Yet, after the possible categorizations, classifications, implicit or
explicit identities, Allah in the Qurān invites all humanity for the true

---

65. Their sights.
66. Allah knows best.
67. Indeed, Allah is over all things competent.
68. All Powerful and Competent.
69. The quality of the causer.
70. Disbelievers.
71. Hypocrites.
72. Explanation of the Qurān.
73. Disbelief.
74. Those before you.
75. And those before you, that you may become righteous.

tawhid[76] as the next ayah starts with this call of [77] يَا أَيُّهَا النَّاسُ. In this call, tawhid in the ubudiyyah of Allah ﷻ is emphasized with يَا أَيُّهَا النَّاسُ اعْبُدُواْ[78] by realizing the tawhid in the Rububiyyah[79] of Allah ﷻ as mentioned [80] يَا أَيُّهَا النَّاسُ اعْبُدُواْ رَبَّكُمُ الَّذِي خَلَقَكُمْ وَالَّذِينَ مِن قَبْلِكُمْ. The result of 'ubudiyyah[81] as presented in the next ayah is taqwa as mentioned لَعَلَّكُمْ تَتَّقُونَ[82].

It is interesting to note that after the following ayahs, the case of Adam as is presented as the source and beginning of all humanity. In this sense, one can realize the bottom-up approach of deductive cases from specific cases or signs to general. In other words, the classifications among humans to all humans, then all humans to beginning of all humanity, purpose, goal and cosmology. This is today's scientific approach or methodology of deductive reasoning, case studies or grounded theory.

On the other hand, one should realize that as the Qurān is a miracle, one can always find both approaches of deductive and inductive methodologies in the same ayah, Sûrah and entire Qurān.

[21–22]

يَا أَيُّهَا النَّاسُ اعْبُدُواْ رَبَّكُمُ الَّذِي خَلَقَكُمْ وَالَّذِينَ مِن قَبْلِكُمْ لَعَلَّكُمْ تَتَّقُونَ[83] {البقرة/21} الَّذِي جَعَلَ لَكُمُ الأَرْضَ فِرَاشاً وَالسَّمَاء بِنَاء وَأَنزَلَ مِنَ السَّمَاء مَاء فَأَخْرَجَ بِهِ مِنَ الثَّمَرَاتِ رِزْقاً لَّكُمْ فَلاَ تَجْعَلُواْ لِلّهِ أَندَاداً وَأَنتُمْ تَعْلَمُونَ[84] {البقرة/22}

The statement of يَا أَيُّهَا النَّاسُ اعْبُدُواْ[85] can signify the Uluhiyyah of Allah ﷻ. When we analyze the above ayahs, one can realize in the ubudiyyah of

---

76. Oneness of Allah
77. O mankind.
78. O mankind, worship [your lord].
79. Lordship. The Attributes of Allah SWT Who takes care of all creation and maintains structure and order.
80. O mankind, worship your lord, who created you and those before you, that you may become righteous.
81. Servanthood. This can be also translated as the responsibility of all creation including humans to worship Allah SWT.
82. That you may become righteous.
83. O mankind, worship your lord, who created you and those before you, that you may become righteous.
84. [He] who made for you the earth a bed [spread out] and the sky a ceiling and sent down from the sky, rain and brought forth thereby fruits as a provision for you. So do not attribute to Allahs equals while you know [that there is nothing similar to him].
85. O mankind, worship.

Allah ﷻ with اعْبُدُواْ[86] , there is the rububiyyah of Allah ﷻ with رَبَّكُمُ[87]. In the Rububiyyah[88] of Allah ﷻ, there is the tawhid as mentioned with [89] فَلَا تَجْعَلُواْ بِلَّهِ أَندَادا. In tawhid, there is the uluhiyyah of Allah ﷻ.

In the part فَلَا تَجْعَلُواْ بِلَّهِ أَندَاداً وَأَنتُمْ تَعْلَمُونَ[90], the word أَندَاداً[91] is the plural of ند. This can mean something similar, or comparable. In this sense, Allah ﷻ does not have any partner. Allah ﷻ is not comparable to anything. Therefore, humans should not assume other things as partners as ند similar to Allah ﷻ. This is called shirk either done implicitly or explicitly. At least, the person should not make shirk to Allah ﷻ knowingly and explicitly as mentioned [92] فَلَا تَجْعَلُواْ بِلَّهِ أَندَاداً وَأَنتُمْ تَعْلَمُونَ. Humans have this much knowledge, 'ilm not to make explicit shirk to Allah ﷻ. Then, inshAllah, one can work on him or herself to remove the implicit shirk, partnerships, with the guidance of Allah ﷻ through the Qurān and sunnah of Rasulullah ﷺ.Here is the case where exactly the social constructions theories [1] fit in that we assign meanings to the things according to the world and habitat that we live in. We make comparisons and analysis according to what we see. Our imaginations and thinking, analysis, and conclusions of assignments are all according to these observations [1]. Yet, approaching to know Allah ﷻ without any guidance can be a full fallacy according to the social construction theories.

The word أَندَاداً indicated in the plural can signify the rejection of any type of partnership, shirk in different varieties, quantities and quantities. One should not make and claim partnership in different Names and Attributes of Allah ﷻ.

The word أَندَاداً[93] indicated in the plural can denote different religious groups such as Christians, Hindus, and other ones in their different divisions and categorizations of shirk[94].

In this sense, the word اندَاداً indicated in the plural can signify any types of internal, spiritual, emotional and mindful engagements of the

---

86. {You all} worship.
87. Your lord.
88. Lordship.
89. So do not attribute to Allah's equals.
90. So do not attribute to Allahs equals while you know [that there is nothing similar to him].
91. Equals. {Of Allah Ta'alah}.
92. So do not attribute to Allahs equals while you know [that there is nothing similar to him].
93. Attribute [to Allahs equals].
94. Believing in someone other than Allah.

person with awareness and without awareness, implicitly or explicitly that induce fear, anxiety, stress, uneasiness, horror, panic, alarm, discomfort, concern, worry, nervousness, other than Allah ﷻ. True tawhid requires the full and only taking refuge, shelter, and going back to Allah ﷻ constantly, continuously, and incessantly.

We have a lot of spiritual sicknesses. Every sickness is due to these engagements as indicated with the word أَندَاداً. Each sickness and piles and multitudes of أَندَاداً can cause darkness on the soul, heart and mind as mentioned أَوْ كَظُلُمَاتٍ فِي بَحْرٍ لُّجِّيٍّ يَغْشَاهُ مَوْجٌ مِّن فَوْقِهِ مَوْجٌ مِّن فَوْقِهِ سَحَابٌ ظُلُمَاتٌ بَعْضُهَا فَوْقَ بَعْضٍ إِذَا أَخْرَجَ يَدَهُ لَمْ يَكَدْ يَرَاهَا وَمَن لَّمْ يَجْعَلِ اللَّهُ لَهُ نُورًا فَمَا لَهُ مِن نُّورٍ [النور/40].

La ilaha illa Allah makes the person get rid of all these sicknesses and spiritual, mental, and emotional piles of darkness as mentioned اللَّهُ وَلِيُّ الَّذِينَ آمَنُواْ يُخْرِجُهُم مِّنَ الظُّلُمَاتِ إِلَى النُّورِ وَالَّذِينَ كَفَرُواْ أَوْلِيَآؤُهُمُ الطَّاغُوتُ يُخْرِجُونَهُم مِّنَ النُّورِ إِلَى الظُّلُمَاتِ أُوْلَئِكَ أَصْحَابُ النَّارِ هُمْ فِيهَا خَالِدُونَ [البقرة/257].

The word أَندَاداً[97] is the plural of نِد. Every نِد has its ضد[98]. Similarly, assuming the opposite with the word ضد is also problem human approach of knowing everything with their opposite as detailed in social construction theories [1]. In this regard, pair or opposites is the quality of creation. Allah ﷻ does not have any partners, opposites, and equivalent.

Every parity, equality, pairness indicated with the word نِد requires divisibility, oppositeness, even numbership.

Allah ﷻ is Unique, al-Ahad[99]. Allah ﷻ is al-Fard[100]. Allah ﷻ is al-Witr. These different Names of Allah ﷻ indicate Oneness, Uniqueness, Oddness, Not having oppositeness, Not Having Partners and all other tanzîh[101] related terms that would take the person away from the standard human logic renderings of deducting meanings from the

---

95. Or [they are] like darknesses within an unfathomable sea which is covered by waves, upon which are waves, over which are clouds—darknesses, some of them upon others. When one puts out his hand [therein], he can hardly see it. And he to whom Allah has not granted light—for him there is no light.

96. Allah is the ally of those who believe. He brings them out from darknesses into the light. And those who disbelieve—their allies are taghut. They take them out of the light into darknesses. Those are the companions of the Fire; they will abide eternally therein.

97. Attribute {to Allahs equals}.

98. Opposite.

99. The one.

100. The single (alone).

101. Disliked.

analogies of partnership or opposites similar to their creation due to their social construction [1].

One of the sunnah tasbihs[102] to do in especially sujûd[103] of prayers is
سبحان ذي الجبروت و الملكوت و الكبرياء و العظمت [4] [5] 6[104].

According to some interpretations, Jabarût[105] are the realities, 'alam[106] of Asma' and Sifah[107]. Jabarût can relate to the Rububiyyah[108] of Allah ﷻ. The real embodiment of Rububiyyah can be represented by humans and other beings as created by Allah ﷻ. One can remember the ayahs in the Qurãn about the creation of Adam as and the parts of Names being acknowledged and known by Adam as. Yet, angels did not know them.

Malakut are the realities, 'alam[109] of angels. Malakût[110] can relate to the U'budiyyah[111] of Allah ﷻ. The real embodiment of 'ubudiyyah are represented by angels and other beings, ruhaniyyûn as created by Allah ﷻ. One can remember hadith narrations about angels embodying the 'ubudiyyah of Allah ﷻ.

Wal Kibriyai[112], Wal A'azamati[113] are related with the Uluhiyyah[114] of Allah ﷻ. No creation can share them. Only, Allah ﷻ has the Kibriya and A'azamah. The hadith mentions

قَالَ اللَّهُ عَزَّ وَجَلَّ الْكِبْرِيَاءُ رِدَائِي وَالْعَظَمَةُ إِزَارِي فَمَنْ نَازَعَنِي وَاحِدًا مِنْهُمَا قَذَفْتُهُ فِي النَّارِ[4]

Allah ﷻ said: "Grandeur is my cloak and greatness is my garment. Whoever competes with me in one of these two, (Whoever tries to take a share then that person becomes lost) I will cast him into the Hellfire." [4]

---

102. Praise.
103. Prostration.
104. Glory be to the One Who has all power, sovereignty, magnificence and might.
105. Realm of power.
106. The world.
107. Descriptions.
108. Lordship.
109. Signs.
110. The world of Angels.
111. Servanthood.
112. Pride.
113. Determination.
114. Divinity.

If we analyze the words of this ayah, below can be some possibilities.
The expression يَا أَيُّهَا[115] is composed of three parts: يَا + أَيُّ + هَا

The first part يَا[116] as the harfun-nidā can indicate warning, caution, notice and counseling.

The second part أَيُّ[117] can be used to find and locate something.

The third part هَا can indicate a harf[118] signifying to remove the ghaflah, heedlessness.

In their totality, the expression[119] يَا أَيُّهَا can indicate different meanings and important points.

In the beginning of the ayah, there is the direct address of Allah ﷻ to the humans. This itself can be considered an honor and elevation of the status of all humans. This can be itself an encouragement and motivation for all humans to perform their 'ibadah[120] but not to be deprived from this honor. They should overcome the problems of laziness, heedlessness, and negligence in performing 'ibadah with this Direct Noble Encouragement of Allah ﷻ.

It is only by means of 'ibadah that one can directly talk and communicate with Allah ﷻ, Rabbul A'lamîn, the Creator, Upholder and Maintainer of all the galaxies, systems, universes and everything.

These three parts in the expression[121] يَا أَيُّهَا can indicate to submit oneself with their heart as a Muslim, to believe fully in tawhid and imān with their mind, and to have the responsibility of 'ibadah and good and virtuous actions as amal with their body.

Heart requires submission. Mind requires conviction. Body requires performance.

Submission and conviction lead to certainty in imān and marifatullah. Performance of this comes naturally as 'ibadah as the expression of adornment for Allah ﷻ.

The address can be mu'min[122], kāfir[123] and munāfiq[124]. There is good news, warning, caution, notice and counseling for the mu'min with the

---

115. O {you}.
116. O.
117. You {people and or things}.
118. Letter.
119. O [you].
120. Worship.
121. O you.
122. Believer.
123. Disbeliever.
124. Hypocrites.

first part يَا. There is an encouragement for the kāfir with the part أَيُّ in order them to struggle aim, find and locate the guidance. There is an urge for the munāfiq with the part هَا to remove the gaflah, heedlessness and have ikhlas[125], sincerity in their engagements.

In social life, the people can be in three categories as upper class (decision makers), middle class (people swinging in between), and general public (laborers). There is a warning, caution, notice and counseling to the decision makers with the first part يَا. There is an urge for the middle class with the word أَيُّ in order to them locate the true guidance. There is an urge for the laborers with the part هَا not to follow everything what they hear and follow but to remove the ghaflah, heedlessness and have critical thinking.

On another perspective, there can be an indication for the phenomena of communication among humans with these three parts. The person first tries to notice someone among many as mentioned with the first part يَا[126]. Then, the person tries to locate and identify this person with the second part [127] أَيُّ. Then, the person tries to communicate with this person in order to deliver the message, explain the need and purpose with the third part هَا, [128]والله اعلم.

The first part يَا as the harfu-nida[129] can indicate the people who are heedless, absent, present, ignorant, preoccupied or busy, a friend or a stranger. Depending on the context and time, its meaning can change. For example, its meaning can be a wake-up call for the heedless. It can be a reminder call the for the absent. It can be an explanation for the ignorant. It can be an encouragement for the friend. It can be a warning for the stranger.

Although there is always the closeness of Allah ﷻ to us, the indication of يَا can entail some meanings. In this sense, how can one understand the part يَا which may indicate distance or farness?

The necessitated 'ibadah[130] is an important responsibility and task for the person. When there is an important task, the distance or farness can indicate an encouragement in order to reach this high and noble goal.

---

125. Sincerity.
126. O.
127. You {people and or things}.
128. Allah knows best.
129. Letters used for calling {someone}.
130. Worship.

The part يَ can indicate farness of 'ibadah from the Uluhiyyah of Allah ﷻ. Most of the time, shirk or deviation from true 'ibadah of Allah ﷻ can entail this problem of mixing 'ubudiyyah and U'luhiyyah of Allah ﷻ. Humans tend to humanize the worship going beyond the limits of adab with Allah ﷻ in the problem of mixing them. For example, people's putting food for deities as a ritual in Eastern religions can be one of the examples of this.

The part يَا[131] indicates the call and teachings of the Qurān going beyond time and place. We may call this today as trans-continental, trans-cultural, and trans-historical. They all indicate these unchanging messages of the Qurān.

The part يَ can indicate different levels of ghaflah, heedlessness that humans have. Everyone can be at different levels of heedlessness or ghaflah. For a person, a small advice can be enough to break this ghaflah. For another, something tragic can happen to break the walls of this ghaflah.

The second part أَيُّ[132] can be used to find and locate something. In this part, the order of 'ibadah is specified to humans with the expression يَا أَيُّهَا النَّاسُ [133]. This can show that other beings naturally with the full appreciation and adornment of Allah ﷻ is already making 'ibadah[134] to Allah ﷻ as: أَلَمْ تَرَ أَنَّ اللَّهَ يُسَبِّحُ لَهُ مَن فِي السَّمَاوَاتِ وَالْأَرْضِ وَالطَّيْرُ صَافَّاتٍ كُلٌّ قَدْ عَلِمَ صَلَاتَهُ وَتَسْبِيحَهُ وَاللَّهُ عَلِيمٌ بِمَا يَفْعَلُونَ [135] {النور/ 41}. They all know their 'ibadah as mentioned كُلٌّ قَدْ عَلِمَ صَلَاتَهُ وَتَسْبِيحَهُ[136]. Yet, heedless humans don't know it. Therefore, the expression يَا أَيُّهَا النَّاسُ[137] directly addresses them to remind and teach them and at the same time, to locate their real positions with Rabbul A'lamìn , ﷻ. Then, the ones who humbly listen and take heed can remove this gaflah with the guidance, Fadl, and Rahmah of Allah ﷻ.

The part أَيُّ can have the indication of hiding something in the general, amm in order to find and locate something. When there is

---

131. O.
132. You {people and or things}.
133. O mankind.
134. Worship.
135. Do you not see that Allah is exalted by whomever is within the heavens and the earth and [by] the birds with wings spread [in flight]? Each [of them] has known his [means of] prayer and exalting [Him], and Allah is Knowing of what they do.
136. Each [of them] has known his [means of] prayer and exalting [Him]
137. O mankind.

ithafah[138] with [139] النَّاسُ, then there is the explanation of this amm, with the hass of humans. In other words, among all the creation, Allah ﷻ orders humans to make 'ibadah to Allah ﷻ. Everything makes already 'ibadah to Allah ﷻ with their fitrah except some humans and jinn. In this regard according to some scholars the word النَّاسُ include both humans and jinn but not only humans [7] .In this sense, يَا as the harfu-nida[140] can indicate calling the humans among all creation for a notice and counseling. The last part هَا can signify to remove the ghaflah, heedlessness from humans.

On another perspective, in the expression يَا أَيُّهَا النَّاسُ[141] , the word النَّاسُ can indicate the forgetfulness, and heedlessness of humans in their nature. Also, this can indicate the promise that all human souls took in qawlu-bala, the initial covenant with Allah ﷻ and now, they forget about it. Yet, this heedlessness may not be due to deliberate stance. It can be related to the human nature of forgetfulness. In this regard, Allah ﷻ gently reminds the people this initial promise-covenant that they took that they would be in recognition of [142]رب العالمين.

In the expression يَا أَيُّهَا النَّاسُ اعْبُدُوا[143], the part اعْبُدُوا[144] can be the answer for the call of the nidā. In this sense, the order of اعْبُدُوا can be continuation and being on istiqamah for the mu'min, submission for the kāfir, and sincerity, iklas[145] for the munāfiq. The order اعْبُدُوا can also indicate the true tawhid[146] for all groups, الله اعلم[147]In the expression يَا[148] أَيُّهَا النَّاسُ اعْبُدُوا رَبَّكُمُ, the name and attribute of Allah ﷻ as the Rabb can be the reason for a person to continue 'ibadah of Allah ﷻ. The attribute and name of Allah ﷻ as the Rabb can indicate that Allah ﷻ takes care of the person's needs. Therefore, this requires thanking, shukr, and appreciation for all the ni'mahs of Allah ﷻ. This thanking and shukur is called as 'ibadah.

---

138. Connected {word}.
139. Mankind.
140. Letters/words using for calling.
141. O mankind.
142. The lord of the worlds.
143. O mankind, worship.
144. {You all} worship.
145. Sincerity.
146. Oneness.
147. Allah knows best.
148. O mankind, worship your lord.

The sila الَّذِي [149] is used to explain something that may not be clear. In the expression, يَا أَيُّهَا النَّاسُ اعْبُدُواْ رَبَّكُمُ الَّذِي خَلَقَكُمْ [150], is connected to Rabb. In this case, this may imply that Allah ﷻ can be more known by humans through the af'al[151] and a'th-hār[152] in the world but not through the Real Uluhiyyah and dhāt of Allah ﷻ.

When we analyze the statement يَا أَيُّهَا النَّاسُ اعْبُدُواْ رَبَّكُمُ الَّذِي خَلَقَكُمْ [153], the relation between خَلَقَكُمْ [154] and اعْبُدُواْ [155] can indicate that we are designed to be religious, and worship Allah ﷻ. In other words, the call with يَا [156] أَيُّهَا النَّاسُ can indicate, all humans are designed to be religious by Allah ﷻ without any exceptions. Although a person can identify him or herself as an atheist, non-religious, materialist, everyone has the starvation and need to be religious and pious similar to eating food, drinking water and breathing. Yet, this spiritual starvation can kill the person if the person does not realize this vital need and feel the soul, heart and mind with the correct and authentic dhikr[157] of Allah ﷻ.

'Ibadah as indicated with religiosity or piety is a positive intrinsic quality of all humans, like seeing, hearing, touching, walking and other given human faculties given and bestowed on us by Allah ﷻ. All these qualities of seeing, hearing, touching, walking etc. are activated without any effort as an autonomous or involuntary action of humans.

The word involuntary is important. It indicates any action done without will or conscious control. Yet, the activation of the intrinsic quality of religiosity or piety in a human can be similar to just pushing a button as indicated with a tiny bit of humans will, intention or inclination (mayalān) as detailed with the belief-aqida schools of asharites and maturidi.

It is critical to understand what is voluntary and involuntary. This forms the essential purpose of our existence as a trial or essence. This tiny inclination or will of humans differentiates us from angels. Angels with their all other qualities have the intrinsic quality of dhikr and

---

149. Who.
150. O mankind, worship your lord who created you.
151. Actions.
152. Public actions.
153. O mankind, worship your lord who created you.
154. [Who] created you.
155. [All of you] Worship.
156. O mankind.
157. Remembrance.

'ibadah of Allah ﷻ in their design without the need of pushing to a button like humans.

On another perspective, the part of the ayah يَا أَيُّهَا النَّاسُ اعْبُدُواْ رَبَّكُمُ[158] الَّذِي خَلَقَكُمْ can indicate that 'ibadah is the payment and result of being created and being in existence. Getting reward from Allah ﷻ for the 'ibadah is from the Fadl, Rahmah[159] and Karam[160] of Allah ﷻ.

The word خَلَقَكُمْ[161] has the meaning of creating a thing from non-existence to existence. In this regard, this word is only to be attributed to Allah ﷻ. Therefore, in the translations of this word and othe similar words to different languages, one should be careful to avoid using words for humans that can only be used for Allah ﷻ. Although the person may not mean it, the adab of language with Uluhiyyah can make the person protected from shirk. It can help the person not implicitly or slowly think, say or do things related with shirk. اللهم احفظنا من هذا، امين[162]

When one reviews[163] يَا أَيُّهَا النَّاسُ اعْبُدُواْ رَبَّكُمُ الَّذِي خَلَقَكُمْ وَالَّذِينَ مِن قَبْلِكُمْ, the part مِن قَبْلِكُمْ[164] makes the connection with the ones who were alive on the earth before but now they are death. Now, you or we are on the earth for their replacement. This knowledge can induce in the person some uneasy, melancholic or sad feelings due to the absence of the ones today from the past and due to the fear of the same consequence of death for the present ones.

Yet, 'ibadah can induce the positive and hope feelings of eternity with absence of death, when we connect ourselves to our Rabb, Allah ﷻ Who is Eternal, Al-Bāqi through 'ibadah. This can be indicated as اعْبُدُواْ رَبَّكُمُ الَّذِي خَلَقَكُمْ وَالَّذِينَ مِن قَبْلِكُمْ[165]. In this regard, a person of 'ibadah can have eternal life in Jannah with the Fadl[166] and Rahmah of Allah ﷻ.

---

158. O mankind, worship your lord who created you.
159. Mercy.
160. Generocity.
161. Created you.
162. O Allah, protect us from this. Ameen
163. O mankind, worship your Lord, who created you and those before you.
164. {Those} before you.
165. Worship your Lord, who created you and those before you.
166. Favor.

The True Hope and How to Hope from Allah ﷻ

When one analyzes the expression لَعَلَّكُمْ تَتَّقُونَ[167] in the totality of the ayah يَا أَيُّهَا النَّاسُ اعْبُدُواْ رَبَّكُمُ الَّذِي خَلَقَكُمْ وَالَّذِينَ مِن قَبْلِكُمْ لَعَلَّكُمْ تَتَّقُونَ[168] {البقرة/21}, one can realize that íbadah leads to taqwa. Yet, the possibility and hope are indicated with the word لَعَلَّكُمْ[169].

The word لَعَلَّكُمْ can signify that if the person is really going to hope and expect from Allah ﷻ that would be through the means of 'ibadah. In other words, making íbadah is a means or a tool of knocking the door of the Rahmah of Allah ﷻ. In other words, Allah ﷻ is teaching us what to hope for and how to hope for and knock the door of hope correctly. This is done through the íbadah of Allah ﷻ.

At another perspective, if the person has a wrong hope which can be called umniyah such as أَمَانِيُّهُمْ[170] as mentioned in وَقَالُوا لَن يَدْخُلَ الْجَنَّةَ إِلاَّ مَن كَانَ هُوداً أَوْ نَصَارَى تِلْكَ أَمَانِيُّهُمْ قُلْ هَاتُواْ بُرْهَانَكُمْ إِن كُنتُمْ صَادِقِينَ[171] {البقرة/111}. If the person has a wrong hope called umniyah, regardless of their 'ibadah then, this hope cannot be fulfilled. This is also mentioned in the case of Firàwn as وَقَالَ فِرْعَوْنُ يَا هَامَانُ ابْنِ لِي صَرْحاً لَّعَلِّي أَبْلُغُ الأَسْبَابَ[172] {غافر/36} أَسْبَابَ السَّمَاوَاتِ فَأَطَّلِعَ إِلَى إِلَهِ مُوسَى وَإِنِّي لَأَظُنُّهُ كَاذِباً وَكَذَلِكَ زُيِّنَ لِفِرْعَوْنَ سُوءُ عَمَلِهِ وَصُدَّ عَنِ السَّبِيلِ وَمَا كَيْدُ فِرْعَوْنَ إِلَّا فِي تَبَابٍ[173] {غافر/37}.

In this case, Firàwn hopes something that is not grounded due to the absence of true imān and tawhid. In this case, instead of 'ibadah leading the person to true hope from Allah ﷻ, his evil acts, سُوءُ عَمَلِهِ[174], as mentioned in وَكَذَلِكَ زُيِّنَ لِفِرْعَوْنَ سُوءُ عَمَلِهِ وَصُدَّ عَنِ السَّبِيلِ وَمَا كَيْدُ فِرْعَوْنَ إِلَّا فِي تَبَابٍ {غافر/37} leads him to ungrounded hopes. اللهم احفظنا من هذا، امين[175].

In this case, both correct hope and using the correct tool of achieving this hope are critical. Many examples of this true hope and tool of achievement are present in the Qurān. A person can hope hidāyah from

---

167. That you may become righteous.
168. O mankind, worship your Lord, who created you and those before you, that you may become righteous—
169. That you may.
170. Their wishful thinking.
171. And they say, "None will enter Paradise except one who is a Jew or a Christian." That is [merely] their wishful thinking. Say, "Produce your proof, if you should be truthful."
172. And Pharaoh said, "O Haman, construct for me a tower that I might reach the ways.
173. The ways into the heavens—so that I may look at the deity of Moses; but indeed, I think he is a liar." And thus was made attractive to Pharaoh the evil of his deed, and he was averted from the [right] way. And the plan of Pharaoh was not except in ruin.
174. The evil of his deed.
175. O Allah, protect us from this. Ameen.

Allah ﷻ by following the Qurān and Rasulullah ﷺ. وَإِذْ آتَيْنَا مُوسَى الْكِتَابَ وَالْفُرْقَانَ لَعَلَّكُمْ تَهْتَدُونَ[176] {البقرة/53}

قُلْ يَا أَيُّهَا النَّاسُ إِنِّي رَسُولُ اللَّهِ إِلَيْكُمْ جَمِيعًا الَّذِي لَهُ مُلْكُ السَّمَاوَاتِ وَالْأَرْضِ لَا إِلَهَ إِلَّا هُوَ يُحْيِي وَيُمِيتُ فَآمِنُوا بِاللَّهِ وَرَسُولِهِ النَّبِيِّ الْأُمِّيِّ الَّذِي يُؤْمِنُ بِاللَّهِ وَكَلِمَاتِهِ وَاتَّبِعُوهُ لَعَلَّكُمْ تَهْتَدُونَ[177] {الأعراف/158}

A person can hope to be among the shakirîn, the ones who always gratitude to Allah ﷻ by having taqwa as mentioned in وَلَقَدْ نَصَرَكُمُ اللَّهُ بِبَدْرٍ وَأَنتُمْ أَذِلَّةٌ فَاتَّقُوا اللَّهَ لَعَلَّكُمْ تَشْكُرُونَ[178] {آل عمران/123}

A person can hope to be among the shakirîn, the ones who always express gratitude to Allah ﷻ by realizing all the bounties, health, wealth, food are all from Allah ﷻ as mentioned in وَاذْكُرُوا إِذْ أَنتُمْ قَلِيلٌ مُّسْتَضْعَفُونَ فِي الْأَرْضِ تَخَافُونَ أَن يَتَخَطَّفَكُمُ النَّاسُ فَآوَاكُمْ وَأَيَّدَكُم بِنَصْرِهِ وَرَزَقَكُم مِّنَ الطَّيِّبَاتِ لَعَلَّكُمْ تَشْكُرُونَ[179]{الأنفال/26}

A person can hope the Rahmah of Allah ﷻ by fully obeying the guidelines set by Allah ﷻ and Rasulullah ﷺ as mentioned in وَأَطِيعُوا اللَّهَ وَالرَّسُولَ لَعَلَّكُمْ تُرْحَمُونَ[180] {آل عمران/132}.

More specifically, a person can hope the Rahmah of Allah ﷻ by praying, giving their zakah and sadaqah, charity and following Rasulullah in all the details of the religion as mentioned in وَأَقِيمُوا الصَّلَاةَ وَآتُوا الزَّكَاةَ وَأَطِيعُوا الرَّسُولَ لَعَلَّكُمْ تُرْحَمُونَ[181] {النور/56}

A person can hope the falāh from Allah ﷻ by taking a means such as working on the path of Allah ﷻ, jihad as mentioned in يَا أَيُّهَا الَّذِينَ آمَنُوا اتَّقُوا اللَّهَ وَابْتَغُوا إِلَيْهِ الْوَسِيلَةَ وَجَاهِدُوا فِي سَبِيلِهِ لَعَلَّكُمْ تُفْلِحُونَ[182] {المائدة/35}

---

176. And [recall] when We gave Moses the Scripture and criterion that perhaps you would be guided.

177. Say, [O Muúammad], "O mankind, indeed I am the Messenger of Allah to you all, [from Him] to whom belongs the dominion of the heavens and the earth. There is no deity except Him; He gives life and causes death." So believe in Allah and His Messenger, the unlettered prophet, who believes in Allah and His words, and follow him that you may be guided.

178. And already had Allah given you victory at [the battle of] Badr while you were weak [i.e., few in number]. Then fear Allah; perhaps you will be grateful.

179. And remember when you were few and oppressed in the land, fearing that people might abduct you, but He sheltered you, supported you with His victory, and provided you with good things—that you might be grateful.

180. And obey Allah and the Messenger that you may obtain mercy.

181. And establish prayer and give Zakah and obey the Messenger—that you may receive mercy.

182. O you who have believed, fear Allah and seek the means [of nearness] to Him and strive in His cause that you may succeed.

A person can hope to be a Dhākir, a person of remembering Allah ﷻ, by constantly making tafakkur, reflection about the creation of Allah ﷻ in the nature and everywhere as mentioned وَهُوَ الَّذِي يُرْسِلُ الرِّيَاحَ بُشْرًا بَيْنَ يَدَيْ رَحْمَتِهِ حَتَّى إِذَا أَقَلَّتْ سَحَابًا ثِقَالًا سُقْنَاهُ لِبَلَدٍ مَّيِّتٍ فَأَنزَلْنَا بِهِ الْمَاء فَأَخْرَجْنَا بِهِ مِن كُلِّ الثَّمَرَاتِ كَذَلِكَ نُخْرِجُ الْمَوْتَى لَعَلَّكُمْ تَذَكَّرُونَ 183 {الأعراف/57}

A person can hope to be a true Muslim by fully realizing all the nímahs[184], bounties, worldly achievements are from Allah ﷻ as mentioned in وَاللّهُ جَعَلَ لَكُم مِّمَّا خَلَقَ ظِلاَلاً وَجَعَلَ لَكُم مِّنَ الْجِبَالِ أَكْنَانًا وَجَعَلَ لَكُمْ سَرَابِيلَ تَقِيكُمُ الْحَرَّ وَسَرَابِيلَ تَقِيكُم بَأْسَكُمْ كَذَلِكَ يُتِمُّ نِعْمَتَهُ عَلَيْكُمْ لَعَلَّكُمْ تُسْلِمُونَ 185 {النحل/81}.

It is interesting to realize as a side note that being in a lot of bounties and realization of these bounties as coming from Allah ﷻ can make the person a true Muslim. This can be seen in the case of Yusuf as when he as was at the highest peak of worldly achievement and his lost family came back, as mentioned رَبِّ قَدْ آتَيْتَنِي مِنَ الْمُلْكِ وَعَلَّمْتَنِي مِن تَأْوِيلِ الأَحَادِيثِ فَاطِرَ السَّمَاوَاتِ وَالأَرْضِ أَنتَ وَلِيِّي فِي الدُّنُيَا وَالآخِرَةِ تَوَفَّنِي مُسْلِمًا وَأَلْحِقْنِي بِالصَّالِحِينَ 186 {يوسف/101}

This can be also realized in the case of Balqis when she saw the bounty of Sulaymān as she fully and truly realized that they were from Allah ﷻ and turned truly as a Muslim to Allah ﷻ when she said قِيلَ لَهَا ادْخُلِي الصَّرْحَ فَلَمَّا رَأَتْهُ حَسِبَتْهُ لُجَّةً وَكَشَفَتْ عَن سَاقَيْهَا قَالَ إِنَّهُ صَرْحٌ مُّمَرَّدٌ مِّن قَوَارِيرَ قَالَتْ رَبِّ إِنِّي ظَلَمْتُ نَفْسِي وَأَسْلَمْتُ مَعَ سُلَيْمَانَ لِلَّهِ رَبِّ الْعَالَمِينَ 187 {النمل/44}

On the other hand, there are people for whom Allah ﷻ gave nímahs[188] but they don't realize and appreciate these nímahs and they are not thankful and grateful to Allah ﷻ. Then, Allah ﷻ opens all other doors of nímah.

---

183. And it is He who sends the winds as good tidings before His mercy [i.e., rainfall] until, when they have carried heavy rainclouds, We drive them to a dead land and We send down rain therein and bring forth thereby [some] of all the fruits. Thus will We bring forth the dead; perhaps you may be reminded.
184. Blessings.
185. And Allah has made for you, from that which He has created, shadows [i.e., shade] and has made for you from the mountains, shelters and has made for you garments which protect you from the heat and garments [i.e., coats of mail] which protect you from your [enemy in] battle. Thus does He complete His favor upon you that you might submit [to Him].
186. My Lord, You have given me [something] of sovereignty and taught me of the interpretation of dreams. Creator of the heavens and earth, You are my protector in this world and the Hereafter. Cause me to die a Muslim and join me with the righteous."
187. She was told, "Enter the palace." But when she saw it, she thought it was a body of water and uncovered her shins [to wade through]. He said, "Indeed, it is a palace [whose floor is] made smooth with glass." She said, "My Lord, indeed I have wronged myself, and I submit with Solomon to Allah, Lord of the worlds."
188. Blessings.

In this case, having and or being in nímah can be an istridrāj, a test or trial that can take the person to an opposite direction further if the person is already embodied ungratefulness or heedlessness because the person does not realize that all nímahs are from Allah ﷻ. They become further arrogant and ungrateful. An example of this mentioned as فَلَمَّا نَسُواْ مَا ذُكِّرُواْ بِهِ فَتَحْنَا عَلَيْهِمْ أَبْوَابَ كُلِّ شَيْءٍ حَتَّى إِذَا فَرِحُواْ بِمَا أُوتُواْ أَخَذْنَاهُم بَغْتَةً فَإِذَا هُم مُّبْلِسُونَ 189 {الأنعام/44}. It is interesting to note that the name of this Sûrah is An'ām and the ayah is emphasizing all the nìmahs being given to this person as mentioned with the part فَتَحْنَا عَلَيْهِمْ أَبْوَابَ كُلِّ شَيْءٍ 190.

Another example of this can be the case of Qarûn as mentioned إِنَّ قَارُونَ كَانَ مِن قَوْمِ مُوسَى فَبَغَى عَلَيْهِمْ وَآتَيْنَاهُ مِنَ الْكُنُوزِ مَا إِنَّ مَفَاتِحَهُ لَتَنُوءُ بِالْعُصْبَةِ أُولِي الْقُوَّةِ إِذْ قَالَ لَهُ قَوْمُهُ لَا تَفْرَحْ إِنَّ اللَّهَ لَا يُحِبُّ الْفَرِحِينَ 191 {القصص/76} وَابْتَغِ فِيمَا آتَاكَ اللَّهُ الدَّارَ الْآخِرَةَ وَلَا تَنسَ نَصِيبَكَ مِنَ الدُّنْيَا وَأَحْسِن كَمَا أَحْسَنَ اللَّهُ إِلَيْكَ وَلَا تَبْغِ الْفَسَادَ فِي الْأَرْضِ إِنَّ اللَّهَ لَا يُحِبُّ الْمُفْسِدِينَ 192 {القصص/77} قَالَ إِنَّمَا أُوتِيتُهُ عَلَى عِلْمٍ عِندِي أَوَلَمْ يَعْلَمْ أَنَّ اللَّهَ قَدْ أَهْلَكَ مِن قَبْلِهِ مِنَ الْقُرُونِ مَنْ هُوَ أَشَدُّ مِنْهُ قُوَّةً وَأَكْثَرُ جَمْعًا وَلَا يُسْأَلُ عَن ذُنُوبِهِمُ الْمُجْرِمُونَ 193 {القصص/78}

The correct and true hope requires true imān and tawhid for this to be not in the category of umniyyah, a wrong and whimsical hope. In this regard, one can find a lot of similarities or engagements of hope of Ahlu-kitāb, Christians or others like Muslims. Yet, when there are no full and complete articles of tawhid, then imperfection and problematic points of their creed can make them display dispositions such as وَقَالُواْ لَن يَدْخُلَ 194 الْجَنَّةَ إِلاَّ مَن كَانَ هُوداً أَوْ نَصَارَى. Then, this becomes a false and incorrect hope as mentioned with أَمَانِيُّهُمْ 195.

Yet, the similar or true dispositions of hope can be also displayed by ahlu-kitāb, especially by the ones who are in the classification of the

---

189. So when they forgot that by which they had been reminded, We opened to them the doors of every [good] thing until, when they rejoiced in that which they were given, We seized them suddenly, and they were [then] in despair.
190. We opened to them the doors of every [good] thing.
191. Indeed, Qaru'n was from the people of Moses, but he tyrannized them. And We gave him of treasures whose keys would burden a band of strong men; thereupon his people said to him, "Do not exult. Indeed, Allah does not like the exultant.
192. But seek, through that which Allah has given you, the home of the Hereafter; and [yet], do not forget your share of the world. And do good as Allah has done good to you. And desire not corruption in the land. Indeed, Allah does not like corrupters."
193. He said, "I was only given it because of knowledge I have." Did he not know that AllŒh had destroyed before him of generations those who were greater than him in power and greater in accumulation [of wealth]? But the criminals, about their sins, will not be asked.
194. And they say, "None will enter Paradise except one who is a Jew or a Christian."
195. Their wishful thinking.

وَإِذَا سَمِعُواْ مَا أُنزِلَ إِلَى الرَّسُولِ تَرَى أَعْيُنَهُمْ تَفِيضُ مِنَ الدَّمْعِ مِمَّا عَرَفُواْ مِنَ الْحَقِّ as ayah

يَقُولُونَ رَبَّنَا آمَنَّا فَاكْتُبْنَا مَعَ الشَّاهِدِينَ[196] {المائدة/83}.

The expression لَعَلَّكُمْ تَتَّقُونَ[197] can signify that the result of taqwa is present at the end of continuation of the 'ibadah. The best thing to hope and achieve at the end of the 'ibadah is taqwa. Yet, in some cases, taqwa may not be achieved due to the absence of ikhlas and core beliefs of tawhid, imān and Islam although there may be the external forms of 'ibadah.

In the expression of لَعَلَّكُمْ تَتَّقُونَ, the word taqwa can have different levels. Some of these can be taqwa from shirk, taqwa from kabāir[198], taqwa from everything except Allah ﷻ, holding the heart to be attached to except Allah ﷻ, staying away from the engagements that may attract punishment, protecting oneself from the anger can be all in the categories of taqwa.

In the classical translations of the word taqwa, one of the common meanings include protecting oneself, avoidance, escaping, safeguarding, and preventing in all self-related engagements in order not to displease Allah ﷻ and maintain this internal state leading to external engagements.

Therefore, the implementation and pillars of taqwa require the categorization of halal and haram as outlined by the fiqh, legal schools. Yet, this classification can be only the beginning and pillars that one should and can excel on it to achieve the level of ihsān in the constant applications of taqwa.

The terms related with taqwa as avoidance, escaping, safeguarding and others have all meanings of vertical Transcendent realities and at the same time, it indicates horizontal human related engagements. For example, a person avoiding quarrel, argument, and possible sources of fitnah with people at the horizontal level can be related with the taqwa of the Transcendent, Allah ﷻ. The person can fill this avoidance with the correct intention as indicated in the Qurān and sunnah of Rasulullah ﷺ. Taqwa in this case can be a state of avoidance and protection from all the possible sources of worldly engagements that may lead to the displeasure of Allah ﷻ. At a higher level, it can be a state of avoidance

---

196. And when they hear what has been revealed to the Messenger, you see their eyes overflowing with tears because of what they have recognized of the truth. They say, "Our Lord, we have believed, so register us among the witnesses.

197. So that you may become righteous.

198. Major sins.

and protection from all possible mind, thought and even emotion related renderings that may lead to the displeasure of Allah ﷻ.

When one analyzes the ayah يَا أَيُّهَا النَّاسُ اعْبُدُواْ رَبَّكُمُ الَّذِي خَلَقَكُمْ وَالَّذِينَ مِن قَبْلِكُمْ لَعَلَّكُمْ تَتَّقُونَ [199] {البقرة/21}, the part لَعَلَّكُمْ تَتَّقُونَ [200] can indicate that the purpose of the 'ibadah is taqwa. In words, 'ibadah is the means to achieve taqwa but it is not the end or goal.

In the ayah يَا أَيُّهَا النَّاسُ اعْبُدُواْ رَبَّكُمُ الَّذِي خَلَقَكُمْ وَالَّذِينَ مِن قَبْلِكُمْ لَعَلَّكُمْ تَتَّقُونَ [201] {البقرة/21}, the word لَعَلَّكُمْ can also indicate the choice of humans with their free will. In other words, the word لَعَلَّكُمْ can imply this possibility of humans without force but their intention, inclination or free choice.

From another perspective, when one observes the nature, Allah ﷻ creates different things for a purpose. For example, a lion has claws to catch, to cut, and to fight. A watermelon is juicy to eat. Similarly, there is a purpose and goal both in physical and spiritual design of a human being. This is taqwa as mentioned لَعَلَّكُمْ تَتَّقُونَ [202]. The person should restore and use his or her faculties for their original design.

The next part of the ayah with الَّذِي جَعَلَ لَكُمُ الأَرْضَ فِرَاشاً وَالسَّمَاء بِنَاء [203] can motivate the person to make 'ibadah to Allah ﷻ. It mentions that Allah ﷻ did you a favor for all these arrangements, therefore, Allah ﷻ has the full and true due and right to be worshipped.

When we analyze the two ayahs ذَلِكَ الْكِتَابُ لاَ رَيْبَ فِيهِ هُدًى لِّلْمُتَّقِينَ [204] and يَا أَيُّهَا النَّاسُ اعْبُدُواْ رَبَّكُمُ الَّذِي خَلَقَكُمْ وَالَّذِينَ مِن قَبْلِكُمْ لَعَلَّكُمْ تَتَّقُونَ [205] {البقرة/2} and {البقرة/21}, the true hidāyah [206] from Allah ﷻ can come with true 'ibadah to Allah ﷻ and this can lead the person to be a muttaqìn [207].

The type of discourse in this ayah can at the same time indicate the high level of human beings. Human beings are created by Allah ﷻ with a noble status. This nobility is also indicated with the direct address in the beginning of the previous ayah as يَا أَيُّهَا النَّاسُ [208].

---

199. O mankind, worship your Lord, who created you and those before you, that you may become righteous.
200. That you may become righteous.
201. O mankind, worship your Lord, who created you and those before you, that you may become righteous.
202. That you may become righteous.
203. [He] who made for you the earth a bed [spread out] and the sky a ceiling.
204. This is the Book about which there is no doubt, a guidance for those conscious of Allah
205. O mankind, worship your Lord, who created you and those before you, that you may become righteous.
206. Guidance.
207. Righteous.
208. O mankind.

On another perspective, the call يَا أَيُّهَا النَّاسُ can indicate expected display of the loyalty of humans to Allah ﷻ by worshipping to Allah ﷻ. In other words, 'ibadah of a person can be this disposition of loyalty after all the favors of Rabbul àlamin.

The part of the ayah with الَّذِي جَعَلَ لَكُمُ الأَرْضَ فِرَاشاً وَالسَّمَاء بِنَاء[209] can also indicate that everything in the nature is created by Allah ﷻ and with the will of Allah ﷻ. In this sense, there is no ambiguous language of nature, science, laws, or mother universe etc. but Allah ﷻ is the Creator of everything.

With all the possibilities, mumkinãt[210], there is the direct will (qast) of Allah ﷻ to create and to assign tasks, qualities, attributes (sifah), in order to maintain a task, as mentioned with الَّذِي جَعَلَ لَكُمُ الأَرْضَ فِرَاشاً[211] وَالسَّمَاء بِنَاء.

In other words, among billions and zillions of possibilities, and among billions and zillions of atoms, each atom forms some specific elements. Among these specific elements, selected elements form bodies such as earth, skies, humans, ants, bees, stars and all different creation with different and similar definite qualities and quantities. All these undeniable obvious realities necessitate certainly and absolutely a direct will called as the Qasd[212] or Divine Will of Allah ﷻ.

In the expression الَّذِي جَعَلَ لَكُمُ[213], the word لَكُمُ[214] is for sababiyah, causality. In other words, the reason for the preparation of the earth with its variety of bounties, nìmahs is human beings. If other creation benefits from earth, it does not negate its primary purpose.

In the part الَّذِي جَعَلَ لَكُمُ الأَرْضَ فِرَاشاً وَالسَّمَاء بِنَاء[215], the word فِرَاشاً[216] is interesting to analyze. This word has the meanings of to spread, widen, make it a place of lying or resting. In this sense, when one considers external shape of the earth as being circular, any round shape object in worldly physical laws would not have anything on it standing still but it would fall down.

---

209. [He] who made for you the earth a bed [spread out] and the sky a ceiling.
210. Possibilities.
211. [He] who made for you the earth a bed [spread out] and the sky a ceiling.
212. Divine will.
213. He who made for you.
214. For you.
215. [He] who made for you the earth a bed [spread out] and the sky a ceiling.
216. A bed {spread out}.

Yet, it is always the sunnatullah to make things possible from the impossibilities in order to amaze us by showing the obvious signs of Allah ﷻ. One may call this as miracle. The real disposition of imān requires the mu'min to be overwhelmed with the constant amazing signs of Allah ﷻ. These amazements expected to lead the person to be in the constant engagements of dhikr with the station of ihsān.

Yet, there are some people who cannot go beyond the laws of physics to find the One Who establishes these laws for a purpose. This purpose is to benefit the humans. Therefore, imān is always recognizing these amazements of Allah ﷻ, appreciating it and verbalizing and embodying in the forms of ìbadah to show gratitude, thankfulness and gratefulness to Allah ﷻ. Our goal should be in being constant amazements with these bounties increasing our yaqîn about the knowledge of Allah ﷻ. The shape, color, mechanism, coordination, structure, micro and macro level analysis of these bounties can constantly make the person to be in the Jannah valleys of imān in this world.In this sense, when a person reviews a college textbook on anatomy, and human physiology, the person can have the similar sparks of imān saying "SubhanAllah!" constantly as if this person is reading the Qurān.

In this sense, when a person reviews a college textbook on astronomy, the person can have the similar sparks of imān saying "SubhanAllah!" naturally as if this person is reading the Qurān.

One can increase these amazements through different specialties, and disciplines as categorized and established different university departments by humans. Yet, looking these amazements without connecting to the Real Doer is a big loss and uncompleted puzzle of this amazement.

It is a loss on the part of the person that he or she does not know how to channel this amazement in a more profitable way in this world and afterlife. The mere amazements of some of the scientists without realizing Allah ﷻ as the Real Doer is similar to a person who is constantly receiving delicious cake every day, eating it and amazed by its taste but does not care to find the person who is sending it. Since he or she does not have this concern of finding, therefore he or she does not have the concern of thanking about it.

One can analyze the word الَّذِي جَعَلَ لَكُمُ الأَرْضَ فِرَاشاً وَالسَّمَاء فِرَاشاً[217] in بِنَاء from the perspective of geography. If one analyzes the continents on the earth, they are simply portion of the lands that are not under water. If we analyze the mountains in these lands, they are the erected parts of the portions of these lands. In other words, Allah ﷻ sets the system in a such a way that certain parts of the earth are land with a livable steepness, slope, gradient and concavity. The parts of the lands under the water are called lake, sea or oceans.

In this regard, the word فِرَاشاً[218] can indicate the suitable conditions for vegetation, and planting with the livable conditions on this land.

The word فِرَاشاً can also imply the base of a building or a house. In this sense, this house is built on a foundation and there is the sustenance of food, air, and other necessary items for humans. The ceiling of this house is the sky as mentioned with وَالسَّمَاء بِنَاء[219].

The base of this house as implied with the word فِرَاشاً[220] is not all solid or all soft. There is the mixed composition of textures to allow both vegetation, agriculture and civil engineering. One can review the amazements in this field in these composition of textures as created by Allah ﷻ with the discipline of material engineering.

In this regard, the word فِرَاشاً can signify this livability among the infinite impossibilities as set by Allah ﷻ referred as the sunnatullah. In other words, Allah ﷻ shows everywhere and in each field of scientific disciplines these possibilities from impossibilities to humble the person and show the Qudrah of Allah ﷻ.

As our teacher used to say, "it is the sunnatullah to make big things or achievements from the trivial looking things and persons." Allah ﷻ can make from trivial-seeming things enormous-looking outcomes as mentioned إِنَّ اللَّهَ لاَ يَسْتَحْيِي أَن يَضْرِبَ مَثَلاً مَّا بَعُوضَةً فَمَا فَوْقَهَا فَأَمَّا الَّذِينَ آمَنُواْ فَيَعْلَمُونَ أَنَّهُ الْحَقُّ مِن رَّبِّهِمْ وَأَمَّا الَّذِينَ كَفَرُواْ فَيَقُولُونَ مَاذَا أَرَادَ اللَّهُ بِهَذَا مَثَلاً يُضِلُّ بِهِ كَثِيراً وَيَهْدِي بِهِ كَثِيراً وَمَا يُضِلُّ بِهِ إِلاَّ الْفَاسِقِينَ[221] {البقرة/26}.

---

217. Bed [Spread out].
218. A bed {spread out}.
219. And the sky [a ceiling].
220. A bed {spread out}.
221. Indeed, Allah is not timid to present an example—that of a mosquito or what is smaller than it. And those who have believed know that it is the truth from their Lord. But as for those who disbelieve, they say, "What did Allah intend by this as an example?" He misleads many thereby and guides many thereby. And He misleads not except the defiantly disobedient.

This itself can show the Divine Interference as a clear sign to show Allah ﷻ 's Qudrah, Will and Tawfiq[222]. Therefore, one should not take credit on any achievement and become arrogant and lose. The person should constantly give all the due true credit in all the engagements of good to Allah ﷻ and make shukr and hamd to Rabbul 'Alamin[223] for being chosen and used as an insignificant and trivial means on the path of Allah ﷻ.

As soon as the person gets on him or herself a due credit or even, thinks that he or she deserves a tiny due of this khayr, good achievement, then the person can be called as a liar, kāfir, mushrik according to the level of his or her engagement. May Allah ﷻ protect us, Amîn!

On another perspective the word[224] فِرَاشاً is used instead of مفروشا[225]. This can indicate that it is not only the geometrical shape of flatness as a livable space but also it can indicate that it is the place of calmness and comfort as the word فِرَاش can signify.

The word بِنَاء[226] can indicate a ceiling and upper limit of a space. The word وَالسَّمَاء[227] in وَالسَّمَاء بِنَاء is generally translated as sky in English. Sky in popular language is the region of the atmosphere and outer space seen from the earth [2]. Then, one can think about stars, planets, moon and other observable objects. Yet, there are a lot of other entities observed and estimated with scientific discoveries such as galaxies, types of stars such as dwarfs, set of galaxies, black holes and others.

Value of a Human: Work of the Heart (Amalul Qulub) or Work of the Body

One can consider the size of a human in all these systems and ask, how can a tiny human in these macroscopic complex systems can be the central focus of the creation? The answer can be that it is not due to his or her physical body but the due to the faculties of heart, mind, soul and other inner faculties. Yet, in this sense, it is not the goal of the humans to make a value system based on amal or action or work of the physical

---

222. Reconcile.
223. Lord of both worlds.
224. Spread out.
225. Furnished.
226. A ceiling.
227. And the sky.

body or worldly achievments as mentioned in the below ayahs with the key expression of أَشَدُّ مِنكُمْ[228].

فَأَمَّا عَادٌ فَاسْتَكْبَرُوا فِي الْأَرْضِ بِغَيْرِ الْحَقِّ وَقَالُوا مَنْ أَشَدُّ مِنَّا قُوَّةً أَوَلَمْ يَرَوْا أَنَّ اللَّهَ الَّذِي خَلَقَهُمْ هُوَ أَشَدُّ مِنْهُمْ قُوَّةً وَكَانُوا بِآيَاتِنَا يَجْحَدُونَ[229] {فصلت/15}

كَالَّذِينَ مِن قَبْلِكُمْ كَانُوا أَشَدَّ مِنكُمْ قُوَّةً وَأَكْثَرَ أَمْوَالاً وَأَوْلَادًا فَاسْتَمْتَعُوا بِخَلَاقِهِمْ فَاسْتَمْتَعْتُم بِخَلَاقِكُمْ كَمَا اسْتَمْتَعَ الَّذِينَ مِن قَبْلِكُمْ بِخَلَاقِهِمْ وَخُضْتُمْ كَالَّذِي خَاضُوا أُولَئِكَ حَبِطَتْ أَعْمَالُهُمْ فِي الدُّنْيَا وَالْآخِرَةِ وَأُولَئِكَ هُمُ الْخَاسِرُونَ[230] {التوبة/69}

أَوَلَمْ يَسِيرُوا فِي الْأَرْضِ فَيَنظُرُوا كَيْفَ كَانَ عَاقِبَةُ الَّذِينَ مِن قَبْلِهِمْ كَانُوا أَشَدَّ مِنْهُمْ قُوَّةً وَأَثَارُوا الْأَرْضَ وَعَمَرُوهَا أَكْثَرَ مِمَّا عَمَرُوهَا وَجَاءَتْهُمْ رُسُلُهُم بِالْبَيِّنَاتِ فَمَا كَانَ اللَّهُ لِيَظْلِمَهُمْ وَلَكِن كَانُوا أَنفُسَهُمْ يَظْلِمُونَ[231] {الروم/9}

أَوَلَمْ يَسِيرُوا فِي الْأَرْضِ فَيَنظُرُوا كَيْفَ كَانَ عَاقِبَةُ الَّذِينَ مِن قَبْلِهِمْ وَكَانُوا أَشَدَّ مِنْهُمْ قُوَّةً وَمَا كَانَ اللَّهُ لِيُعْجِزَهُ مِن شَيْءٍ فِي السَّمَاوَاتِ وَلَا فِي الْأَرْضِ إِنَّهُ كَانَ عَلِيمًا قَدِيرًا[232] {فاطر/44}

أَوَلَمْ يَسِيرُوا فِي الْأَرْضِ فَيَنظُرُوا كَيْفَ كَانَ عَاقِبَةُ الَّذِينَ كَانُوا مِن قَبْلِهِمْ كَانُوا هُمْ أَشَدَّ مِنْهُمْ قُوَّةً وَآثَارًا فِي الْأَرْضِ فَأَخَذَهُمُ اللَّهُ بِذُنُوبِهِمْ وَمَا كَانَ لَهُم مِّنَ اللَّهِ مِن وَاقٍ[233] {غافر/21}

---

228. Greater then them.

229. As for Aad, they were arrogant upon the earth without right and said, "Who is greater than us in strength?" Did they not consider that Allah who created them was greater than them in strength? But they were rejecting Our signs.

230. [You disbelievers are] like those before you; they were stronger than you in power and more abundant in wealth and children. They enjoyed their portion [of worldly enjoyment], and you have enjoyed your portion as those before you enjoyed their portion, and you have engaged [in vanities] like that in which they engaged. [It is] those whose deeds have become worthless in this world and in the Hereafter, and it is they who are the losers.

231. Have they not traveled through the earth and observed how was the end of those before them? They were greater than them in power, and they plowed [or excavated] the earth and built it up more than they [i.e., the Makkans] have built it up, and their messengers came to them with clear evidences. And Allah would not ever have wronged them, but they were wronging themselves.

232. Have they not traveled through the land and observed how was the end of those before them? And they were greater than them in power. But Allah is not to be caused failure [i.e., prevented] by anything in the heavens or on the earth. Indeed, He is ever Knowing and Competent.

233. Have they not traveled through the land and observed how was the end of those who were before them? They were greater than them in strength and in impression on the land, but Allah seized them for their sins. And they had not from Allah any protector.

فَأَهْلَكْنَا أَشَدَّ مِنْهُم بَطْشًا وَمَضَى مَثَلُ الْأَوَّلِينَ²³⁴ {الزخرف/8}

وَكَمْ أَهْلَكْنَا قَبْلَهُم مِّن قَرْنٍ هُمْ أَشَدُّ مِنْهُم بَطْشًا فَنَقَّبُوا فِي الْبِلَادِ هَلْ مِن مَّحِيصٍ²³⁵ {ق/36}

In other words, humans should not have a value system with their evaluations of physical achievements in the world. Allah ﷻ created so much enormous and complex systems in their physical and material compositions and relationships as mentioned لَخَلْقُ السَّمَاوَاتِ وَالْأَرْضِ أَكْبَرُ مِنْ خَلْقِ النَّاسِ وَلَكِنَّ أَكْثَرَ النَّاسِ لَا يَعْلَمُونَ²³⁶ {غافر/57}.

Perhaps, since our immediate judgment or valuation of the people is through physical achievements, there is a suggestion to travel different places to see the physical strength of people as how it used to be in order to take a heed and lesson as mentioned أَوَلَمْ يَسِيرُوا فِي الْأَرْضِ فَيَنظُرُوا كَيْفَ²³⁷ كَانَ عَاقِبَةُ الَّذِينَ مِن قَبْلِهِمْ. Possibly, this may help the person to convince him or herself about this reality.

There is a difference in methodology of the value systems present itself here in Western Philosophy detached from religion and true Muslim philosophy.

Western philosophy gives values and meanings to everything around them according to their apparent meaning only through the faculties of mind by only using deductive reasoning.

Muslim philosophy gives values and meanings to everything around them according to their both apparent and wholistic meanings through the faculties of mind and heart imbedded in wahiy/revelation of the Qurãn and Sunnah by using both deductive and inductive reasonings.

In other words, deductive reasoning is the apparent and immediate meanings of this data empirically accessible to the person.

Inductive reasoning is the meanings and understanding of this piece in the whole system as being part of the whole.

In this sense, our mind can give immediate empirical data of inductive reasoning through mind.

234. And We destroyed greater than them in [striking] power, and the example of the former peoples has preceded.
235. And how many a generation before them did We destroy who were greater than them in [striking] power and had explored throughout the lands. Is there any place of escape?
236. The creation of the heavens and earth is greater than the creation of mankind, but most of the people dont know.
237. Have they not traveled through the land and observed how was the end of those who were before them?

In Muslim philosophy, both inductive reasoning of piece analysis and deductive reasoning of whole analysis have its true value in their reference to imān, their reference to being creation of Allah ﷻ and their reference to their purpose of creation as created by Allah ﷻ.

In secular understanding of deductive and inductive reasoning, all the piece and whole analysis are performed within the world of apparent of alam-shadah without their reference to their real meanings to imān, and their reference to Allah ﷻ.

In Muslim philosophy of deductive reasoning in piece analysis, everything shows Allah ﷻ with the Name al-Ahad[238]. In their deductive reasoning of group analysis, everything shows Allah ﷻ with the Name al-Wahid[239]. The piece has a purpose, goal and meaning in the whole with the reference point of imān as explained by Allah ﷻ. Although every piece has a value with their reference point to imān, there are assigned meanings to each piece of creation as mentioned with the word of (jàla) [240] جعل in many parts of the Qurān.

In this sense, giving value or meaning beyond their defined and assigned meanings to these pieces by Allah ﷻ is considered incorrect, falsehood, zulm, oppression and darkness. The value of system of religion is therefore different than the Western Philosophy of value system based only on mind.

For example, in the terminologies and assigned meanings of basic physics, electrons were first assigned with negative charges and protons were assigned with positive changes. Then this, in the popular meanings of physics carried to the gender relations of man and women. Then, implicit meanings and interpretations were given to indicate oppositeness with opposite sex or contradicting features. Yet, later positron was discovered carrying the features of electron with positive charges. Then, with the quantum physics, electron and positron merging became popular with the word annihilation. With the detailed findings of quantum physics another term was developed as pairs instead of opposites. Distinction between opposites and parity was better and further branched.

Analyzing the above cases as given by natural scientists increasingly derived assigning meanings with the Western philosophy of empirical

---

238. The One.
239. The Unique.
240. Assigned or made.

meanings, the religion in scriptures approached the cases of genders of male and female not as opposites minimizing the conflicts but as more close pairs with complementary roles and aiming to have harmony.

In this sense, true, authentic and original religious teachings from God gives and shows, presents and makes humans accessible to the universal truths and knowledge. If humans don't accept them, the journeys of life in scientific discoveries will accumulate over the course of hundreds and thousands of years will end up with the same results as given by inductive reasoning in revelations in the true scriptures.

Therefore, genuine and smart people use the notion of "submit" and "follow" with these true and authentic teachings of God instead of going constantly in the mind struggles and worries of theories, premises and assumptions and methodology of mere logic.

That does not mean that mind is not important. Mind is important. Yet, it should be accepted that it has limits and it needs guidance. Mind pumped with arrogance is nothing more than a balloon filled with air that has no mass. As humans discover more galaxies, a true scientist will be expected to be more humble for the limitations of their own selves as humans but not become more arrogant.

The similarities of both systems of philosophy stem from the fact that Allah ﷻ wants humans to use their mind in the guidance of wahiy[241]. The similarities stem from the fact that Allah ﷻ does order or assign meanings that have the inclusive and complete meanings of logic, wisdom, care and mercy.

Yet, the goal is the amalul qulub[242]. In other words, there are the works of the heart and soul. They all start with the proper intention, niyyah[243]. In this sense, amalul qulub, the actions and works of the heart, can be sidq[244], ikhlas[245], khashyah[246], muraqabah[247], khudue[248], rida[249], faqr[250], dhull[251] and others.

---

241. Revealation from God.
242. Works of the heart and soul.
243. Intention.
244. Truthful.
245. Sincerity.
246. Fear.
247. Internal reflection. { to reflect using your heart and mind}
248. Submission.
249. Pleasure.
250. Poverty.
251. Humiliation.

In this sense, amal of the body follows the amalul qulub as mentioned by Rasulullah ﷺ that all the value of the actions are according to their intentions [3] [4]. According to many ulamāh, scholars, including the founder of usul, methodology in Islam, Imam Shafi (Rh), the hadith about value of the actions is according to intentions is the basis of one third of the religion of Islam [3] [4].

Due to absence of amalul qulub, Shaytān lost. Shaytān did not have Dhull [252] (الذل) but claim to have izzah (عزه[253]) by comparing the physicality, or composition of the creation material of fire versus dust.

The similar wrong and deadly comparison are performed by humans following these footsteps as:

إِنَّ قَارُونَ كَانَ مِن قَوْمِ مُوسَى فَبَغَى عَلَيْهِمْ وَآتَيْنَاهُ مِنَ الْكُنُوزِ مَا إِنَّ مَفَاتِحَهُ لَتَنُوءُ بِالْعُصْبَةِ أُولِي الْقُوَّةِ إِذْ قَالَ لَهُ قَوْمُهُ لَا تَفْرَحْ إِنَّ اللَّهَ لَا يُحِبُّ الْفَرِحِينَ[254] {القصص/76}

قَالَ إِنَّمَا أُوتِيتُهُ عَلَى عِلْمٍ عِندِي أَوَلَمْ يَعْلَمْ أَنَّ اللَّهَ قَدْ أَهْلَكَ مِن قَبْلِهِ مِنَ الْقُرُونِ مَنْ هُوَ أَشَدُّ مِنْهُ قُوَّةً وَأَكْثَرُ جَمْعًا وَلَا يُسْأَلُ عَن ذُنُوبِهِمُ الْمُجْرِمُونَ[255] {القصص/78}

فَخَرَجَ عَلَى قَوْمِهِ فِي زِينَتِهِ قَالَ الَّذِينَ يُرِيدُونَ الْحَيَاةَ الدُّنْيَا يَا لَيْتَ لَنَا مِثْلَ مَا أُوتِيَ قَارُونُ إِنَّهُ لَذُو حَظٍّ عَظِيمٍ[256] {القصص/79}

Amalul Qulûb: Ikhlas-Everything for Allah ﷻ

قَالَ أَنَا خَيْرٌ مِّنْهُ خَلَقْتَنِي مِن نَّارٍ وَخَلَقْتَهُ مِن طِينٍ[257] {ص/76} قَالَ فَاخْرُجْ مِنْهَا فَإِنَّكَ رَجِيمٌ[258] {ص/77} وَإِنَّ عَلَيْكَ لَعْنَتِي إِلَى يَوْمِ الدِّينِ[259] {ص/78} قَالَ رَبِّ فَأَنظِرْنِي إِلَى

---

252. Humbleness and Humility
253. Pride.
254. Indeed, Qarun was from the people of Moses, but he tyrannized them. And We gave him of treasures whose keys would burden a band of strong men; thereupon his people said to him, "Do not exult. Indeed, Allah does not like the exultant.
255. He said, "I was only given it because of knowledge I have." Did he not know that Allah had destroyed before him of generations those who were greater than him in power and greater in accumulation [of wealth]? But the criminals, about their sins, will not be asked.
256. So he came out before his people in his adornment. Those who desired the worldly life said, "Oh, would that we had like what was given to Qarun. Indeed, he is one of great fortune."
257. He said, "I am better than him. You created me from fire and created him from clay."
258. [Allah] said, "Then get out of it [i.e., Paradise], for indeed, you are expelled.
259. And indeed, upon you is My curse until the Day of Recompense."

يَوْمِ يُبْعَثُونَ 260 {ص/79} قَالَ فَإِنَّكَ مِنَ الْمُنظَرِينَ 261 {ص/80} إِلَى يَوْمِ الْوَقْتِ الْمَعْلُومِ 262 {ص/81} قَالَ فَبِعِزَّتِكَ لَأُغْوِيَنَّهُمْ أَجْمَعِينَ 263 {ص/82} إِلاَّ عِبَادَكَ مِنْهُمُ الْمُخْلَصِينَ 264 {ص/83}

قَالَ فَالْحَقُّ وَالْحَقَّ أَقُولُ 265 {ص/84}

It is very interesting to note in the above ayahs that Shaytān makes a true statement about something that he himself does not do. He mentions that the core of the action is ikhlas as {ص/83} 266 إِلَّا عِبَادَكَ مِنْهُمُ الْمُخْلَصِينَ, yet he himself does not do it. Allah ﷻ approves this truth as قَالَ فَالْحَقُّ وَالْحَقَّ أَقُولُ 267 {ص/84}.

Ikhlas is doing everything to please solely and only for Allah ﷻ. This is called pure and true religion.

Adab and ikhlas, doing everything for Allah ﷻ requires following the command of Allah ﷻ as angels did as mentioned إِذْ قَالَ رَبُّكَ لِلْمَلَائِكَةِ إِنِّي خَالِقٌ بَشَرًا مِن طِينٍ 268 {ص/71} فَإِذَا سَوَّيْتُهُ وَنَفَخْتُ فِيهِ مِن رُّوحِي فَقَعُوا لَهُ سَاجِدِينَ 269 {ص/72} فَسَجَدَ الْمَلَائِكَةُ كُلُّهُمْ أَجْمَعُونَ 270 {ص/73}

Shaytān could have had a question about the position of Adam. Yet, he did not have ikhlas and adab to please Allah ﷻ as mentioned إِلَّا إِبْلِيسَ اسْتَكْبَرَ وَكَانَ مِنَ الْكَافِرِينَ 271 {ص/74}.

One should understand that every person is different. Some people can have more strong self-identity. Everything is fine if we know our limits with the shi'ār 272 and accordingly with Allah ﷻ. If this boundary is broken as mentioned with قَالَ يَا إِبْلِيسُ مَا مَنَعَكَ أَن تَسْجُدَ لِمَا خَلَقْتُ بِيَدَيَّ أَسْتَكْبَرْتَ أَمْ

---

260. He said, "My Lord, then reprieve me until the Day they are resurrected."
261. [Allah] said, "So indeed, you are of those reprieved.
262. Until the Day of the time well-known."
263. [Iblees] said, "By Your might, I will surely mislead them all.
264. Except, among them, Your chosen servants."
265. [Allah] said, "The truth [is My oath], and the truth I say.
266. Except, among them, Your chosen servants."
267. [Allah] said, "The truth [is My oath], and the truth I say.
268. [So mention] when your Lord said to the angels, "Indeed, I am going to create a human being from clay.
269. So when I have proportioned him and breathed into him of My [created] soul, then fall down to him in prostration."
270. So the angels prostrated—all of them entirely,
271. Except Iblees; he was arrogant and became among the disbelievers.
272. The assigned items by Allah that deserve respect.

{75/ص} 273كُنتَ مِنَ الْعَالِينَ, then the person falls into the endless punishment of undeserved, lying, disrespectful punishments of arrogance, kibir as mentioned أَسْتَكْبَرْتَ274.

This kibir275 is only removed then with fear and Jahannam as mentioned a person who has a tiny kibir in their will not enter Jannah [4] [8] [9], May Allah ﷻ protect us.

There are many indications of ikhlas, doing everything for Allah ﷻ to be the essence of religion, amalul qulub276 as:

وَمَا أُمِرُوا إِلَّا لِيَعْبُدُوا اللَّهَ مُخْلِصِينَ لَهُ الدِّينَ حُنَفَاءَ وَيُقِيمُوا الصَّلَاةَ وَيُؤْتُوا الزَّكَاةَ وَذَلِكَ دِينُ الْقَيِّمَةِ277 {البينة/5}

قُلْ أَتُحَاجُّونَنَا فِي اللَّهِ وَهُوَ رَبُّنَا وَرَبُّكُمْ وَلَنَا أَعْمَالُنَا وَلَكُمْ أَعْمَالُكُمْ وَنَحْنُ لَهُ مُخْلِصُونَ278 {البقرة/139}

إِنَّ الْمُنَافِقِينَ فِي الدَّرْكِ الْأَسْفَلِ مِنَ النَّارِ وَلَن تَجِدَ لَهُمْ نَصِيرًا279 {النساء/145} إِلَّا الَّذِينَ تَابُوا وَأَصْلَحُوا وَاعْتَصَمُوا بِاللَّهِ وَأَخْلَصُوا دِينَهُمْ لِلَّهِ فَأُولَئِكَ مَعَ الْمُؤْمِنِينَ وَسَوْفَ يُؤْتِ اللَّهُ الْمُؤْمِنِينَ أَجْرًا عَظِيمًا280 {النساء/146}

قُلْ أَمَرَ رَبِّي بِالْقِسْطِ وَأَقِيمُوا وُجُوهَكُمْ عِندَ كُلِّ مَسْجِدٍ وَادْعُوهُ مُخْلِصِينَ لَهُ الدِّينَ كَمَا بَدَأَكُمْ تَعُودُونَ281 {الأعراف/29}

---

273. [Allah] said, "O Iblees, what prevented you from prostrating to that which I created with My hands? Were you arrogant [then], or were you [already] among the haughty?"
274. You became arrogant.
275. Pride.
276. Works of the heart and soul.
277. And they were not commanded except to worship Allah, [being] sincere to Him in religion, inclining to truth, and to establish prayer and to give zakaah. And that is the correct religion.
278. Say, [O Muhammad], "Do you argue with us about Allah while He is our Lord and your Lord? For us are our deeds, and for you are your deeds. And we are sincere [in deed and intention] to Him."
279. Indeed, the hypocrites will be in the lowest depths of the Fire—and never will you find for them a helper –
280. Except for those who repent, correct themselves, hold fast to Allah, and are sincere in their religion for Allah, for those will be with the believers. And Allah is going to give the believers a great reward.
281. Say, [O Muhammad], "My Lord has ordered justice and that you direct yourselves [to the Qiblah] at every place [or time] of prostration, and invoke Him, sincere to Him in religion." Just as He originated you, you will return [to life].

One can realize that the Prophets of Allah ﷻ has this level as mentioned

وَاذْكُرْ فِي الْكِتَابِ مُوسَى إِنَّهُ كَانَ مُخْلَصًا وَكَانَ رَسُولًا نَبِيًّا[282] {مريم/51}

One of the experimental ways of testing ikhlas or meaning of ikhlas that fully and only turning to Allah ﷻ is the case that when all apparent means, reasons and people disappear. An example of this can be فَإِذَا رَكِبُوا

فِي الْفُلْكِ دَعَوُا اللَّهَ مُخْلِصِينَ لَهُ الدِّينَ فَلَمَّا نَجَّاهُمْ إِلَى الْبَرِّ إِذَا هُمْ يُشْرِكُونَ[283] {العنكبوت/65}

Another example of this can be a person afflicted with a disease that no one can help such as cancer. Then, they fully turn to Allah ﷻ. Another example of this can be a person in prison. There is no means or freedom to attach oneself. Therefore, in these instances one can find drastic changes in people's lives to fully, sincerely, and only turn to Allah ﷻ. Some may call these changes as sudden changes or conversion as religious texts [10] can refer. Yet, the important part is that this is an experimental part of understanding what ikhlas or sincerity for Allah ﷻ is. One can ask ikhlas and sincerity to Allah with àfiyah without being tested with these difficult trials. [284]. اللهم احفظنا منه. امين.   Yes, a human being is tiny creature with his or her physical body. Yet, this world and universe with all its galaxies, stars, and other systems may not be enough for humans with their potentialities of the faculties of heart, mind, and soul as translated from qalb[285], àqil[286], and rûh[287].

The only place that would satisfy the needs of rûh, soul, the ideas of àqil, mind, and engagements of qalb, heart with all their potentialities is àkhirah, afterlife.

If we take each faculty separately, for example, heart is always in the dynamic changing of emotions. Mind is always wandering positions of thinking. Soul is being affected with all the engagements of heart and mind. There are yearning potentialities for each.

Philosophers' mind wanderings can be an example of these potentialities. All today's religions can be examples of these potentialities with the yearnings of heart and mind. Yet, when there is no guidance, the pitfalls of dark black holes can absorb these people and they can be

---

282. And mention in the Book, Moses. Indeed, he was chosen, and he was a messenger and a prophet.

283. And when they board a ship, they supplicate Allah, sincere to Him in religion [i.e., faith and hope]. But when He delivers them to the land, at once they associate others with Him.

284. Oh Allah, protect us from this.

285. Heart.

286. Mind.

287. Soul.

in purposeless wanderings. Then, they may be in cyclical positions of forgetting about their own selves, goal and purpose as mentioned:

وَلَا تَكُونُوا كَالَّذِينَ نَسُوا اللَّهَ فَأَنسَاهُمْ أَنفُسَهُمْ أُوْلَئِكَ هُمُ الْفَاسِقُونَ[288] {الحشر/19}

قَالَ فَإِنَّهَا مُحَرَّمَةٌ عَلَيْهِمْ أَرْبَعِينَ سَنَةً يَتِيهُونَ فِي الْأَرْضِ فَلَا تَأْسَ عَلَى الْقَوْمِ الْفَاسِقِينَ[289] {المائدة/26}

The expression يَتِيهُونَ فِي الْأَرْضِ [290] can indicate these wanderings without any guidance and purpose. اللهم احفظنا منه. امين[291] The Qurān and Sunnah establish and guide the person to these true potentialities established with the actions and works of the heart, amalul qulûb.

Depending on the level of the person, he or she explores them with this guidance. Yet, an unveiled and direct opening of all these potentialities will be given with the Fadl[292] and Rahmah[293] of Allah ﷻ in the afterlife due to their struggle of following the Qurān and sunnah as the true guidance in this world. Then, the person becomes satisfied with all his or her faculties of their potentials as mentioned يَا أَيَّتُهَا النَّفْسُ الْمُطْمَئِنَّةُ[294] {الفجر/27} ارْجِعِي إِلَى رَبِّكِ رَاضِيَةً مَّرْضِيَّةً[295] {الفجر/28} فَادْخُلِي فِي عِبَادِي[296] {الفجر/29} وَادْخُلِي جَنَّتِي[297] {الفجر/30}. اللهم اجعلنا منهم[298]

There are a lot of creation of Allah ﷻ in the universe other than the humans. Although humans can be central focus of the all creation, this does not mean other creation does not benefit from the bounties of Allah ﷻ. Their benefit does not nullify humans to be the central focus of the creation.

---

288. And be not like those who forgot Allah, so He made them forget themselves. Those are the defiantly disobedient.
289. [Allah] said, "Then indeed, it is forbidden to them for forty years [in which] they will wander throughout the land. So do not grieve over the defiantly disobedient people."
290. They get lost on earth.
291. Oh allah, protect us from this.
292. Favor.
293. Mercy.
294. [To the righteous it will be said], "O reassured soul,
295. Return to your Lord, well-pleased and pleasing [to Him],
296. And enter among My [righteous] servants,
297. And enter My Paradise."
298. Oh Allah, make us from among them.

وَأَنزَلَ مِنَ السَّمَاء مَاء فَأَخْرَجَ بِهِ مِنَ الثَّمَرَاتِ رِزْقاً When we analyze the part[299] لَكُمْ, the part وَأَنزَلَ مِنَ السَّمَاء مَاء[300] is directly attributed to Allah ﷻ. This can possibly indicate that each drop of the rain is not random. It has a purpose and goal. It serves a purpose of fulfilling a specific need in the perfect and complex structure of the nature as created by Allah ﷻ.

Each raindrop falls separately without mixing with the other drop. They don't hit each other. It has a final or terminal velocity [2] that it does not accelerate to a speed that it can hurt and damage the person and even very sturdy buildings. Terminal velocity is a constant speed that a freely falling object eventually reaches when the resistance of the medium through which it is falling, prevents further acceleration [2]. All these arrangements in a single raindrop can indicate how Allah ﷻ magnificently originates, maintains and keeps the order in the nature and universe. Yet, some worship these physical laws referred as nature or science. They miss a very simple point that they are expecting a benefit from something that does not hear.

It is interesting to analyze the word السَّمَاء[301] in the part of the ayah [302] الَّذِي جَعَلَ لَكُمُ الأَرْضَ فِرَاشاً وَالسَّمَاء بِنَاء وَأَنزَلَ مِنَ السَّمَاء مَاء. One ask the question what is the hikmah or wisdom of this word السَّمَاء[303] being repeated twice instead of using a pronoun-dhamir?

The first time, the word السَّمَاء in [304] الَّذِي جَعَلَ لَكُمُ الأَرْضَ فِرَاشاً وَالسَّمَا can indicate sky. Sky in English is defined as the region of the atmosphere and outer space seen from the earth [2]. In this regard, the blue atmosphere with clouds can be sky. As well as, viewing the outer space with stars, moon and other planets in a clear night can be also sky. Therefore, in its general comprehensive definition of sky, there is no harf-jar, preposition مِنَ[305] in the first appreance compared to the second case as وَأَنزَلَ مِنَ السَّمَاء مَاء[306]. The word السَّمَاء can indicate a general observable and measurable term of sky as galaxies, outer space.

---

299. And sent down rain from the sky and produced thereby some fruits as provisions for you.

300. And sent down rain from the sky.

301. The sky.

302. [He] who made for you the earth a bed [spread out] and the sky [a ceiling] and sent down from the sky rain.

303. The sky.

304. [He] who made for you the earth a bed [spread out] and the sky [a ceiling].

305. From.

306. And sent down rain from the sky.

The second time, the word السَّمَاء in وَأَنزَلَ مِنَ السَّمَاء مَاء [307] can indicate a specific and closer location called clouds. Clouds are defined as a visible mass of condensed water vapor floating in the atmosphere, typically high above the ground. In this regard, the preposition, harf-jar, مِنَ[308] in وَأَنزَلَ مِنَ السَّمَاء مَاء can emphasize this directionality that rain comes from above.

In both cases there is the common theme of the emphasis for the directionality of the sky in reference to the humans' frame. They need to look up in both cases.

In the expression وَأَنزَلَ مِنَ السَّمَاء مَاء [309], the word مَاء [310] can indicate different phases such as rain (liquid water), snow (soft water as flakes), or hail (frozen water). All of their essential form is water. Therefore, these three different phases are not mentioned separately.

In addition, the word مَاء is mentioned as rain, liquid water to possibly indicate that out of three phases of water, rain is the most useful and it is the most observable and common form in different continents with different climates.

The word مَاء[311] is indicated in the form of tanwin. This can indicate the complexity of a water molecule. Water is a compound of oxygen and hydrogen (chem. formula: H_2O) with highly distinctive physical and chemical properties: it is able to dissolve many other substances; its solid form (ice) is *less* dense than the liquid form; its boiling point, viscosity, and surface tension are unusually high for its molecular weight, and it is partially dissociated into hydrogen and hydroxyl ions [2].

The word مَاء indicated in the form of tanwin[312] can also indicate the complex structure of rain drops that when it falls down on the earth they fall as a separate drop that it is not a gushing water or a water fall coming from the sky like Niagara Falls. The raindrop does not come as a very speedy particle like a bullet that can damage the people's head but it has a terminal velocity [2] as an exceptional law for gravitational attractional force, SubhanAllah!

---

307. And sent down rain from the sky
308. From.
309. And sent down from the sky rain.
310. Water [rain].
311. Water [rain].
312. A double short vowel that leads to slight ghunna. Gives letters sound or movement.

We are living in the world of amazements if we can open our eyes and realize it, SubhanAllah! This just a tiny example among billons and zillions of amazements in the creation showing constantly Allah ﷻ. That means that there are zillions of amazements that would lead the person to say and practice subhanAllah as mentioned:

سبحان الله عدد خلقه ورضا نفسه وزنه عرشه ومداد كلماته. سبحان الله عدد ملئ
السماوات وملئ الرض وملئ بينهما³¹³". Then because of this realization, zillions of true gratitude is required as Alhamdulillah, as mentioned الحمد الله عدد خلقه ورضا نفسه وزنه عرشه ومداد كلماته. الحمد الله عدد ملئ السماوات وملئ الرض وملئ بينهما³¹⁴" Then remembering that Allah SWT ﷻ is Exalted and Greater with Allahu Akbar with these zillions of amazements, "الله أكبر عدد خلقه ورضا نفسه وزنه عرشه ومداد كلماته الله أكبر عدد ملئ السماوات وملئ الرض وملئ بينهما³¹⁵"Finally, concluding with the true dhikr and embodiments of tawhid as " لا اله الا الله"in each of these zillions of amazements as mentioned below is critical:

"لا إله الا الله عدد خلقه ورضا نفسه وزنه عرشه ومداد كلماته لا إله الا الله عدد ملئ السماوات وملئ الرض وملئ بينهما ³¹⁶"

The different versions of the above azkār comes with some variation in different narrations of the hadith [6][8] [11].

Another perspective of amazement can reveal itself, when we analyze a small looking word بِهِ³¹⁷in the part of the ayah ³¹⁸ وَأَنزَلَ مِنَ السَّمَاء مَاء فَأَخْرَجَ بِهِ مِنَ الثَّمَرَاتِ

The word بِه can indicate the system of nutrition supplied with water for the life of a plant similar to the blood carrying the required nutrients

---

313. Glory be to God, the number of his creations, his contentment, his throne weight, and the outpouring of his worlds. Glory be to God, the number is full of heavens, the number is full of earth, the number is full of between them.
314. Praise be God, the number of his creations, his contentment, his throne weight, and the outpouring of his worlds. Praise be to God, the number is full of heavens, the number is full of earth, the number is full of between them.
315. God is the greatest, the number of his creations, his contentment, his throne weight, and the outpouring of his worlds. God is the greatest the number is full of heavens, the number is full of earth, the number is full of between them.
316. There is no god but Allah, the number of his creations, his contentment, his throne weight, and the outpouring of his worlds. Theres no god but Allah, the number is full of heavens, the number is full of earth, the number is full of between them.
317. With it.
318. And sent down rain from the sky and produced thereby some fruits [as a provision for you].

for a human. There is a constant flow and circulation, like human circulatory system.

The word بِهِ can indicate the mechanism of transport of water in the trunks of the trees through the branches, and leaves. The word بِهِ can indicate all different sciences evolving and focusing on fluid-dynamics and fluid-mechanics related with water in the growth of a plan.

In the part فَأَخْرَجَ بِهِ مِنَ الثَّمَرَاتِ رِزْقاً لَكُمْ[319], the preposition, harf-jar مِنَ can indicate that there are a lot of end products or fruits as mentioned with الثَّمَرَاتِ[320]. Yet, from those there are especially ones that humans will mostly benefit and use constantly as mentioned with رِزْقاً لَكُمْ[321]. In other words, the expression مِنَ الثَّمَرَاتِ [322] can indicate specificity for these sustenance items with another specificity as especially for humans mentioned with رِزْقاً لَكُمْ[323].

In this case, one can think about vitamins for example. The word vitamin is combined from a Greek word vita "life" + amine because vitamins were originally thought to contain an amino acid. These are any group of organic compounds that are life essentials for normal growth and nutrition and are required in small quantities in the diet because they cannot be synthesized by the body [2]. One can think about vitamins such as A, B, C, D, E, H, K, M and P. Each vitamin can have specific essentiality among its own categorization further such as B1, B2, B6 or B12 to address the specific needs of human body. Each of these vitamins can come from different fruits and vegetables as well as from animal sources.

When we analyze the word رِزْقاً لَكُمْ[324] in فَأَخْرَجَ بِهِ مِنَ الثَّمَرَاتِ[325] , this word comes in the form of nakrah. This form of nakrah can indicate that rizq[326] can come to the person in an indefinite, undefined, and unfixed means. It can indicate that the means of barakah from Allah is covered and can come not with the means of causality. One can also call this as a mysterious way of the Divine Delivery as mentioned also in فَتَقَبَّلَهَا رَبُّهَا بِقَبُولٍ حَسَنٍ وَأَنبَتَهَا نَبَاتًا حَسَنًا وَكَفَّلَهَا زَكَرِيَّا كُلَّمَا دَخَلَ عَلَيْهَا زَكَرِيَّا الْمِحْرَابَ

---

319. And brought forth with its fruits as a sustenance for you.
320. Fruits.
321. Sustenance for you.
322. With its fruits
323. As a sustenance for you.
324. A sustenance.
325. And brought forth with its fruits as a sustenance for you.
326. Sustenance.

وَجَدَ عِندَهَا رِزْقاً قَالَ يَا مَرْيَمُ أَنَّى لَكِ هَذَا قَالَتْ هُوَ مِنْ عِندِ اللّهِ إِنَّ اللّهَ يَرْزُقُ مَن يَشَاء بِغَيْرِ
حِسَابٍ[327] {آل عمران/37}.

When we analyze the part of the ayah فَأَخْرَجَ بِهِ مِنَ الثَّمَرَاتِ رِزْقاً لَّكُمْ[328],
the preposition-harf-jar ل in the word لَّكُمْ[329] can indicate the main reason
or specificity. In other words, the main reason for the presence of the
rizq or sustenance is the humans. Yet, this does not mean that other
creation cannot benefit from it.

Similarly, as Allah ﷻ specified the existence, delivery and structure
of rizq-sustenance mainly for humans, then it is expected from humans
that they should only specify their shukr, gratitude, and hamd to Allah
ﷻ as mentioned with فَلاَ تَجْعَلُواْ لِلّهِ أَندَاداً[330]

When one observes and estimates the cosmos with all available tools
of physics, astronomy and other sciences, cosmos is the universe seen
as a well-ordered whole as defined in a simple dictionary [2] as humans
agree in their secular curriculums. In this perspective, regardless of the
person's belief, humans agree with scientific discoveries about this order
and structure in nature, universe and cosmos. In other words, there is a
running system, being maintained, and taken care of. Rabbul Alamin is
the most closest Attribute and Name of Allah ﷻ that can be translated
as the Sustainer, Maintainer, and Care Taker of this system as frequently
comes in the Qurān.

It is expected from humans to make constantly deductive reasoning
by observing, discovering, critical thinking and analyzing the nature,
universe and cosmos in order to realize, recognize and appreciate Allah
ﷻ with gratitude and amazement. As mind and heart should be in the
states of these constant amazements, the tongue should be in constant
expression of these amazements as SubhanAllah, Alhamdulillah, Allahu
Akbar, and La ilaha illa Allah.

Yet Allah ﷻ is the Most Merciful with the Divine Fadl[331] and
Rahmah.[332] Allah ﷻ also gives opportunity for inductive reasoning by

---

327. So her Lord accepted her with good acceptance and caused her to grow in a good
manner and put her in the care of Zechariah. Every time Zechariah entered upon her in the
prayer chamber, he found with her provision. He said, "O Mary, from where is this [coming] to
you?" She said, "It is from Allah. Indeed, Allah provides for whom He wills without account."
328. And brought forth with its fruits as a sustenance for you.
329. For you.
330. So do not set up rivals to Allah.
331. Thanks.
332. Mercy.

sending directly scriptures and the prophets. The Qurān and Rasulullah ﷺ's teachings are direct, pure and exact to make the person access this mystery of humans without spending years of mind and heart wanderings by observation. This is called wahy or absolute content.

In a logical system, both inductive and deductive reasoning should match, harmonize and triangulate to the same realities. The next step comes living these realities, experience them and confirming them, like a scientist following the guidelines of a theory, applying on a data and confirming the results. For some, experience can be called the field of tasawwuf.

In another perspective, one is Islam, the other is Imān and further is ihsān.

In an another viewpoint, deductive reasoning is I'lm-al-yaqin[333], inductive reasoning is a'yn-al-yaqin[334] and experience is haqq-al-yaqin[335].

In another perspective, Allah ﷻ sends the Qurān and Rasulullah ﷺ as direct instruction with Uluhiyyah of Allah ﷻ. We as humans need to observe in the universe, nature and cosmos all different signs with the Rububiyyah of Allah ﷻ. The result of this should be 'ubudiyyah[336] leading to taqwa as the experience and true embodiment as mentioned with the ayah [337] يَا أَيُّهَا النَّاسُ اعْبُدُواْ رَبَّكُمُ الَّذِي خَلَقَكُمْ وَالَّذِينَ مِن قَبْلِكُمْ لَعَلَّكُمْ تَتَّقُونَ {البقرة/21}.

In the part فَلَا تَجْعَلُواْ بِلَّهِ أَندَاداً[338], the harf ﻑ can indicate sababiyah, causality. One can think the beginning of these two ayahs and translate this ﻑ as consecutive "therefore." Then, a meaning can be "Allah ﷻ is al-Màbûd as indicated with the word اعْبُدُواْ[339] therefore, don't make shirk-partnership as mentioned with

لَا تَجْعَلُواْ بِلَّهِ أَندَاداً[340]. Allah ﷻ is al-Khāliq as indicated with the word خَلَقَكُمْ[341] therefore, don't make shirk-partnership with that لَا تَجْعَلُواْ بِلَّهِ أَندَاداً.

---

333. Certainty with knowledge.
334. Certainty with witnessing.
335. Certainty with tasting and experiencing it.
336. Divineness.
337. O mankind, worship your Lord, who created you and those before you, that you may become righteous.
338. So do not set up rivals to Allah.
339. You all worship.
340. So do not set up rivals to Allah.
341. Created you.

Allah ﷻ is al-Munìm[342], al-Razzāq[343], al-Qādir[344], and all other related Names and Attributes of Allah ﷻ as indicated the portion of the ayah [345]الَّذِي جَعَلَ لَكُمُ الأَرْضَ فِرَاشاً وَالسَّمَاء بِنَاء وَأَنزَلَ مِنَ السَّمَاء مَاء فَأَخْرَجَ بِهِ مِنَ الثَّمَرَاتِ رِزْقاً لَّكُمْ فَلاَ تَجْعَلُواْ لِلّهِ أَندَاداً. Therefore, don't make shirk-partnership with Allah.

In this perspective, 'ibadah to Allah ﷻ is not necessarily the disposition of getting reward from Allah ﷻ in the future such as in the afterlife. Yet, it is the disposition of thanking and expressing our gratitude to Allah ﷻ for all the things that we already received from Allah ﷻ. Examples of these can be being alive and existent, seeing, hearing, ability to eat, breath, and relieving oneself in the restroom and being in the habitat/world that we live in and being in a family and all others.

Yet, Allah ﷻ constantly gives and promises us to give more in the afterlife and in this world, if we adopt this notion of recognition and appreciating that these nimahs are showering on us from Allah ﷻ. This recognition and appreciation should be through true tawhid[346] and 'ibadah[347]. This is mentioned in وَإِذْ تَأَذَّنَ رَبُّكُمْ لَئِن شَكَرْتُمْ لأَزِيدَنَّكُمْ وَلَئِن كَفَرْتُمْ إِنَّ عَذَابِي لَشَدِيدٌ[348] {إبراهيم/7}.

This recognition, appreciation and shukr is to be only for Allah ﷻ. This is of the gist of amalul-qulub, action of the heart. This is one of the gists of ikhlas. If one embodies this true shukr, then the person can be safer of the fears of accountability and afterlife as mentioned مَّا يَفْعَلُ اللّهُ بِعَذَابِكُمْ إِن شَكَرْتُمْ وَآمَنتُمْ وَكَانَ اللّهُ شَاكِرًا عَلِيمًا[349] {النساء/147}.

In this sense, the true complete 'ubudiyyah is a means to establish 'ubudiyyah with the heart through the means of 'ubudiyyah with the body as ordered by Allah ﷻ. In other words, amalu salih, good actions are the means to reach and maintain the level of amalu salihul qulub, good actions of the heart. One can call this as the embodiment of 'ibadah.

---

342. The guardian of faith.

343. The provider.

344. The Able.

345. He] who made for you the earth a bed [spread out] and the sky [a ceiling] and sent down from the sky rain, and brought forth with its fruits as a sustenance for you.

346. Oneness.

347. Worship.

348. And [remember] when your Lord proclaimed, 'If you are grateful, I will surely increase you [in favor]; but if you deny, indeed, My punishment is severe.'"

349. What would Allah do with [i.e., gain from] your punishment if you are grateful and believe? And ever is Allah Appreciative and Knowing.

In this sense, heart as denoted with qalb in terminology has a special place in Islamic terminology with its own faculties and spiritual organs. Knowing Allah ﷻ, experiencing and witnessing Allah ﷻ, truly happens in this essential part called heart.

In this sense, the Qurān mentions that belief or disbelief, appreciation or unrecognition of Allah ﷻ all happens at this level. The Qurānic verse mentions about blindness of heart but not blindness of physical eye as not witnessing Allah ﷻ :

أَفَلَمْ يَسِيرُوا فِي الْأَرْضِ فَتَكُونَ لَهُمْ قُلُوبٌ يَعْقِلُونَ بِهَا أَوْ آذَانٌ يَسْمَعُونَ بِهَا فَإِنَّهَا لَا تَعْمَى الْأَبْصَارُ وَلَكِن تَعْمَى الْقُلُوبُ الَّتِي فِي الصُّدُورِ ³⁵⁰ {الحج/46}

لاَ يُؤَاخِذُكُمُ اللّهُ بِاللَّغْوِ فِيَ أَيْمَانِكُمْ وَلَكِن يُؤَاخِذُكُم بِمَا كَسَبَتْ قُلُوبُكُمْ وَاللّهُ غَفُورٌ حَلِيمٌ ³⁵¹ {البقرة/225}

هُمْ لِلْكُفْرِ يَوْمَئِذٍ أَقْرَبُ مِنْهُمْ لِلإِيمَانِ يَقُولُونَ بِأَفْوَاهِهِم مَّا لَيْسَ فِي قُلُوبِهِمْ وَاللّهُ أَعْلَمُ بِمَا يَكْتُمُونَ ³⁵² {آل عمران/167}

وَلَقَدْ ذَرَأْنَا لِجَهَنَّمَ كَثِيرًا مِّنَ الْجِنِّ وَالإِنسِ لَهُمْ قُلُوبٌ لاَّ يَفْقَهُونَ بِهَا وَلَهُمْ أَعْيُنٌ لاَّ يُبْصِرُونَ بِهَا وَلَهُمْ آذَانٌ لاَّ يَسْمَعُونَ بِهَا أُوْلَئِكَ كَالأَنْعَامِ بَلْ هُمْ أَضَلُّ أُوْلَئِكَ هُمُ الْغَافِلُونَ ³⁵³ {الأعراف/179}

As reviewed in above ayahs, everything happens at the level of qulub or qalb. The judgment in akhirah, the value of a person for Allah ﷻ and the reality of pleasure of Allah ﷻ is all at the level of qalb as mentioned

لَقَدْ رَضِيَ اللَّهُ عَنِ الْمُؤْمِنِينَ إِذْ يُبَايِعُونَكَ تَحْتَ الشَّجَرَةِ فَعَلِمَ مَا فِي قُلُوبِهِمْ فَأَنزَلَ السَّكِينَةَ عَلَيْهِمْ وَأَثَابَهُمْ فَتْحًا قَرِيبًا ³⁵⁴ {الفتح/18}

---

350. So have they not traveled through the earth and have hearts by which to reason and ears by which to hear? For indeed, it is not eyes that are blinded, but blinded are the hearts which are within the breasts.

351. Allah does not impose blame upon you for what is unintentional in your oaths, but He imposes blame upon you for what your hearts have earned. And Allah is Forgiving and Forbearing.

352. They were nearer to disbelief that day than to faith, saying with their mouths what was not in their hearts. And Allah is most knowing of what they conceal.

353. And We have certainly created for Hell many of the jinn and mankind. They have hearts with which they do not understand, they have eyes with which they do not see, and they have ears with which they do not hear. Those are like livestock; rather, they are more astray. It is they who are the heedless.

354. Certainly was Allah pleased with the believers when they pledged allegiance to you, [O Muhammad], under the tree, and He knew what was in their hearts, so He sent down tranquility upon them and rewarded them with an imminent conquest..

"اللهم ثبت قلوبنا على دينك و طاعتك"[355]

The ayah إِنَّمَا الصَّدَقَاتُ لِلْفُقَرَاءِ وَالْمَسَاكِينِ وَالْعَامِلِينَ عَلَيْهَا وَالْمُؤَلَّفَةِ قُلُوبُهُمْ وَفِي الرِّقَابِ
وَالْغَارِمِينَ وَفِي سَبِيلِ اللَّهِ وَابْنِ السَّبِيلِ فَرِيضَةً مِّنَ اللَّهِ وَاللَّهُ عَلِيمٌ حَكِيمٌ[356] {التوبة/60}
indicate that there is a training for the a'mal of the qulub. It may take
time to sail with the correct direction of ikhlas. On a side note, one of
the highest numbers that this word qalb[357] is mentioned is in Sûrah
Tawbah. This can indicate that the maintainince of qulûb on the right
path can be with tawbah and istigfar, اللهم اجعلنا منهم[358]

It is interesting to analyze the word rabt with qalb in the ayah وَرَبَطْنَا
عَلَى قُلُوبِهِمْ إِذْ قَامُوا فَقَالُوا رَبُّنَا رَبُّ السَّمَاوَاتِ وَالْأَرْضِ لَن نَّدْعُوَ مِن دُونِهِ إِلَهًا لَّقَدْ قُلْنَا إِذًا
شَطَطًا[359] {الكهف/14}. A similar word is used in a hadith with ribāt[360] [11]
in order to indicate the firmness of the heart with wudhu, salah, and
masjid to show the means and avenues of solidifying the heart in one's
relationship with Allah.

Heart is the place to take a position to guide the emotions, feelings,
thoughts and intentions. Therefore, this control can be also called taqwa
especially when emotions or thoughts are trying to disrespect for shi'ar
as assigned by Allah as mentioned:

ذَلِكَ وَمَن يُعَظِّمْ شَعَائِرَ اللَّهِ فَإِنَّهَا مِن تَقْوَى الْقُلُوبِ[361] {الحج/32}

One of the biggest shi'ar is Rasulullah who the person requires
to have adab with and requires hearts to adapt taqwa with this biggest
shia'ar[362] as the Qurān mentioned إِنَّ الَّذِينَ يَغُضُّونَ أَصْوَاتَهُمْ عِندَ رَسُولِ اللَّهِ
أُولَئِكَ الَّذِينَ امْتَحَنَ اللَّهُ قُلُوبَهُمْ لِلتَّقْوَى لَهُم مَّغْفِرَةٌ وَأَجْرٌ عَظِيمٌ[363] {الحجرات/3}.

---

355. Oh Allah, fix our hearts on your religion and obedience.
356. Zakah expenditures are only for the poor and for the needy and for those employed for
it and for bringing hearts together [for Islam] and for freeing captives [or slaves] and for those
in debt and for the cause of Allah and for the [stranded] traveler—an obligation [imposed] by
Allah. And Allah is Knowing and Wise.
357. Heart.
358. Oh Allah, make us from among them.
359. And We bond [i.e., made firm] their hearts when they stood up and said, "Our Lord is
the Lord of the heavens and the earth. Never will we invoke besides Him any deity. We would
have certainly spoken, then, an excessive transgression.
360. To bond.
361. That [is so]. And whoever honors the symbols [i.e., rites] of Allah—indeed, it is from the
piety of hearts.
362. Symbols assigned by Allah SWT that deem respect.
363. Indeed, those who lower their voices before the Messenger of Allah—they are the ones
whose hearts Allah has tested for righteousness. For them is forgiveness and great reward.

One can also realize that shaytān can have affect on two types of hearts. One is sick and unsound heart, and the other is hard but not soft heart in their relationship with Allah ﷻ as mentioned لِيَجْعَلَ مَا يُلْقِي الشَّيْطَانُ
فِتْنَةً لِّلَّذِينَ فِي قُلُوبِهِم مَّرَضٌ وَالْقَاسِيَةِ قُلُوبُهُمْ وَإِنَّ الظَّالِمِينَ لَفِي شِقَاقٍ بَعِيدٍ[364] {الحج/53}.

One of the ways to test the soundness of heart if there is a positive change of heart with the remembrance of Allah ﷻ as mentioned: الَّذِينَ إِذَا
ذُكِرَ اللَّهُ وَجِلَتْ قُلُوبُهُمْ وَالصَّابِرِينَ عَلَى مَا أَصَابَهُمْ وَالْمُقِيمِي الصَّلَاةِ وَمِمَّا رَزَقْنَاهُمْ يُنفِقُونَ[365]
{الحج/35}

It is interesting to analyze the ayah وَإِذْ يَقُولُ الْمُنَافِقُونَ وَالَّذِينَ فِي قُلُوبِهِم
لَئِن لَّمْ يَنتَهِ الْمُنَافِقُونَ and مَّرَضٌ مَّا وَعَدَنَا اللَّهُ وَرَسُولُهُ إِلَّا غُرُورًا[366] {الأحزاب/12}
وَالَّذِينَ فِي قُلُوبِهِم مَّرَضٌ وَالْمُرْجِفُونَ فِي الْمَدِينَةِ لَنُغْرِيَنَّكَ بِهِمْ ثُمَّ لَا يُجَاوِرُونَكَ فِيهَا
إِلَّا قَلِيلًا[367] {الأحزاب/60} that not all the people who has sickness in their heart can be considered as munāfiq[368]. There is a separation of these groups in the ayah. In this sense, if a Muslim has sickness of their heart, they should really be alarmed to take care of it by making istigfar, and dua. Rasulullah ﷺ teaches us to read اللهم[369] [طهر قلبي من النفاق 12]. One can also realize that the teachings of legal rulings and fiqh in their apparent form is really to instill this soundness of heart as mentioned وَإِذَا سَأَلْتُمُوهُنَّ مَتَاعًا فَاسْأَلُوهُنَّ مِن وَرَاءِ
حِجَابٍ ذَلِكُمْ أَطْهَرُ لِقُلُوبِكُمْ وَقُلُوبِهِنَّ وَمَا كَانَ لَكُمْ أَن تُؤْذُوا رَسُولَ اللَّهِ وَلَا أَن تَنكِحُوا
أَزْوَاجَهُ مِن بَعْدِهِ أَبَدًا إِنَّ ذَلِكُمْ كَانَ عِندَ اللَّهِ عَظِيمًا[370]{الأحزاب/53}.

In other words, taqwal qulub requires filtering the unwanted thoughts, ideas, and emotions entering to the heart as mentioned before. Following the guidelines of shariah and fiqh, makes easier for the

---

364. [That is] so He may make what Satan throws in [i.e., asserts] a trial for those within whose hearts is disease and those hard of heart. And indeed, the wrongdoers are in extreme dissension.
365. Who, when Allah is mentioned, their hearts are fearful, and [to] the patient over what has afflicted them, and the establishers of prayer and those who spend from what We have provided them.
366. And [remember] when the hypocrites and those in whose hearts is disease said, "Allah and His Messenger did not promise us except delusion,"
367. If the hypocrites and those in whose hearts is disease and those who spread rumors in al-Madinah do not cease, We will surely incite you against them; then they will not remain your neighbors therein except for a little.
368. Hypocrite.
369. Oh Allah, purify my heart from hypocricy.
370. There is no blame upon them [i.e., women] concerning their fathers or their sons or their brothers or their brothers' sons or their sisters' sons or their women or those their right hands possess [i.e., slaves]. And fear Allah. Indeed Allah is ever, over all things, Witness.

person to control one's heart. This shows that controlling the heart is not mere effort of indulging oneself with only self awareness of dhikr and 'ibadah but at the same time, following the guidelines of fiqh in order to minimize and eliminate possible poisonous effects that can disturb the heart and make heart sick.

Below is an interesting ayah where both heart and human body can reach to the same goal. In other words, they can both work separately in their engagements of pleasure and desire. Yet, with the true guidance, they converge overtime and unite for the same goal of dhikr of Allah ﷻ as mentioned اللَّهُ نَزَّلَ أَحْسَنَ الْحَدِيثِ كِتَابًا مُتَشَابِهًا مَثَانِيَ تَقْشَعِرُّ مِنْهُ جُلُودُ الَّذِينَ يَخْشَوْنَ رَبَّهُمْ ثُمَّ تَلِينُ جُلُودُهُمْ وَقُلُوبُهُمْ إِلَى ذِكْرِ اللَّهِ ذَلِكَ هُدَى اللَّهِ يَهْدِي بِهِ مَنْ يَشَاءُ وَمَنْ يُضْلِلْ اللَّهُ فَمَا لَهُ مِنْ هَادٍ[371] {الزمر/23}

One can see the heart of a kāfir can have full problems with their heart if they die with kufr, then their problems in their heart will be exposed in the akhirah as mentioned أَمْ حَسِبَ الَّذِينَ فِي قُلُوبِهِم مَّرَضٌ أَن لَّن يُخْرِجَ اللَّهُ أَضْغَانَهُمْ[372] {محمد/29}. On the other hand, a Muslim can have some disease in their heart, but they should constantly seek solution with istigfar from Allah ﷻ and avoid implementing them as mentioned وَلَا تَجْعَلْ فِي قُلُوبِنَا غِلًّا لِّلَّذِينَ آمَنُوا رَبَّنَا إِنَّكَ رَؤُوفٌ رَّحِيمٌ[373] {الحشر/10}

If a person sometimes fails to control their heart, they need to make tawbah as mentioned إِن تَتُوبَا إِلَى اللَّهِ فَقَدْ صَغَتْ قُلُوبُكُمَا وَإِن تَظَاهَرَا عَلَيْهِ فَإِنَّ اللَّهَ هُوَ مَوْلَاهُ وَجِبْرِيلُ وَصَالِحُ الْمُؤْمِنِينَ وَالْمَلَائِكَةُ بَعْدَ ذَلِكَ ظَهِيرٌ[374] {التحريم/4}.

In this sense, the beatification of the hearts is made with imān as mentioned وَاعْلَمُوا أَنَّ فِيكُمْ رَسُولَ اللَّهِ لَوْ يُطِيعُكُمْ فِي كَثِيرٍ مِّنَ الْأَمْرِ لَعَنِتُّمْ وَلَكِنَّ اللَّهَ حَبَّبَ إِلَيْكُمُ الْإِيمَانَ وَزَيَّنَهُ فِي قُلُوبِكُمْ وَكَرَّهَ إِلَيْكُمُ الْكُفْرَ وَالْفُسُوقَ وَالْعِصْيَانَ أُولَئِكَ هُمُ الرَّاشِدُونَ[375]

---

371. Allah has sent down the best statement: a consistent Book wherein is reiteration. The skins shiver therefrom of those who fear their Lord; then their skins and their hearts relax at the remembrance [i.e., mention] of Allah. That is the guidance of Allah by which He guides whom He wills. And one whom Allah leaves astray—for him there is no guide.

372. Or do those in whose hearts is disease think that Allah would never expose their [feelings of] hatred?

373. And [there is a share for] those who came after them, saying, "Our Lord, forgive us and our brothers who preceded us in faith and put not in our hearts [any] resentment toward those who have believed. Our Lord, indeed You are Kind and Merciful."

374. If you two [wives] repent to Allah, [it is best], for your hearts have deviated. But if you cooperate against him—then indeed Allah is his protector, and Gabriel and the righteous of the believers and the angels, moreover, are [his] assistants.

375. And know that among you is the Messenger of Allah. If he were to obey you in much of the matter, you would be in difficulty, but Allah has endeared to you the faith and has made it pleasing in your hearts and has made hateful to you disbelief, defiance and disobedience. Those are the [rightly] guided.

{الحجرات/7}. In this perspective, imãn is at the level of the heart and Islam is at the level tongue and body as mentioned قَالَتِ الْأَعْرَابُ آمَنَّا قُل لَّمْ تُؤْمِنُوا وَلَكِن قُولُوا أَسْلَمْنَا وَلَمَّا يَدْخُلِ الْإِيمَانُ فِي قُلُوبِكُمْ وَإِن تُطِيعُوا اللَّهَ وَرَسُولَهُ لَا يَلِتْكُم مِّنْ أَعْمَالِكُمْ شَيْئًا إِنَّ اللَّهَ غَفُورٌ رَّحِيمٌ[376] {الحجرات/14}. There is an order of Islam, Imãn and Ihsãn as mentiond in Hadith Jibril [11] [12]. Amalu salih of body of Islam helps the amalu salih of heart of imãn to exist. This co-existence is expressed at the highest level of ihsãn.

The rusting and hardening of the heart like an iron occurs as mentioned in Sûrah Hadid due to the lack and absence of true remembrance of Allah ﷻ as mentioned أَلَمْ يَأْنِ لِلَّذِينَ آمَنُوا أَن تَخْشَعَ قُلُوبُهُمْ لِذِكْرِ اللَّهِ وَمَا نَزَلَ مِنَ الْحَقِّ وَلَا يَكُونُوا كَالَّذِينَ أُوتُوا الْكِتَابَ مِن قَبْلُ فَطَالَ عَلَيْهِمُ الْأَمَدُ فَقَسَتْ قُلُوبُهُمْ وَكَثِيرٌ مِّنْهُمْ فَاسِقُونَ[377] {الحديد/16}.

Amalul qulub[378] requires doing everything for Allah ﷻ with ikhlas but not due to our kinship or other interest based relationships as mentioned لَا تَجِدُ قَوْمًا يُؤْمِنُونَ بِاللَّهِ وَالْيَوْمِ الْآخِرِ يُوَادُّونَ مَنْ حَادَّ اللَّهَ وَرَسُولَهُ وَلَوْ كَانُوا آبَاءَهُمْ أَوْ أَبْنَاءَهُمْ أَوْ إِخْوَانَهُمْ أَوْ عَشِيرَتَهُمْ أُولَئِكَ كَتَبَ فِي قُلُوبِهِمُ الْإِيمَانَ وَأَيَّدَهُم بِرُوحٍ مِّنْهُ وَيُدْخِلُهُمْ جَنَّاتٍ تَجْرِي مِن تَحْتِهَا الْأَنْهَارُ خَالِدِينَ فِيهَا رَضِيَ اللَّهُ عَنْهُمْ وَرَضُوا عَنْهُ أُولَئِكَ حِزْبُ اللَّهِ أَلَا إِنَّ حِزْبَ اللَّهِ هُمُ الْمُفْلِحُونَ[379] {المجادلة/22}.

When the hearts are not together with the same goal and purpose, there may not be a group identity although people think they are a group or a body as mentioned لَا يُقَاتِلُونَكُمْ جَمِيعًا إِلَّا فِي قُرًى مُّحَصَّنَةٍ أَوْ مِن وَرَاءِ جُدُرٍ بَأْسُهُمْ بَيْنَهُمْ شَدِيدٌ تَحْسَبُهُمْ جَمِيعًا وَقُلُوبُهُمْ شَتَّى ذَلِكَ بِأَنَّهُمْ قَوْمٌ لَّا يَعْقِلُونَ[380] {الحشر/14}.

Measurement of Ikhlãs One can ask how to measure the quantity and quality of the ikhlas?

---

376. The Bedouins say, "We have believed." Say, "You have not [yet] believed; but say [instead], 'We have submitted,' for faith has not yet entered your hearts. And if you obey Allah and His Messenger, He will not deprive you from your deeds of anything. Indeed, Allah is Forgiving and Merciful."
377. Has the time not come for those who have believed that their hearts should become humbly submissive at the remembrance of Allah and what has come down of the truth? And let them not be like those who were given the Scripture before, and a long period passed over them, so their hearts hardened; and many of them are defiantly disobedient.
378. Work/actions of the heart.
379. You will not find a people who believe in Allah and the Last Day having affection for those who oppose Allah and His Messenger, even if they were their fathers or their sons or their brothers or their kindred. Those—He has decreed within their hearts faith and supported them with spirit from Him. And We will admit them to gardens beneath which rivers flow, wherein they abide eternally. Allah is pleased with them, and they are pleased with Him— those are the party of Allah. Unquestionably, the party of Allah—they are the successful.
380. They will not fight you all except within fortified cities or from behind walls. Their violence [i.e., enmity] among themselves is severe. You think they are together, but their hearts are diverse. That is because they are a people who do not reason.

The entire and full creed of believing in akhirah based on the quality and quantity of ikhlas. In other words, when a person does something, he or she may expect an outcome from it. This outcome or expectation can be in the world from people or others.

Yet, tawhid requires all expectations to be only from Allah ﷻ.

The ayah وَلاَ تَهِنُواْ فِي ابْتِغَاءِ الْقَوْمِ إِن تَكُونُواْ تَأْلَمُونَ فَإِنَّهُمْ يَأْلَمُونَ كَمَا تَأْلَمُونَ وَتَرْجُونَ مِنَ اللّهِ مَا لاَ يَرْجُونَ وَكَانَ اللّهُ عَلِيمًا حَكِيمًا [381] {النساء/104} can indicate the critical word with raja', تَرْجُونَ[382], hope, the expectation for their outcomes regardless of being a Muslim or not.

A believer expects something from Allah ﷻ in their engagements. A disbeliever expects from others. A believer expects things to happen to him or her in the akhirah, afterlife and given to him or her by Allah ﷻ.

A religion with an absence of afterlife does not teach any expectations for its followers in the afterlife. Or, they can have teachings instilling expectations from other things other than Allah ﷻ. Therefore, either they don't expect at anything after death as mentioned:

أَيَعِدُكُمْ أَنَّكُمْ إِذَا مِتُّمْ وَكُنتُمْ تُرَابًا وَعِظَامًا أَنَّكُم مُّخْرَجُونَ[383] {المؤمنون/35} هَيْهَاتَ هَيْهَاتَ لِمَا تُوعَدُونَ[384] {المؤمنون/36} إِنْ هِيَ إِلاَّ حَيَاتُنَا الدُّنْيَا نَمُوتُ وَنَحْيَا وَمَا نَحْنُ بِمَبْعُوثِينَ[385] {المؤمنون/37}

Or they expect from other things other than Allah ﷻ as expressed especially with the word زعم[386] as mentioned:

وَيَوْمَ يُنَادِيهِمْ فَيَقُولُ أَيْنَ شُرَكَائِيَ الَّذِينَ كُنتُمْ تَزْعُمُونَ[387] {القصص/62}

وَيَوْمَ يُنَادِيهِمْ فَيَقُولُ أَيْنَ شُرَكَائِيَ الَّذِينَ كُنتُمْ تَزْعُمُونَ[388] {القصص/74}

---

381. And do not weaken in pursuit of the enemy. If you should be suffering—so are they suffering as you are suffering, but you expect from Allah that which they expect not. And Allah is ever Knowing and Wise.

382. You except.

383. Does he promise you that when you have died and become dust and bones that you will be brought forth [once more]?

384. How far, how far, is that which you are promised.

385. It [i.e., life] is not but our worldly life—we die and live, but we will not be resurrected.

386. To claim.

387. And [warn of] the Day He will call them and say, "Where are My 'partners' which you used to claim?"

388. And [warn of] the Day He will call them and say, "Where are My 'partners' which you used to claim?"

وَلَقَدْ جِئْتُمُونَا فُرَادَى كَمَا خَلَقْنَاكُمْ أَوَّلَ مَرَّةٍ وَتَرَكْتُم مَّا خَوَّلْنَاكُمْ وَرَاء ظُهُورِكُمْ وَمَا نَرَى مَعَكُمْ شُفَعَاءكُمُ الَّذِينَ زَعَمْتُمْ أَنَّهُمْ فِيكُمْ شُرَكَاء لَقَد تَّقَطَّعَ بَيْنَكُمْ وَضَلَّ عَنكُم مَّا كُنتُمْ تَزْعُمُونَ﴿389﴾.{الأنعام/94}

وَيَوْمَ يَقُولُ نَادُوا شُرَكَائِيَ الَّذِينَ زَعَمْتُمْ فَدَعَوْهُمْ فَلَمْ يَسْتَجِيبُوا لَهُمْ وَجَعَلْنَا بَيْنَهُم مَّوْبِقًا﴿390﴾ {الكهف/52}

The person is awarded according to their expectations. Therefore, the word or words implying raja'a[391], تَرْجُونَ[392] are critical. One should ask to him or herself: What is my expectation in each of my action? Why? Who am I trying to get recognition for? Even, the people who are at a higher level, can ask: What is my expectation in each of my thoughts and ideas? Why?

Rasulullah ﷺ mentions that Allah ﷻ treats the person according to their expectation and zann about Allah 11] ﷻ.

One can call all these expectations as the creed of akhirah, afterlife. Accountability is the subset of afterlife. Believing in afterlife and having expectation from Allah ﷻ is the primary, usul of the imān.

Therefore, one can look at the categorizations of religions such as ahlu-kitab versus others due to this presence or absence of expectations from Allah ﷻ which is structured as afterlife, akhirah.

Therefore, a true mumin is expected to have full yaqîn and expectation only from Allah ﷻ as mentioned وَبِالآخِرَةِ هُمْ يُوقِنُونَ[393] {البقرة/4}. In this sense, yaqîn requires the full expectation and all engagements only from Allah ﷻ. One can refer this taqwa as well.

The quantity and quality of ikhlas can be measured according to the ability of a person having this full expectation only from Allah ﷻ in the akhirah or not. For example, when a person feeds someone, a person

---

389. [It will be said to them], "And you have certainly come to Us alone [i.e., individually] as We created you the first time, and you have left whatever We bestowed upon you behind you. And We do not see with you your 'intercessors' which you claimed that they were among you associates [of Allah]. It has [all] been severed between you, and lost from you is what you used to claim."

390. And [warn of] the Day when He will say, "Call 'My partners' whom you claimed," and they will invoke them, but they will not respond to them. And We will put between them [a valley of] destruction.

391. Expectation.

392. You except.

393. And who believe in what has been revealed to you, [O Muhammad], and what was revealed before you, and of the Hereafter they are certain [in faith].

may expect an appreciation or gratitude from others. Yet, the true ikhlas requires expectation only from Allah ﷻ as mentioned:

وَيُطْعِمُونَ الطَّعَامَ عَلَى حُبِّهِ مِسْكِينًا وَيَتِيمًا وَأَسِيرًا {الإنسان/8}³⁹⁴ إِنَّمَا نُطْعِمُكُمْ لِوَجْهِ اللَّهِ لَا نُرِيدُ مِنكُمْ جَزَاءً وَلَا شُكُورًا {الإنسان/9}³⁹⁵ إِنَّا نَخَافُ مِن رَّبِّنَا يَوْمًا عَبُوسًا قَمْطَرِيرًا³⁹⁶ {الإنسان/10} فَوَقَاهُمُ اللَّهُ شَرَّ ذَلِكَ الْيَوْمِ وَلَقَّاهُمْ نَضْرَةً وَسُرُورًا³⁹⁷ {الإنسان/11}

One can remember the hadith about the first three people among Muslims to be punished in the akhirah: a preacher & a reciter, activist and a philanthropist [11]. They expected something in their engagements from people other than an expectation from Allah ﷻ. They received what they wanted. Therefore, they will have an enormous disappointment in the akhirah.

One can also examine any person's intention and ikhlas in helping the poor, trying to solve social problems and in other ethical engagements. Depending on their expectations and intention, they receive their results from Allah ﷻ in the form of worldly achievements, recognition, being remembered in the history or not as mentioned:

اللَّهُ لَطِيفٌ بِعِبَادِهِ يَرْزُقُ مَن يَشَاءُ وَهُوَ الْقَوِيُّ الْعَزِيزُ³⁹⁸ {الشورى/19} مَن كَانَ يُرِيدُ حَرْثَ الْآخِرَةِ نَزِدْ لَهُ فِي حَرْثِهِ وَمَن كَانَ يُرِيدُ حَرْثَ الدُّنْيَا نُؤْتِهِ مِنْهَا وَمَا لَهُ فِي الْآخِرَةِ مِن نَّصِيبٍ³⁹⁹ {الشورى/20}

Going back to previous questions such as what is my expectation in each of my action? Or, Who am I trying to get recognition for?

It is possible that the person can be striving in life to get recognition in educational, social or professional life especially by their superiors, supervisors, or departments. Yes, it is possible to get recognized in the society or among peers. It is possible to get applauded, congratulated, become famous and remembered in the history.

Yet, any simple person who has a little bit of experience in life through the means of social interactions or through the means of aging can simply and fully realize that everyone is a human like this

---

394. And they give food in spite of love for it to the needy, the orphan, and the captive...
395. [Saying], "We feed you only for the countenance [i.e., approval] of Allah. We wish not from you reward or gratitude.
396. Indeed, We fear from our Lord a Day austere and distressful."
397. So Allah will protect them from the evil of that Day and give them radiance and happiness.
398. And [then] you did your deed which you did, and you were of the ungrateful."
399. [Moses] said, "I did it, then, while I was of those astray [i.e., ignorant].

person. Everyone is mortal. Everyone has problems, needs, fears and helplessness regardless of being the president or king of a country or a having different medical, academic, or social degrees, ranks or positions.

A human who is mortal and who has full needs incline to be egocentric. This may not be always due to selfish reasons of not caring others but due to overwhelming needs of this person for his or her own needs. In other words, the self-related problems, self-related needs, self-related fears and helplessness of a person can put the person in a mesmerizing terror of self-focus.

If this self-focus goes to the direction of not caring of others, then, as a sociological technical word, we can call this person as selfish. If this self-focus goes to the direction of focusing one's own problem, we can call this as self-accountability.

In both cases, due to temporal and mortal nature of humans and due to their egocentric approaches of the self-focus, humans give worth of other humans can have limited and temporal value.

Humans can seem to applaud or congratulate others for their achievements, but it is all time-based, superficial and peripheral.

Most of the time these recognitions or applaud of humans can be insincere, shallow, narrow, artificial, pony, hypocritical, deceitful or two-faced.

If their recognition for this person is insincere then, it is a social phenomenon that the people may not want to be rude for this person's achievement. It may not be related to a position of real applaud. The recognizer has their own self-focus related problems or issues as a human being. Therefore, he or she may recognize it in order not to be rude. The common English expression as "good for you!" can very well and vividly depict this reality.

If their recognition for this person is shallow or narrow, then the achiever, the person who desires for recognition, can be disappointed because he or she was not recognized and awarded in the way he or she expected.

If their recognition for this person is deceitful or two-faced, then the recognizer has the spiritual sickness of jealousy that, in reality, this person aspires for the achiever to lose this recognition and have it on him or herself.

If their recognition for this person is sincere then, it is all time-based because the sincere recognizers need to move in life for their own problems and issues. Yet, the achiever wants his or her recognition not be forgotten but constantly to be remembered. The achiever wants intrinsicly constant appreciation by others. One can review the millions of books in the library shelves sitting there about expecting recognition from others, yet no one reads them and knows about them, SubhanAllah.

In all cases, if the person expects recognition only from Allah ﷻ, then his or her achievement transforms to be an infinite but not time-based or temporal compared to humans. We don't say the word recognizer for Allah ﷻ but the Knower, al-Alìm, Allah ﷻ knows everything. Allah ﷻ appreciates as al-Shakur.

When Allah ﷻ appreciates this person's aim and goal then, Allah ﷻ tells Jibril as to recognize this person as pleasing and loving Allah ﷻ. Then, Jibril as does it. Then, Jibril calls all angels and a recognition (wudd) [11] is given to all earth for this person's position of aiming to please Allah ﷻ. اللهم اجعلنا منهم [400]

Therefore, for this appreciation, Allah ﷻ gives and rewards the person an infinite reward as Jannah. Allah ﷻ is Infinite, al-Baki. Therefore, this appreciation for this human is given as an infinite form as khalidina fiha abada in Jannah as mentioned in parts of the Qurãn, SubhanAllah!

There is no disappointment on the achiever's side in this case. Allah ﷻ asks this person as the hadith mentions if he or she is satisfied [11].

The people in Jannah even in the lowest part of it confirms full heartedly that they got enormously more than what they expected. Even in one of the hadith, a person thinks in the Judgement Day that it is a joke [11] that all are given for this person, yet he did not do anything to deserve it, SubhanAllah!

So, one can choose, who they want to target, aim in life for their recognition, temporal humans with their own problems of needs and fear? Or, pleasing Allah ﷻ Who appreciates and rewards the person without any disappointment with خالدين فيها [401]

Assigning Just Values. It is interesting to note that the word جَعَلَ[402] is used twice in the same ayah as الَّذِي جَعَلَ لَكُمُ الْأَرْضَ فِرَاشاً وَالسَّمَاء[403] and بِنَاءً[404] فَلَا تَجْعَلُوا لِلَّهِ أَنْدَاداً[405]. As we discussed before, this word جَعَلَ can

---

400. Oh Allah, make us from among them.
401. Immoortal in it.
402. Made.
403. [He] who made for you.
404. [He] who made for you the earth a bed [spread out] and the sky a ceiling.
405. So do not attribute to Allah equals.

indicate assigning responsibility and purpose with choice and will. In this regard, Allah ﷻ creates the earth and makes and assigns it with a responsibility and purpose of being a livable and comfortable space for humans as mentioned الأَرْضَ فِرَاشاً[1406] with the Divine Mashiyyah Choice and Will. Allah ﷻ creates the sky, atmosphere and outer space and makes and assigns it with a responsibility and purpose of being a livable and comfortable covered dwelling, similar to a house with a ceiling, for humans as mentioned فِرَاشاً وَالسَّمَاء بِنَاء[407] with the Divine Masihiyyah Choice and Will.

Similarly, humans have the free will and they can assign purpose, goal and meaning to things. One of the distinctness of humans is that they have the free will and fee choice to assign responsibilities and values in their very limited and weak capacity. One can remember the hadith about Allah ﷻ created Adam in the Divine image can indicate this free will or free choice of humans in their limited capacity of assigning roles, and responsibilities.

In this regard, their assignment can be false or true, correct or wrong. One of the utmost incorrect and false assignment of humans is that when they assign responsibility of partnerships of things with Allah ﷻ. In that sense, Allah ﷻ reminds them about their wrong and false assignment as mentioned as mentioned فَلَا تَجْعَلُواْ لِلّهِ أَندَاداً[408].

The word تَجْعَلُواْ[409] in فَلَا تَجْعَلُواْ لِلّهِ أَندَاداً can indicate what humans assign and view as partners with Allah ﷻ does not have any basis, truth, and knowledge. They are all made-up, fictitious, imaginary, untrue, false, fabricated, and wrong assumptions.

In other words, true ilm requires assignment of correct meanings, purpose, and responsibilities. One may call this as the level of objectivity. Therefore, a person who knows as mentioned وَأَنتُمْ تَعْلَمُونَ[410] as mentioned in the ayah will not assign incorrect and false meanings, purpose and responsibilities as mentioned with فَلَا تَجْعَلُواْ لِلّهِ أَندَاداً.

In this case, the ayah mentions فَلَا تَجْعَلُواْ لِلّهِ أَندَاداً وَأَنتُمْ تَعْلَمُونَ[411] {البقرة/22}. If the person knows and does not give real due, correct assignment,

---

406. The earth a bed [spread out].
407. [spread out] and the sky a ceiling.
408. So do not attribute to Allah equals.
409. Attribute.
410. While you know {that there is nothing similar to him}.
411. So do not attribute to Allah equals while you know [that there is nothing similar to Him].

meaning and responsibility to its due, then it is not objective, correct, and true.

Then, this can show alternative motifs such as arrogance, jealousy, laziness, and others. The case of Abu Jahil as reported that he knew by knowledge about the risālah of Rasulullah ﷺ but he did not assign the true value by accepting the Islam and nubuwwah [14]. In his statement, this purposeful wrong choice was due to jealousy.

In this regard, it is interesting to note that after the word جَعَلَ[412] being used twice in the same ayah of 22 in this Sûrah as الَّذِي جَعَلَ لَكُمُ الْأَرْضَ[413] وَإِذْ قَالَ and فَلَا تَجْعَلُوا لِلَّهِ أَنْدَاداً وَالسَّمَاءَ بِنَاءً[414] فِرَاشاً, then its next usage comes as رَبُّكَ لِلْمَلَائِكَةِ إِنِّي جَاعِلٌ فِي الْأَرْضِ خَلِيفَةً قَالُوا أَتَجْعَلُ فِيهَا مَن يُفْسِدُ فِيهَا وَيَسْفِكُ الدِّمَاءَ وَنَحْنُ نُسَبِّحُ بِحَمْدِكَ وَنُقَدِّسُ لَكَ قَالَ إِنِّي أَعْلَمُ مَا لَا تَعْلَمُونَ[415] {البقرة/30}.

Similar part in different parts of the Qurān are also mentioned as for example وَهُوَ الَّذِي جَعَلَكُمْ خَلَائِفَ الْأَرْضِ وَرَفَعَ بَعْضَكُمْ فَوْقَ بَعْضٍ دَرَجَاتٍ لِيَبْلُوَكُمْ فِي مَا آتَاكُمْ إِنَّ رَبَّكَ سَرِيعُ الْعِقَابِ وَإِنَّهُ لَغَفُورٌ رَّحِيمٌ[416] {الأنعام/165}.

The purpose of humans on earth is to first have the correct realization about Allah ﷻ as our Creator, Rabb[417], Khaliq[418], Mun'im[419], Razzaq[420] as indicated with the word جَعَلَ[421]. Therefore, the person should not make incorrect renderings of partnerships with Allah ﷻ as mentioned فَلَا[422] تَجْعَلُوا لِلَّهِ أَنْدَاداً. This initial, first, and utmost reference point of assignment, recognition, value and purpose determines the secondary cases of valuation.

Then, after this initial and correct realization, assigning a value to everything on the earth with their true due and justice, adl as mentioned

---

412. Made.
413. [He] who made for you the earth a bed [spread out] and the sky a ceiling.
414. So do not attribute to Allah equals.
415. And [mention, O Muhammad], when your Lord said to the angels, "Indeed, I will make upon the earth a successive authority." They said, "Will You place upon it one who causes corruption therein and sheds blood, while we declare Your praise and sanctify You?" He [Allah] said, "Indeed, I know that which you do not know.
416. And it is He who has made you successors upon the earth and has raised some of you above others in degrees [of rank] that He may try you through what He has given you. Indeed, your Lord is swift in penalty; but indeed, He is Forgiving and Merciful.
417. Lord.
418. The ceater.
419. The giver of peace.
420. The provider.
421. Made.
422. So do not attribute to Allah equals.

again with the same word جَعَلَ in the ayah جَعَلَكُمْ خَلَائِفَ الْأَرْضِ[423] can be considered as the secondary case of valuation.

Therefore, one can say that the purpose of our existence is our constant struggle of making the correct and true assignments without injustice, oppression and falsehood.

In our Western terminologies, one calls this as constant and intrinsic valuation.

In other words, we constantly and intrinsically give value to everything every day. If it is a wrong and unfair valuation or value, we call them as injustice, discrimination, unfairness and sometimes refer them as backwardness or fundamentalism. If it is the correct one, then we call them as justice, fairness and sometimes open-mindedness or modernity.

One can always ask who determines this valuation system? Allah ﷻ and Rasulullah ﷺ teaches us directly, clearly, and openly in the Qurān and sunnah a valuation system. Yet, it is expected that a non-Muslim can arrive at the same results with their mind through their objective and collective efforts practice, trial and error systems and guidelines after many centuries. Yet regardless of being Muslim or not, this valuation and correct assignment is not easy but indeed very difficult as mentioned إِنَّا عَرَضْنَا الْأَمَانَةَ عَلَى السَّمَاوَاتِ وَالْأَرْضِ وَالْجِبَالِ فَأَبَيْنَ أَن يَحْمِلْنَهَا وَأَشْفَقْنَ مِنْهَا وَحَمَلَهَا الْإِنسَانُ إِنَّهُ كَانَ ظَلُومًا جَهُولًا[424] {الأحزاب/72}. In this ayah, this expected true, fair, and just assignment of everything is mentioned with the word as the responsibility الْأَمَانَةَ. Yes, having free will and free choice requires responsibility. True fulfillment of the responsibility requires assigning everything in their proper place with their proper, correct and true meanings without making injustice, unfairness and discrimination.

Responsibility requires accountability. Accountability in this life and afterlife stems from this responsibility. Therefore, being responsible of something is like a poisonous honey. One can remember the ayah in the Qurān {النبأ/40}[425] وَيَقُولُ الْكَافِرُ يَا لَيْتَنِي كُنتُ تُرَابًا.

---

423. Has made you successors upon the earth.
424. Indeed, We offered the Trust to the heavens and the earth and the mountains, and they declined to bear it and feared it; but man [undertook to] bear it. Indeed, he was unjust and ignorant.
425. And the disbeliever will say, "Oh, I wish that I were dust!"

Therefore, one can remember the statements of Abu Bakr (RA) to be a bird or a tree but not being a human [15]. One can remember the statements of Omar ra.

These were the people who understood the realities and tried at their highest capacity and levels to assign the proper valuation to everything due to being accountable with their choice in front of Allah ﷻ.

Not assigning the proper valuation of everything can be defined as Dhulm[426] or oppression. The biggest Dhulm[427], oppression is the person's not recognition and appreciation of Allah ﷻ. Therefore, each Dhulm or oppression entails lies.

When we don't recognize Allah ﷻ in the way that Allah ﷻ should be recognized, these attitudes, behaviors and lies do not have any effect in the Divine Reality. Yet, the person is deemed to be questioned.

Similarly, if we don't give the proper just value of things in life, then the person can be questioned in this world with even secular laws.

In zulm or transliterated as dhulm, in oppression related with shirk such as giving divinity to Isa as or other things, is in reality an improper valuation to Isa as and other things. Both the shirk attributed and attributor are questioned in the afterlife due to clarification and engagements of these dhulm, oppressions.Giving divinity to a human or anything other than Allah ﷻ is an improper valuation. Any improper valuation called oppression called dhulm which can instill darkness, uneasiness, fear and others in this dunya and akhirah as mentioned [16] by Rasulullah ﷺ[428]، فَإِنَّ الظُّلْمَ ظُلُمَاتٌ يَوْمَ الْقِيَامَةِ When the person attributes randomness and statistical evolution theories to the countless number of creations, then they make Dhulm, oppression to each creation. Therefore, this attribution of zulm or lies to each creation deems the person in an unlimited accountability of punishment. May Allah ﷻ protect us.

Again, khalifah is the one who has the responsibility of implementation of the just and fair valuation for everything as indicated with جَعَلَكُمْ خَلَائِفَ الأَرْض[429].

Yet, a Muslim at least can recognize Allah ﷻ as mentioned in the Qurãn and sunnah. Yet, if the Muslim lacks in their proper valuation of

426. Opression.
427. Opression.
428. Injustice will appear as darkness on the Day of Rising.
429. And it is He who has made you successors upon the earth.

justice with other things, beings or humans, then this is called a sin that needs accountability with the person and that being.

Yet, a person of not believer cannot truly locate everything in their true disposition in reference to the Original and True point of Reference, Allah ﷻ. They can approximate meanings but not get the essence due the lack of this core principle.

In the above perspectives, one can view the inductive reasoning similar to a case of an experienced manager who have workers working under him. A young and novice worker can come to the manager to solve a technical issue in his assembly of work. With his best judgment, this work can present some possible reasons, meanings and solutions to the problem. Yet, the experienced manager who knows the type of work and overall line of production stages can suggest some tweaking and guidance about this worker's reasoning, meaning and solution considering both general line of production stages and his own experience and expertise on this line of assembly. In this case, although the worker may not fully grasp the logic, he follows the guidance suggested by the experienced manager. After many years of working, the novice worker many years ago now becomes an experienced manager. He now understands perfectly about the suggestion of his boss, the experienced manager. He now appreciates him so much that by showing a solution at the time, his boss saved his job at the time. He himself now is promoted.

Similarly, above is just an example. We cannot truly compare and replace the Reality of Allah ﷻ with our humanly renderings. Yet, the Qurān and Sunnah are like the examples of giving us guidance by considering our past, present and future. In all these engagements and following this guidance from Allah ﷻ and Rasulullah ﷺ, the person appreciates both in this dunya and afterlife about this guidance and fully realizes the reality and truth, al-haqq as mentioned:

$$\text{وَلَا تَنفَعُ الشَّفَاعَةُ عِندَهُ إِلَّا لِمَنْ أَذِنَ لَهُ حَتَّى إِذَا فُرِّعَ عَن قُلُوبِهِمْ قَالُوا مَاذَا قَالَ رَبُّكُمْ قَالُوا}$$
$$\text{الْحَقَّ وَهُوَ الْعَلِيُّ الْكَبِيرُ}^{430} \ \{23/\text{سبأ}\}$$

---

430. And intercession does not benefit with Him except for one whom He permits. [And those wait] until, when terror is removed from their hearts, they will say [to one another], "What has your Lord said?" They will say, "The truth." And He is the Most High, the Grand.

وَنَادَى أَصْحَابُ الْجَنَّةِ أَصْحَابَ النَّارِ أَن قَدْ وَجَدْنَا مَا وَعَدَنَا رَبُّنَا حَقًّا فَهَلْ وَجَدتُّم مَّا
وَعَدَ رَبُّكُمْ حَقًّا قَالُواْ نَعَمْ فَأَذَّنَ مُؤَذِّنٌ بَيْنَهُمْ أَن لَّعْنَةُ اللّهِ عَلَى الظَّالِمِينَ431 {الأعراف/44}

وَسِيقَ الَّذِينَ كَفَرُوا إِلَى جَهَنَّمَ زُمَرًا حَتَّى إِذَا جَاؤُوهَا فُتِحَتْ أَبْوَابُهَا وَقَالَ لَهُمْ خَزَنَتُهَا
أَلَمْ يَأْتِكُمْ رُسُلٌ مِّنكُمْ يَتْلُونَ عَلَيْكُمْ آيَاتِ رَبِّكُمْ وَيُنذِرُونَكُمْ لِقَاء يَوْمِكُمْ هَذَا قَالُوا بَلَى وَلَكِنْ
حَقَّتْ كَلِمَةُ الْعَذَابِ عَلَى الْكَافِرِينَ432 {الزمر/71}

وَسِيقَ الَّذِينَ اتَّقَوْا رَبَّهُمْ إِلَى الْجَنَّةِ زُمَرًا حَتَّى إِذَا جَاؤُوهَا وَفُتِحَتْ أَبْوَابُهَا وَقَالَ لَهُمْ
خَزَنَتُهَا سَلَامٌ عَلَيْكُمْ طِبْتُمْ فَادْخُلُوهَا خَالِدِينَ433 {الزمر/73}

May Allah ﷻ make us follow the guidance of the Qurān and Sunnah, Amìn.

Asking the Hidayah from Allah ﷻ

In this regard, one can ask: can or should the person ask correct fulfilment of this responsibility and hidayah from Allah ﷻ? Can Allah ﷻ give the attribute of hidayah[434] on the earth for all humans?

Yes definitiely, as mentioned وَلَوْ شَاء رَبُّكَ لآمَنَ مَن فِي الأَرْضِ كُلُّهُمْ جَمِيعًا أَفَأَنتَ تُكْرِهُ النَّاسَ حَتَّى يَكُونُواْ مُؤْمِنِينَ435 {يونس/99}. One can realize the word شَاء is used.

The answer is that this is one of the secret parts of this responsibility of humans. In other words, we should not have any attitude or claim to have any power. We should not carry any claim in the assignment of the true value of everything that we or I did or we or I was successful. These cases can be also related with the matters of hidayah. We can claim or

---

431. And the companions of Paradise will call out to the companions of the Fire, "We have already found what our Lord promised us to be true. Have you found what your Lord promised to be true?" They will say, "Yes." Then an announcer will announce among them, "The curse of Allah shall be upon the wrongdoers

432. And those who disbelieved will be driven to Hell in groups until, when they reach it, its gates are opened and its keepers will say, "Did there not come to you messengers from yourselves, reciting to you the verses of your Lord and warning you of the meeting of this Day of yours?" They will say, "Yes, but the word [i.e., decree] of punishment has come into effect upon the disbelievers."

433. But those who feared their Lord will be driven to Paradise in groups until, when they reach it while its gates have been opened and its keepers say, "Peace be upon you; you have become pure; so enter it to abide eternally therein," [they will enter].

434. Guidance.

435. And had your Lord willed, those on earth would have believed—all of them entirely. Then, [O Muhammad], would you compel the people in order that they become believers?

say the words I or we guided people, except we all beg the guidance from Allah ﷻ.

For example, رَبَّنَا وَاجْعَلْنَا مُسْلِمَيْنِ لَكَ وَمِن ذُرِّيَّتِنَا أُمَّةً مُّسْلِمَةً لَّكَ وَأَرِنَا مَنَاسِكَنَا وَتُبْ عَلَيْنَآ إِنَّكَ أَنتَ التَّوَّابُ الرَّحِيمُ[436] {البقرة/128}, Ibrahim as uses the same word with وَاجْعَلْنَا, and asks for this trait of مُسْلِمَيْنِ لَكَ. In this case, hidayah is given by Allah ﷻ. The person should be in the recognition of the constant need of Allah ﷻ for everything.In other words, a person can be in hidayah and trying to fulfill this true attributing of valuation with everything by sincerely asking from Allah ﷻ. This can be one of the secrets of hidayah which is the knowing and acting on true valuation. This can be called being the true khalifah on earth.

The attribute of hidayah is given by Allah ﷻ after recognition of this need of asking the hidayah of assignment as [437] رَبَّنَا وَاجْعَلْنَا مُسْلِمَيْنِ لَكَ. Then, one can have a glimpse of why the preference of شَاء[438] is used in the above ayah. This is in order to emphasize this tiny but very critical human disposition or inclination (mayil[439]) of the person for the Constant and Full Need for Allah ﷻ.

One can analyze the duas mentioned in the Qurān and sunnah with the word جعل and try to understand the expected dispositions of humans in their relationship with Allah ﷻ.

When we analyze the expression فَلاَ تَجْعَلُواْ لِلَّهِ أَندَاداً, the structure is not فَلاَ تَجْعَلُواْ أَندَادا لِلَّهِ[440]. The precedence of the Name of Allah لِلَّهِ, ﷻ before أَندَادا[441] can indicate that the negation of partners with Allah ﷻ is not due to the quality or quantity of partners but it is due to Who, Allah ﷻ is in the Divine Uluhiyyah. In other words, Allah ﷻ is al-Ahad[442] and al-Wahid[443]. Therefore, this requires not to associate implicitly or explicitly any partners with Allah ﷻ.

The expression وَأَنتُمْ تَعْلَمُونَ[444] in the ayah can indicate that the essence of Islam is 'ilm and its essence is mind, intellect, and logic. Therefore,

---

436. Our Lord, and make us Muslims [in submission] to You and from our descendants a Muslim nation [in submission] to You. And show us our rites [of hajj and Umrah] and accept our repentance. Indeed, You are the Accepting of repentance, the Merciful.
437. Our Lord, and make us Muslims [in submission] to You.
438. Willed.
439. Inclination.
440. So do not attribute to Allah equals.
441. Equals.
442. The One.
443. The Unique.
444. And you know.

Islam rejects irrational, unreasonable, illogical, whimsical, unfounded and groundless approaches in both belief and practice. Therefore, Islam rejects imaginative and unoriginal teachings in religion. Muslim is not the name of a follower of a religion started with Rasulullah ﷺ. But, it is the name of all humans since the first human being, Adam as who have been truly following these logical and rational teachings of Allah ﷻ.

In the above ayah, the expression وَأَنتُمْ تَعْلَمُونَ {البقرة/22} without any objects, maful can make ijaz to avoid itnab in balagah. Yet, by having no maful[445], it can make itnab be open to many possibilities. In other words, Allah ﷻ mentions that the person can know a lot of things by using their mind, intellect, by observing their own body, anatomy, by observing nature, by observing spiritual faculties of heart, emotions and experience. Yet, with all this knowledge, the person should embody[446] فَلَا تَجْعَلُواْ لِلّهِ أَندَاداً.

"In the expression of فَلاَ تَجْعَلُواْ لِلّهِ أَندَاداً, sometimes the person knows and still does not recognize and appreciate Allah ﷻ.

Sometimes, the person knows, tries and yet, implicitly and explicitly falls in the category of فَلاَ تَجْعَلُواْ لِلّهِ أَندَاداً. Therefore, the dua of Rasulullah ﷺ as اللهم اني اعوذ بك ان اشرك بك شيء و انا اعلم واستغفرك بما لم اعلم [16][447] is a dua for Muslims. In other words, we engage in the valleys of shirk implicitly or explicitly, knowingly or unknowingly.

Sometimes, the person engages himself or herself in a sin. Each sin or each engagement leading to sin can have a way to a shirk. Each shirk[448] can lead to the displeasure of Allah ﷻ.

For the beginner, the displeasure of Allah ﷻ can mean fear from Allah ﷻ. For the elect, the displeasure of Allah ﷻ can mean embarrassment, hayã or shyness from Allah ﷻ that the person feels sad about displeasing Allah ﷻ after Allah ﷻ gives this person everything. For the elect of the elect, regardless of a sin or not, the person sees him or herself always at a position of not truly appreciating Allah ﷻ as mentioned wa ma qadarullahi haqqa qadrihi [39:67].

---

445. What the action is being done upon.
446. So do not attribute to Allah equals.
447. Oh Allah, I seek refuge on you to make something shirk with you and I know, and ask forgiveness for what I did not know.
448. To share partners with Allah.

Remembering our discussion about tawhid in Uluhiyyah[449], Rububiyyah[450] and Ubudiyyah[451] of Allah ﷻ, we need to express the tawhid of Uluhiyyah[452] of Allah ﷻ with our tawhid in ubudiyyah of Allah ﷻ. These expressions should be embodied in a person as a trait and quality with sincerity through the engagements of the mind and heart by constantly witnessing, observing, living and experiencing the tawhid in Rububiyyah[453] of Allah ﷻ.

Yes, one of the hikmahs and wisdoms of having instinctive, unconscious, involuntary continuous engagements of thinking with our brain and cognitive faculties and engagements of dynamically changing emotions with our heart and other spiritual faculties is to embody true tawhid by constantly engaging them with Rububiyyah[454] of Allah ﷻ.

In other words, tawhid in Uluhiyyah[455] and tawhid in Ubudiyyah[456] of Allah ﷻ requires submission and following. Tawhid in Rububiyyah of Allah ﷻ requires constant critical thinking, observing, evaluation, inference, and conclusion with knowledge and asking hidayah for true interpretation of them from Allah ﷻ.

In all these engagements, knowing your-self, constant self-check and accountability with your temporal and creation qualities as the a'bd of Allah ﷻ is critical and default to remind oneself.

In other words, one should be always in the constant heart and mind related states of the need for Allah ﷻ. He or she should embody the mind and heart states as for example "Oh Allah, I can't do without you even less than a second, please do not leave me by myself alone." This is mentioned by Rasulullah ﷺ in his duas as "O Allah! It is Your mercy that I hope for, so leave me not to myself for the blinking of an eye, and put right for me all my affairs! There is no god but You—O All—Living, Self-Subsistent [Lord]! (Ya Hayy[457], Ya Qayyum[458]), in Your mercy do I seek relief" [5].

---

449. Divinity.
450. Lordship.
451. Divinity.
452. Divinity.
453. Lordship.
454. Lordship.
455. Divinity.
456. Divinity.
457. The Alive.
458. O Protector.

Tawhidi Uluhiyyah requires submission, humbleness, humility, and following. Tawhidi Rububiyyah requires using the mind and critical thinking. The form of embodiment of accepting and understanding requires the representation in the form of Tawhidi U'budiyyah.

Tawhidi Uluhiyyah requires the works of heart and experience with the realization of the true self with its needs for Allah ﷻ like the people of the heart such as mutassawiffin, mystics. For example, it is mentioned that Shayhul Karkhi was not an intellectual but the genuine person of the heart on the path of Allah ﷻ and Rasulullah ﷺ. Tawhidi Rububiyyah[459] requires the works of mind, thinking, using the methodology of logic like philosophers such as Aristotle who can go to the steps of mind by giving meanings to prove the existence of Allah ﷻ Who is One and Unique.

For some people who take the religion from their parents, culture or society can start the journey with Tawhidi Uluhiyyah. Yet, this should be supported to reach the level of yaqin and certainty with Tawhidi Rububiyyah.

For some people who do take incorrect form of religion or don't take the correct form of religion can start the journey with Tawhidi Rububiyyah and guided by Allah ﷻ with Tawhidi Uluhiyyah which requires authentic and original revelation from Allah ﷻ that are the Qurān and Hadith.

In both possible cases of inheritance of religious teachings from parents, society or culture, Tawhid U'budiyyah[460] is the expected outcome of the display of Tawhidi Uluhiyyah and Tawhidi Rububiyyah. In other words, although Allah ﷻ knows our inner renderings of heart and intention, the general rule is that the internal disposition is to be expressed by the external. It can be difficult to understand a case of a person sitting inside the garbage can with filth and telling that "my internal feelings are smelling flowers, jasmine and roses." Although there can be some exceptions through the mystical understandings of engagements, the religion is for everyone. The religion sets internal intended meanings that are not apparently contradicting with their external meanings in our worldly views of social constructs.

In other words, 'ibadah is the tool of embodiment of the aqidah[461].

---

459. The effort of reaching to the full yaqeen.
460. The experiential intellect working through experience.
461. Belief.

In terminology, some may distinguish and use two types of mind or intellect. One is theoretical intellect by observing the nature and systems working through abstraction, assumptions and models. The other is experiential intellect working through experience, real personal actions and engagements. One can call this sense-experience or empiricism.

Tawhid Uluhiyyah[462] is given to us in the Qurān and Sunnah. We follow, submit and accept as they are given to us by Allah ﷻ and explained by Rasulullah ﷺ. The level of this submission can be called taqwa and reached with the applications of Tawhid Rububiyyah[463] and Ubudiyyah[464].

Tawhid Rububiyyah[465] is the effort of reaching to the full yaqeen, full certainty through the theoretical intellect by observing the nature and systems working through abstraction, assumptions and models.

Tawhid Ubudiyyah[466] is the experiential intellect working through experience, engagements of 'ibadah and real personal actions of deeds as outlined in the Qurān and sunnah of Rasulullah ﷺ.Yet, a human's pure mind and intellect should be guided by the Qurān and sunnah. Today, people may assign values, and meanings to the things by only using the mind. Tomorrow, these assignments and meanings can change and updated due to the limited tools of human mind in the accessibility of meanings. An example of this can be for the initial assignment of Pluto as a planet after its discovery then it was changed as a dwarf in astronomy as mentioned:

From the time of its discovery it was regarded as the ninth (outermost) planet of the solar system, but in the 1990s its unusual characteristics led astronomers to question its planetary nature. In August 2006, the International Astronomical Union formally declared Pluto to be a dwarf planet rather than a planet proper [2].

When Allah ﷻ gives us the meanings and their assigned values, our position should be to understand and detail these meanings and values in order to increase our yaqîn. The knowledge in the guidance of the Qurān and sunnah can lead us to constant meaningful, beneficial and

---

462. Oneness of divineness.
463. The effort of reaching to the full yaqeen.
464. Is the experiential intellect working through experience.
465. Oneness of lordship.
466. Oneness of divineness.

optimized results. The knowledge without the guidance of the wahiy can lead the person to long unclear and changing results.

Scientific changing findings or results can lead the people to lose trust in science with mere mind engagements.

Scientific findings with the engagements of the mind under guidance of wahiy can lead the person to the trusted universal constants and laws as established by Allah ﷻ. This can be called sunnatullah or a'adatullah as well.

Complementary Roles of Science and the Qurān and Hadith

There are two different sources or books of laws, guidelines, principles and facts in religion. One is instructed through scriptures, from the Qurān as an inductive source of reasoning. The other is through scientific natural and social laws, guidelines, principles and facts called sunnatullah as a deductive source of reasoning.

Nature is another Divine Book from Allah ﷻ and its exploration can be called science or sunnatullah. The Qurān is a Divine Book from Allah ﷻ and its exploration can be called studying the scriptural analysis in the light of the hadith, teachings of Rasulullah ﷺ.

The first exploration is referred as scientific exploration. Everyone can do it with different purposes. A non-Muslim can do it with the purpose of knowing the nature and universe and making use of it and taking advantage of it. A Muslim scientist can do it with the purpose of amazement to increase their imān and at the same time, it can benefit them further by using them for the benefits of humans. A Muslim has a wider and broader purpose to derive purpose, meaning and value from all these explorations by relating them all to the Creator with recognition, appreciation, thankfulness and gratefulness. A non-Muslim can approach it with more capitalist, egocentric and consumerist perspectives of viewing them as simple means, and tools to satisfy one's greed with the attitude of "I don't care about its broader and divine purpose, as long as I get benefit, pleasure and advantage from it, that is how I use it."

The second exploration is referred as scriptural exploration. Everyone can do it with different purposes. A non-Muslim can do it with the purpose of knowing and using for the means of taking advantage of it to hold a position, title and wealth. A true Muslim can do it with the purpose of amazement to increase their imān and at the same, it can benefit them further by sharing them with other humans. A Muslim has a wider and broader purpose to derive purpose, meaning and value from all these explorations by relating them all to the Creator with recognition, appreciation, thankfulness and gratefulness. A non-Muslim can approach it with more capitalist, egocentric and consumerist perspectives of viewing them as simple means, and tools to satisfy one's greed with the attitude of "I don't care about its broader and divine purpose, as long as I get benefit and advantage from it, that is how I use it."

In the case of the non-Muslim, science and scripture are separate. Church and state are separate. Religion and real life are separate. They contradict. Religion does not have a purpose as long as it can be used for benefit. Then, it can be dumbed as any type of commodity. Science does not have a purpose as long as it can be used to benefit. Everything is based on egocentric perspective of life. The pronoun "I" is at the center of everything.

In the case of the true Muslim, both science and the Qurān are complementary. Both science and the Qurān are harmonious. Both science and the Qurān agree. Both science and the Qurān harmonize. Both science and the Qurān are two Divine Books from Allah ﷻ. One is the Book as the Qurān. The other is the workbook as the nature. The applications of science show the correspondence, validity, harmony, and pairing feature of the theory in reality. Therefore, a true Muslim is in constant engagements of amazement of imān in their life journeys until they die. They live in the world a life of Jannah-Heaven through these constant amazements. Then, they reach to the real Jannah-Heaven the world of absolute amazements after death.

Ideal Human Being

If one really reviews the expected outcome of both inductive reasoning as expressed by the Qurān and sunnah as يَا أَيُّهَا النَّاسُ اعْبُدُواْ رَبَّكُمُ الَّذِي خَلَقَكُمْ وَالَّذِينَ مِن قَبْلِكُمْ لَعَلَّكُمْ تَتَّقُونَ [467] {البقرة/21} and the deductive reasoning as expressed by الَّذِي جَعَلَ لَكُمُ الأَرْضَ فِرَاشاً وَالسَّمَاء بِنَاء وَأَنزَلَ مِنَ السَّمَاء مَاء فَأَخْرَجَ

---

467. O mankind, worship your Lord, who created you and those before you, that you may become righteous—

بِهِ مِنَ الثَّمَرَاتِ رِزْقاً لَّكُمْ فَلاَ تَجْعَلُواْ لِلّهِ أَندَاداً وَأَنتُمْ تَعْلَمُونَ[468] {البقرة/22}, then one can realize that both have the complementary roles and lead to the natural, fitrah[469] state of being true a'abd[470] as Abdullah or al-insān al-kāmil, the ideal human being.

In other words, a person deprived of one part, either inductive or deductive reasoning, may not be in a complete, ideal, and natural disposition of being an ideal human being.

For a person following the scriptures without the guidance of mind, it can be very difficult to reach ideal states of imān with certainty. The rare claims can be present by the mystics to emphasize that certainty can be achieved by the experience. Yet, knowledge in the realms of the mind is the key to follow with the guidelines of the scriptures and experiential learning.

A person following the scriptures without the guidance of mind can be easily manipulated and misguided on the path of Allah ﷻ and Rasulullah ﷺ. In other words, the tools of religion can be very powerful to motivate people in a good or a bad cause. When people are motivated to an end goal given by Allah ﷻ in this world and afterlife, any genuine person may not want to take a risk of displeasing Allah ﷻ. Yet, if the motivation of the people with religious content is not checked through the mind of the individual, then one can see devastating results. One of the prime examples of this is called as religious extremism due to absence of check of the mind in religious motivational discourses. Although these individuals or groups are minority who have the absence of the guidance of mind in religious engagements, their voices are more popularized and become widespread causing an unfair stigma on religions.

On the other hand, a person following the mind without the guidance of the Qurān and Rasulullah ﷺ becomes trapped in the arrogant states of self in the guidance of illusionary and pseudo mind. This person does not accept and realize the simple realities of his own self as a needy creature who is fully dependent on Allah ﷻ in his breathing,

---

468. [He] who made for you the earth a bed [spread out] and the sky a ceiling and sent down from the sky, rain and brought forth thereby fruits as provision for you. So do not attribute to Allah equals while you know [that there is nothing similar to Him].
469. Religion of Allah.
470. Servant {of Allah}.

seeing, hearing, digestion and excretion. Yet, he makes claims with the end goals of recognition, fame, popularity, wealth or position.

A person following the mind without the guidance of the Qurān and Rasulullah 🌸 cannot help himself and cannot help others. A sincere philosopher can come out with a very detailed methodological meaning, purpose, and value of everything in life in order to help himself and others. Yet, if he or she does not realize the importance of the mind through the guidance of the Qurān and Rasulullah 🌸, he may be a lost-wanderer in this life-long struggle ending up in very dark depressive state. One can look at the historical engagements of philosophers who committed suicide due to absence of the wahiy, the Divine Guidance of Allah 🕮 through belief and practice in their own lives [17].

Yes, being an ideal human being requires embodying both the mind and wahiy, the Qurān and sunnah of Rasulullah 🌸.

Social Responsibilities, Self, and 'ibadah

One of the roles of 'ibadah is to make this ideal human an individual of a socially responsible person as the a'abd of Allah 🕮.

When the person is in 'ibadah of Allah 🕮, one of the essence of 'ibadah, as mentioned يَا أَيُّهَا النَّاسُ اعْبُدُواْ رَبَّكُمُ[471] is to be responsible with one's relationship with Allah 🕮 and at the same time carry the social and communal responsibilities through I'badah.

Salah as an 'ibadah and worship carries this social responsibility as the collectivity body of u'budiyyah to Allah 🕮. The indication of plurality in Sûrah Fatiha as read in every salah, the requirements of praying with jama'a of every salah and Jum'a prayers can indicate this collective form of 'ibadah being presented to Rabbul A'lamîn . Even in this collectivity, it is not only humans but all other beings with humans become one collective body as the a'bd of Allah 🕮 to present their gift of 'ibadah for the display of their gratitude, thankfulness, and appreciation for Allah 🕮, al-Ahad[472], and al-Wahid[473].

Sawm as an 'ibadah and worship carries this social responsibility of fasting at the same time in the month of Ramadan together as a group

---

471. O mankind, worship your lord.
472. The Unique.
473. The One.

presented to Allah ﷻ. Yet, at the same, the person has the empathy with the poor and needy by depriving themselves from food and drink.

Zakah and sadaqa as an 'ibadah and worship carries the social responsibility of directly helping others through the charity wealth, knowledge, and good and kind treatment of others. This is an explicit manifestation of social responsibility as instructed in Islam, Christianity, Judaism as an unchanging rule of Allah ﷻ.

Hajj as an 'ibadah and worship carries the social responsibility of meeting and visiting each other at a certain time and place as a one collective body of Muslims who have different ethnic and languages. This ritual breaks the fragmentation and segregation of people due to their color, gender, ethnic and identities and but unifies them as a collective and social solidarity as the a'bd of Allah ﷻ.

A person gains his or her value with their 'ubudiyyah to Allah ﷻ. In other words, human being is a tiny creature in their size in the universe. Yet, he or she becomes the master of the universe by relating him or herself to the Creator of the universe. The simple looking phrase bismillah is the expression of this relation of the person with the Creator.

'Ubudiyyah is the embodiment of all these phrases such as bismillah, subhanAllah, alhamdulillah, Allahuakbar, la ilaha illa Allah and other forms of verbal and bodily expressions performed only and sincerely for Allah ﷻ as instructed and practiced by Rasulullah ﷺ.

If the person does not have this relation and ascription of himself or herself to Allah ﷻ, then he is and should be the most fearful, uneasy, anxious, nervous and worried person. He or she does not know what may happen to him or her a few seconds later. He or she doesn't have anyone that can protect them from these infinite unknowns. He can crack his spiritual back due to carrying loads of fear, anxieties, and things that he can't handle.

The people of indulgence with addictions such as alcohol, drugs, and with other things happen in order to forget their own realities which are in spiritual crack downs and explosions.

In all of the above cases, 'ibadah has a role both for personal and social engagements. A person who is not in i'badah of Allah ﷻ cannot truly and enjoyably fulfill their social responsibilities for others. Everything starts with the self and, then can extend to others.

Most of the time the person carries his or her own self-consciously. When he or she is engaged in social responsibilities of 'ibadah, he may forget his own conscious self but join the group identity for social solidarity of the collective self.

Therefore, as mentioned by Rasulullah ﷺ with small struggle-Jihad and big one [18] , the person's self engagements with their ascription to Allah ﷻ determines the real value of the person for Allah ﷻ.

If this order is not carefully watched or realized with small and big struggle, one can find a lot of people in the flow of social groups without much critical engagement of self with 'ibadah. In these cases, the motivation for social responsibility can be leaving a legacy behind, fame, position, or recognition. Yet, Rasulullah ﷺ warns about the first three people who were lacking these self-related engagements that they would be questioned and punished in the afterlife [11]. In other words, the value goes back to original discussion of ikhlas, and amalul qulûb.

Philosophers try to give meaning to humans for their purpose, goal and value. Accordingly, other fields such as sociology, psychology, anthropology, and other social sciences try to formalize and apply these initial premises, thoughts and approaches to the apparent world of our lives.

These mental deductions of philosophers as the empirical data can be sometimes hit or miss and sometimes it can come to a point and sometimes, it can be stuck and signal for dead ends. Sometimes, an idea can be popularized through philosophers' abstract gauges but, yet the social applicability of these philosophical teachings can show their impracticality.

Sometimes an idea can be popular with some people, at a certain time of the history and with at a certain period. Then, it can fade away fully. One can review the dead philosophical thoughts buried in the million books of libraries that are sitting in the shelves or data storage devices as unused knowledge like the people buried in the grave.

The above methodology can show the trial and error method of deductive reasoning through empirical data or experiments. It shows the changing character of this scientific knowledge. In other words, what is considered science today may be considered unscientific tomorrow. If something has its changing nature, then it requires critical thinking by the person constantly opposite to submission and following nature of religion. Therefore, the popularized phrase of "critical thinking" in colleges and universities is developed due to its needed application on scientific process and explorations.

In other words, critical thinking requires not to submit and follow to the findings of science, philosophy, psychology, sociology and other disciplines today. But, it requires the possibility of error in these results. It requires the subjective interpretation of the scientist. It requires the possibility of changing this finding tomorrow with better understanding of scientific tools and interpretations. There are many examples of this. One can consider Newtonian laws of physics when some of its problematic themes were pointed through theories of relativistic physics by Einstein.

On the other hand, the religion of Allah ﷻ with the true teachings such as the Qurān and Sunnah of Rasulullah ﷺ presents these objective initial values and meanings simply. It requires submission and following. This can be called inductive reasoning. It explains everything similar to the manual of the manufacturer about this machine as human with their purpose and meaning.

Its guidelines are very clear, simple and straightforward. The Creator is One. A human being is a created being which has an end and beginning. Unlikely, the Creator does not have an end or beginning, the Creator is infinite. Therefore, the Creator is unique, one and different than the creation.

A human as the creation of the Creator has a purpose in life. The life is short but it has a purpose. The innate desire of humans not to die and live infinitely proves that there is an endless life after death. The case of injustices in the world requires a full and thorough justice and accountability in a place by the One who is aware of all the details of the true intentions and actions.

The value of a human is measured in his or her initial recognition of their Creator. This recognition can be called belief, imān. This recognition requires appreciation and thanking in the form of practice. This can be called worship, 'ibadah or Islam.

The lowest human being even lower than innate beings is the one who does not recognize this simple fact when they do not recognize their one, unique and true Creator. It is like a person who comes home every day, eats, sleeps, takes shower and dress nice and clean clothes. Everything is free. He doesn't pay for anything. He doesn't clean after himself. He doesn't do laundry. Everything is for his service. Yet, he does not say "hi" or "salām" to the people in this house who makes all these for him. This is not one day. Maybe, his attitude is for 60–70 years or until he dies. One can imagine this person and say "What a lowly selfish useless this person is! At least say hi or salam to the people who are doing all this for you!"

This is exactly the person of kufr. This is exactly the case of the person who do not recognize their one, unique, and true Creator. Allah ﷻ gives this person a functioning body, health, life and other means of livable conditions such as nature, air, and others. In their life, they even don't recognize this similar to the person saying "hi or salam" in a house with a full and free service.

When this person in the above story of the house says "hi", then this is similar to the belief and imān to the One and Unique Creator. When this person thanks the people in the house, then, this is similar to the practice of showing thanking and gratitude to Allah ﷻ through practice and worship, ʿibadah. All the worship rituals are performed with the intention of thanking to Allah ﷻ.

In the case of the philosophers without the guidance of the Qurān and Rasulullah, a life and afterlife can be wasted with the lollipop effects of the position, title, and self-sufficiency of the mind induced by arrogance, fears, spiritual devastations and losses. In the other case of the aʿbd of Allah ﷻ following the true teachings from the Creator of all universes, a life and afterlife can be used efficiently and with achievements with the humbleness and guidance of the mind with the Qurān and Sunna of Rasulullah ﷺ. To prove the above points, one can review the statistical analysis of the last moments of philosophers dying in very devastating manners such as committing suicide, dying due to addictions and other unhappy endings [17]. On the other hand, one can review the reports about the friends of Allah ﷻ who tried to follow these Divine Guidance of the Qurān and sunnah how they ended their lives in pleasant ways of departure but not in agony.

ʿIbadah and ʿubudiyyah is a noble link between the person and Allah ﷻ. Whatever the high titles and positions of the person can be, he or she can reach the highest position of their real and expected achievement through the means of ʿibadah and ʿubudiyyah.

The people of position, title and authority seek recognition, respect, and distinction. A person affliated with a prestigious university such as Harvard can assume and expect recognition or distinction from outsiders due to his or her association with this university. A person in a university with a title of a department chair can have this special recognition with this title especially for the ones who are under him. This normalized expectancy due to titles or wealth is expressed in وَكَانَ لَهُ ثَمَرٌ فَقَالَ لِصَاحِبِهِ وَهُوَ يُحَاوِرُهُ أَنَا أَكْثَرُ مِنكَ مَالًا وَأَعَزُّ نَفَرًا [474] {الكهف/34}.

Yet, all these expectations of a person for recognitions can show the human desire, seeking and zeal for these recognitions, distinguishedness or respect through these titles and positions which somehow hold some type of authority. One can also argue that these titles or recognitions are the secondary cause of holding a position to help others or to be part of the social life. One can also argue that these secondary results are social constructions and their meaning and value are all relative.

Yet, the true 'ibadah for only Allah ﷻ is the primary cause of this true fulfilment of human desire for the fulfilment of recognition, respect and distinguishedness. When Allah ﷻ, the Infinite, al-Baki, appreciates your effort of attachment to Allah ﷻ through the vehicle of 'ibadah, then you can have the permanent, real and absolute disposition of recognition, respect and distinguishedness compared to the temporary, fake and relative dispositions of recognition of humans through humanly credited titles and worldly positions.

In this sense, if a person of title such as MD, PhD, president, commissioner, mayor, chair, provost, dean, professor, and others really want to transform their temporary humanly pseudo, and relative and social constructed recognitions and distinguishedness into a permanent, real and absolute recognition, respect and distinguishedness, then they need to relate themselves with the One Who is al-Baqi[475], the Infinite Source of all the merits. This relation and association with Allah ﷻ is displayed with 'ibadah.

One cannot claim that I have an association with Allah ﷻ but I don't do 'ibadah. 'Ibadah is the form of this concrete form of association in our worldly human means of social constructions as ordered by Allah ﷻ in the Qurān in this ayah as يَا أَيُّهَا النَّاسُ اعْبُدُواْ رَبَّكُمُ الَّذِي خَلَقَكُمْ.Now, one can analyze this lowly case of believers looking this recognition through

---

474. And he had fruit, so he said to his companion while he was conversing with him, "I am greater than you in wealth and mightier in [numbers of] men."
475. The everlasting.

titles and associations with the forsake of sacrificing their absolute association with Allah ﷻ. This very lowly case is presented as

الَّذِينَ يَتَّخِذُونَ الْكَافِرِينَ أَوْلِيَاء مِن دُونِ الْمُؤْمِنِينَ أَيَبْتَغُونَ عِندَهُمُ الْعِزَّةَ فَإِنَّ الْعِزَّةَ لِلَّهِ جَمِيعًا[476] {النساء/139}

The real absolute and permanent case of recognition, respect, and distinguishedness is achieved through the association with Allah ﷻ as mentioned فَإِنَّ الْعِزَّةَ لِلَّهِ جَمِيعًا[477]. Here, the word جَمِيعًا[478] can indicate these individual cases of respect, recognition, or respect. Yet, their reflection on the true servants of Allah ﷻ and the self-claimed or pseudo reflections through titles and positions asserting authority, wealth or power is truly, absolutely, collectively and altogether belongs to Allah ﷻ.

In this regard, one can analyze the ayah وَلَا يَحْزُنكَ قَوْلُهُمْ إِنَّ الْعِزَّةَ لِلَّهِ جَمِيعًا هُوَ السَّمِيعُ الْعَلِيمُ[479] {يونس/65} that the people can manifest these self-claimed and fake expressions of power, authority, wealth, title and positions as mentioned قَوْلُهُمْ[480]. Their expressions can really hurt the genuine people of imān, and tabligh as embodied by Rasulullah ﷺ. Therefore, this normalization point is given as an advice with[481] وَلَا يَحْزُنكَ قَوْلُهُمْ. The real absolute appreciation and recognition only fully and truly belongs to Allah ﷻ as mentioned[482] إِنَّ الْعِزَّةَ لِلَّهِ جَمِيعًا. The real authority of holding everything is mentioned in the next ayah as أَلا إِنَّ لِلَّهِ مَن فِي السَّمَاوَاتِ وَمَن فِي الْأَرْضِ but yet they follow these pseudo fake social constructs as وَمَا يَتَّبِعُ الَّذِينَ يَدْعُونَ مِن دُونِ اللّهِ شُرَكَاء إِن يَتَّبِعُونَ إِلاَّ الظَّنَّ وَإِنْ هُمْ إِلاَّ يَخْرُصُونَ[483] {يونس/66}.

---

476. Those who take disbelievers as allies instead of the believers. Do they seek with them honor [through power]? But indeed, honor belongs to Allah entirely.
477. But indeed honor belongs to Allah entirely.
478. Entirely.
479. And let not their speech grieve you. Indeed, honor [due to power] belongs to Allah entirely. He is the Hearing, the Knowing.
480. Their speech.
481. Let not their speech grieve you.
482. Indeed honor belongs to Allah entirely.
483. Unquestionably, to Allah belongs whoever is in the heavens and whoever is on the earth. And those who invoke other than Allah do not [actually] follow [His] "partners." They follow not except assumption, and they are not but falsifying.

Spiritual Diseases and their Cure

If we analyze this spiritual disease further, one can focus on the following ayahs of the Qurān diagnosing the disease and making surgery about it as mentioned:

وَكَانَ لَهُ ثَمَرٌ فَقَالَ لِصَاحِبِهِ وَهُوَ يُحَاوِرُهُ أَنَا أَكْثَرُ مِنكَ مَالًا وَأَعَزُّ نَفَرًا ⁴⁸⁴ {الكهف/34}

وَدَخَلَ جَنَّتَهُ وَهُوَ ظَالِمٌ لِّنَفْسِهِ قَالَ مَا أَظُنُّ أَن تَبِيدَ هَذِهِ أَبَدًا⁴⁸⁵ {الكهف/35} وَمَا أَظُنُّ السَّاعَةَ قَائِمَةً وَلَئِن رُّدِدتُّ إِلَى رَبِّي لَأَجِدَنَّ خَيْرًا مِّنْهَا مُنقَلَبًا⁴⁸⁶ {الكهف/36} قَالَ لَهُ صَاحِبُهُ وَهُوَ يُحَاوِرُهُ أَكَفَرْتَ بِالَّذِي خَلَقَكَ مِن تُرَابٍ ثُمَّ مِن نُّطْفَةٍ ثُمَّ سَوَّاكَ رَجُلًا⁴⁸⁷ {الكهف/37} لَّكِنَّا هُوَ اللَّهُ رَبِّي وَلَا أُشْرِكُ بِرَبِّي أَحَدًا⁴⁸⁸ {الكهف/38} وَلَوْلَا إِذْ دَخَلْتَ جَنَّتَكَ قُلْتَ مَا شَاء اللَّهُ لَا قُوَّةَ إِلَّا بِاللَّهِ إِن تَرَنِ أَنَا أَقَلَّ مِنكَ مَالًا وَوَلَدًا⁴⁸⁹ {الكهف/39} فَعَسَى رَبِّي أَن يُؤْتِيَنِ خَيْرًا مِّن جَنَّتِكَ وَيُرْسِلَ عَلَيْهَا حُسْبَانًا مِّنَ السَّمَاء فَتُصْبِحَ صَعِيدًا زَلَقًا⁴⁹⁰ {الكهف/40} أَوْ يُصْبِحَ مَاؤُهَا غَوْرًا فَلَن تَسْتَطِيعَ لَهُ طَلَبًا⁴⁹¹ {الكهف/41} وَأُحِيطَ بِثَمَرِهِ فَأَصْبَحَ يُقَلِّبُ كَفَّيْهِ عَلَى مَا أَنفَقَ فِيهَا وَهِيَ خَاوِيَةٌ عَلَى عُرُوشِهَا وَيَقُولُ يَا لَيْتَنِي لَمْ أُشْرِكْ بِرَبِّي أَحَدًا⁴⁹² {الكهف/42} وَلَمْ تَكُن لَّهُ فِئَةٌ يَنصُرُونَهُ مِن دُونِ اللَّهِ وَمَا كَانَ مُنتَصِرًا ⁴⁹³{الكهف/43} هُنَالِكَ الْوَلَايَةُ لِلَّهِ الْحَقِّ هُوَ خَيْرٌ ثَوَابًا وَخَيْرٌ عُقْبًا ⁴⁹⁴{الكهف/44}

---

484. And he had fruit, so he said to his companion while he was conversing with him, "I am greater than you in wealth and mightier in [numbers of] men."
485. And he entered his garden while he was unjust to himself. He said, "I do not think that this will perish—ever.
486. And I do not think the Hour will occur. And even if I should be brought back to my Lord, I will surely find better than this as a return."
487. His companion said to him while he was conversing with him, "Have you disbelieved in He who created you from dust and then from a sperm-drop and then proportioned you [as] a man?
488. But as for me, He is Allah, my Lord, and I do not associate with my Lord anyone.
489. And why did you, when you entered your garden, not say, 'What Allah willed [has occurred]; there is no power except in Allah'? Although you see me less than you in wealth and children,
490. It may be that my Lord will give me [something] better than your garden and will send upon it a calamity from the sky, and it will become a smooth, dusty ground,
491. Or its water will become sunken [into the earth], so you would never be able to seek it."
492. And his fruits were encompassed [by ruin], so he began to turn his hands about [in dismay] over what he had spent on it, while it had collapsed upon its trellises, and said, "Oh, I wish I had not associated with my Lord anyone."
493. And there was for him no company to aid him other than Allah, nor could he defend himself.
494. There the authority is [completely] for Allah, the Truth. He is best in reward and best in outcome.

The underlined disease is the attachment to titles, recognitions, positions, wealth, and accordingly the outcomes of prestige as mentioned أَنَا أَكْثَرُ مِنكَ مَالًا وَأَعَزُّ نَفَرًا {الكهف/34} [495]. The diagnosis of these diseases is emphasized by the doctor or psychologist as إِن تَرَنِ أَنَا أَقَلَّ مِنكَ مَالًا وَوَلَدًا {الكهف/39} [496]

Then, the spread of this disease can cause secondary diseases similar to metastasis as مَا أَظُنُّ أَن تَبِيدَ هَذِهِ أَبَدًا {الكهف/35} [497]. The disease here is about not realizing the worldly attachments are temporary, fake and socially constructed.

The secondary metastasis is وَمَا أَظُنُّ السَّاعَةَ قَائِمَةً وَلَئِن رُّدِدتُّ إِلَى رَبِّي لَأَجِدَنَّ خَيْرًا مِّنْهَا مُنقَلَبًا {الكهف/36} [498]. The false expectations of dhann, illusions, and expectations about the unseen. In other words, one forms these expectations of the unseen and future according to their present state. If their present state is in false, deceptive and fake illusions, then their expectations for future and unseen would be illusionary, false, deceptive and fake.

In this case, the doctor shows the true, and real reality as قَالَ لَهُ صَاحِبُهُ وَهُوَ يُحَاوِرُهُ أَكَفَرْتَ بِالَّذِي خَلَقَكَ مِن تُرَابٍ ثُمَّ مِن نُّطْفَةٍ ثُمَّ سَوَّاكَ رَجُلًا {الكهف/37} [499] لَّكِنَّا هُوَ اللَّهُ رَبِّي وَلَا أُشْرِكُ بِرَبِّي أَحَدًا {الكهف/38} [500] وَلَوْلَا إِذْ دَخَلْتَ جَنَّتَكَ قُلْتَ مَا شَاء اللَّهُ لَا قُوَّةَ إِلَّا بِاللَّهِ [501].

Here is an evil-seeming surgery which may include pain at the end, yet the removal of these diseases with their metastatis effects is mentioned as: فَعَسَى رَبِّي أَن يُؤْتِيَنِ خَيْرًا مِّن جَنَّتِكَ وَيُرْسِلَ عَلَيْهَا حُسْبَانًا مِّنَ السَّمَاء فَتُصْبِحَ صَعِيدًا زَلَقًا {الكهف/40} [502] أَوْ يُصْبِحَ مَاؤُهَا غَوْرًا فَلَن تَسْتَطِيعَ لَهُ طَلَبًا {الكهف/41} [503]

After this painful surgery, if the person is not a person of imãn, then it is expected that either the person can go through depressive states of

---

495. I am greater than you in wealth and mightier in [numbers of] men."
496. ? Although you see me less than you in wealth and children,
497. And he entered his garden while he was unjust to himself. He said, "I do not think that this will perish—ever.
498. And I do not think the Hour will occur. And even if I should be brought back to my Lord, I will surely find better than this as a return."
499. His companion said to him while he was conversing with him, "Have you disbelieved in He who created you from dust and then from a sperm-drop and then proportioned you [as] a man?
500. But as for me, He is Allah, my Lord, and I do not associate with my Lord anyone.
501. And why did you, when you entered your garden, not say, 'What Allah willed [has occurred]; there is no power except in Allah'?
502. It may be that my Lord will give me [something] better than your garden and will send upon it a calamity from the sky, and it will become a smooth, dusty ground,
503. Or its water will become sunken [into the earth], so you would never be able to seek it."

وَأُحِيطَ بِثَمَرِهِ فَأَصْبَحَ يُقَلِّبُ كَفَّيْهِ عَلَى مَا أَنفَقَ فِيهَا وَهِيَ خَاوِيَةٌ عَلَى
loss as mentioned
عُرُوشِهَا وَيَقُولُ يَا لَيْتَنِي لَمْ أُشْرِكْ بِرَبِّي أَحَدًا504 {الكهف/42}

Or, it is hoped that with the hidayah of Allah ﷻ the person can have hidayah and understand the reality before they die.

The prior case is an example of increase in agony and spiritual destruction of the person further. One can remember spiritual chaos of people when they leave or removed from their position of authority and their related deaths.

After this painful surgery, if the person is a person of imān, then it is expected that the person can change their position, ask forgiveness as mentioned وَأُحِيطَ بِثَمَرِهِ فَأَصْبَحَ يُقَلِّبُ كَفَّيْهِ عَلَى مَا أَنفَقَ فِيهَا وَهِيَ خَاوِيَةٌ عَلَى عُرُوشِهَا
وَيَقُولُ يَا لَيْتَنِي لَمْ أُشْرِكْ بِرَبِّي أَحَدًا505 {الكهف/42}

The expected result of a successful surgery is for the person to embody the reality of وَلَمْ تَكُن لَّهُ فِئَةٌ يَنصُرُونَهُ مِن دُونِ اللَّهِ وَمَا كَانَ مُنتَصِرًا
{الكهف/43}506. هُنَالِكَ الْوَلَايَةُ لِلَّهِ الْحَقِّ هُوَ خَيْرٌ ثَوَابًا وَخَيْرٌ عُقْبًا507 {الكهف/44}

The reality is that these positions, titles, human recognitions and wealth are all helpless, lowly, worthless, valueless, insignificant, empty or hollow, abandoned and useless as mentioned وَلَمْ تَكُن لَّهُ فِئَةٌ يَنصُرُونَهُ مِن
دُونِ اللَّهِ وَمَا كَانَ مُنتَصِرًا508 {الكهف/43}.

Yet, these associations, in order to gain positions, wealth and recognition as mentioned 509وَاتَّخَذُوا مِن دُونِ اللَّهِ آلِهَةً لِّيَكُونُوا لَهُمْ عِزًّا {مريم/81}
كَلَّا سَيَكْفُرُونَ 510 will turn against them in front of Allah ﷻ as mentioned
بِعِبَادَتِهِمْ وَيَكُونُونَ عَلَيْهِمْ ضِدًّا {مريم/82}.

So, stop and take a heed!

Turn away from them before they turn against you!

---

504. And his fruits were encompassed [by ruin], so he began to turn his hands about [in dismay] over what he had spent on it, while it had collapsed upon its trellises, and said, "Oh, I wish I had not associated with my Lord anyone."

505. And his fruits were encompassed [by ruin], so he began to turn his hands about [in dismay] over what he had spent on it, while it had collapsed upon its trellises, and said, "Oh, I wish I had not associated with my Lord anyone."

506. And there was for him no company to aid him other than Allah, nor could he defend himself.

507. There the authority is [completely] for Allah, the Truth. He is best in reward and best in outcome.

508. And there was for him no company to aid him other than Allah, nor could he defend himself.

509. And they have taken besides Allah [false] deities that they would be for them [a source of] honor.

510. No! They [i.e., those "gods"] will deny their worship of them and will be against them opponents [on the Day of Judgement].

Here is an example and embodiment of the people of taking heed, making a full U-turn from their position as: فَأَلْقَوْا حِبَالَهُمْ وَعِصِيَّهُمْ وَقَالُوا بِعِزَّةِ فِرْعَوْنَ إِنَّا لَنَحْنُ الْغَالِبُونَ{44/الشعراء} [511] فَأَلْقَى مُوسَى عَصَاهُ فَإِذَا هِيَ تَلْقَفُ مَا يَأْفِكُونَ{45/الشعراء} [512] فَأُلْقِيَ السَّحَرَةُ سَاجِدِينَ{46/الشعراء} [513] قَالُوا آمَنَّا بِرَبِّ الْعَالَمِينَ [514] {47/الشعراء} رَبِّ مُوسَى وَهَارُونَ [515] {48/الشعراء}

Magicians initially wanted to take position, and recognition by associating themselves with fira'wn as mentioned [516] وَقَالُوا بِعِزَّةِ فِرْعَوْنَ إِنَّا لَنَحْنُ الْغَالِبُونَ {44/الشعراء} as the word بِعِزَّةِ is critical to focus. This is also mentioned in the ayah فَلَمَّا جَاءَ السَّحَرَةُ قَالُوا لِفِرْعَوْنَ أَئِنَّ لَنَا لَأَجْرًا إِن كُنَّا نَحْنُ الْغَالِبِينَ [517] {41/الشعراء} قَالَ نَعَمْ وَإِنَّكُمْ إِذًا لَّمِنَ الْمُقَرَّبِينَ [518] {42/الشعراء}

The reality of position, recognition and association only but only comes with Allah ﷻ as mentioned هُنَالِكَ الْوَلَايَةُ لِلَّهِ الْحَقِّ[519]. This is the best, true, real and permanent position, recognition and success in this world and after death as mentioned هُوَ خَيْرٌ ثَوَابًا وَخَيْرٌ عُقْبًا[520] {44/الكهف}. The person gains value with their 'ibadah to Allah ﷻ.

Spanning of Signs

When the Qurān explores different signs of Allah ﷻ and presents them to the reader, the accessibility measures sometimes change. These changing accessibilities can serve the purpose of covering all different spans of understandings, mind, intellectual and rational level reasoning. At the same time, this presentation can span different spiritual and emotional states and faculties of humans emerging at different times, places, and contexts. Sometimes, this inclusive and comprehensive level of spanning of the Qurān can aim to increase the limits of humans in their experiential and intellectual levels in the approximations of marifatullah and taqwa.

---

511. So they threw their ropes and their staffs and said, "By the might of Pharaoh, indeed it is we who are predominant."
512. Then Moses threw his staff, and at once it devoured what they falsified.
513. So the magicians fell down in prostration [to Allah].
514. They said, "We have believed in the Lord of the worlds,
515. The Lord of Moses and Aaron."
516. So they threw their ropes and their staffs and said, "By the might of Pharaoh, indeed it is we who are predominant."
517. And when the magicians arrived, they said to Pharaoh, "Is there indeed for us a reward if we are the predominant?"
518. He said, "Yes, and indeed, you will then be of those near [to me]."
519. There the authority is [completely] for Allah, the Truth
520. He is best in reward and best in outcome.

One can review the below ayahs in this concept of inclusive and comprehensive levels of spanning as the key word[521] سَيُرِيكُمْ can indicate :

وَقُلِ الْحَمْدُ لِلَّهِ سَيُرِيكُمْ آيَاتِهِ فَتَعْرِفُونَهَا وَمَا رَبُّكَ بِغَافِلٍ عَمَّا تَعْمَلُونَ[522] {النمل/93}

بَنُرِيهِمْ آيَاتِنَا فِي الْآفَاقِ وَفِي أَنفُسِهِمْ حَتَّى يَتَبَيَّنَ لَهُمْ أَنَّهُ الْحَقُّ أَوَلَمْ يَكْفِ بِرَبِّكَ أَنَّهُ عَلَى كُلِّ شَيْءٍ شَهِيدٌ[523] {فصلت/53}

خُلِقَ الْإِنسَانُ مِنْ عَجَلٍ سَأُرِيكُمْ آيَاتِي فَلَا تَسْتَعْجِلُونِ[524] {الأنبياء/37}

If one reviews the above ayahs around the common word سَيُرِيكُمْ[525], سَنُرِيهِمْ[526], and سَأُرِيكُمْ, they all have سَ. This can indicate the certainty and absolutism. This certainty and absolute disposition can be related to each person's exposure of different signs of Allah ﷻ during their lifespan. Some of these signs can only be known by the person. Some can be also known by the others around and with this person as كُمْ and هِمْ can indicate. This disposition can be related with al-Adl[527], the Just Attribute of Allah ﷻ.

In other words, Allah ﷻ shows everyone their customized individual and collective signs about the secrecy of this life, about its purpose, and goal in their expected relation with Allah ﷻ as mentioned[528] سَنُرِيهِمْ آيَاتِنَا فِي الْآفَاقِ وَفِي أَنفُسِهِمْ حَتَّى يَتَبَيَّنَ لَهُمْ أَنَّهُ الْحَقُّ. The true meaning, purpose and goal of everything in their relation with Allah ﷻ as the Creator can be called الْحَقُّ[529], the true and objective reality. Here, the word يَتَبَيَّنَ can indicate the revealing realities compared to the acquired knowledge or I'lm level renderings of [530] سَيُرِيكُمْ آيَاتِهِ فَتَعْرِفُونَهَا.

---

521. He will show you.
522. And say, "[All] praise is [due] to Allah. He will show you His signs, and you will recognize them. And your Lord is not unaware of what you do."
523. We will show them Our signs in the horizons and within themselves until it becomes clear to them that it is the truth But is it not sufficient concerning your Lord that He is, over all things, a Witness?
524. Man was created of haste [i.e., impatience]. I will show you My signs [i.e., vengeance], so do not impatiently urge Me.
525. I will show you.
526. We will show you.
527. The Just.
528. We will show them Our signs in the horizons and within themselves until it becomes clear to them that it is the truth.
529. The truth.
530. We will show you the signs so that you will recognize them.

In other words, if the true 'ilm, knowledge with the expression سَيُرِيكُمْ آيَاتِهِ فَتَعْرِفُونَهَا can indicate 'ilmal yaqin, then[531] يَتَبَيَّنَ لَهُمْ أَنَّهُ الْحَقُّ can indicate haqqal yaqin. Lastly, خُلِقَ الْإِنسَانُ مِنْ عَجَلٍ [532] [533] سَأُرِيكُمْ آيَاتِي فَلَا تَسْتَعْجِلُونِ, with the words عَجَلٍ[534] and[535] تَسْتَعْجِلُونِ with their implied opposite, mafhumul mukhafala, can indicate this full witnessing in the akhirah with the 'aynal yaqin.

The pronoun of هو [536] in سَيُرِيكُمْ آيَاتِهِ[537] can indicate the multiplicity of signs for al-Ahad in tawhid of La ilaha illa Allah. The pronoun نحن[538] can indicate the multiplicity of signs for al-Wahid in tawhid of La ilaha illa Allah. The pronoun انا[539] in سَأُرِيكُمْ آيَاتِي[540] can indicate different Attributes and Names of Allah ﷻ for the Zat, Allah الله اعلم[541] ﷻ.

Realizing and knowing these signs requires appreciation, thankfulness and gratitude to Allah ﷻ as mentioned وَقُلِ الْحَمْدُ لِلَّهِ سَيُرِيكُمْ[542] آيَاتِهِ فَتَعْرِفُونَهَا.

اللهم ارنا الحق حقا و ارزقنا اتباعه و ارنا الباطل باطل و ارزقنا اجتنابه.[543]

One should remember in any of the renderings of the Qurān that one should primarily consider the initial and primary meanings through the methodology of muffasirûn. In this methodology, the understanding of riwayah, narrations as explained by Rasulullah ﷺ with their sabab nuzûl, and early salaf of the sahabah and tabiûn precedes the engagements of dirāyah by using other analysis in the contexts of intellect, time and context.

---

531. It becomes clear to them that it is the truth.
532. Man was created of haste [i.e., impatience].
533. I will show you My signs [i.e., vengeance], so do not impatiently urge Me.
534. Haste, [impatience].
535. Impatiently urging.
536. Him.
537. I will show you my signs.
538. We.
539. Me.
540. I will show u my signs.
541. Allah knows best.
542. And say, "[All] praise is [due] to Allah. He will show you His signs, and you will recognize them.
543. Oh Alllah, show us the truth, and grant us the following. And show us the falsehood and grant us the ability to avoid it.

Personalization

When one reviews the ayah ﴾سَنُرِيهِمْ آيَاتِنَا فِي الْأَفَاقِ وَفِي أَنفُسِهِمْ حَتَّى يَتَبَيَّنَ لَهُمْ أَنَّهُ الْحَقُّ﴾[544], one can realize the personalization of these signs in order to break the gaflah and bring the person at a very rational state. At this rational state, the person can see what is right and wrong clearly, then the only step that is expected from this person is to make a choice with their free-will.

One can review the case of Abu Jahil [19] that he uttered and declared the truthfulness of the Prophet ﷺ yet, he made a opposite choice with full awareness due to his jealousy.

One can see the effect of the diseases of the heart that they can overtake the person. They can overtake the person's mind, intellect and rational faculties. Jealousy overtakes the intellect. Arrogance overtakes the reason. This is the ultimate and finale of the fight between the mind and emotions, diseased and healthy heart.

One can see this fight as Shaytān representing emotions, his diseased heart overtook his reasoning. The embodiment of arrogance and jealousy represented by Shaytān overtook his faculties of mind, reason, and reasonability.

In this sense, Adam as represents the balanced form of reason and emotions. His emotions prevailed when they made a choice although there were clear instructions from Allah ﷻ. His reason helped him understand his mistake and ran back to Allah ﷻ and made tawbah. On the other hand, Shaytān lost his reasoning fully, and wandering in the valleys of the diseased heart of emotions represented by arrogance and jealousy. A reasonable individual would ask forgiveness after a mistake. There is no reasoning with Shaytān. He did not use:

Therefore, in the realms of the religion Islam, mind precedes the heart representing emotions good or bad. Mind is a compass.

In the fight between the reason and emotions, it is expected that one should follow the reason. In other words, one cannot follow the emotions if there are logical clear guidelines. In these cases, emotions can serve the purpose of whimsical ideas without any grounds but unsupported assumptions.

---

544. We will show them Our signs in the horizons and within themselves until it becomes clear to them that it is the truth.

Therefore, the core principles of Islam are always but always logical and based on reason. It is after stages of this reasonability, the person goes to states of tawakkul[545], taslím[546] and tawfidh[547]. In order words, when a person is in need and finds these reasonable quenching teachings about both mind and heart related engagements, then the person follows, submits and adapts a new life of Islam. Yet, in all parts, reason and mind is a compass and tool to use it for check and balance.

Breaking the Gaflah

One can see in the ayah[548] سَنُرِيهِمْ آيَاتِنَا فِي الْأَفَاقِ وَفِي أَنفُسِهِمْ حَتَّى يَتَبَيَّنَ لَهُمْ أَنَّهُ الْحَقُّ, one of the purpose of spanning of the signs is that to break the gaflah, heedlessness of the person. Then, bring this person back into their normal states of mind and heart.

In this regard, the spanning of the signs from macro levels الَّذِي جَعَلَ لَكُمُ الْأَرْضَ فِرَاشاً وَالسَّمَاء بِنَاءً[549] to micro levels[550] وَأَنزَلَ مِنَ السَّمَاء مَاء فَأَخْرَجَ بِهِ مِنَ الثَّمَرَاتِ رِزْقاً is another way of breaking this gaflah, the blindness of daily routines. Again, breaking the gaflah is personalized according to each person. This person can experience these openings and breaking points at different times of their age, at different times of day and with different types of social and natural engagements.

Today, a pandemic virus can be a delusional reason to make the people imprison in their homes with no social engagements. Yet, Allah ﷻ as the Real Reason of all reason breaks the blindness of people's daily routines referred as gaflah through different means. People who are not used to staying in their homes, now have time hopefully with less distraction to re-evaluate their simple purpose,meaning and goal in life.

The ayahs of the Qurān emphasize this point with a critical word نُفَصِّلُ[551] as:

كَذَلِكَ نُفَصِّلُ الآيَاتِ لِقَوْمٍ يَعْلَمُونَ[552] {الأعراف/32}

---

545. Trust.
546. Peace.
547. Provision.
548. We will show them Our signs in the horizons and within themselves until it becomes clear to them that it is the truth
549. [He] who made for you the earth a bed [spread out] and the sky a ceiling.
550. And sent down from the sky, rain and brought forth thereby fruits as provision [for you].
551. We detail.
552. Thus do We detail the verses for a people who know.

وَكَذَلِكَ نُفَصِّلُ الآيَاتِ وَلَعَلَّهُمْ يَرْجِعُونَ [553]{الأعراف/174}

وَنُفَصِّلُ الآيَاتِ لِقَوْمٍ يَعْلَمُونَ [554] {التوبة/11}

كَذَلِكَ نُفَصِّلُ الآيَاتِ لِقَوْمٍ يَتَفَكَّرُونَ [555] {يونس/24}

كَذَلِكَ نُفَصِّلُ الآيَاتِ لِقَوْمٍ يَعْقِلُونَ [556]{الروم/28}

وَكَذَلِكَ نفَصِّلُ الآيَاتِ وَلِتَسْتَبِينَ سَبِيلُ الْمُجْرِمِينَ [557] {الأنعام/55}

In this sense, one can understand the word نُفَصِّلُ [558] with different spanning of the ayahs is to break the gaflah of humans. Analyzing the stages of breaking, the first stage is to know as mentioned كَذَلِكَ نُفَصِّلُ [559] الآيَاتِ لِقَوْمٍ يَعْلَمُونَ {الأعراف/32} and then, make tawbah as mentioned [560] وَكَذَلِكَ نُفَصِّلُ الآيَاتِ وَلَعَلَّهُمْ يَرْجِعُونَ {الأعراف/174}. It is interesting to note that this critical word mentioned twice in Sûrah a'raf, الأعراف [561] which has the root meaning of to know.

At another level, if the person knows as mentioned وَنُفَصِّلُ الآيَاتِ لِقَوْمٍ يَعْلَمُونَ [562]{التوبة/11}, then they can think and reflect on this knowledge as mentioned كَذَلِكَ نُفَصِّلُ الآيَاتِ لِقَوْمٍ يَتَفَكَّرُونَ{يونس/24} [563]. Then, they can become the people or person of true reason and aqil following al-haqq as mentioned كَذَلِكَ نُفَصِّلُ الآيَاتِ لِقَوْمٍ يَعْقِلُونَ{الروم/28} [564].

In all of these spanning of these signs at different levels of personalization, time, and context, the goal is to break the ghaflah. This indeed can reveal the cases of people and dispositions on the contrary, which are not al-haqq, not reasonable as mentioned وَكَذَلِكَ نفَصِّلُ الآيَاتِ وَلِتَسْتَبِينَ سَبِيلُ الْمُجْرِمِينَ [565] {الأنعام/55}

---

553. And thus do We [explain in] detail the verses, and perhaps they will return.
554. And We detail the verses for a people who know.
555. Thus do We explain in detail the signs for a people who give thought.
556. Thus do We detail the verses for a people who use reason.
557. And thus do We detail the verses, and [thus] the way of the criminals will become evident.
558. We detail [the verse].
559. Thus do We detail the verses for a people who know.
560. And thus do We [explain in] detail the verses, and perhaps they will return.
561. To know.
562. And We detail the verses for a people who know.
563. Thus do We explain in detail the signs for a people who give thought.
564. Thus do We detail the verses for a people who use reason.
565. And thus do We detail the verses, and [thus] the way of the criminals will become evident.

Human Beings at the Center

When one considers all the creation of Allah ﷻ in the universe, one can realize everything is helping the humans in their existence. In other words, Allah ﷻ has placed humans at the center of creation as mentioned وَلَقَدْ كَرَّمْنَا بَنِي آدَمَ وَحَمَلْنَاهُمْ فِي الْبَرِّ وَالْبَحْرِ وَرَزَقْنَاهُم مِّنَ الطَّيِّبَاتِ وَفَضَّلْنَاهُمْ عَلَى كَثِيرٍ مِّمَّنْ خَلَقْنَا تَفْضِيلاً [566] {الإسراء/70}.

In other words, the fruits and vegetables created in the form, taste and smell that humans would eat. The amount of oxygen and gas composition is created to form a livable atmosphere for humans. The amount of sun light, changing of day and light, the location of stars and all others benefit humans in their bodily and spiritual existence. These are all from the Karam of Allah ﷻ as mentioned[567] وَلَقَدْ كَرَّمْنَا بَنِي آدَمَ.

Countless nimahs of Allah ﷻ on us

Sometimes, as we do not remember different nimahs of Allah ﷻ, the Qurān explicitly reminds us these nimahs. In the inductive cases of reasoning, explicit guidelines are expected as in the case of scriptures. In the case of deductive reasoning, it is expected that the person would observe and deduce meanings to appreciate all different nimahs of Allah ﷻ.

Yes, in this perspective, this ayah reminds the nimahs of Allah ﷻ. Sūrah Rahmān with the repetition of the ayah as فَبِأَيِّ آلَاءِ رَبِّكُمَا تُكَذِّبَانِ [568] {الرحمن/13} reminds us the nimahs of Allah ﷻ on us as humans are at the center of creation.

In another perspective, everything is serving, easing, and comforting the humans as they are at the center of the creation. These nimahs are in this world as mentioned يَخْرُجُ مِنْهُمَا اللُّؤْلُؤُ وَالْمَرْجَانُ [569] {الرحمن/22} فَبِأَيِّ آلَاءِ رَبِّكُمَا تُكَذِّبَانِ [570] {الرحمن/23} وَلَهُ الْجَوَارِ الْمُنشَآتُ فِي الْبَحْرِ كَالْأَعْلَامِ [571] {الرحمن/24} فَبِأَيِّ آلَاءِ رَبِّكُمَا تُكَذِّبَانِ [572] {الرحمن/25}.

---

566. And We have certainly honored the children of Adam and carried them on the land and sea and provided for them of the good things and preferred them over much of what We have created, with [definite] preference.
567. And We have certainly honored the children of Adam.
568. So which of the favors of your Lord would you deny?
569. From both of them emerge pearl and coral.
570. So which of the favors of your Lord would you deny?
571. And to Him belong the ships [with sails] elevated in the sea like mountains.
572. So which of the favors of your Lord would you deny?

These ni'mahs also continue in the afterlife as well, as mentioned: فِيهِمَا عَيْنَانِ تَجْرِيَانِ 573{الرحمن/50} فَبِأَيِّ آلَاءِ رَبِّكُمَا تُكَذِّبَانِ 574{الرحمن/51} فِيهِمَا مِن كُلِّ فَاكِهَةٍ زَوْجَانِ 575{الرحمن/52} فَبِأَيِّ آلَاءِ رَبِّكُمَا تُكَذِّبَانِ 576{الرحمن/53} مُتَّكِئِينَ عَلَى فُرُشٍ بَطَائِنُهَا مِنْ إِسْتَبْرَقٍ وَجَنَى الْجَنَّتَيْنِ دَانٍ 577{الرحمن/54} فَبِأَيِّ آلَاءِ رَبِّكُمَا تُكَذِّبَانِ 578{الرحمن/55}

In this perspective, Allah ﷻ gives us countless ni'mahs as mentioned وَآتَاكُم مِّن كُلِّ مَا سَأَلْتُمُوهُ وَإِن تَعُدُّواْ نِعْمَتَ اللّهِ لاَ تُحْصُوهَا إِنَّ الإِنسَانَ لَظَلُومٌ كَفَّارٌ 579{إبراهيم/34}. If the person does not still realize and appreciate Allah ﷻ after all this, then the disposition of the person is إِنَّ الإِنسَانَ لَظَلُومٌ كَفَّارٌ 580{إبراهيم/34}.

On the other hand, the person cannot truly appreciate Allah ﷻ وَمَا قَدَرُوا اللَّهَ حَقَّ قَدْرِهِ وَالْأَرْضُ جَمِيعًا قَبْضَتُهُ يَوْمَ الْقِيَامَةِ وَالسَّماوَاتُ as mentioned مَطْوِيَّاتٌ بِيَمِينِهِ سُبْحَانَهُ وَتَعَالَى عَمَّا يُشْرِكُونَ 581{الزمر/67}. Yet, if he or she realizes the countless nimahs of Allah ﷻ as mentioned وَإِن تَعُدُّواْ نِعْمَةَ اللّهِ لاَ تُحْصُوهَا إِنَّ اللّهَ لَغَفُورٌ رَّحِيمٌ 582{النحل/18}, then one can understand that it is impossible to truly appreciate and thank Allah ﷻ. Realizing and understanding this can make the person be forgiven by al-Gaffār and given more nimahs by al- Rahîm as mentioned إِنَّ اللّهَ لَغَفُورٌ رَّحِيمٌ 583{النحل/18}.

Absurdity of Unrecognition

One can witness countless nimahs of Allah ﷻ in different witnessing experiential signs spanning from anfus[584] to afāq[585] internal to external, from our own bodies to external habitat of clouds, galaxies, and skies.

---

573. In both of them are two springs, flowing.
574. So which of the favors of your Lord would you deny?
575. In both of them are of every fruit, two kinds.
576. So which of the favors of your Lord would you deny?
577. [They are] reclining on beds whose linings are of silk brocade, and the fruit of the two gardens is hanging low.
578. So which of the favors of your Lord would you deny?
579. And He gave you from all you asked of Him. And if you should count the favor [i.e., blessings] of Allah, you could not enumerate them. Indeed, mankind is [generally] most unjust and ungrateful.
580. Indeed, mankind is [generally] most unjust and ungrateful.
581. They have not appraised Allah with true appraisal, while the earth entirely will be [within] His grip on the Day of Resurrection, and the heavens will be folded in His right hand. Exalted is He and high above what they associate with Him.
582. And if you should count the favors of Allah, you could not enumerate them. Indeed, Allah is Forgiving and Merciful.
583. Indeed, Allah is Forgiving and Merciful.
584. Internal self.
585. Extrernal self.

In this perspective, one of the closest nimah from anfus, internal is the person's existence after creation as mentioned [586] يَا أَيُّهَا النَّاسُ اعْبُدُواْ رَبَّكُمُ الَّذِي خَلَقَكُمْ. It is expected that the person can discover their own selves and appreciate their own existence by thanking Allah ﷻ.

In this regard, there are a lot of ayahs in the Qurān and the hadith that can allude to the need for the self-discovery of the person. We don't assume but try to discover ourselves. Looking our own hands, feet, hair, nose, eyes, cheeks, and others are all amazing and very interesting that we find ourselves with these organs. These organs are granted to us without any effort and we are using them constantly. We are dependent on them. These are some of the closest signs, nimahs of Allah ﷻ for the person that one can categorize them as anfus, internal.

These self-discoveries are all related to knowing Allah ﷻ as mentioned [587] وَلَا تَكُونُوا كَالَّذِينَ نَسُوا اللَّهَ فَأَنسَاهُمْ أَنفُسَهُمْ أُوْلَئِكَ هُمُ الْفَاسِقُونَ {الحشر/19}. In this regard, without the guidance of the Qurān and Rasulullah, there are books written in the fields of philosophy, humanities, literature, anthropology, education, sociology, and psychology. Yet, the discoveries in these books have hit and miss approach due to its absence of inductive comprehensive approach of wahiy, revelation. In other words, Allah ﷻ as the Creator sets the guidelines what and who the real self is and the self's critical relation with the Creator through the Qurān and Sunnah of Rasulullah ﷺ. Today, one can give example from the defense industry selling guns or other mechanisms to other countries to protect themselves. Yet, at one point, these countries purchasing these defense mechanisms tend to use them against the ones who they purchased them from. In a common sense, this idea can be absurd. Manufacturer knows the problems and potentials of these applications. Yet, the absurd purchaser tries to use this mechanism or application against the manufacturer.

This analogy is like the case of above disciplines of social sciences and philosophy as the purchaser. Allah ﷻ creates everything from nothing. Allah ﷻ knows the potentials and problems of the humans. Yet, the above disciplines tend to use this given tool, application, or mechanism of self against their Manufacturer, Allah ﷻ as mentioned أَوَلَمْ

---

586. O mankind, worship your lord who created you.
587. And be not like those who forgot Allah, so He made them forget themselves. Those are the defiantly disobedient.

يَرَ الْإِنسَانُ أَنَّا خَلَقْنَاهُ مِن نُطْفَةٍ فَإِذَا هُوَ خَصِيمٌ مُّبِينٌ {يس/77} 588 وَضَرَبَ لَنَا مَثَلاً وَنَسِيَ خَلْقَهُ قَالَ مَنْ يُحْيِي الْعِظَامَ وَهِيَ رَمِيمٌ {يس/78} 589 قُلْ يُحْيِيهَا الَّذِي أَنشَأَهَا أَوَّلَ مَرَّةٍ وَهُوَ بِكُلِّ خَلْقٍ عَلِيمٌ {يس/79} 590.

أَوَلَمْ يَرَ الْإِنسَانُ أَنَّا خَلَقْنَاهُ مِن نُطْفَةٍ فَإِذَا هُوَ خَصِيمٌ مُّبِينٌ 591 SubhanAllah, the ayah {يس/77} exactly points to this absurd logic of humans. Allah ☙ created or manufactured humans from nothing. Yet, humans absurdly try to go against their Manufacturer, similar to an enemy or opponent.

In other words, these disciplines bring arguments, theories, and premises by using this self, intelligence, mind, logic, and rationality given by Allah ☙ against their Creator, similar to the people purchasing these mechanisms from the manufacturer and using them against them. Yet, this gun analogy may not be fully good analogy due to the destructive power of the guns.

In this regard, humans' stance by assuming and overlooking the existence of the Creator and trying to develop theories with different approaches, interpretations and explanations about the purpose, meaning and value of life is very absurd and illogical.

Existence of the Self

When a person thinks about his or her existence and pre-existence, that can open some doors of amazement for the person.

This ayah begins as592 يَا أَيُّهَا النَّاسُ اعْبُدُواْ رَبَّكُمُ الَّذِي خَلَقَكُمْ. The expression593 رَبَّكُمُ الَّذِي خَلَقَكُمْ can indicate this required reflection and critical thinking about one's pre-existence. This critical thinking should lead the person to ask the critical questions of "What was I doing before I was born?"

Being in existence and tracing our own personal memories about our own selves until a certain time of childhood can fill us with different feelings and emotions.

---

588. Does man not consider that We created him from a [mere] sperm-drop—then at once he is a clear adversary?

589. And he presents for Us an example and forgets his [own] creation. He says, "Who will give life to bones while they are disintegrated?"

590. Say, "He will give them life who produced them the first time; and He is, of all creation, Knowing."

591. Does man not consider that We created him from a [mere] sperm-drop—then at once he is a clear adversary?

592. O mankind, worship your lord who created you.

593. Your lord who created you.

Yet, we don't remember our date of delivery, how we cried or not. We don't remember our initial year as a one year old or when were a few months old as a baby being existent in this world. Yet, we depend on the narrations and records as mentioned by our mothers, fathers, relatives and elders about our own past. So, what does all above tell us? This is a question to think about. Let's go to another level.

The Qurān mentions about the pre-delivery stages in the wombs and uterus about ourselves, myself and yourself approximately 1500 years ago. These stagings are confirmed today with the advances in medicine with the imaging devices [20]. Our mothers, fathers and family members can know us after we were born. Yet, these information of the events in the womb even are not realized, recognized and known by our mothers, fathers and relatives. These stagings are mentioned ثُمَّ جَعَلْنَاهُ نُطْفَةً فِي قَرَارٍ مَّكِينٍ [594] {المؤمنون/13} ثُمَّ خَلَقْنَا النُّطْفَةَ عَلَقَةً فَخَلَقْنَا الْعَلَقَةَ مُضْغَةً فَخَلَقْنَا الْمُضْغَةَ عِظَامًا فَكَسَوْنَا الْعِظَامَ لَحْمًا ثُمَّ أَنشَأْنَاهُ خَلْقًا آخَرَ فَتَبَارَكَ اللهُ أَحْسَنُ الْخَالِقِينَ [595] {المؤمنون/14}

The mother only serves as a carrier mentioned with the word حَمَلَتْهُ or حَمْلُهُ in the ayah وَوَصَّيْنَا الْإِنسَانَ بِوَالِدَيْهِ إِحْسَانًا حَمَلَتْهُ أُمُّهُ كُرْهًا وَوَضَعَتْهُ كُرْهًا وَحَمْلُهُ وَفِصَالُهُ ثَلَاثُونَ شَهْرًا حَتَّى إِذَا بَلَغَ أَشُدَّهُ وَبَلَغَ أَرْبَعِينَ سَنَةً قَالَ رَبِّ أَوْزِعْنِي أَنْ أَشْكُرَ نِعْمَتَكَ الَّتِي أَنْعَمْتَ عَلَيَّ وَعَلَى وَالِدَيَّ وَأَنْ أَعْمَلَ صَالِحًا تَرْضَاهُ وَأَصْلِحْ لِي فِي ذُرِّيَّتِي إِنِّي تُبْتُ إِلَيْكَ وَإِنِّي مِنَ الْمُسْلِمِينَ {الأحقاف/15} and similar ayahs of the Qurān. The mother is not aware of the process in her womb, and does not have any control of these events except and only to wait until the delivery of the child.

In another detailing, one can see the process in the womb as يَخْلُقُكُمْ فِي بُطُونِ أُمَّهَاتِكُمْ خَلْقًا مِن بَعْدِ خَلْقٍ فِي ظُلُمَاتٍ ثَلَاثٍ ذَلِكُمُ اللهُ رَبُّكُمْ لَهُ الْمُلْكُ لَا إِلَهَ إِلَّا هُوَ فَأَنَّى تُصْرَفُونَ [596] {الزمر/6}

So, what does all above tell us?

This is a question to think about.

Let's go to another level.

The Qurān mentions the interaction between the husband and wife before the case of womb or uterus as هُوَ الَّذِي خَلَقَكُم مِّن نَّفْسٍ وَاحِدَةٍ وَجَعَلَ مِنْهَا

---

594. Then We placed him as a sperm-drop in a firm lodging [i.e., the womb].
595. Then We made the sperm-drop into a clinging clot, and We made the clot into a lump [of flesh], and We made [from] the lump, bones, and We covered the bones with flesh; then We developed him into another creation. So blessed is Allah, the best of creators.
596. He created you from one soul. Then He made from it its mate, and He produced for you from the grazing livestock eight mates. He creates you in the wombs of your mothers, creation after creation, within three darknesses. That is Allah, your Lord; to Him belongs dominion. There is no deity except Him, so how are you averted?

زَوْجَهَا لِيَسْكُنَ إِلَيْهَا فَلَمَّا تَغَشَّاهَا حَمَلَتْ حَمْلاً خَفِيفًا فَمَرَّتْ بِهِ فَلَمَّا أَثْقَلَت دَّعَوَا اللهَ رَبَّهُمَا لَئِنْ آتَيْتَنَا صَالِحاً لَّنَكُونَنَّ مِنَ الشَّاكِرِينَ ⁵⁹⁷{الأعراف/189}.

Yet, the answer of all the questions are the same. We do not know, are aware and recognize about our own selves in the staging of formations.

We don't know and remember our delivery times coming into this world.

We don't know and remember our early child and baby times of existence.

We don't know and remember the stage of formation in the womb or uterus.

Yet, we claim that we know ourselves and we oversee our existence and abilities. In all above stages, there is the process of coming into existence, staging, change, and formation. Neither our mothers nor our fathers or anyone has any say, or anything do to with it. Except, the mothers has a platform of womb or uterus as a carrier delivering the message, or word that is sent as " كُنْ", "be!" by Allah ﷻ. This process of creation continues from the beginning from Adam as until now.

In this sense, Allah ﷻ is the one Who Creates, forms us and brings us in existence as mentioned[598] رَبَّكُمُ الَّذِي خَلَقَكُمْ.

In all above stages, the critical word خَلَقَ[599] is used as attributed to Allah ﷻ. Then, how does a person not realize this simple reality but still act in the absurdity of unrecognition?

The above process and constant creation, formation and bringing in existence is the case for all of us as mentioned رَبَّكُمُ الَّذِي خَلَقَكُمْ وَالَّذِينَ[600] مِن قَبْلِكُمْ.

In this regard, the critical word خَلَقَ[601] can indicate our natural and innate given disposition of being in existence as given and bestowed by Allah ﷻ. Not remembering the details of our existence can indicate the same given bounty, payment and gift of being existence as given, created and bestowed by Allah ﷻ.

---

597. It is He who created you from one soul and created from it its mate that he might dwell in security with her. And when he [i.e., man] covers her, she carries a light burden [i.e., a pregnancy] and continues therein. And when it becomes heavy, they both invoke Allah, their Lord, "If You should give us a good [child], we will surely be among the grateful."
598. Your lord who created you.
599. Created.
600. Your lord who created you and those before you.
601. Created.

In this sense, existence is a nìmah[602], and light from Allah ﷻ. Identifiability, self, and being known is an honor, dignity, and light. Non-existence is a darkness of infinite unknowns. Therefore, even the case of a kãfir being punished in afterlife is nìmah compared to unexistence of unknowns of darknesses. A mumin recognizes this nìmah of existence from Allah ﷻ and shows their recognition, appreciation and gratitude with imãn, Islãm and ihsãn. [603] اللهم اجعلنا منهم. امين,Our self gets dignified as we increase our connection with the One Who has the Source of All Existence with Full Honor as mentioned مَن كَانَ يُرِيدُ الْعِزَّةَ فَلِلَّهِ الْعِزَّةُ جَمِيعًا إِلَيْهِ يَصْعَدُ الْكَلِمُ الطَّيِّبُ وَالْعَمَلُ الصَّالِحُ يَرْفَعُهُ وَالَّذِينَ يَمْكُرُونَ السَّيِّئَاتِ لَهُمْ عَذَابٌ شَدِيدٌ وَمَكْرُ أُولَئِكَ هُوَ يَبُورُ [604]{فاطر/10}

Our self gets lowered as we disconnect ourselves from Allah ﷻ لَقَدْ خَلَقْنَا الْإِنسَانَ فِي أَحْسَنِ تَقْوِيمٍ [605]{التين/4} ثُمَّ رَدَدْنَاهُ أَسْفَلَ سَافِلِينَ [606]{التين/5} إِلَّا الَّذِينَ آمَنُوا وَعَمِلُوا الصَّالِحَاتِ فَلَهُمْ أَجْرٌ غَيْرُ مَمْنُونٍ [607]{التين/6}

All the creation except some humans and jinn know about this nìmah of existence and in recognition as mentioned أَلَمْ تَرَ أَنَّ اللَّهَ يُسَبِّحُ لَهُ مَن فِي السَّمَاوَاتِ وَالْأَرْضِ وَالطَّيْرُ صَافَّاتٍ كُلٌّ قَدْ عَلِمَ صَلَاتَهُ وَتَسْبِيحَهُ وَاللَّهُ عَلِيمٌ بِمَا يَفْعَلُونَ [608] {النور/41}

[23–24]

وَإِن كُنتُمْ فِي رَيْبٍ مِّمَّا نَزَّلْنَا عَلَى عَبْدِنَا فَأْتُواْ بِسُورَةٍ مِّن مِّثْلِهِ وَادْعُواْ شُهَدَاءكُم مِّن دُونِ اللَّهِ إِنْ كُنتُمْ صَادِقِينَ [609]{البقرة/23} فَإِن لَّمْ تَفْعَلُواْ وَلَن تَفْعَلُواْ فَاتَّقُواْ النَّارَ الَّتِي وَقُودُهَا النَّاسُ وَالْحِجَارَةُ أُعِدَّتْ لِلْكَافِرِينَ [610] {البقرة/24}

---

602. Blessing.
603. Oh Allah, make us from amongst them. Ameen.
604. Whoever desires honor [through power]—then to Allah belongs all honor. To Him ascends good speech, and righteous work raises it. But they who plot evil deeds will have a severe punishment, and the plotting of those—it will perish.
605. We have certainly created man in the best of stature;
606. Then We return him to the lowest of the low,
607. Except for those who believe and do righteous deeds, for they will have a reward uninterrupted.
608. Do you not see that Allah is exalted by whomever is within the heavens and the earth and [by] the birds with wings spread [in flight]? Each [of them] has known his [means of] prayer and exalting [Him], and Allah is Knowing of what they do.
609. And if you are in doubt about what We have sent down [i.e., the Qurãn] upon Our Servant [i.e., Prophet Muhammad (PBUH)], then produce a Sûrah the like thereof and call upon your witnesses [i.e., supporters] other than Allah, if you should be truthful.
610. But if you do not—and you will never be able to—then fear the Fire, whose fuel is men and stones, prepared for the disbelievers.

These ayahs are related with risālah[611], nabuwwah[612], prophethood of Rasulullah ﷺ. As mentioned in the beginning of the book, one can realize four main themes in the Qurān as a methodology. The previous ayahs have the theme of tawhid. In these current ayahs, the theme of nubuwwah, prophethood of Rasulullah ﷺ is presented.

The focus is on the proof of the prophethood of Rasulullah ﷺ as mentioned with عَبْدِنَا. In this methodology of reasoning, if one proves one case, then one can show its application in other cases as well. This may be called sampling as a technical word that a small part or quantity intended to show what the whole is like [2]. In this case, the whole is the task of prophethood as represented by the all prophets sent by Allah ﷻ.

In this sense, one of the biggest proofs of the prophethood of Rasulullah ﷺ is his biggest and still present mujizah[613], the Noble and Honorable Qurān. This mujizah, miracle will be present and existent until the Day of Qiyamah in the world among humans as it is revealed by Allah ﷻ unlike to the fate of previous scriptures as mentioned:

$$ \{ الحجر/9\} \ ^{614} إِنَّا نَحْنُ نَزَّلْنَا الذِّكْرَ وَإِنَّا لَهُ لَحَافِظُونَ $$

Yet, it is always the choice and free will of human beings to engage, follow and adopt the teachings of the Qurān.

Existence of the Qurān as an available miracle of Allah ﷻ among all humans until Day of Qiyamah can also indicate the Adl, Just Name of Allah ﷻ.

In other words, one can ask and say that other nations before Islam constantly received guidance from Allah ﷻ in the form of prophets being sent to them in many numbers. Yet, Rasulullah ﷺ was alive among people as the last prophet almost 1500 years ago. We don't have a prophet among us, living with us, teaching and guiding us. How can one explain this with the justice, adalah of Allah ﷻ?

The previous nations did not have what we have currently have about scriptures. The previous nations did not have access to the original teachings of their scriptures. There was the constant effort of changing,

---

611. A message.
612. Prophethood.
613. A miracle.
614. Indeed, it is We who sent down the message [i.e., the Qurān], and indeed, We will be its guardian.

hiding, and limiting the accessibility of original scriptures sent by Allah ﷻ after their prophets and messengers died.

In our case, Allah ﷻ promised with the Divine Assurance that the Qurān will be original, authentic, accessible until the Day of Qiyamah as mentioned:

$$ \text{إِنَّا نَحْنُ نَزَّلْنَا الذِّكْرَ وَإِنَّا لَهُ لَحَافِظُونَ}^{615} \{9/\text{الحجر}\} $$

The previous nations with scriptures did not have what we have currently in terms of very mind-numbing, critical, careful and scientific scholarship of separating the Qurān from all other writings even from the hadith. When one reviews the methodology of previous scriptures today, there are many fundamental problems and issues relating with authenticity, and originality. There is another problem of the mixture of the original revelation with saintly teachings.

In this regard, the Qurān is authentic and original as revelaed from Allah ﷻ. In addition, there is a clear separation between the Qurān and hadith in their methodology of preservation, and analysis. Even when one reviews the historical development of scholarship in the previous scriptures, there was an immense effect of the usul, methodology of Islamic scholarship affecting ahlu-kitāb how they should approach and develop their own scholarship.One can review many objective texts written by the scholars of ahlu-kitāb about their acknowledgements of these critical effects of Islamic usuli-methodolgial scholarship on Jewish scholarship developing their rules of fiqh as structuralized in four schools of mazhab, developing their own dictionary and aqidah.

One can view this huge Islamic scholarly usuli-methodological effects at the times of Andalusia, effecting the Jewish and Christian scholarships, and then how today's scholarship has been built on both Jewish and Christian scholarships [21].

The previous nations especially their common people did not have access to the original teachings of their scriptures. There was the effort of changing, hiding, and limiting the accessibility of original scriptures sent by Allah ﷻ after their prophets and messengers died.

When we look at today and historical preservation of authenticity, availability, accessibility of the Qurān from the time of Rasulullah ﷺ

---

615. Indeed, it is We who sent down the message [i.e., the Qurān], and indeed, We will be its guardian.

1500 years ago until our time, there is no really issue of authenticity, and accessibility of the Qurān. The teachings of the Qurān is all open source.

It is again the case of free choice and free will of all humans, including the Muslims if they want to engage and how much they want to engage with the Qurān in their own and social lives.

As mentioned in the ayah, {الحجر/9} [616] إِنَّا نَحْنُ نَزَّلْنَا الذِّكْرَ وَإِنَّا لَهُ لَحَافِظُونَ, Allah ﷻ disabled the humans in their free will choice of changing the authentic teachings of the Qurān as a successful venture as they did with the other books and scriptures sent by Allah ﷻ.

There can be very fading attempts but these attempts were so fade as mentioned [617] يُرِيدُونَ لِيُطْفِئُوا نُورَ اللَّهِ بِأَفْوَاهِهِمْ وَاللَّهُ مُتِمُّ نُورِهِ وَلَوْ كَرِهَ الْكَافِرُونَ {الصف/8} that they were not even referenced in some of zealous non-Muslim literatures who have been very thirsty to point them out.

Now, this huge, breath-taking, clear, obvious and strong miracle of Qurān is available. The real question is how many people truly know about it? How much do we benefit from it?

Similarly, the tedious scientific methodology of hadith in its authenticity is the complementary source that were not available for the people of the book. What they have currently in their scriptures is similar to our hadith literature, yet the issues of authenticity really do not seem to be a big concern in these scriptures. Yet, one can review the critical authentication process of each hadith and their categorization and their applications in Islam.

One can ask why the authenticity is so important?

Because a person who is in their normal mind should not want to adopt and follow a teaching if that is not from Allah ﷻ.

Therefore, the entire field of authenticity of the Qurān and hadith with its rationality, completeness, availability to be accessible by everyone with its thoroughness gives comfort, and assurance. As a result of this, one can find Muslims fully grasping their religion compared to others. The heart and mind are all fully satisfied. It is a separate question if a Muslim practices what is available to them or not.

One of the possible reasons of Western societies leaving their religious identities and identifying themselves as "nones" or "spiritual"

---

616. Indeed, it is We who sent down the message [i.e., the Qurān], and indeed, We will be its guardian.
617. They want to extinguish the light of Allah with their mouths, but Allah will perfect His light, although the disbelievers dislike it.

is due to this lack of comfort, assurance and thoroughness established with its authenticity [6]. Consequently, the relationship with the religion and scripture becomes very lose and volatile. This is very normal. This is not unfortunately much underlined in Western societies.

People make sociological researches of religious identity changes. Then, the analyzes of the data lean to the need that "we need to change our religion, it is old and backwards." Yet, not many asks this very simple and critical sociological question of "what we follow, is this authentic?"

There is no full heart and mind assurance of authenticity. Even a small insertion or change in the authenticity the teachings and scripture can open a big crack and make the foundation fall apart. Therefore, there is this constant assurance and reminder in the Qurān as:

الْحَمْدُ لِلَّهِ الَّذِي أنزَلَ عَلَى عَبْدِهِ الْكِتَابَ وَلَمْ يَجْعَل لَّهُ عِوَجَا 618 {الكهف/1}

أَفَلاَ يَتَدَبَّرُونَ الْقُرْآنَ وَلَوْ كَانَ مِنْ عِندِ غَيْرِ اللّهِ لَوَجَدُواْ فِيهِ اخْتِلاَفًا كَثِيرًا 619 {النساء/82}

Prophethood-Nubuwwah

When we review the cases of the responsibility of prophethood given to other prophets, one can realize:

Their prophethood indicates about Rasulullah ﷺ.Rasulullah ﷺ collects in his prophethood all the separate individual emerging prominent features of each prophet.

Therefore, Rasulullah ﷺ is called the lead prophet and human being. As all the prophets are role models for humans, the lead prophet necessitates to be the lead of all humans, sayyidul-bashar.

Therefore, focusing on the prophethood of Rasulullah ﷺ as a case of proof after tawhid can prove also the prophethood of other messengers sent by Allah ﷻ.

---

618. [All] praise is [due] to Allah, who has sent down upon His Servant [Muhammad (PBUH)] the Book and has not made therein any deviance.
619. Then do they not reflect upon the Qurān? If it had been from [any] other than Allah, they would have found within it much contradiction.

Truthfulness-as-Sidq

When we try to understand anything in our world means of complexity, we try to do segmentation in order to put these events, cases, materials or incidents in smaller pieces to analyze. Then, as we do summation of all these individual pieces, we arrive to the aggregate result about this case, incident, or scientific problem.

Similarly, as we approach to the life of Rasulullah ﷺ with this concept of segmentation of each incident, there is a one common theme among many that emerges in all cases. That is the sidq, the truthfulness and reliability of Rasulullah ﷺ. In other words, a person in his entire life emphasizing and embodying the truthfulness, sidq in each of his small segments and incidents of social, family, legal, military, business, and personal life will be called in deductive reasoning as sadiqul-amîn[620], the most truthful ﷺ. A person's life is collected and defined with all the small intervals of life time intervals. An established trait or character of a person is defined how and what this person displays in each small intervals of time of their life in different engagements. If the person in majority of the cases shows this trait or quality, a person may still be called or identified with this trait or quality.

If the person without any exception all the time displays this quality, then it becomes an absolute pure quality and trait of a person. In this sense, truthfulness is the full and pure embodied trait of Rasulullah ﷺ.

There are a lot of reports about his truthfulness, honesty, and conflict resolution of Rasulullah ﷺ before the prophethood. How can a person known to be the epitome of truthfulness and honesty before prophethood not continue the same trait of truthfulness-sidq even with more diligence after receiving revelation from Allah ﷻ? Below ayahs underline these critical points with this impossibility with the question structure of مَا كَانَ لِ:

وَمَا كَانَ لِنَبِيٍّ أَن يَغُلَّ وَمَن يَغْلُلْ يَأْتِ بِمَا غَلَّ يَوْمَ الْقِيَامَةِ ثُمَّ تُوَفَّى كُلُّ نَفْسٍ مَّا كَسَبَتْ وَهُمْ لاَ يُظْلَمُونَ [621] {آل عمران/161}

---

620. The Most Truthful.
621. It is not [attributable] to any prophet that he would act unfaithfully [in regard to war booty]. And whoever betrays, [taking unlawfully], will come with what he took on the Day of Resurrection. Then will every soul be [fully] compensated for what it earned, and they will not be wronged.

The Qurãn mentions the impossibility of deceitfulness opposite to sidq for the true prophet of Allah ﷻ.

مَا كَانَ لِبَشَرٍ أَن يُؤْتِيَهُ اللّهُ الْكِتَابَ وَالْحُكْمَ وَالنُّبُوَّةَ ثُمَّ يَقُولَ لِلنَّاسِ كُونُواْ عِبَادًا لِّي مِن دُونِ اللّهِ وَلَكِن كُونُواْ رَبَّانِيِّينَ بِمَا كُنتُمْ تُعَلِّمُونَ الْكِتَابَ وَبِمَا كُنتُمْ تَدْرُسُونَ ٢٢٢ {آل عمران/79}

Although the context of the above ayah can be Isa as, there is a generally rule for the true prophethood given by Allah ﷻ. It is not logical for a person to falsely claim prophethood if it is truly given by Allah ﷻ. In each claim, one can analyze what is false and true. There are thousands of signs about the true prophethood of Rasulullah ﷺ. The prophethood of Rasulullah ﷺ is an absolute truth. When one reviews the claims by the false prophethoods such as Musaylama al-Kathãb, it is very apparent that it is an absolute false claim.

وَلَقَدْ أَرْسَلْنَا رُسُلاً مِّن قَبْلِكَ وَجَعَلْنَا لَهُمْ أَزْوَاجًا وَذُرِّيَّةً وَمَا كَانَ لِرَسُولٍ أَن يَأْتِيَ بِآيَةٍ إِلاَّ بِإِذْنِ اللّهِ لِكُلِّ أَجَلٍ كِتَابٌ ٢٢٣ {الرعد/38}

وَلَقَدْ أَرْسَلْنَا رُسُلًا مِّن قَبْلِكَ مِنْهُم مَّن قَصَصْنَا عَلَيْكَ وَمِنْهُم مَّن لَّمْ نَقْصُصْ عَلَيْكَ وَمَا كَانَ لِرَسُولٍ أَنْ يَأْتِيَ بِآيَةٍ إِلَّا بِإِذْنِ اللّهِ فَإِذَا جَاء أَمْرُ اللّهِ قُضِيَ بِالْحَقِّ وَخَسِرَ هُنَالِكَ الْمُبْطِلُونَ ٢٢٤ {غافر/78}

In the above ayahs as mentioned in different places as an emphasis with the part وَمَا كَانَ لِ stresses the impossibility of any emergence of true prophethood and the acceptance of his teachigs among people and the survival of these teachings unless it is with the permission of Allah ﷻ.

In other words, an individual.who embodied truthfulness and reliability in all details of life will not incline to any type of contrary

---

622. It is not for a human [prophet] that Allah should give him the Scripture and authority and prophethood and then he would say to the people, "Be servants to me rather than Allah," but [instead, he would say], "Be pious scholars of the Lord because of what you have taught of the Scripture and because of what you have studied."

623. And We have already sent messengers before you and assigned to them wives and descendants. And it was not for a messenger to come with a sign except by permission of Allah. For every term is a decree.

624. And We have already sent messengers before you. Among them are those [whose stories] We have related to you, and among them are those [whose stories] We have not related to you. And it was not for any messenger to bring a sign [or verse] except by permission of Allah. So when the command of Allah comes, it will be concluded [i.e., judged] in truth, and the falsifiers will thereupon lose [all].

actions, ideas and assertions at the boundaries of Divine Reality, Allah 🕮.

Purity-al-Haqq

If there is a flaw in a teaching, the sustainability and continuality of it will be questionable. In other words, something that is not original, pure and authentic will not survive universally. Universal truths survive as agreed teachings due to their sustainability, continuality and harmony in their contents, assumptions and premises making these contents.

Substitutes cannot replace the original and pure teachings. Humans effort of using mind without religion to establish structure and order in personal and social lives are another representation of filtering aboriginal teachings and replacing them with the original and pure ones. Yet, they arrive to the same conclusions after hundred years of effort and with the accumulation of data. On the other hand, the Qurān and the sunnah presents these valuable teachings immediately accessible to everyone without any effort. One is the long struggle of mind. The other is the barakah of submission of being a Muslim.

Therefore, the teachings of Allah 🕮 as presented in the previous scriptures in their original forms affected the social values of ethics and morality and survived in our societies. Today, people acknowledge it or not, the inherited values of universal morality and ethics stem from the scriptures as sent originally by Allah 🕮 and confirmed by the intellectual renderings of philosophers and trial and error systems of humans in their efforts of establishing civilized societies [10].

Similarly, the content of the teachings of the Qurān and Rasulullah 🕮 are these pure, harmonious, and flawless ones available to all humans until the End of Days.

Therefore, their pure full and complete content requires these teachings to be universal as mentioned وَقُلْ جَاء الْحَقُّ وَزَهَقَ الْبَاطِلَ إِنَّ الْبَاطِلُ [625]. The word الْحَقُّ[626] can indicate these universal truths as replacing the truths with flaws and problems. This can be also considered as a sunnatullah, a social law as established by Allah 🕮.

---

625. And say, "Truth has come, and falsehood has departed. Indeed is falsehood, [by nature], ever bound to depart."
626. The Truth.

If there is a slight impurity in something, although it may survive sometime with its longevity, it is deemed to change, disappear, and updated with their original and pure teachings as in the case of trinity for example in Christianity. Rasulullah ﷺ mentions [13] that at the end of days, the trinity will disappear and replaced with the tawhid. Although Christianity is considered as monotheistic, the impurity in the creed of tawhid with trinity will be filtered as part of this process of sunnatullah. This is an example for جَاءَ الْحَقُّ وَزَهَقَ الْبَاطِلُ إِنَّ الْبَاطِلَ كَانَ زَهُوقًا.

This can indicate survival of a teaching with its longevity depends on its purity or pureness in its content. Imam Ghazali 's work to be still valid and used today can be example of this purity and harmonious content as it stems from the original source of the Qurān and Sunnah.

In all these discussions, one can have a glimpse of how something becomes accepted in generations and survive from one to another generation. First, it is the Divine Will, Ma'isha of Allah ﷻ. Allah ﷻ establishes sunnatullah as the social law of al-Haqq as mentioned وَقُلْ

جَاءَ الْحَقُّ وَزَهَقَ الْبَاطِلُ إِنَّ الْبَاطِلَ كَانَ زَهُوقًا [627] {الإسراء/81}

In other words, the more something is the truth, the more it has its longevity and survival. Depending on its flawless, something may survive accordingly.

In another perspective, one can say Allah ﷻ is the Absolute Truth al-Haqq. Therefore, there is no beginning and end for Allah ﷻ. Allah ﷻ as the Absolute Truth is and should be Infinitely Continuously Existent as the al-Qayyum, al-Hayy, al-Awwal and al-Akhir names can indicate. The Absolute Truth as necessitated by Absolute Perfectness can be indicated with all the Asmau al-Husna.

After this one can remember the dua of this full embodiment in tahajjud to be engraved to the minds and hearts as [5][628] اَللَّهُمَّ لَكَ الْحَمْدُ

---

627. And say, "Truth has come, and falsehood has departed. Indeed is falsehood, [by nature], ever bound to depart."

628. O Allah! To You is due all praise for You are the Sustainer of the heavens and the earth and all that is within them. All praise is Yours, for You are the King of the heavens and the earth and all that is within them. All praise is Yours, for You are the Light of the heavens and the earth and all that is within them. All praise is Yours, for You are the Truth, Your promise is true, the meeting with You is true and Your word is true. Paradise is true, the Hellfire is true, the Prophets are true, Muhammad (peace and blessings be upon him) is true, and the Last Hour is true. O Allah! To You I have submitted, in You do I believe, in You have I put my trust, and unto You I turn in repentance. For Your sake I have disputed, and from You I seek judgment, so forgive me for what I have done and for what I will do, for what I have concealed and what I have declared, and for that [in me] that You know best about. You are the Hastener and the Postponer, there is no god but You, and there is no strength or power except in Allah.

أَنْتَ قَيُّومُ السَّمْوَاتِ وَالْأَرْضِ وَمَنْ فِيهِنَّ، وَلَكَ الْحَمْدُ أَنْتَ مَلِكُ السَّمَوَاتِ وَالْأَرْضِ وَمَنْ فِيهِنَّ،
وَلَكَ الْحَمْدُ أَنْتَ نُورُ السَّمَوَاتِ وَالْأَرْضِ وَمَنْ فِيهِنَّ، وَلَكَ الْحَمْدُ أَنْتَ الْحَقُّ وَوَعْدُكَ الْحَقُّ وَلِقَاءُكَ
حَقٌّ وَقَوْلُكَ حَقٌّ وَالْجَنَّةُ حَقٌّ وَالنَّارُ حَقٌّ وَالنَّبِيُّونَ حَقٌّ وَمُحَمَّدٌ ﷺ حَقٌّ وَالسَّاعَةُ حَقٌّ. اَللَّهُمَّ لَكَ
أَسْلَمْتُ وَبِكَ أَمَنْتُ وَعَلَيْكَ تَوَكَّلْتُ وَإِلَيْكَ أَنَبْتُ وَبِكَ خَاصَمْتُ وَإِلَيْكَ حَاكَمْتُ فَاغْفِرْ لِي مَا قَدَّمْتُ
وَمَا أَخَّرْتُ وَمَا أَسْرَرْتُ وَمَا أَعْلَنْتُ وَمَا أَنْتَ أَعْلَمُ بِهِ مِنِّي. أَنْتَ الْمُقَدِّمُ وَأَنْتَ الْمُؤَخِّرُ لَا إِلَهَ إِلَّا
أَنْتَ وَلاَ حَوْلَ وَلاَ قُوَّةَ إِلاَّ بِاللهِ

Other things become the haqq, reality and truth as Allah ﷻ establishes the sunnatullah, as the haqq. If Allah ﷻ has established something else as haqq, then that would be al-haqq.

Sidq and Haqq gives bonding for the continuity and longevity.

Collective Character Traits

A unit or a group is formed by pieces or individuals. One of the appealing features of a group or a unit is that the individuals are stronger when they are associated with a group. Each individual has the intrinsic quality of supporting each other in a group. This ensures a good and successful group harmony and teamwork. If each piece or individual do not have shared values and do not support each other for a common goal, then this group cannot survive. It breaks and goes apart as individuals.

The same logic can be reflected on the collective character traits of a person. A person's collective character is formed with different individual traits. Each individual trait will have the tendency to support another trait. Being generous can indicate courage. Courage can indicate avoidance from lying. Avoidance from lying can indicate truthfulness.

Similarly, when one analyzes the individual character traits of Rasulullah ﷺ, they all support each other. Some of these character traits are nobility, truthfulness, justice, impartiality, objectivity, integrity, courage, generosity, altruism, caring for others, graciousness, civility, politeness, balance, sociability, friendliness, pleasantness, dignity, approachability, honesty, thoughtfulness, reliability, kindness, big-heartedness, gentleness, easiness, compassion, and mercifulness.

One can see some of these above character traits mentioned as لَقَدْ جَاءَكُمْ رَسُولٌ مِّنْ أَنفُسِكُمْ عَزِيزٌ عَلَيْهِ مَا عَنِتُّمْ حَرِيصٌ عَلَيْكُم بِالْمُؤْمِنِينَ رَؤُوفٌ رَّحِيمٌ [629] {التوبة/128}.

---

629. There has certainly come to you a Messenger from among yourselves. Grievous to him is what you suffer; [he is] concerned over you [i.e., your guidance] and to the believers is kind and merciful.

With some of these above character traits, one can visualize a person among human beings as a human and as the messenger of Allah ﷻ relating and calling humans with a profoundly serious, critical and important message from Allah ﷻ. In this regard, if one considers some of the above character traits, one can better understand the ayah as وَمَا أَرْسَلْنَاكَ إِلَّا رَحْمَةً لِّلْعَالَمِينَ [630]{الأنبياء/107}.

In other words, a critical and important message coming from Allah ﷻ can put a person and all of us as normal humans in a shattered state of mind and heart. Yet, Rasulullah ﷺ is a mercy for us to relate and tune this high frequency message to our low mode of reception system. Rasulullah ﷺ brings this message with a very gentle, caring and merciful tuning in the realms of human tolerance limits as mentioned :

وَمَا أَرْسَلْنَاكَ إِلَّا رَحْمَةً لِّلْعَالَمِينَ {الأنبياء/107}[631] قُلْ إِنَّمَا يُوحَى إِلَيَّ أَنَّمَا إِلَهُكُمْ إِلَهٌ وَاحِدٌ فَهَلْ أَنتُم مُّسْلِمُونَ [632]{الأنبياء/108}.

In other words, this message of قُلْ إِنَّمَا يُوحَى إِلَيَّ أَنَّمَا إِلَهُكُمْ إِلَهٌ وَاحِدٌ فَهَلْ أَنتُم مُّسْلِمُونَ [633]{الأنبياء/108} is tuned with rahmah, mercy, caring, and love as always humans attracted to and as embodied by Rasulullah ﷺ as mentioned {الأنبياء/107}[634] وَمَا أَرْسَلْنَاكَ إِلَّا رَحْمَةً لِّلْعَالَمِينَ.

If this tuning is not done in the encounters of Transcendent Reality, Allah ﷻ and with the Qurān, we or anything can be destroyed as mentioned:

وَلَمَّا جَاء مُوسَى لِمِيقَاتِنَا وَكَلَّمَهُ رَبُّهُ قَالَ رَبِّ أَرِنِي أَنظُرْ إِلَيْكَ قَالَ لَن تَرَانِي وَلَكِنِ انظُرْ إِلَى الْجَبَلِ فَإِنِ اسْتَقَرَّ مَكَانَهُ فَسَوْفَ تَرَانِي فَلَمَّا تَجَلَّى رَبُّهُ لِلْجَبَلِ جَعَلَهُ دَكًّا وَخَرَّ موسَى صَعِقًا فَلَمَّا أَفَاقَ قَالَ سُبْحَانَكَ تُبْتُ إِلَيْكَ وَأَنَا أَوَّلُ الْمُؤْمِنِينَ [635]{الأعراف/143}

---

630. And We have not sent you, [O Muhammad], except as a mercy to the worlds.
631. And We have not sent you, [O Muhammad], except as a mercy to the worlds.
632. Say, "It is only revealed to me that your god is but one God; so will you be Muslims [in submission to Him]?"
633. Say, "It is only revealed to me that your god is but one God; so will you be Muslims [in submission to Him]?"
634. And We have not sent you, [O Muhammad], except as a mercy to the worlds.
635. And when Moses arrived at Our appointed time and his Lord spoke to him, he said, "My Lord, show me [Yourself] that I may look at You." [Allah] said, "You will not see Me, but look at the mountain; if it should remain in place, then you will see Me." But when his Lord appeared to the mountain, He rendered it level, and Moses fell unconscious. And when he awoke, he said, "Exalted are You! I have repented to You, and I am the first of the believers."

لَوْ أَنزَلْنَا هَذَا الْقُرْآنَ عَلَى جَبَلٍ لَّرَأَيْتَهُ خَاشِعًا مُّتَصَدِّعًا مِّنْ خَشْيَةِ اللَّهِ وَتِلْكَ الْأَمْثَالُ
نَضْرِبُهَا لِلنَّاسِ لَعَلَّهُمْ يَتَفَكَّرُونَ 636 {الحشر/21}

This tuning is done by Rasulullah ﷺ in such a way that we still enjoy our lives in our humanly engagements and shortcomings and still we can appreciate and please Allah ﷻ.

Most of the time, people are in heedless states of gaflah, they don't realize about Who Allah ﷻ, the Qurān and Rasulullah are. In these states, humans' enjoyments of life are not due to tuning but it is due to heedlessness.

In one case, people enjoy this world and afterlife by knowing Allah ﷻ and following the footsteps of Rasulullah ﷺ in the modes of humanly tuned forms. In the other case, people seem to enjoy this world with a lot of internal fears but with no enjoyment in the eternal afterlife due to being in the states of "I don't care."

To prove the above points, one can review the life of Rasulullah ﷺ with different perspectives to analyze his character, temperament, dispositions, and personality at different times, in different contexts with different people. One can find clear common themes in his personality, character, and temperament in all these dispositions. If there is any seeming difference in his character disposition, the sahabah immediately brings the contextualization through the case, person or time in hadith narrations in order to eliminate any type of misunderstandings for the people like us coming in later generations, not witnessing but only hearing the reports of these incidents.

To give some examples, in one case, depending on the person's level, Rasulullah ﷺ may use direct language about his advice compared to the ones who may not be at that level. Rasulullah ﷺ has all the time truthfulness, as- sidq. Delivery of this message is optimized with the person according to their level.

Depending on the time, this delivery method can be more intense and straightforward as mentioned in Juma' khutbahs [11] as his khutbas[637] were short but dense.

---

636. If We had sent down this Qurān upon a mountain, you would have seen it humbled and splitting from fear of Allah. And these examples We present to the people that perhaps they will give thought.
637. Islamic lectures.

Depending on the case of injustice, Rasulullah ﷺ can display an anger on his face, then sahabah immediately understands the case.

In all these cases, if there is anything that may not seem to be fitting in general charming character of Rasulullah ﷺ with all above traits, the sahabah immediately brings these explanations or footnotes for the contextualization of the case, person or time in hadith narrations in order to eliminate any type of misunderstanding for the people like us coming in later generations, not witnessing but hearing the reports of these incidents.

One should realize that when even non-Muslims witnessed these traits of Rasulullah ﷺ in their society. They unanimously and naturally gave him the title of Muhammad al-Amìn[638]. Still, today, non-Muslims analyze people in the history with their different tools of complex parameters of character traits and achievements with their computational analysis. It constantly shows the same results that Rasulullah ﷺ is the one who has been distinctive in all these virtuous traits in human history [22].

One should realize that the collectivity of good traits necessitates the absence of bad traits in a person. Existence of honesty, truthfulness and trustworthiness as a character of a person necessitates the absence of dishonesty, lying, and deceit or duplicity.

One can review the aggregate character trait of Rasulullah ﷺ with the title of Muhammad al-Amìn given by non-Muslims during his time and ask the question, how a person like him can incline to the lowly states of lying or deceit in the claims of prophethood? Is that possible?

WAllahi, that is impossible! Rasulullah ﷺ is Al-Sadiqul Al-Amìn[639].

Job of Prophethood

If there is a profession or a field, there are certain training and expertise required in that field and profession to practice. People write guidelines, training manuals, and establish academic and professional journals in order to transfer this acquired knowledge over the course of years. This acquired knowledge in that field can be called literature.

---

638. The Trustworthy.
639. The Truthful, the Trustworthy.

If one analyzes the field and responsibility of prophethood, one can find similar guidelines. The person should have the utmost traits of care, concern, love for others including the traits of trustworthiness, honesty and yet at the same, the skills to deliver them in society with justice and wisdom in order to remind tawhid and help them with their social problems.

Yet, one of the most commons traits for this field is that the person is chosen by Allah ﷻ. In this case, they are equipped with some tools beyond physical laws called miracles in order to support their authenticity of prophethood from Allah ﷻ and choosiness by Allah ﷻ.

In this field of responsibility of prophethood, the associates of prophets are given the information and knowledge of other peers before and after them by Allah ﷻ as mentioned الَّذِينَ يَتَّبِعُونَ الرَّسُولَ النَّبِيَّ الْأُمِّيَّ الَّذِي يَجِدُونَهُ مَكْتُوبًا عِندَهُمْ فِي التَّوْرَاةِ وَالْإِنجِيلِ يَأْمُرُهُم بِالْمَعْرُوفِ وَيَنْهَاهُمْ عَنِ الْمُنكَرِ وَيُحِلُّ لَهُمُ الطَّيِّبَاتِ وَيُحَرِّمُ عَلَيْهِمُ الْخَبَائِثَ وَيَضَعُ عَنْهُمْ إِصْرَهُمْ وَالْأَغْلَالَ الَّتِي كَانَتْ عَلَيْهِمْ فَالَّذِينَ آمَنُواْ بِهِ وَعَزَّرُوهُ وَنَصَرُوهُ وَاتَّبَعُواْ النُّورَ الَّذِي أُنزِلَ مَعَهُ أُوْلَئِكَ هُمُ الْمُفْلِحُونَ 640{الأعراف/157}.

This knowledge can be somehow in different capacities. One can remember the statements of Rasulullah ﷺ as "all the prophets are brothers" [16] to remind us this common responsibility in the field of prophethood.

Below are some examples of the ayahs for some of the definition and responsibility of the prophethood as:

وَمَا أَرْسَلْنَا مِن قَبْلِكَ مِن رَّسُولٍ إِلَّا نُوحِي إِلَيْهِ أَنَّهُ لَا إِلَهَ إِلَّا أَنَا فَاعْبُدُونِ 641{الأنبياء/25}

كَمَا أَرْسَلْنَا فِيكُمْ رَسُولاً مِّنكُمْ يَتْلُو عَلَيْكُمْ آيَاتِنَا وَيُزَكِّيكُمْ وَيُعَلِّمُكُمُ الْكِتَابَ وَالْحِكْمَةَ وَيُعَلِّمُكُم مَّا لَمْ تَكُونُواْ تَعْلَمُونَ 642{البقرة/151}

---

640. Those who follow the Messenger, the unlettered prophet, whom they find written [i.e., mentioned] in what they have of the Torah and the Gospel, who enjoins upon them what is right and forbids them what is wrong and makes lawful for them the good things and prohibits for them the evil and relieves them of their burden and the shackles which were upon them. So they who have believed in him, honored him, supported him and followed the light which was sent down with him—it is those who will be the successful.
641. And We sent not before you any messenger except that We revealed to him that, "There is no deity except Me, so worship Me."
642. Just as We have sent among you a messenger from yourselves reciting to you Our verses and purifying you and teaching you the Book and wisdom and teaching you that which you did not know.

وَمَا أَرْسَلْنَا مِن رَّسُولٍ إِلاَّ بِلِسَانِ قَوْمِهِ لِيُبَيِّنَ لَهُمْ فَيُضِلُّ اللّهُ مَن يَشَاء وَيَهْدِي مَن يَشَاء وَهُوَ الْعَزِيزُ الْحَكِيمُ [643] {إبراهيم/4}

وَبِالْحَقِّ أَنزَلْنَاهُ وَبِالْحَقِّ نَزَلَ وَمَا أَرْسَلْنَاكَ إِلاَّ مُبَشِّرًا وَنَذِيرًا [644] {الإسراء/105}

As every job or responsibility has limits, prophethoods have limits as well such as:

مَّنْ يُطِعِ الرَّسُولَ فَقَدْ أَطَاعَ اللّهَ وَمَن تَوَلَّى فَمَا أَرْسَلْنَاكَ عَلَيْهِمْ حَفِيظًا [645] {النساء/80}

رَّبُّكُمْ أَعْلَمُ بِكُمْ إِن يَشَأْ يَرْحَمْكُمْ أَوْ إِن يَشَأْ يُعَذِّبْكُمْ وَمَا أَرْسَلْنَاكَ عَلَيْهِمْ وَكِيلاً [646] {الإسراء/54}

In this responsibility, there is always normalization of some features and traits of a prophet. As people can expect that since prophets are chosen by Allah ﷻ, therefore, they should be beyond humans and supernatural. Yet, the normalization of human prophets as humans with human qualities among humans is emphasized as:

وَما أَرْسَلْنَا قَبْلَكَ مِنَ الْمُرْسَلِينَ إِلَّا إِنَّهُمْ لَيَأْكُلُونَ الطَّعَامَ وَيَمْشُونَ فِي الْأَسْوَاقِ وَجَعَلْنَا بَعْضَكُمْ لِبَعْضٍ فِتْنَةً أَتَصْبِرُونَ وَكَانَ رَبُّكَ بَصِيرًا [647] {الفرقان/20}

وَمَا مَنَعَ النَّاسَ أَن يُؤْمِنُواْ إِذْ جَاءهُمُ الْهُدَى إِلاَّ أَن قَالُواْ أَبَعَثَ اللّهُ بَشَرًا رَّسُولاً [648] {الإسراء/94} قُل لَّوْ كَانَ فِي الأَرْضِ مَلآئِكَةٌ يَمْشُونَ مُطْمَئِنِّينَ لَنَزَّلْنَا عَلَيْهِم مِّنَ السَّمَاء مَلَكًا رَّسُولاً [649] {الإسراء/95}

---

643. And We did not send any messenger except [speaking] in the language of his people to state clearly for them, and Allah sends astray [thereby] whom He wills and guides whom He wills. And He is the Exalted in Might, the Wise.

644. And with the truth We have sent it [i.e., the Qurān] down, and with the truth is has descended. And We have not sent you, [O Muhammad], except as a bringer of good tidings and a warner.

645. He who obeys the Messenger has obeyed Allah; but those who turn away—We have not sent you over them as a guardian.

646. Your Lord is most knowing of you. If He wills, He will have mercy upon you; or if He wills, He will punish you. And We have not sent you, [O Muhammad], over them as a manager.

647. And We did not send before you, [O Muhammad], any of the messengers except that they ate food and walked in the markets. And We have made some of you [people] as trial for others—will you have patience? And ever is your Lord, Seeing.

648. And what prevented the people from believing when guidance came to them except that they said, "Has Allah sent a human messenger?"

649. Say, "If there were upon the earth angels walking securely, We would have sent down to them from the heaven an angel [as a] messenger."

In other words, the above ayahs can indicate that every species is to be represented by their own peers and species. It can be a sign of an arrogance not to be pleased how the person is created by Allah ﷻ but the person wants to be something or someone other than Allah ﷻ created the person. One can extrapolate the concepts of tattooing, gender identity issues, and other artificial self-denial renderings.

The primary example of this is Shaytān on one side. As he was a jinn among the angels and lost this position due to being arrogant وَإِذْ قُلْنَا لِلْمَلَائِكَةِ اسْجُدُوا لِآدَمَ فَسَجَدُوا إِلَّا إِبْلِيسَ كَانَ مِنَ الْجِنِّ فَفَسَقَ عَنْ أَمْرِ رَبِّهِ أَفَتَتَّخِذُونَهُ وَذُرِّيَّتَهُ أَوْلِيَاءَ مِن دُونِي وَهُمْ لَكُمْ عَدُوٌّ بِئْسَ لِلظَّالِمِينَ بَدَلًا﴾ [650] {الكهف/50}.

His arrogance possibly stemmed from not being among its species as a jinn and not being pleased as what and how Allah ﷻ created him among his own species. This is an interpretation, الله اعلم [651]. Yes, his representation of arrogance can be his desire to be with angels. He has been a Jinn and possibly showing the signs of displeasure in the Divine Choice about his creation. Again, the display of displeasure emerges also when he does not follow the order of Allah ﷻ to make sajdah to Allah ﷻ but he follows his own argument and logic. Shaytān wanted to be somethingelse other than what he was.

The opposite example of this is Rasulullah ﷺ on another side. When Rasulullah ﷺ was asked if he wanted to be a king or an a'bd prophet, Rasululullah ﷺ preferred the fitrah, natural disposition of creation of as being the a'bd of Allah ﷻ . One of Rasulullah's ﷺ preferred names were Abdullah and AbdurRahman to name the children to show this embodiment and acceptance of being 'abd of Allah ﷻ as a human [4].

The middle example of this can be Adam as. Adam as was also attracted to be like angels as mentioned [652] وَقَالَ مَا نَهَاكُمَا رَبُّكُمَا عَنْ هَذِهِ الشَّجَرَةِ إِلَّا أَن تَكُونَا مَلَكَيْنِ أَوْ تَكُونَا مِنَ الْخَالِدِينَ {الأعراف/20}. Our father Adam as and our mother Hawwa as was not appealed to be like angels not because of the renderings and intention of arrogance but for other reasons,[653] الله اعلم.

---

650. And [mention] when We said to the angels, "Prostrate to Adam," and they prostrated, except for Iblees. He was of the jinn and departed from [i.e., disobeyed] the command of his Lord. Then will you take him and his descendants as allies other than Me while they are enemies to you? Wretched it is for the wrongdoers as an exchange.

651. Allah knows best.

652. Shaytān said, "Your Lord did not forbid you this tree except that you become angels or become of the immortal."

653. Allah knows best.

In this perspective, the person can choose who to follow. One is the arrogant, artificial, and unnatural dispositions of Shaytān. The other is pure, humble, peaceful and natural dispositions of Rasulullah ﷺ. The difference between them is similar to an unclean smelling filth and a clean pure smell of musk.

اللهم اجعلنا من اتباع سنت نبينا و حبيبنا و امامنا رسول الله صلى الله عليه و سلم. آمين. 654

The challenges of this responsibility of prophethood is mentioned for example as

{سبأ/34} 655 وَمَا أَرْسَلْنَا فِي قَرْيَةٍ مِّن نَّذِيرٍ إِلَّا قَالَ مُتْرَفُوهَا إِنَّا بِمَا أُرْسِلْتُم بِهِ كَافِرُونَ

وَكَذَلِكَ مَا أَرْسَلْنَا مِن قَبْلِكَ فِي قَرْيَةٍ مِّن نَّذِيرٍ إِلَّا قَالَ مُتْرَفُوهَا إِنَّا وَجَدْنَا آبَاءَنَا عَلَى أُمَّةٍ وَّإِنَّا عَلَى آثَارِهِم مُّقْتَدُونَ 656 {الزخرف/23}

One of the interesting features of prophethood is that the values or teachings that they bring have been viewed as conflicting with the social norms of the society.

We as social beings tend to follow our social norms of the society. One can reviews the case of Rasulullah ﷺ, presenting some very strong dense teachings which are challenging the social norms of the society.

On the other hand, this person is ummi, illiterate not from a highly educated part of the society. He is known to be an orphan. He has a history of being a shepherd. He is known not to be a leader. Yet, this person, Rasulullah ﷺ has known to be al-sadiq, the truthful before the prophethood. Yet, his social status does not seem to fit at a position for his initial claim to be accepted by the society at large with our current parameters of claims making in sociology [1]. Yet, he presented his case ﷺ in a very serious, determined, logical, and merciful way of love, kindness and care. Initially, his presentation seemed to be addressing his own people. Then, it has immediately become apparent and clear that his message was for all humanity until the End of Days.

Now, one can review this case with its emergence parameters from a place in the middle of a desert but not from a civilized society and

654. Oh Allah, make us from the followers of our Prophet, our Beloved, and the Messenger og God. May God bless him and grant him peace. Ameen.
655. And We did not send into a city any warner except that its affluent said, "Indeed we, in that with which you were sent, are disbelievers."
656. And similarly, We did not send before you any warner into a city except that its affluent said, "Indeed, we found our fathers upon a religion, and we are, in their footsteps, following."

from a person of illiterate but not a highly educated intellectual. Then, one can immediately, and only call this as a miracle of Allah ﷻ to show another possibility from impossibilities as it is usual in sunnatullah in order to prove and authenticate that this is message is truth and from Allah ﷻ, Rabbul A'lamim. Therefore, one should really listen carefully, take a heed and follow the teachings of Rasulullah ﷺ, al-Habíb ﷺ.

Authenticity

One can see the challenge, clear confrontation, and absolute declaration in the style of these two ayahs وَإِن كُنتُمْ فِي رَيْبٍ مِّمَّا نَزَّلْنَا عَلَى عَبْدِنَا فَأْتُواْ بِسُورَةٍ مِّن مِّثْلِهِ وَادْعُواْ شُهَدَاءكُم مِّن دُونِ اللّهِ إِنْ كُنْتُمْ صَادِقِينَ [657] {البقرة/23} فَإِن لَّمْ تَفْعَلُواْ وَلَن تَفْعَلُواْ فَاتَّقُواْ النَّارَ الَّتِي وَقُودُهَا النَّاسُ وَالْحِجَارَةُ أُعِدَّتْ لِلْكَافِرِينَ [658] {البقرة/24}.

The part[659] فَأْتُواْ بِسُورَةٍ مِّن مِّثْلِهِ is one challenge that as if it tells the person to support your argument with even with a Sûrah in the Qurãn, but you can't do it.

Within مِّثْلِهِ فَأْتُواْ بِسُورَةٍ مِّن[660], the part بِسُورَةٍ[661] is an additional challenge that you don't need to bring entire similar book like the Qurãn but only a Sûrah, but you can't even do this.

The next is another challenge وَادْعُواْ شُهَدَاءكُم[662] that encourages the person to have everyone help him or her in this, but neither you or they can do it.

The next is another challenger as إِنْ كُنْتُمْ صَادِقِينَ[663], as if declaring that but you can't do it because you are a liar if you are claiming it. This is another challenge to them.

Here is another very strong absolute declaration and challenge as mentioned فَإِن لَّمْ تَفْعَلُواْ وَلَن تَفْعَلُو[664]. This declaration mentions that it is impossible for a person to this. Your humanly weak and limited abilities are disabled in the realms of the Divine Reality of Allah ﷻ.

---

657. And if you are in doubt about what We have sent down [i.e., the Qurãn] upon Our Servant [i.e., Prophet Muhammad (PBUH)], then produce a Sûrah the like thereof and call upon your witnesses [i.e., supporters] other than Allah, if you should be truthful.

658. But if you do not—and you will never be able to—then fear the Fire, whose fuel is men and stones, prepared for the disbelievers.

659. Then produce a Sûrah the like thereof.

660. Then produce a Sûrah the like thereof.

661. A Sûrah.

662. And call upon your witnesses [i.e., supporters].

663. If you should be truthful.

664. But if you do not—and you will never be able to.

The part of the ayah as وَإِن كُنتُمْ فِي رَيْبٍ مِّمَّا نَزَّلْنَا عَلَىٰ عَبْدِنَا[665] can indicate that the audience is the kuffar in its contextual and apparent form of siyāk and sibāk. Yet, each ayah of the Qurān has an indication for personal lives for everyone.

In other words, in the expression[666] وَإِن كُنتُمْ فِي رَيْبٍ مِّمَّا نَزَّلْنَا عَلَىٰ عَبْدِنَا, the word[667] رَيْبٍ can be a whimsical, waswasa of Shaytān and nafs that Muslims can also sometimes be in. Yet, it is important remind the nafs about the disposition of the Qurān related with رَيْبٍ, these whimsical effects.

In its broader sense, some of the branches of the current Western philosophy promotes رَيْبٍ[668], these illusionary states. The branching of these philosophical approaches of raybiyah, skepticism leading to illusionary states and then, calling everything as social constructs are some examples of this unguided renderings of mind without the light of the Qurān and Sunnah of Rasulullah ﷺ.

Although one can see this guidance of wahy with the original teachings of other prophets such as Musa as and Isa as, because the originality of these scriptures of ahlu-kitāb are questionable currently, then one can sympathize with their misguidance. In other words, promoting value of the religion for the Westerns can be a fallacy when they think about their own religions with their fallacies. This really impedes a sense of sympathy for the ones who do not view religion as the essential element of life. Therefore, the Muslims who realize the true value of their religion should be sympathetic in their judgment of others, especially the ones who do not value religion.

One can promote the value of the religion when there is a filtering, tasaffi of the problematic teachings in Christianity and others. In other words, then promotion of the value of the religion becomes valid when original teachings are returns and again embedded in Christianity.

In other words, today only true guidance of the mind through the scriptures and wahiy can be achieved through the guidance of the Qurān and Sunnah of Rasulullah ﷺ.Rasulullah ﷺ mentions about this process of tasaffi, filtering of Christinaity from the problematic teachings [13] before the End of Day.

---

665. And if you are in doubt about what We have sent down [i.e., the Qurān].
666. And if you are in doubt about what We have sent down [i.e., the Qurān].
667. Doubt.
668. Doubt.

This is one of the biggest reasons of isolation of people from the religion and promoting and epitomizing, the philosophy based only on mind. We are all in life, looking for meanings and values for our present and future times. If a religion with their scriptures believed to be the word of God does not fully satisfy the people due to its loss of original content, then it is normal to look for the alternatives such as philosophy, to re-assign meanings and values for the present and future times in the life of an individual. In the past, when there were prevalent native societies that they used to assign bātil, wrong intrinsic ungrounded meanings to the icons, objects or images to assume some meanings. Today, due to civilized forms of societies, mind, logic and rationality are promoted to assume meanings with the empirical data.

Both the intrinsic ungrounded mystical meanings as performed in native societies and mind based meanings as often performed in the world today can be misleading without the guidance of the wahiy, true revelation from Allah ﷻ.

Sometimes, after all the logical discussions, people can still want to entertain these whimsical attitudes of rayb or doubts. Yet, now, the notion of fear, punishment and accountability is mentioned to really shake the person and bring them to their normal and objective clear faculties of reason.

For example, there may be a child with a lot of tantrums. The parents can give all the reasons, options and explanations in order this naughty child to stop his tantrums and come back to his normal and peaceful state. Yet, the child jumps up and down, break things, cries and asks things that are really out of the line of reason. Then, the parents may tell the child "if you don't stop your tantrum, you will go to your room and stay there for five minutes." Then, the child may now stop due to fear and hopefully become normal, think and consider for his next actions of choice.

Similarly, our nafs, egos are like small children. When there is something clear and reasonable, the person may still want to continue in the unreasonable attitudes of tantrums. This may be a case in the renderings of kāfir with their kufr with whimsical or ungrounded dispositions of mind. The fear can at least make them think and reconsider their disposition and choice.

In the case of a Muslim, sometimes the ego and nafs may want to wander in the whimsical dispositions with the encouragement of

Shaytān. In this case, fear imbedded with istigfar can make the person come back to his normal and expected position with Allah ﷻ.

In both cases of a kāfir and a sinful Muslim, these above cases of rayb[669] pumbed with nafs and Shaytān can put the person in layers of darkness, dhulumat[670] taking away from the joy, happiness and peace of imān. In the case of a kāfir, these layers of darkness can be so overwhelming, consistent and increasing as the person ages and gets close to death and encounters evil-seeming incidents.

In the case of a Muslim, this darkness can be disgusting as the person knows the sweetness of imān. This spiritiual darkness can be present each time the person leaves the shores of imān with the pump of Shaytān and nafs. Therefore, he or she can remove this disgust or filth with istigfar and go back to their normal states of fitrah. In the case of a kafir, there is no notion of disgust because he or she did not taste the sweetness of imān.

[671]اللهم احفظنا منه. امين,

[672]... و اعوذ بك ان اشرك بك شيء و انا اعلم و استغفرك بما لم اعلم

[673]. اللهم صلى على سيدنا محمد و على ال سيدنا محمد

Content Knowledge & Being an Ummi

When a person is explaining a content of something, it is impossible to give a factual data unless it is either through direct experience of being with them if happened in the past and then narrating what happened. Or, he or she can explain this incident through literature review in that content, field or discipline. By using the mind and reason, the person can do some analysis and try to fill the missing points or th egaps of continuity by them extrapoloating with some possibilities. For the first case, Rasulullah ﷺ did not live in the past before his time. Yet, he ﷺ

---

669. Doubt.
670. Darkness.
671. Oh Allah, protect us from this.
672. And I seek refuge in you to share with you something while I know, and I seek forgiveness for what I did not know.
673. Oh Allah, blessings and peace upon our master Muhammed ﷺ., and upon our Master Muhammad ﷺ.'s family.

reported them as if he 🕊 had witnessed and 🕊 all these cases, or events as reported in the Qurān and sunnah. For example,

وَمَا كُنتَ بِجَانِبِ الْغَرْبِيِّ إِذْ قَضَيْنَا إِلَى مُوسَى الْأَمْرَ وَمَا كُنتَ مِنَ الشَّاهِدِينَ
{القصص/44} ٦٧٤ وَلَٰكِنَّا أَنشَأْنَا قُرُونًا فَتَطَاوَلَ عَلَيْهِمُ الْعُمُرُ وَمَا كُنتَ ثَاوِيًا فِي أَهْلِ
مَدْيَنَ تَتْلُو عَلَيْهِمْ آيَاتِنَا وَلَٰكِنَّا كُنَّا مُرْسِلِينَ {القصص/45} ٦٧٥ وَمَا كُنتَ بِجَانِبِ الطُّورِ
إِذْ نَادَيْنَا وَلَٰكِن رَّحْمَةً مِّن رَّبِّكَ لِتُنذِرَ قَوْمًا مَّا أَتَاهُم مِّن نَّذِيرٍ مِّن قَبْلِكَ لَعَلَّهُمْ يَتَذَكَّرُونَ ٦٧٦
{القصص/46}.

The methodology of incident reporting as the witness of the case for the basis of a factual data are presented in these ayahs as some examples. Rasulullah 🕊 reported them as if he was the witness of these historical incidents.

Furthermore, in these historical cases of reporting, Rasulullah 🕊 narrated us through the Qurān, these inner secret mind and heart related thoughts of them. For example, قَالُوا إِن يَسْرِقْ فَقَدْ سَرَقَ أَخٌ لَّهُ مِن قَبْلُ فَأَسَرَّهَا One يُوسُفُ فِي نَفْسِهِ وَلَمْ يُبْدِهَا لَهُمْ قَالَ أَنتُمْ شَرٌّ مَّكَانًا وَاللَّهُ أَعْلَمُ بِمَا تَصِفُونَ ٦٧٧ {يوسف/77} can ask who can know, as in the above case, about what happened in the past before Rasulullah 🕊? In addition, who can know the thoughts and feelings of Yusuf as at that time as mentioned ٦٧٨فَأَسَرَّهَا يُوسُفُ فِي نَفْسِهِ ? The answer is only Allah 🕊. Allah 🕊 is the al-A'lim[679], al-Bātin[680], al-Qayyum[681] and al-Hakîm[682].

One can think and claim as some people claimed that Rasulullah 🕊 were aware of the earlier of scriptures. Therefore, there is the content of the Qurān. One should remember there are very many refuting the cases of this claim such as Rasulullah 🕊 was being an ummi, illeterate.

---

674. And you, [O Muhammad], were not on the western side [of the mount] when We revealed to Moses the command, and you were not among the witnesses [to that].
675. But We produced [many] generations [after Moses], and prolonged was their duration. And you were not a resident among the people of Madyan, reciting to them Our verses, but We were senders [of this message].
676. And you were not at the side of the mount when We called [Moses] but [were sent] as a mercy from your Lord to warn a people to whom no warner had come before you that they might be reminded.
677. They said, "If he steals—a brother of his has stolen before." But Joseph kept it within himself and did not reveal it to them. He said, "You are worse in position, and Allah is most knowing of what you describe."
678. But Joseph kept it within himself.
679. The All Knower.
680. The Hidden One.
681. The Sustainer.
682. The All-Wise.

Or, there were really no ahlu-kitāb in Makkah. There are no incidents or any reports from his early opponents that they were able to cite that Rasulullah ﷺ spent any time with any person of ahlu kitāb of knowledge.

One of the obvious case is the content of the Qurān is perfect unlike the altered prior scriptures. There is no contraction. The amazing case is that the Qurān's uphold of Torah and Gospel through the narratives related with alteration and losing authenticity, referring to similar stories with both similar different content.

One can find an amazing example of this when especially the scholarship and readers of Judaism who seem to have more concerns related with the authenticity of revealation compared to the readers and scholarship of Christianity where mystical and personal relevant experientail religious interperations are wide spread without much concern of authenticity. In this regard, one can find Tawrah in English for a Jewish reader with the footnotes of Quranic passages about the same Sûrah such as Sûrah Yusuf. This can imply that there is a respect to scholarship and also, there is an inclination to learn about the authentic narratives in the Qurān. Following them is a separate question between the person and Allah SWT. Below is a quote to indicate [23]

The people of the Torah used to conceal the story of Joseph. When God sent Muhammad as a prophet, the Jews came to him, among them 'Abdallāh ibn Salām and many of the tribe of Ahbār, and said to him, "Muhammad if you be a prophet, tell us the story of Joseph and his brethren." An he began to recite it, sometimes, raising his voice and sometimes lowering it. The Jews wept and said, "Muhammad has been given more of the story of Joseph than is in our Torah." Then, they asked him, "where did you learn this, Muhammad, for we conceal this chapter?" Muhammad said, "My Lord has revealed it to me." — "You speak the truth (sadaqta), Muhammad," they said (Tales of the Prophets, 192).

Allah ﷻ informs Rasulullah ﷺ through the Qurān about these all detailed cases of the past with their inner and secret dispositions of thoughts and emotions only possibly known by the people themselves, and even not known by the other people at their time, if not publicized.

If one analyzes the case of فَأَسَرَّهَا يُوسُفُ فِي نَفْسِهِ[683], the inner disposition of Yusuf as[684] قَالَ أَنتُمْ شَرٌّ مَّكَانًا وَاللهُ أَعْلَمُ بِمَا تَصِفُونَ is a true and exact statement

---

683. But Joseph kept it within himself.
684. He said, "You are worse in position, and Allah is most knowing of what you describe."

685قَالُواْ إِن يَسْرِقْ فَقَدْ سَرَقَ أَخٌ لَّهُ when his brothers blamed Yusuf as by saying مِن قَبْلُ . This was on top of their evil engagements of their attempt to kill Yusuf as. Yet, one can realize that this inner response of Yusuf as قَالَ أَنتُمْ شَرٌّ مَّكَانًا وَاللّهُ أَعْلَمُ بِمَا تَصِفُونَ is a secret and inner statement of Yusuf as but not never verbalized. This secret was buried in the history.

Especially, one can analyze the character of Yusuf as in قَالَ لاَ تَثْرِيبَ عَلَيْكُمُ الْيَوْمَ يَغْفِرُ اللّهُ لَكُمْ وَهُوَ أَرْحَمُ الرَّاحِمِينَ686 {يوسف/92}. When Yusuf as had the opportunity to verbalize the real evil engagements of his brothers, he did not do it but stated قَالَ لاَ تَثْرِيبَ عَلَيْكُمُ الْيَوْمَ يَغْفِرُ اللّهُ لَكُمْ وَهُوَ أَرْحَمُ الرَّاحِمِينَ687 {يوسف/92}. 688قَالَ أَنتُمْ شَرٌّ مَّكَانًا In this case, one can realize that وَاللّهُ أَعْلَمُ بِمَا تَصِفُونَ was a secret and an inner statement of Yusuf as but not verbalized and this secret was buried in the history until it was revealed by Allah ﷻ Who is all Al-A'lim[689], Al-Batin[690], Al-Qādir[691], Al-Hayy[692], Al-Qayyum[693], and Al-Hakim[694]. Allah ﷻ revealed it to Rasulullah ﷺ through the Qurān.

Then, how can a person who is ummi can know all these except he ﷺ is the true prophet of Allah ﷻ. He ﷺ does not talk on his account or engage on his account but all his life is a revelation and guided by Allah ﷻ through the revelation of the Qurān as a matluw wahiy and the sunnah and hadith as a gayru-matluw wahiy.

In the second case of the methodology of acquiring a factual data is through literature review in that content, field or discipline and by using the mind, they can do some analysis. Yet, Rasulullah ﷺ was an ummi. The general character of the society at that time has the feature of ummi. Ummi here can be understood as someone or people who were illiterate, not affected with civilized discourses, pure, and natural. In this case, being an ummi can indicate a desert society with the people of badawins (desert Arabs) who may not be civilized and may not carry

---

685. They said, "If he steals—a brother of his has stolen before."
686. He said, "No blame will there be upon you today. Allah will forgive you; and He is the most merciful of the merciful.
687. He said, "No blame will there be upon you today. Allah will forgive you; and He is the most merciful of the merciful.
688. He said, "You are worse in position, and Allah is most knowing of what you describe."
689. The All-Knower.
690. The Hidden One.
691. The Powerful.
692. The Ever-Living.
693. The Sustainer.
694. The All-Wise.

civil manners according to civil communities. On the other hand, the word ummi for Rasulullah ﷺ can indicate especially the pure, sincere and motherly nature of caring, love, truthfulness, sidq, genuininenss and kindness. This approach can be viewed in the ayah as:

هُوَ الَّذِي بَعَثَ فِي الْأُمِّيِّينَ رَسُولًا مِّنْهُمْ يَتْلُو عَلَيْهِمْ آيَاتِهِ وَيُزَكِّيهِمْ وَيُعَلِّمُهُمُ الْكِتَابَ وَالْحِكْمَةَ وَإِن كَانُوا مِن قَبْلُ لَفِي ضَلَالٍ مُّبِينٍ 695 {الجمعة/2}

In this sense, the word ummi can be opposite of the term of "ahlu-kitāb". One is people of the book, people of education or people of civilization and the other is people of instinct as mentioned وَمِنْهُمْ أُمِّيُّونَ لَا يَعْلَمُونَ الْكِتَابَ إِلَّا أَمَانِيَّ وَإِنْ هُمْ إِلَّا يَظُنُّونَ 696 {البقرة/78}. Here, ahlu-kitāb in its technical term is Christians and Jews. In its broader meaning, the ones who have the knowledge of the book, scriptures, guidelines from Allah ﷻ. The opposite of ahlu-kitāb[697] are the people who don't know about the book as mentioned أُمِّيُّونَ لَا يَعْلَمُونَ الْكِتَابَ[698] and accordingly they don't have the guidance from the book and they follow their instincts as mentioned [699] إِلَّا أَمَانِيَّ.

These instincts without the guidance of the book can be wrong assumptions as mentioned إِلَّا أَمَانِيَّ وَإِنْ هُمْ إِلَّا يَظُنُّونَ[700]. In the case of Rasulullah ﷺ., the word ummi[701] can indicate the most pure, honest, caring and truthful. When this intrinsic and innate character and feature of umm was combined in Rasulullah with prophethood, he ﷺ became the highest holder of guidance for people with knowledge and practice as mentioned

وَكَذَلِكَ أَوْحَيْنَا إِلَيْكَ رُوحًا مِّنْ أَمْرِنَا مَا كُنتَ تَدْرِي مَا الْكِتَابُ وَلَا الْإِيمَانُ وَلَكِن جَعَلْنَاهُ نُورًا نَّهْدِي بِهِ مَن نَّشَاء مِنْ عِبَادِنَا وَإِنَّكَ لَتَهْدِي إِلَى صِرَاطٍ مُّسْتَقِيمٍ[702] {الشورى/52}

---

695. It is He who has sent among the unlettered [Arabs] a Messenger from themselves reciting to them His verses and purifying them and teaching them the Book [i.e., the Qurān] and wisdom [i.e., the sunnah]—although they were before in clear error—

696. And among them are unlettered ones who do not know the Scripture except [indulgement in] wishful thinking, but they are only assuming.

697. The people of the Book.

698. Unlettered ones who do not know the Scripture.

699. Except [indulgement in] wishful thinking,

700. Except [indulgement in] wishful thinking, but they are only assuming.

701. Illiterate.

702. And thus We have revealed to you an inspiration of Our command [i.e., the Qurān]. You did not know what is the Book or [what is] faith, but We have made it a light by which We guide whom We will of Our servants. And indeed, [O Muhammad], you guide to a straight path

صِرَاطِ اللَّهِ الَّذِي لَهُ مَا فِي السَّمَاوَاتِ وَمَا فِي الْأَرْضِ أَلَا إِلَى اللَّهِ تَصِيرُ الْأُمُورُ
{الشورى/53}703.

There are people who may not have much knowledge, but they can
be sincere, determined and honest about what they do. There are people
who may be educated and have expertise and specialities but they may
not act on this knowledge but carry them as a mere carrier. Yet, when
both features were combined in Rasulullah ﷺ with the guidance of
Allah ﷻ, then he ﷺ became a person of guidance both for the ahlu-
kitāb and ummiyun. This guidance was with the authentic and original
scripture from Allah ﷻ, the Qurān and his genuine practice on these
teachings with this genuine collective character of being an ummi,
referred as sunnah or hadith. This is mentioned as:

فَإِنْ حَاجُّوكَ فَقُلْ أَسْلَمْتُ وَجْهِيَ لِلَّهِ وَمَنِ اتَّبَعَنِ وَقُل لِّلَّذِينَ أُوتُواْ الْكِتَابَ وَالأُمِّيِّينَ
أَأَسْلَمْتُمْ فَإِنْ أَسْلَمُواْ فَقَدِ اهْتَدَواْ وَّإِن تَوَلَّوْاْ فَإِنَّمَا عَلَيْكَ الْبَلاَغُ وَاللّهُ بَصِيرٌ بِالْعِبَادِ 704{آل
عمران/20}

الَّذِينَ يَتَّبِعُونَ الرَّسُولَ النَّبِيَّ الأُمِّيَّ الَّذِي يَجِدُونَهُ مَكْتُوبًا عِندَهُمْ فِي التَّوْرَاةِ وَالإِنْجِيلِ
يَأْمُرُهُم بِالْمَعْرُوفِ وَيَنْهَاهُمْ عَنِ الْمُنكَرِ وَيُحِلُّ لَهُمُ الطَّيِّبَاتِ وَيُحَرِّمُ عَلَيْهِمُ الْخَبَآئِثَ
وَيَضَعُ عَنْهُمْ إِصْرَهُمْ وَالأَغْلاَلَ الَّتِي كَانَتْ عَلَيْهِمْ فَالَّذِينَ آمَنُواْ بِهِ وَعَزَّرُوهُ وَنَصَرُوهُ
وَاتَّبَعُواْ النُّورَ الَّذِيَ أُنزِلَ مَعَهُ أُوْلَـئِكَ هُمُ الْمُفْلِحُونَ 705{الأعراف/157}

---

703. The path of Allah, to whom belongs whatever is in the heavens and whatever is on the
earth. Unquestionably, to Allah do [all] matters evolve [i.e., return].
704. So if they argue with you, say, "I have submitted myself to Allah [in Islam], and [so have]
those who follow me." And say to those who were given the Scripture and [to] the unlearned,
"Have you submitted yourselves?" And if they submit [in Islam], they are rightly guided; but if
they turn away—then upon you is only the [duty of] notification. And Allah is Seeing of [His]
servants.
705. Those who follow the Messenger, the unlettered prophet, whom they find written [i.e.,
mentioned] in what they have of the Torah and the Gospel, who enjoins upon them what
is right and forbids them what is wrong and makes lawful for them the good things and
prohibits for them the evil and relieves them of their burden and the shackles which were
upon them. So they who have believed in him, honored him, supported him and followed the
light which was sent down with him—it is those who will be the successful.

Therefore, both compelling and charming features of Rasulullah ﷺ demand all the humanity to follow Rasulullah ﷺ as mentioned:

قُلْ يَا أَيُّهَا النَّاسُ إِنِّي رَسُولُ اللّهِ إِلَيْكُمْ جَمِيعًا الَّذِي لَهُ مُلْكُ السَّمَاوَاتِ وَالأَرْضِ لا إِلَهَ إِلاَّ هُوَ يُحْيِي وَيُمِيتُ فَآمِنُواْ بِاللّهِ وَرَسُولِهِ النَّبِيِّ الأُمِّيِّ الَّذِي يُؤْمِنُ بِاللّهِ وَكَلِمَاتِهِ وَاتَّبِعُوهُ لَعَلَّكُمْ تَهْتَدُونَ 706 {الأعراف/158}

From the above analysis, one can witness that an ummi person is bringing counter cases to the people of knowledge and scripture pointing out their both their fallacies in order to make corrections. The methodology of his approach with the Qurān is very rational and logical. This methodology includes their existing approaches to the belief as one may call literature review in today's scientific world. Then, he ﷺ very genuinely and logically presents an update for the correct creed without emphasizing group or other identities. In other words, in this methodology of update content is emphasized rather than mere following or submission. Following can be secondary until one understands the purpose of the content, the need and goal of Rasulullah ﷺ.

If this is not realized, then people may view Islām as another religion from God with different interpretations. Then, due to this, they ask "if they are all from God and acceptable with different interpretations, what is the need for three religions? Why are these religions in conflict? Why do people interpret differently?...etc." All these questions stem from lack of the content knowledge what the Qurān is about, the teachings of Rasulullah ﷺ and Islam. In other words, these questions are due to not properly understanding the need of existence for Christianity after Judaism and Islam after Christianity. In other words, one of the main goals of the Qurān and Rasulullah in his teachings is to reinstate the original teachings of prior messengers and prophets such as Musa as and Isa as.

All these prove the prophethood of Rasulullah ﷺ that Rasulullah ﷺ is Al-Haqq[707] with certainty is the messenger of Allah ﷻ.

---

706. Say, [O Muhammad], "O mankind, indeed I am the Messenger of Allah to you all, [from Him] to whom belongs the dominion of the heavens and the earth. There is no deity except Him; He gives life and causes death." So believe in Allah and His Messenger, the unlettered prophet, who believes in Allah and His words, and follow him that you may be guided.
707. The Absolute Truth.

Context

It is important to analyze the social norms and beliefs and context that prophethood of Rasulullah was present initially in the Arabian society.

One can especially focus individual changes leading to communal and social changes.

If we analyze the concept of change and its opposite as inertia in different fields such as physics, psychology, and sociology, they may have some common and different meanings.

Inertia in simple physics is a property of matter by which it continues in its existing state of rest or uniform motion in a straight line, unless that state is changed by an external force [2].

A phase change in chemistry is the change of homogeneous form of matter from one state such as liquid, solid or gas to another state with the external change of temperature applied on the matter.

In social and individual changes, the change is more complex and depending on multiple variables compared to the notions in natural sciences such as physics or chemistry.

Especially, if there is a society like the original Arabian desert society in the initial encounters of Islam, change was not understood as something positive and commendable compared to our present times with the promotion of the open-mindedness, acceptance, tolerance, and dispositions against discrimination.

Yes, in a tribal society such as the people of Arabia before Islam, people strongly held positions due to tribal and lineage associations leading to different positions in that society. Change or going against the teachings of ancestors was unanimously viewed as betrayals to the social norms, unappreciation to parents, and as being outcast by the friends.

Instead of meritocracy, or a government run by selected or elected people on the basis of their ability [2], people were in positions and decision making due to their mere lineage asociations.

Following inherited norms from ancestry and forefathers was required and it was considered as nobility.

One can view that all these strong associations standing against to change were multiplied with the illiterate, untaught and ignorant positions of these Arabs in the desert. Giving ritualistic values for following the teachings of ancestors was a prime example of these people being against to change but rather they further divinized or sanctified these inherited norms, cultures and beliefs from the forefathers as something that needed to be blindly followed. They did not critically think about these inherited teachings and did not assess their plausibility, consistency and logic.

In other words, if Islam was originally revealed to the civilized people in the cities who were used to reading, understanding and critically thinking, then one can possibly think about the easiness of change. Yet, it was originally revealed with very high values, logical and methodical guidelines and spiritual and heart related teachings and transformations to the illiterate desert people. One day Omar ra mentioned this point as "We were the people of desert. Allah ﷻ elevated our status with Islam" [23].

This impossible transformation of this type of society and spreading the world as the most intellectual and spiritual religion with the most followers is another miracle of Rasulullah ﷺ enabled by Allah ﷻ, SubhanAllah!

Time Length of Change

When one considers the process and time length of change in societies, it is generally gradual process [24]. Communal change generally follows the steps of acceptance of the change among the individuals, spread of this change, and adaptation of this change by the majority of or all the society and community to form policies, laws and guidelines about this change.

One can review the process of change through claims making and policymaking in sociology [25]. There are emergency policies, and abrupt changes through policy making. The content of these changes are genereally considered as short term [25].

The general process of change is made through the natural process of the certain cyclical process to become a long-term policy, principle, or law.

In this sense, one can really see the depth of change and time length of change that Rasulullah ﷺ made during his lifetime ﷺ. In 23 years of prophethood, people almost totally leave all their prior beliefs and valuation system of their lives. Then, the same people established a country. Then, this message in these 23 years spread to many countries and was adapted by them. All this was at a time, communication and traveling was not even close to our time. Today's one hour distance with plane was weeks of travel at that time.

One can compare the dense amount of natural communal change with the case of Isa as. Christianity was also spread to many places by the disciplines and adapted by many countries.

Yet, there is a big difference. The communal adaptation of Christianity at a country level was only done after 300 to 400 years later after the departure of Isa as. In other words, after Isa as, the disciples' effect as a communal change was first adapted at a country level after 300–400 years of Isa as existence among people.In the case of Rasulullah ﷺ during 23 years of his life time, there were countries adapted Islam as a religion as a communal change. Then, after a few years later of demise of Rasulullah ﷺ, during the life of time of Omar ra, Islam was adapted at continental levels, SubhanAllah!, What a fast change and adaptation with the Fadl and Tawfiq of Allah ﷻ!

This itself can be another proof of enablement of Allah ﷻ as a miracle to show the true prophethood of Rasulullah ﷺ.

Quality of Change

When the change is done abruptly and by force, it is sustainability and longevity can be always questionable. Yet, this change has an effect of changing people's minds, ideas, customs, beliefs and spiritual practices in a very short time and keeping its longevity with close to two billion followers today. This permanent change itself in this short time can indicate the authenticity of the prophethood of Rasulullah ﷺ.It is possible to direct people's attention with threats, terrorizations, pressure, and instilling in them fear. An example of this can be:

قَالَ آمَنتُمْ لَهُ قَبْلَ أَنْ آذَنَ لَكُمْ إِنَّهُ لَكَبِيرُكُمُ الَّذِي عَلَّمَكُمُ السِّحْرَ فَلَسَوْفَ تَعْلَمُونَ لَأُقَطِّعَنَّ أَيْدِيَكُمْ وَأَرْجُلَكُم مِّنْ خِلَافٍ وَلَأُصَلِّبَنَّكُمْ أَجْمَعِينَ[708] {الشعراء/49}.

Yet, these effects can be transitory, peripheral, and short-lived. In other words, when the iman enters to hearts of people, it has a permanent, rooted and long-lived effect in this world and afterlife.

---

708. [Pharaoh] said, "You believed him [i.e., Moses] before I gave you permission. Indeed, he is your leader who has taught you magic, but you are going to know. I will surely cut off your hands and your feet on opposite sides, and I will surely crucify you all."

Imān makes such a transformation in humans minds, hearts, emotions, and cognitive states that there is another human being that is formed although the body may look the same. Now, this person has a new character, trait, moral values, purpose and goal in life. He or she has a new valuation system to evaluate things around them. Now, everything has a marvelous optimistic positive meaning compared to their prior dark states and pessimistic meanings of purposeless, uselessness, and randomness. One can view this transformation in:

اللّهُ وَلِيُّ الَّذِينَ آمَنُواْ يُخْرِجُهُم مِّنَ الظُّلُمَاتِ إِلَى النُّورِ وَالَّذِينَ كَفَرُواْ أَوْلِيَاؤُهُمُ الطَّاغُوتُ يُخْرِجُونَهُم مِّنَ النُّورِ إِلَى الظُّلُمَاتِ أُوْلَئِكَ أَصْحَابُ النَّارِ هُمْ فِيهَا خَالِدُونَ709 {البقرة/257}

This can be in the response of a group as mentioned who were threatened and terrorized but yet, their imān transformed them at a permanent station and they responded to above threats as : قَالُوا لَا ضَيْرَ إِنَّا إِلَى رَبِّنَا مُنقَلِبُونَ{الشعراء/50}710 إِنَّا نَطْمَعُ أَن يَغْفِرَ لَنَا رَبُّنَا خَطَايَانَا أَن كُنَّا أَوَّلَ الْمُؤْمِنِينَ711 {الشعراء/51}

In the above case, one can realize this quality of change in the prophethood of Musa as with the case of magicians.

When one compares the case of Musa as and Rasulullah ﷺ, the quality of change they instilled through imān were permanent, transformational and long-lived. This is one of the similarities in the job of prophethood among different prophets.

One difference is that Musa as had magicians and some possible local people other than Bani-Israel who did not know about imān fully. These few magicians and local people from qibti ethnicity did not know much about true imān. In this regard, one can realize the effect of the transformation of the imān in magicians in the above ayahs.

Most of the people following Musa as were Bani-Israel and they already had the articles of imān as inherited from their forefathers as most of them were previous prophets. Musa as led them as the prophet of Allah ﷻ in order to instill and remind the original message that they were already familiar.

---

709. Allah is the ally of those who believe. He brings them out from darknesses into the light. And those who disbelieve—their allies are Taghut. They take them out of the light into darknesses. Those are the companions of the Fire; they will abide eternally therein.
710. They said, "No harm. Indeed, to our Lord we will return.
711. Indeed, we aspire that our Lord will forgive us our sins because we were the first of the believers."

وَلَقَدْ آتَيْنَا مُوسَى الْهُدَى وَأَوْرَثْنَا بَنِي إِسْرَائِيلَ الْكِتَابَ⁷¹²{غافر/53}

وَلَقَدْ آتَيْنَا مُوسَى الْكِتَابَ فَلَا تَكُن فِي مِرْيَةٍ مِّن لِّقَائِهِ وَجَعَلْنَاهُ هُدًى لِّبَنِي إِسْرَائِيلَ
⁷¹³{السجدة/23}

In the case of Rasulullah ﷺ, almost all the people in pre-Islamic Arabia were like magicians. They did not know about imān like the case of bani-Israìl. In that sense, the position of Rasulullah ﷺ was mentioned هُوَ الَّذِي بَعَثَ فِي الْأُمِّيِّينَ رَسُولًا مِّنْهُمْ يَتْلُو عَلَيْهِمْ آيَاتِهِ وَيُزَكِّيهِمْ وَيُعَلِّمُهُمُ الْكِتَابَ وَالْحِكْمَةَ as وَإِن كَانُوا مِن قَبْلُ لَفِي ضَلَالٍ مُّبِينٍ⁷¹⁴{الجمعة/2}

In other words, the full transformational effect of Rasulullah ﷺ happened in all the thousands, and millions of initial Muslims similar to some magicians at the time of Musa as.

At the time of Rasulullah ﷺ, before Islam, there were such barbaric commons customs and habits such as burying alive the female children due to their femininity. One can observe a phenomenal transformation in the habits of the same group of people after Islam. The same people who were able kill their own children now were hesitant to step on an ant by accident on the sidewalk.

These comprehensive, wide-ranging, rapid, permanent, and stationary changes cannot be explained by social theories based only on mind. The primary explanation is the miraculous effect of prophethood similar to the case of Musa as with magicians as their imān was enabled by Allah ﷻ. This enablement of Allah ﷻ for Rasulullah is mentioned as:

وَأَلَّفَ بَيْنَ قُلُوبِهِمْ لَوْ أَنفَقْتَ مَا فِي الْأَرْضِ جَمِيعاً مَّا أَلَّفْتَ بَيْنَ قُلُوبِهِمْ وَلَكِنَّ اللّهَ أَلَّفَ بَيْنَهُمْ
إِنَّهُ عَزِيزٌ حَكِيمٌ⁷¹⁵{الأنفال/63}

فَلَمْ تَقْتُلُوهُمْ وَلَكِنَّ اللّهَ قَتَلَهُمْ وَمَا رَمَيْتَ إِذْ رَمَيْتَ وَلَكِنَّ اللّهَ رَمَى وَلِيُبْلِيَ الْمُؤْمِنِينَ مِنْهُ بَلَاء
حَسَناً إِنَّ اللّهَ سَمِيعٌ عَلِيمٌ⁷¹⁶{الأنفال/17}

---

712. And We had certainly given Moses guidance, and We caused the Children of Israel to inherit the Scripture

713. And We certainly gave Moses the Scripture, so do not be in doubt over his meeting. And We made it [i.e., the Torah] guidance for the Children of Israel.

714. It is He who has sent among the unlettered [Arabs] a Messenger from themselves reciting to them His verses and purifying them and teaching them the Book [i.e., the Qurān] and wisdom [i.e., the sunnah]—although they were before in clear error—

715. And brought together their hearts. If you had spent all that is in the earth, you could not have brought their hearts together; but Allah brought them together. Indeed, He is Exalted in Might and Wise.

716. And you did not kill them, but it was Allah who killed them. And you threw not, [O Muhammad], when you threw, but it was Allah who threw that He might test the believers with a good test. Indeed, Allah is Hearing and Knowing.

One can realize that when there is a change in one's life, it may be only through one aspect of their life. Yet, making a change in all different aspects of life for a person is a miracle of Rasulullah ﷺ. If this is not only one person but for many, billions today, then this can indicate another miracle proving the prophethood of Rasulullah ﷺ.One can consider an imaginary case. Let's assume contemporary most famous hundred philosophers living at the time of Rasulullah ﷺ whether they could make the same immense permanent change in the life and addictions of the people. These people are not college graduates or students but they are the people of desert who were on the tribal value system.

The change that Rasulullah ﷺ brought had a such a transformative format that the same people who used to bury their girls alive and did not feel sad about it became the people of sensitivity and genuineness that they had the concern and worry about stepping on the ants by accident while walking on the sidewalks.

One of the basic difference of philosophers' effect of change is that they affect ideas. Their effect may not be seen immediately. An idea of a philosopher can be used in policy making and applications of social rules through formal teachings in colleges in today's societies. Philosophers or other fields of social scientists such as psychologists do not generally emerge as activists trying to implement their ideas and convince people. Yet, they try to address the social problem and concepts by observing people and make claims and premises about it. Then, either these ideas fade away and become unused.

Or, if they catch attention by the power holders such as governments, kings, rulers, then it can have a forced application on the society such as the cases of emergence of Karl Marx, Freud, Weber, Stalin, and Durkheim and others on the communist and capitalist societies. Or, it can receive attention in different diciplines of academia for the basis of a theory and then, it can be promoted from there. Philosophers' content can be complicated and detailed. Philosophers' effect of change on the societies can be top-down approach of inductive cases.

In the case of religious movements, the initiator of a movement can also display action or work in the field as a person. They can also be called as activists. Then, they can move the masses with few ideas or doctrinal changes. Religious movements' content may not be as detailed and complicated compared as the cases of philosophers. The effect of change on the societies can be through both inductive approach of the true teachings of scripture and the cases of relevancy with activism of deductive pieces.

When we compare the case of Rasulullah ﷺ with above two cases, Rasulullah ﷺ brings a very detailed full applicable change for the lives of people with the Qurān and practice referred as sunnah and hadith[717]. These applications and teachings can have relevancy direct application, meanings and openings for all levels of learners. From simple minded people of purity referred as ummi to the complicated and genius minded people of scholars following scientific methodology can have direct access and regular and endless benefit from these teachings.

Therefore, this uniqueness and miraculous case of Rasulullah ﷺ can be better understood with comparison to the historical similar cases. Rasulullah ﷺ was not a simple religious movement leader like others in the history due to his grassroot association and activism. Rasulullah ﷺ was not a person like philosophers making detailed complex ideological changes and his ideas were adapted by the powerholders leading to change due to his extensive new teachings with the Qurān and sunnah.

Rasulullah ﷺ was the messenger of Allah ﷻ who miraculously was enabled by Allah ﷻ to enable a comprehensive change from personal and social lives in a very short time with a very dense strong authentic source of knowledge and practice in people's minds and hearts unlike to traditional religious movements and unlike to the cases of philosophers.

Therefore, the number of Muslims will increase over time due to the strong genuine and authentic content of Islam with the Qurān and hadith as mentioned by Rasulullah ﷺ and by the end of days that the number of Muslims will be abundance. The effect of this increase can be in that sense slow, similar to the effect of ideas on minds over centuries. This increase or adaptation is not necessarily related with the practice by Muslims but due to the strong and authentic message of the Qurān and sunnah. The practice of Muslims as the examples and representatives of the Qurān and sunnah can accelerate the rate of this adaptation of these teachings by others or decelerate it depending on how they are

---

717. One can remember comprehensive of the Qurān and hadith is similar to the New Testament and Old Testament together. In this sense, the original and true doctrines of two religions Judaism and Christianity in thousands of years is compiled into one religion, Islām with the Qurān and Sunnah. Islām includes all the inclusive information for all religions with updates sufficing changes of time and culture until the End of Day.

represented. So, from the perspective of Qadar[718], it is only a matter of time whether we are involved in this change or not as mentioned:

{الصف/8}[719] يُرِيدُونَ لِيُطْفِئُوا نُورَ اللَّهِ بِأَفْوَاهِهِمْ وَاللَّهُ مُتِمُّ نُورِهِ وَلَوْ كَرِهَ الْكَافِرُونَ

{يونس/82}[720] وَيُحِقُّ اللَّهُ الْحَقَّ بِكَلِمَاتِهِ وَلَوْ كَرِهَ الْمُجْرِمُونَ

In this sense, other ideas as promoted and popularized by philosophers and their fellow social scientists have very thin effects as mentioned[721] بِأَفْوَاهِهِمْ. The message of Allah ﷻ as mentioned with نُورَ اللَّهِ[722] is so strong, robust, and fully and absolutely convincing [723] الْحَقَّ that no conflicting philosophical ideas or practices can stand in front of it:

بَلْ نَقْذِفُ بِالْحَقِّ عَلَى الْبَاطِلِ فَيَدْمَغُهُ فَإِذَا هُوَ زَاهِقٌ وَلَكُمُ الْوَيْلُ مِمَّا تَصِفُونَ[724]{الأنبياء/18}

فَوَقَعَ الْحَقُّ وَبَطَلَ مَا كَانُواْ يَعْمَلُونَ[725] {الأعراف/118}

It is al-haqq, the truth. It has the overpowering effect on bātil, falsehood as mentioned:

وَقُلْ جَاء الْحَقُّ وَزَهَقَ الْبَاطِلُ إِنَّ الْبَاطِلَ كَانَ زَهُوقًا[726] {الإسراء/81}

One can also review this ayah [727] قُلْ جَاء الْحَقُّ وَمَا يُبْدِئُ الْبَاطِلُ وَمَا يُعِيدُ {سبأ/49}. When humans assign universal teachings and it becomes agreed upon, it can be likely that this universality or acceptance is one of the established truths as mentioned with the word al-haqq,[728] الْحَقَّ. In other words, we have established social and natural laws and constants. If this is not changing, then it becomes a constant referred as universal truth.

---

718. Decree.
719. They want to extinguish the light of Allah with their mouths, but Allah will perfect His light, although the disbelievers dislike it.
720. And Allah will establish the truth by His words, even if the criminals dislike it."
721. With their mouths.
722. The light of Allah.
723. The truth.
724. Rather, We dash the truth upon falsehood, and it destroys it, and thereupon it departs. And for you is destruction from that which you describe.
725. So the truth was established, and abolished was what they were doing.
726. And say, "Truth has come, and falsehood has departed. Indeed is falsehood, [by nature], ever bound to depart."
727. Say, "The truth has come, and falsehood can neither begin [anything] nor repeat [it]."
728. The truth.

In this regard, all the teachings of Allah ﷻ are الْحَقُّ whether humans refer them as universal constants or truths. In these truths as assigned by Allah ﷻ, there is no reversibility and disappearance[729] وَمَا يُبْدِئُ الْبَاطِلُ وَمَا يُعِيدُ compared to the cases of al-batil[730], false, illusionary and inauthentic interpretations or assigned values as mentioned[731] هُوَ زَاهِقٌ.

With the above approach, once the Qurān and hadith are in reality of the realms of humans, then it is going to stay with the people until the end of days. One can ask why the cases such as Tawrah and Injil did not stay in their originality with people? Injil and Tawrah were were initially sent to a certain group of people. Yet, due to the strength and robust teachings of Allah ﷻ, they were spread and followed by billions of people. Their original messages affected the societies and established social and universal constants. Yet, the accessibility of the original teachings of these books were altered. It access to their original and authentic forms were prevented. Yet, some of their original teachings remained in the societies. The questions of originality and authenticity always have remained for these books of tawrah or injil due to their different available versions among people.

With the Divine Mashiyyah of Allah ﷻ, Qurān was sent for all mankind and its assurance of accessibility measures was given for all humans until the end of days by Allah ﷻ. Now, one can realize that when the Qurān is there with its original teachings until end of days, then جَاءَ الْحَقُّ وَمَا يُبْدِئُ الْبَاطِلُ وَمَا يُعِيدُ[732], the ideas of batil will not remain and will fade away as mentioned[733] هُوَ زَاهِقٌ. There is the full accessible and full robust teaching of al-haqq, the Qurān, among humans at all times. The Qurān will be there with the Divine Protection.

One can also view the notion of الْحَقُّ[734] with its opposite of illusionary, artificial, and pseudo concepts and meanings of social constructions[735] الظَّنَّ as mentioned وَمَا لَهُم بِهِ مِنْ عِلْمٍ إِن يَتَّبِعُونَ إِلَّا الظَّنَّ وَإِنَّ الظَّنَّ لَا يُغْنِي مِنَ الْحَقِّ شَيْئًا {النجم/28}[736]. In this sense, every الْحَقّ is in accordance with true 'ilm,

---

729. Falsehood can neither begin [anything] nor repeat [it]."
730. Falsehood.
731. It departs.
732. The truth has come, and falsehood can neither begin [anything] nor repeat [it]."
733. It departs.
734. The truth.
735. Assumption
736. And they have thereof no knowledge. They follow not except assumption, and indeed, assumption avails not against the truth at all.

knowledge or science. Every zann leading to bātil is not in accordance with true 'ilm. Every bātil is not scientific.

As humans have tendency for waswasa[737], whimsical thoughts, uncertainties, and hesitance of assigning meanings, Allah ﷻ assures us with this critical word[738] الْحَقُّ, which one can write volumes of books only on this word alone. Therefore, the person should not be in illusionary states of uncertainty but follow the certain and absolute truths. If the person is sincerely looking for the absolute truth and reality then, they will follow the Qurān and sunnah of Rasulullah ﷺ, as mentioned {147/البقرة} الْحَقُّ مِن رَّبِّكَ فَلاَ تَكُونَنَّ مِنَ الْمُمْتَرِينَ[739]. This is so critical to remind to oneself that this ayah is repeated in different parts of the Qurān to give assurance as {60/آل عمران} الْحَقُّ مِن رَّبِّكَ فَلاَ تَكُن مِّن الْمُمْتَرِينَ[740]

أَفَغَيْرَ اللَّهِ أَبْتَغِي حَكَمًا وَهُوَ الَّذِي أَنزَلَ إِلَيْكُمُ الْكِتَابَ مُفَصَّلاً وَالَّذِينَ آتَيْنَاهُمُ الْكِتَابَ يَعْلَمُونَ أَنَّهُ مُنَزَّلٌ مِّن رَّبِّكَ بِالْحَقِّ فَلاَ تَكُونَنَّ مِنَ الْمُمْتَرِينَ[741] {114/الأنعام}

فَإِن كُنتَ فِي شَكٍّ مِّمَّا أَنزَلْنَا إِلَيْكَ فَاسْأَلِ الَّذِينَ يَقْرَؤُونَ الْكِتَابَ مِن قَبْلِكَ لَقَدْ جَاءَكَ الْحَقُّ مِن رَّبِّكَ فَلاَ تَكُونَنَّ مِنَ الْمُمْتَرِينَ[742] {94/يونس}

In other words, the Qurān constantly repeats this word,[743] الْحَقُّ, to assure the person that our human dispositions need constant assurance due to our choices of assigning values, meanings and choices in life. The doubts or uncertainties are like sneaky and devious creatures trying to enter from any tiny hole that they can find. Therefore, seeking refuge in Allah ﷻ with ta'wwuz and dua is very critical. May Allah ﷻ protect us, Amìn.

Especially, one can see in philosophy the concept of viewing everything as an illusionary state of mind and heart as a social construct is becoming more and more popular. This concept affects all the social sciences and build some traces in the foundations of

---

737. Whispers in the heart.
738. The truth.
739. The truth is from your Lord, so never be among the doubters.
740. The truth is from your Lord, so do not be among the doubters.
741. [Say], "Then is it other than Allah I should seek as judge while it is He who has revealed to you the Book [i.e., the Qurān] explained in detail?" And those to whom We [previously] gave the Scripture know that it is sent down from your Lord in truth, so never be among the doubters.
742. So if you are in doubt, [O Muhammad], about that which We have revealed to you, then ask those who have been reading the Scripture before you. The truth has certainly come to you from your Lord, so never be among the doubters.
743. The truth.

different disciplines due to secularism. Therefore, one can realize the critical repetition of this word الْحَقُّ, to destroy these human fallacies of assigning false meanings and subsequently building on it with world views and disciplines.

In that sense, الْحَقُّ is the position of the absolute reality of the true assignment of the correct meanings. To remove these doubts, the Qurān assures the person with the repetition of this word.Everything in life is certain as the creation of Allah ﷻ. Everything has a meaning and purpose as assigned by Allah ﷻ and as explained by Allah ﷻ. This can be something that humans may not pay attention in small scales. One may not give much attention to a small bug, fly or mosquito. Yet it is mentioned as: إِنَّ اللَّهَ لاَ يَسْتَحْيِي أَن يَضْرِبَ مَثَلاً مَّا بَعُوضَةً فَمَا فَوْقَهَا فَأَمَّا الَّذِينَ آمَنُواْ فَيَعْلَمُونَ أَنَّهُ الْحَقُّ مِن رَّبِّهِمْ وَأَمَّا الَّذِينَ كَفَرُواْ فَيَقُولُونَ مَاذَا أَرَادَ اللَّهُ بِهَذَا مَثَلاً يُضِلُّ بِهِ كَثِيراً وَيَهْدِي بِهِ كَثِيراً وَمَا يُضِلُّ بِهِ إِلاَّ الْفَاسِقِينَ 744{البقرة/26} الَّذِينَ يَنقُضُونَ عَهْدَ اللَّه مِن بَعْدِ مِيثَاقِهِ وَيَقْطَعُونَ مَا أَمَرَ اللَّهُ بِهِ أَن يُوصَلَ وَيُفْسِدُونَ فِي الأَرْضِ أُولَئِكَ هُمُ الْخَاسِرُونَ745 {البقرة/27} كَيْفَ تَكْفُرُونَ بِاللَّهِ وَكُنتُمْ أَمْوَاتاً فَأَحْيَاكُمْ ثُمَّ يُمِيتُكُمْ ثُمَّ يُحْيِيكُمْ ثُمَّ إِلَيْهِ تُرْجَعُونَ746 {البقرة/28}

It can be something in macro levels from the reference point of humans as mentioned: وَهُوَ الَّذِي خَلَقَ السَّمَاوَاتِ وَالأَرْضَ بِالْحَقِّ وَيَوْمَ يَقُولُ كُن فَيَكُونُ قَوْلُهُ الْحَقُّ وَلَهُ الْمُلْكُ يَوْمَ يُنفَخُ فِي الصُّورِ عَالِمُ الْغَيْبِ وَالشَّهَادَةِ وَهُوَ الْحَكِيمُ الْخَبِيرُ747 {الأنعام/73}

For example, we analyze this critical word الْحَقُّ besides many examples in the Qurān, one can realize about the strong emphasis and repetition about the Qurān with the word الْحَقُّ that the Qurān and teachings of Rasulullah ﷺ are certain, truth and absolute from Allah ﷻ:

إِنَّا أَنزَلْنَا عَلَيْكَ الْكِتَابَ لِلنَّاسِ بِالْحَقِّ فَمَنِ اهْتَدَى فَلِنَفْسِهِ وَمَن ضَلَّ فَإِنَّمَا يَضِلُّ عَلَيْهَا وَمَا أَنتَ عَلَيْهِم بِوَكِيلٍ748 {الزمر/41}

---

744. Indeed, Allah is not timid to present an example—that of a mosquito or what is smaller than it. And those who have believed know that it is the truth from their Lord. But as for those who disbelieve, they say, "What did Allah intend by this as an example?" He misleads many thereby and guides many thereby. And He misleads not except the defiantly disobedient,

745. Who break the covenant of Allah after contracting it and sever that which Allah has ordered to be joined and cause corruption on earth. It is those who are the losers.

746. How can you disbelieve in Allah when you were lifeless and He brought you to life; then He will cause you to die, then He will bring you [back] to life, and then to Him you will be returned.

747. And it is He who created the heavens and earth in truth. And the day [i.e., whenever] He says, "Be," and it is, His word is the truth. And His is the dominion [on] the Day the Horn is blown. [He is] Knower of the unseen and the witnessed; and He is the Wise, the Acquainted.

748. Indeed, We sent down to you the Book for the people in truth. So whoever is guided—it is for [the benefit of] his soul; and whoever goes astray only goes astray to its detriment. And you are not a manager [i.e., authority] over them.

اللَّهُ الَّذِي أَنزَلَ الْكِتَابَ بِالْحَقِّ وَالْمِيزَانَ وَمَا يُدْرِيكَ لَعَلَّ السَّاعَةَ قَرِيبٌ 749{الشورى/17}

إِنَّا أَرْسَلْنَاكَ بِالْحَقِّ بَشِيرًا وَنَذِيرًا وَلاَ تُسْأَلُ عَنْ أَصْحَابِ الْجَحِيمِ 750{البقرة/119}

تِلْكَ آيَاتُ اللهِ نَتْلُوهَا عَلَيْكَ بِالْحَقِّ وَإِنَّكَ لَمِنَ الْمُرْسَلِينَ 751{البقرة/252}

نَزَّلَ عَلَيْكَ الْكِتَابَ بِالْحَقِّ مُصَدِّقاً لِّمَا بَيْنَ يَدَيْهِ وَأَنزَلَ التَّوْرَاةَ وَالإِنجِيلَ 752{آل عمران/3}

تِلْكَ آيَاتُ اللهِ نَتْلُوهَا عَلَيْكَ بِالْحَقِّ وَمَا اللهُ يُرِيدُ ظُلْمًا لِّلْعَالَمِينَ 753{آل عمران/108}

يَا أَيُّهَا النَّاسُ قَدْ جَاءكُمُ الرَّسُولُ بِالْحَقِّ مِن رَّبِّكُمْ فَآمِنُواْ خَيْرًا لَّكُمْ وَإِن تَكْفُرُواْ فَإِنَّ لِلّهِ مَا فِي السَّمَاوَاتِ وَالأَرْضِ وَكَانَ اللهُ عَلِيمًا حَكِيمًا 754{النساء/170}

المر تِلْكَ آيَاتُ الْكِتَابِ وَالَّذِيَ أُنزِلَ إِلَيْكَ مِن رَّبِّكَ الْحَقُّ وَلَـكِنَّ أَكْثَرَ النَّاسِ لاَ يُؤْمِنُونَ 755{الرعد/1}

The hidayah[756] to this truth and reality, الْحَقَّ[757] is from Allah ﷻ that one should thank and appreciate Allah ﷻ for this hidayah as mentioned: وَنَزَعْنَا مَا فِي صُدُورِهِم مِّنْ غِلٍّ تَجْرِي مِن تَحْتِهِمُ الأَنْهَارُ وَقَالُواْ الْحَمْدُ لِلّهِ الَّذِي هَدَانَا لِهَـذَا وَمَا كُنَّا لِنَهْتَدِيَ لَوْلا أَنْ هَدَانَا اللهُ لَقَدْ جَاءتْ رُسُلُ رَبِّنَا بِالْحَقِّ وَنُودُواْ أَن تِلْكُمُ الْجَنَّةُ أُورِثْتُمُوهَا بِمَا كُنتُمْ تَعْمَلُونَ 758{الأعراف/43}

---

749. It is Allah who has sent down the Book in truth and [also] the balance [i.e., justice]. And what will make you perceive? Perhaps the Hour is near.
750. Indeed, We have sent you, [O Muhammad], with the truth as a bringer of good tidings and a warner, and you will not be asked about the companions of Hellfire.
751. These are the verses of Allah which We recite to you, [O Muhammad], in truth. And indeed, you are from among the messengers.
752. He has sent down upon you, [O Muhammad], the Book in truth, confirming what was before it. And He revealed the Torah and the Gospel.
753. These are the verses of Allah. We recite them to you, [O Muhammad], in truth; and Allah wants no injustice to the worlds [i.e., His creatures].
754. O mankind, the Messenger has come to you with the truth from your Lord, so believe; it is better for you. But if you disbelieve—then indeed, to Allah belongs whatever is in the heavens and earth. And ever is Allah Knowing and Wise.
755. Alif, Lam, Meem, Ra. These are the verses of the Book; and what has been revealed to you from your Lord is the truth, but most of the people do not believe.
756. Guidance.
757. The truth.
758. And We will have removed whatever is within their breasts of resentment, [while] flowing beneath them are rivers. And they will say, "Praise to Allah, who has guided us to this; and we would never have been guided if Allah had not guided us. Certainly the messengers of our Lord had come with the truth." And they will be called, "This is Paradise, which you have been made to inherit for what you used to do."

قُلْ هَلْ مِن شُرَكَآئِكُم مَّن يَهْدِي إِلَى إِلْحَقِّ قُلِ اللَّهُ يَهْدِي لِلْحَقِّ أَفَمَن يَهْدِي إِلَى الْحَقِّ
أَحَقُّ أَن يُتَّبَعَ أَمَّن لاَّ يَهِدِّيَ إِلاَّ أَن يُهْدَى فَمَا لَكُمْ كَيْفَ تَحْكُمُونَ 759 {يونس/35} وَمَا يَتَّبِعُ
أَكْثَرُهُمْ إِلاَّ ظَنًّا إِنَّ الظَّنَّ لاَ يُغْنِي مِنَ الْحَقِّ شَيْئًا إِنَّ اللَّهَ عَلِيمٌ بِمَا يَفْعَلُونَ 760 {يونس/36}

Yet, the person has the free will and choice for hidayah for the truth and reality, الْحَقَّ as this is the purpose in life as mentioned: قُلْ يَا أَيُّهَا النَّاسُ قَدْ
جَاءكُمُ إِلْحَقُّ مِن رَّبِّكُمْ فَمَنِ اهْتَدَى فَإِنَّمَا يَهْتَدِي لِنَفْسِهِ وَمَن ضَلَّ فَإِنَّمَا يَضِلُّ عَلَيْهَا وَمَا أَنَاْ عَلَيْكُم
بِوَكِيلٍ 761 {يونس/108}

وَقُلِ إِلْحَقُّ مِن رَّبِّكُمْ فَمَن شَاء فَلْيُؤْمِن وَمَن شَاء فَلْيَكُفُرْ إِنَّا أَعْتَدْنَا لِلظَّالِمِينَ نَارًا أَحَاطَ
بِهِمْ سُرَادِقُهَا وَإِن يَسْتَغِيثُوا يُغَاثُوا بِمَاء كَالْمُهْلِ يَشْوِي الْوُجُوهَ بِئْسَ الشَّرَابُ وَسَاءتْ
مُرْتَفَقًا 762 {الكهف/29}

Prophets and messengers of Allah ﷻ are only ordered, equipped and instructed to teach and deliver الْحَقَّ, the certain and absolute teachings from Allah ﷻ as mentioned:

وَإِذْ قَالَ اللّهُ يَا عِيسَى ابْنَ مَرْيَمَ أَأَنتَ قُلتَ لِلنَّاسِ اتَّخِذُونِي وَأُمِّيَ إِلَهَيْنِ مِن دُونِ اللّهِ قَالَ
سُبْحَانَكَ مَا يَكُونُ لِي أَنْ أَقُولَ مَا لَيْسَ لِي بِحَقٍّ إِن كُنتُ قُلْتُهُ فَقَدْ عَلِمْتَهُ تَعْلَمُ مَا فِي نَفْسِي
وَلاَ أَعْلَمُ مَا فِي نَفْسِكَ إِنَّكَ أَنتَ عَلاَّمُ الْغُيُوبِ 763 {المائدة/116} مَا قُلْتُ لَهُمْ إِلاَّ مَا أَمَرْتَنِي
بِهِ أَنِ اعْبُدُواْ اللّهَ رَبِّي وَرَبَّكُمْ وَكُنتُ عَلَيْهِمْ شَهِيدًا مَّا دُمْتُ فِيهِمْ فَلَمَّا تَوَفَّيْتَنِي كُنتَ أَنتَ

---

759. Say, "Are there of your 'partners' any who guides to the truth?" Say, "Allah guides to the truth. So is He who guides to the truth more worthy to be followed or he who guides not unless he is guided? Then what is [wrong] with you—how do you judge?"

760. And most of them follow not except assumption. Indeed, assumption avails not against the truth at all. Indeed, Allah is Knowing of what they do.

761. Say, "O mankind, the truth has come to you from your Lord, so whoever is guided is only guided for [the benefit of] his soul, and whoever goes astray only goes astray [in violation] against it. And I am not over you a manager."

762. And say, "The truth is from your Lord, so whoever wills—let him believe; and whoever wills—let him disbelieve." Indeed, We have prepared for the wrongdoers a fire whose walls will surround them. And if they call for relief, they will be relieved with water like murky oil, which scalds [their] faces. Wretched is the drink, and evil is the resting place.

763. And [beware the Day] when Allah will say, "O Jesus, Son of Mary, did you say to the people, 'Take me and my mother as deities besides Allah?'" He will say, "Exalted are You! It was not for me to say that to which I have no right. If I had said it, You would have known it. You know what is within myself, and I do not know what is within Yourself. Indeed, it is You who is Knower of the unseen.

الرَّقِيبَ عَلَيْهِمْ وَأَنتَ عَلَى كُلِّ شَيْءٍ شَهِيدٌ 764{المائدة/117} إِن تُعَذِّبْهُمْ فَإِنَّهُمْ عِبَادُكَ وَإِن تَغْفِرْ لَهُمْ فَإِنَّكَ أَنتَ الْعَزِيزُ الْحَكِيمُ 765{المائدة/118}

In this case, if the prophets don't do that then they themselves become responsible therefore, the initial response of Isa as to the question of Allah is 766 سُبْحَانَكَ مَا يَكُونُ لِي أَنْ أَقُولَ مَا لَيْسَ لِي بِحَقٍّ. It can imply that "Ya Allah! We as messengers and prophets only tell humans what You instruct us of, as mentioned767 مَا قُلْتُ لَهُمْ إِلاَّ مَا أَمَرْتَنِي بِهِ أَنِ اعْبُدُواْ اللَّهَ رَبِّي وَرَبَّكُمْ which is الْحَقَّ768.

This is another teaching method of the Qurān about the positions of the prophets and messengers that only they relate the message as revealed from Allah as769 الْحَقَّ. Therefore, they have the sidq and truthfulness as mentioned in the following ayah as قَالَ اللَّهُ هَذَا يَوْمُ يَنفَعُ الصَّادِقِينَ صِدْقُهُمْ لَهُمْ جَنَّاتٌ تَجْرِي مِن تَحْتِهَا الأَنْهَارُ خَالِدِينَ فِيهَا أَبَدًا رَّضِيَ اللَّهُ عَنْهُمْ وَرَضُواْ عَنْهُ ذَلِكَ الْفَوْزُ الْعَظِيمُ {المائدة/119}770.

Allah created everything with الْحَقَّ that is certain and absolute as مَا خَلَقْنَاهُمَا إِلَّا بِالْحَقِّ وَلَكِنَّ أَكْثَرَهُمْ لَا يَعْلَمُونَ {الدخان/39}771. The arguments of assigning partners, shares and roles for others are all false. Allah creates all creation. Allah assign their meanings, purpose and value. Therefore, one should discard the illusionary assigned explanations. Below are the two cases of people: one is following the certain and the other following the uncertain, illusionary and false assigned values and meanings as:

---

764. I said not to them except what You commanded me—to worship Allah, my Lord and your Lord. And I was a witness over them as long as I was among them; but when You took me up, You were the Observer over them, and You are, over all things, Witness.
765. If You should punish them, indeed they are Your servants; but if You forgive them, indeed it is You who is the Exalted in Might, the Wise."
766. "Exalted are You! It was not for me to say that to which I have no right.
767. I said not to them except what You commanded me—to worship Allah, my Lord and your Lord.
768. The truth.
769. The truth.
770. Allah will say, "This is the Day when the truthful will benefit from their truthfulness." For them are gardens [in Paradise] beneath which rivers flow, wherein they will abide forever, Allah being pleased with them, and they with Him. That is the great attainment.
771. We did not create them except in truth, but most of them do not know.

وَالَّذِينَ آمَنُوا وَعَمِلُوا الصَّالِحَاتِ وَآمَنُوا بِمَا نُزِّلَ عَلَى مُحَمَّدٍ وَهُوَ الْحَقُّ مِن رَّبِّهِمْ كَفَّرَ عَنْهُمْ سَيِّئَاتِهِمْ وَأَصْلَحَ بَالَهُمْ 772{محمد/2} ذَلِكَ بِأَنَّ الَّذِينَ كَفَرُوا اتَّبَعُوا الْبَاطِلَ وَأَنَّ الَّذِينَ آمَنُوا اتَّبَعُوا الْحَقَّ مِن رَّبِّهِمْ كَذَلِكَ يَضْرِبُ اللَّهُ لِلنَّاسِ أَمْثَالَهُمْ 773{محمد/3}

وَلاَ تَلْبِسُوا الْحَقَّ بِالْبَاطِلِ وَتَكْتُمُوا الْحَقَّ وَأَنتُمْ تَعْلَمُونَ 774{البقرة/42}

The reality of death is certain as mentioned وَجَاءَتْ سَكْرَةُ الْمَوْتِ بِالْحَقِّ ذَلِكَ مَا كُنتَ مِنْهُ تَحِيدُ 775{ق/19}

One of the effects of the certainty and truth is that it affects hearts as mentioned أَلَمْ يَأْنِ لِلَّذِينَ آمَنُوا أَن تَخْشَعَ قُلُوبُهُمْ لِذِكْرِ اللَّهِ وَمَا نَزَلَ مِنَ الْحَقِّ وَلَا يَكُونُوا كَالَّذِينَ أُوتُوا الْكِتَابَ مِن قَبْلُ فَطَالَ عَلَيْهِمُ الْأَمَدُ فَقَسَتْ قُلُوبُهُمْ وَكَثِيرٌ مِّنْهُمْ فَاسِقُونَ 776{الحديد/16}.

Among them, there can be still the ones when they encounter with the absolute truth and reality of the Qurān and sunnah, they can be in the positions of وَإِذَا سَمِعُوا مَا أُنزِلَ إِلَى الرَّسُولِ تَرَى أَعْيُنَهُمْ تَفِيضُ مِنَ الدَّمْعِ مِمَّا عَرَفُوا مِنَ الْحَقِّ يَقُولُونَ رَبَّنَا آمَنَّا فَاكْتُبْنَا مَعَ الشَّاهِدِينَ 777{المائدة/83} وَمَا لَنَا لَا نُؤْمِنُ بِاللهِ وَمَا جَاءَنَا مِنَ الْحَقِّ وَنَطْمَعُ أَن يُدْخِلَنَا رَبُّنَا مَعَ الْقَوْمِ الصَّالِحِينَ 778{المائدة/84}

When absolute complete and all-inclusive religion Islam comes with its certainty all the other religions will be secondary although they may have some pieces of truth but not all as mentioned هُوَ الَّذِي أَرْسَلَ رَسُولَهُ بِالْهُدَى وَدِينِ الْحَقِّ لِيُظْهِرَهُ عَلَى الدِّينِ كُلِّهِ وَلَوْ كَرِهَ الْمُشْرِكُونَ 779{الصف/9}. هُوَ الَّذِي أَرْسَلَ رَسُولَهُ بِالْهُدَى وَدِينِ الْحَقِّ لِيُظْهِرَهُ عَلَى الدِّينِ كُلِّهِ وَلَوْ كَرِهَ الْمُشْرِكُونَ 780 {التوبة/33}

---

772. And those who believe and do righteous deeds and believe in what has been sent down upon Muhammad—and it is the truth from their Lord—He will remove from them their misdeeds and amend their condition.

773. That is because those who disbelieve follow falsehood, and those who believe follow the truth from their Lord. Thus does Allah present to the people their comparisons.

774. And do not mix the truth with falsehood or conceal the truth while you know [it].

775. And the intoxication of death will bring the truth; that is what you were trying to avoid.

776. Has the time not come for those who have believed that their hearts should become humbly submissive at the remembrance of Allah and what has come down of the truth? And let them not be like those who were given the Scripture before, and a long period passed over them, so their hearts hardened; and many of them are defiantly disobedient.

777. And when they hear what has been revealed to the Messenger, you see their eyes overflowing with tears because of what they have recognized of the truth. They say, "Our Lord, we have believed, so register us among the witnesses.

778. And why should we not believe in Allah and what has come to us of the truth? And we aspire that our Lord will admit us [to Paradise] with the righteous people."

779. It is He who sent His Messenger with guidance and the religion of truth to manifest it over all religion, although those who associate others with Allah dislike it.

780. It is He who has sent His Messenger with guidance and the religion of truth to manifest it over all religion, although they who associate others with Allah dislike it.

In other words, complete, perfect and healthy systems and institutions survive and unhealthy systems with bugs and holes will not have longevity. One of the hikmahs that the above ayahs are repeated in the Qurān due to its importance in religious affiliations when people are updating or choosing their religion.

Due to its importance, this notion of certainty with the word al-haqq is given both to a Sûrah and as to be the name of judgment day and accountability due to its pivotal role in human's worldly actions of decision making as mentioned {الحاقة/51}[781] وَإِنَّهُ لَحَقُّ الْيَقِينِ.

It is important to use the teachings of the Qurān and sunnah to give dawah and nasi'ah to people as mentioned إِلَّا الَّذِينَ آمَنُوا وَعَمِلُوا الصَّالِحَاتِ وَتَوَاصَوْا بِالْحَقِّ وَتَوَاصَوْا بِالصَّبْرِ[782] {العصر/3}.

It is important to know about Allah ﷻ with true knowledge and expectations as assigned by Allah ﷻ in the Qurān and sunnah of Rasulullah ﷺ as:

ثُمَّ أَنزَلَ عَلَيْكُم مِّن بَعْدِ الْغَمِّ أَمَنَةً نُّعَاسًا يَغْشَى طَآئِفَةً مِّنكُمْ وَطَآئِفَةٌ قَدْ أَهَمَّتْهُمْ أَنفُسُهُمْ يَظُنُّونَ بِاللّهِ غَيْرَ الْحَقِّ ظَنَّ الْجَاهِلِيَّةِ يَقُولُونَ هَل لَّنَا مِنَ الأَمْرِ مِن شَيْءٍ قُلْ إِنَّ الأَمْرَ كُلَّهُ للّهِ يُخْفُونَ فِي أَنفُسِهِم مَّا لاَ يُبْدُونَ لَكَ يَقُولُونَ لَوْ كَانَ لَنَا مِنَ الأَمْرِ شَيْءٌ مَّا قُتِلْنَا هَاهُنَا قُل لَّوْ كُنتُمْ فِي بُيُوتِكُمْ لَبَرَزَ الَّذِينَ كُتِبَ عَلَيْهِمُ الْقَتْلُ إِلَى مَضَاجِعِهِمْ وَلِيَبْتَلِيَ اللّهُ مَا فِي صُدُورِكُمْ وَلِيُمَحَّصَ مَا فِي قُلُوبِكُمْ وَاللّهُ عَلِيمٌ بِذَاتِ الصُّدُورِ[783] {آل عمران/154}

This is a divine assurance by Allah ﷻ about the unseen, afterlife and accountability as:وَالَّذِينَ آمَنُواْ وَعَمِلُواْ الصَّالِحَاتِ سَنُدْخِلُهُمْ جَنَّاتٍ تَجْرِي مِن تَحْتِهَا الأَنْهَارُ خَالِدِينَ فِيهَا أَبَدًا وَعْدَ اللّهِ حَقًّا وَمَنْ أَصْدَقُ مِنَ اللّهِ قِيلاً[784]{النساء/122}. In this

---

781. And indeed, it is the truth of certainty.
782. Except for those who have believed and done righteous deeds and advised each other to truth and advised each other to patience.
783. Then after distress, He sent down upon you security [in the form of] drowsiness, overcoming a faction of you, while another faction worried about themselves, thinking of Allah other than the truth—the thought of ignorance, saying, "Is there anything for us [to have done] in this matter?" Say, "Indeed, the matter belongs completely to Allah." They conceal within themselves what they will not reveal to you. They say, "If there was anything we could have done in the matter, we [i.e., some of us] would not have been killed right here." Say, "Even if you had been inside your houses, those decreed to be killed would have come out to their death beds." [It was] so that Allah might test what is in your breasts and purify what is in your hearts. And Allah is Knowing of that within the breasts.
784. But the ones who believe and do righteous deeds—We will admit them to gardens beneath which rivers flow, wherein they will abide forever. [It is] the promise of Allah, [which is] truth, and who is more truthful than Allah in statement.

ayah, the expression وَمَنْ أَصْدَقُ مِنَ اللهِ قِيلًا[785] puts another level of certainty to remove the doubts after وَعْدَ اللهَ حَقًّا[786]. It is like [787]نور على نور,

[788]اللهم اجعلنا من المنورين من نورك Here is a case of an absolute kāfir, may Allah ﷻ protect us, Ameen:

إِنَّ الَّذِينَ يَكْفُرُونَ بِاللهِ وَرُسُلِهِ وَيُرِيدُونَ أَن يُفَرِّقُواْ بَيْنَ اللهِ وَرُسُلِهِ وَيَقُولُونَ نُؤْمِنُ بِبَعْضٍ وَنَكْفُرُ بِبَعْضٍ وَيُرِيدُونَ أَن يَتَّخِذُواْ بَيْنَ ذَلِكَ سَبِيلًا[789] {النساء/150} أُوْلَئِكَ هُمُ الْكَافِرُونَ حَقًّا وَأَعْتَدْنَا لِلْكَافِرِينَ عَذَابًا مُهِينًا[790] {النساء/151}.

This case are the people who pick and choose, especially in the dispositions of the Qurān and sunnah. May Allah ﷻ protect us, Ameen.

This is an important ayah وَاتْلُ عَلَيْهِمْ نَبَأَ ابْنَيْ آدَمَ بِالْحَقِّ إِذْ قَرَّبَا قُرْبَانًا فَتُقُبِّلَ مِنْ أَحَدِهِمَا وَلَمْ يُتَقَبَّلْ مِنَ الآخَرِ قَالَ لَأَقْتُلَنَّكَ قَالَ إِنَّمَا يَتَقَبَّلُ اللهُ مِنَ الْمُتَّقِينَ[791] {المائدة/27}. Especially, in our renderings of religiosity and piety what is accepted by Allah ﷻ and not. It is not the apparent but our inner dispositions of heart and intention. The word بِالْحَقِّ[792] can indicate the necessity of teaching this core point of religiosity. The case of jealousy as indicated in the context of this ayah can be the same possible reason of religious acts of not acceptance by Allah ﷻ, similar to Shaytān in his rendering of Adam as.

Here are some cases of destruction of illusions, uncertainties, and doubts as:

وَلَوْ تَرَى إِذْ وُقِفُواْ عَلَى رَبِّهِمْ قَالَ أَلَيْسَ هَذَا بِالْحَقِّ قَالُواْ بَلَى وَرَبِّنَا قَالَ فَذُوقُواْ العَذَابَ بِمَا كُنتُمْ تَكْفُرُونَ[793] {الأنعام/30}

---

785. And who is more truthful than Allah in statement.
786. [It is] the promise of Allah, [which is] truth.
787. Light upon Light.
788. Oh Allah, make us enlightened by your light.
789. Indeed, those who disbelieve in Allah and His messengers and wish to discriminate between Allah and His messengers and say, "We believe in some and disbelieve in others," and wish to adopt a way in between—
790. Those are the disbelievers, truly. And We have prepared for the disbelievers a humiliating punishment.
791. O my people, enter the Holy Land [i.e., Palestine] which Allah has assigned to you and do not turn back [from fighting in Allah's cause] and [thus] become losers."
792. With the truth.
793. If you could but see when they will be made to stand before their Lord. He will say, "Is this not the truth?" They will say, "Yes, by our Lord." He will [then] say, "So taste the punishment for what you used to deny."

وَنَادَى أَصْحَابُ الْجَنَّةِ أَصْحَابَ النَّارِ أَن قَدْ وَجَدْنَا مَا وَعَدَنَا رَبُّنَا حَقًّا فَهَلْ وَجَدتُّم مَّا وَعَدَ رَبُّكُمْ حَقًّا قَالُواْ نَعَمْ فَأَذَّنَ مُؤَذِّنٌ بَيْنَهُمْ أَن لَّعْنَةُ اللّهِ عَلَى الظَّالِمِينَ ⁷⁹⁴{الأعراف/44}

May Allah ﷻ protect us, Ameen. These ayahs have shocking points because humans really need to think this disease of skepticism and doubt. These ayahs are antidotes with reality, certainty and full absoluteness to shock the person and destroy these diseases if the person can really open their eyes, astagfirullah, as mentioned: وَقُلْ جَاء الْحَقُّ وَزَهَقَ الْبَاطِلُ إِنَّ الْبَاطِلَ كَانَ زَهُوقًا⁷⁹⁵ {الإسراء/81} وَنُنَزِّلُ مِنَ الْقُرْآنِ مَا هُوَ شِفَاء وَرَحْمَةٌ لِّلْمُؤْمِنِينَ وَلاَ يَزِيدُ الظَّالِمِينَ إَلاَّ خَسَارًا ⁷⁹⁶{الإسراء/81}

One can see that the certainity of the reality from Allah ﷻ destroys all these skepticsims, doubts, fears, uncertainities. Then, the heart of the person has a healing effect with the Qurān, the absolute truth reality from Allah ﷻ as mentioned

Here is one of the Names and Attributes of Allah ﷻ as al-Haqq, the Real, ثُمَّ رُدُّواْ إِلَى اللّهِ مَوْلاَهُمُ الْحَقِّ أَلاَ لَهُ الْحُكْمُ وَهُوَ أَسْرَعُ الْحَاسِبِينَ ⁷⁹⁷ {الأنعام/62}.

هُنَالِكَ تَبْلُو كُلُّ نَفْسٍ مَّا أَسْلَفَتْ وَرُدُّواْ إِلَى اللّهِ مَوْلاَهُمُ الْحَقِّ وَضَلَّ عَنْهُم مَّا كَانُواْ يَفْتَرُونَ {يونس/30}

فَذَلِكُمُ اللّهُ رَبُّكُمُ الْحَقُّ فَمَاذَا بَعْدَ الْحَقِّ إِلاَّ الضَّلاَلُ فَأَنَّى تُصْرَفُونَ {يونس/32}

The reality of ours become full reality when we go back to Allah ﷻ, the Real. May Allah ﷻ protect us from a bad return of full reality and realization, Ameen.

In its reality, the illusionary states, doubts and uncertainties induce and instill fear because there is no basis for it. Everything is built on possibilities. Yet, there is a clear strong message as a book, the Qurān and as a messenger, Rasulullah ﷺ asserting with a full certain assertion about the reality, and the absolute unchanging truth. Then, one can ask

---

794. And the companions of Paradise will call out to the companions of the Fire, "We have already found what our Lord promised us to be true. Have you found what your Lord promised to be true?" They will say, "Yes." Then an announcer will announce among them, "The curse of Allah shall be upon the wrongdoers.
795. And say, "Truth has come, and falsehood has departed. Indeed is falsehood, [by nature], ever bound to depart."
796. And We send down of the Qurān that which is healing and mercy for the believers, but it does not increase the wrongdoers except in loss.
797. Then they [i.e., His servants] are returned to Allah, their true Lord. Unquestionably, His is the judgement, and He is the swiftest of accountants.

which group has or should be more in fear? The people of doubts don't have anything concrete in their hand. The people of imān they have a concrete Book and Messenger ﷺ. This theme is indicated in وَكَيْفَ أَخَافُ

مَا أَشْرَكْتُمْ وَلاَ تَخَافُونَ أَنَّكُمْ أَشْرَكْتُم بِاللّهِ مَا لَمْ يُنَزِّلْ بِهِ عَلَيْكُمْ سُلْطَانًا فَأَيُّ الْفَرِيقَيْنِ أَحَقُّ بِالأَمْنِ إِن كُنتُمْ تَعْلَمُونَ ⁷⁹⁸{الأنعام/81}

Allah ﷻ is al-Baqi⁷⁹⁹.Our knowledge about Allah ﷻ will always be in the approximations of the knowledge given by Allah ﷻ and Rasulullah ﷺ. The indication or practice of this knowledge can be called taqwa. As we increase and approximate the knowledge about Allah ﷻ on a pattern as guided by the Qurān and sunnah of Rasulullah ﷺ, we can really come to one conclusion that "we never can truly approximate our knowledge about Allah ﷻ" because Allah ﷻ is al-Baki, Our Creator. Yet we are all limited creation as mentioned ⁸⁰⁰ مَا قَدَرُوا اللَّهَ حَقَّ قَدْرِهِ إِنَّ اللَّهَ لَقَوِيٌّ عَزِيزٌ {الحج/74}

On the other hand, these approximations of knowledge about Allah ﷻ can be sometimes totally off the correct pattern when there is no guidance or the person is in their effect of nafs and Shaytān as mentioned: وَمَا قَدَرُوا اللَّهَ حَقَّ قَدْرِهِ إِذْ قَالُوا مَا أَنزَلَ اللَّهُ عَلَى بَشَرٍ مِّن شَيْءٍ قُلْ مَنْ أَنزَلَ الْكِتَابَ الَّذِي جَاء بِهِ مُوسَى نُورًا وَهُدًى لِّلنَّاسِ تَجْعَلُونَهُ قَرَاطِيسَ تُبْدُونَهَا وَتُخْفُونَ كَثِيرًا وَعُلِّمْتُم مَّا لَمْ تَعْلَمُوا أَنتُمْ وَلاَ آبَاؤُكُمْ قُلِ اللَّهُ ثُمَّ ذَرْهُمْ فِي خَوْضِهِمْ يَلْعَبُونَ ⁸⁰¹{الأنعام/91}

In the above verses one can translate قَدَرُوا as the approximation of knowledge of about Allah ﷻ. Having an idea or understanding about Allah ﷻ that Allah ﷻ did not send any prophets or books to humans for their guidance, is a full wrong pattern of human thoughts about Allah ﷻ. Similar approaches of incorrect human approximations can be seen when they associate partners or children with the One Who is Far from these claims,⁸⁰² سبحان الله عما يصفون . This itself is a big slander as mentioned:

---

798. And how should I fear what you associate while you do not fear that you have associated with Allah that for which He has not sent down to you any authority? So which of the two parties has more right to security, if you should know?"

799. The Everlasting.

800. They have not appraised Allah with true appraisal. Indeed, Allah is Powerful and Exalted in Might.

801. And they did not appraise Allah with true appraisal when they said, "Allah did not reveal to a human being anything." Say, "Who revealed the Scripture that Moses brought as light and guidance to the people? You [Jews] make it into pages, disclosing [some of] it and concealing much. And you291 were taught that which you knew not—neither you nor your fathers." Say, "Allah [revealed it]." Then leave them in their [empty] discourse, amusing themselves.

802. Glory be to god about what they describe.

وَمَنْ أَظْلَمُ مِمَّنِ افْتَرَى عَلَى اللّهِ كَذِبًا أَوْ قَالَ أُوحِيَ إِلَيَّ وَلَمْ يُوحَ إِلَيْهِ شَيْءٌ وَمَن قَالَ سَأُنزِلُ مِثْلَ مَا أَنزَلَ اللّهُ وَلَوْ تَرَى إِذِ الظَّالِمُونَ فِي غَمَرَاتِ الْمَوْتِ وَالْمَلآئِكَةُ بَاسِطُواْ أَيْدِيهِمْ أَخْرِجُواْ أَنفُسَكُمُ الْيَوْمَ تُجْزَوْنَ عَذَابَ الْهُونِ بِمَا كُنتُمْ تَقُولُونَ عَلَى اللّهِ غَيْرَ الْحَقِّ وَكُنتُمْ عَنْ آيَاتِهِ تَسْتَكْبِرُونَ803 {الأنعام/93}

One review the definition of a mu'min with its reality and certainty as وَالَّذِينَ آمَنُواْ وَهَاجَرُواْ وَجَاهَدُواْ فِي سَبِيلِ اللّهِ وَالَّذِينَ آوَواْ وَّنَصَرُواْ أُولَئِكَ هُمُ الْمُؤْمِنُونَ حَقًّا لَّهُم مَّغْفِرَةٌ وَرِزْقٌ كَرِيمٌ804 {الأنفال/74}

805.اللهم اجعلنا منهمOne can see that these realities of truth, certainty, and absolute reality is not new with the Qurān, Rasulullah ﷺ and the Islam but Allah ﷻ mentioned these unchanging realities, these universals, in the Tawrah and injil, before as mentioned:

إِنَّ اللّهَ اشْتَرَى مِنَ الْمُؤْمِنِينَ أَنفُسَهُمْ وَأَمْوَالَهُم بِأَنَّ لَهُمُ الجَنَّةَ يُقَاتِلُونَ فِي سَبِيلِ اللّهِ فَيَقْتُلُونَ وَيُقْتَلُونَ وَعْدًا عَلَيْهِ حَقًّا فِي التَّوْرَاةِ وَالإِنجِيلِ وَالْقُرْآنِ وَمَنْ أَوْفَى بِعَهْدِهِ مِنَ اللّهِ فَاسْتَبْشِرُواْ بِبَيْعِكُمُ الَّذِي بَايَعْتُم بِهِ وَذَلِكَ هُوَ الْفَوْزُ الْعَظِيمُ806 {التوبة/111}

The categorization of real versus not real, illusionary, or correct versus and incorrect, or certainty versus doubts leading to going off track is mentioned with فَذَلِكُمُ اللّهُ رَبُّكُمُ الْحَقُّ فَمَاذَا بَعْدَ الْحَقِّ إِلاَّ الضَّلاَلُ فَأَنَّى تُصْرَفُونَ807 {يونس/32}

Here is a very logical case of choice: if one is leading you to a certain, correct and real then why don't you follow? Are you still going to follow uncertain, incorrect and illusionary? This can be rendered from قُلْ هَلْ

---

803. And who is more unjust than one who invents a lie about Allah or says, "It has been inspired to me," while nothing has been inspired to him, and one who says, "I will reveal [something] like what Allah revealed." And if you could but see when the wrongdoers are in the overwhelming pangs of death while the angels extend their hands, [saying], "Discharge your souls! Today you will be awarded the punishment of [extreme] humiliation for what you used to say against Allah other than the truth and [that] you were, toward His verses, being arrogant."

804. But those who have believed and emigrated and fought in the cause of Allah and those who gave shelter and aided—it is they who are the believers, truly. For them is forgiveness and noble provision.

805. Oh Allah, Make us from among them.

806. Indeed, Allah has purchased from the believers their lives and their properties [in exchange] for that they will have Paradise. They fight in the cause of Allah, so they kill and are killed. [It is] a true promise [binding] upon Him in the Torah and the Gospel and the Qurān. And who is truer to his covenant than Allah? So rejoice in your transaction which you have contracted. And it is that which is the great attainment.

807. For that is Allah, your Lord, the Truth. And what can be beyond truth except error? So how are you averted?

مِن شُرَكَآئِكُم مَّن يَهْدِي إِلَى الْحَقِّ قُلِ اللَّهُ يَهْدِي لِلْحَقِّ أَفَمَن يَهْدِي إِلَى الْحَقِّ أَحَقُّ أَن يُتَّبَعَ أَمَّن لاَّ يَهِدِّيَ إِلاَّ أَن يُهْدَى فَمَا لَكُمْ كَيْفَ تَحْكُمُونَ 808 {يونس/35} وَمَا يَتَّبِعُ أَكْثَرُهُمْ إِلاَّ ظَنًّا إِنَّ الظَّنَّ لاَ يُغْنِي مِنَ الْحَقِّ شَيْئًا إِنَّ اللَّهَ عَلَيمٌ بِمَا يَفْعَلُونَ 809 {يونس/36} Still, even they see this difference they still run behind the whimsical claims of assertions, doubts and uncertainties.

The importance of the unchanging assurance and promise of Allah ﷻ is mentioned in the ayah as 810 وَيُحِقُّ اللَّهُ الْحَقَّ بِكَلِمَاتِهِ وَلَوْ كَرِهَ الْمُجْرِمُونَ {82/يونس} with the word811 بِكَلِمَاتِهِ. It is interesting to see that Shaytān also reveals one of the sources of doubt and exposes about the disposition of certainty, reality and truth are all from Allah ﷻ as mentioned وَقَالَ الشَّيْطَانُ لَمَّا قُضِيَ الأَمْرُ إِنَّ اللَّهَ وَعَدَكُمْ وَعْدَ الْحَقِّ وَوَعَدتُّكُمْ فَأَخْلَفْتُكُمْ وَمَا كَانَ لِيَ عَلَيْكُم مِّن سُلْطَانٍ إِلاَّ أَن دَعَوْتُكُمْ فَاسْتَجَبْتُمْ لِي فَلاَ تَلُومُونِي وَلُومُوا أَنفُسَكُم مَّا أَنَاْ بِمُصْرِخِكُمْ وَمَا أَنتُمْ بِمُصْرِخِيَّ إِنِّي كَفَرْتُ بِمَا أَشْرَكْتُمُونِ مِن قَبْلُ إِنَّ الظَّالِمِينَ لَهُمْ عَذَابٌ أَلِيمٌ 812 {إبراهيم/22}

Sometimes, malaikah813 can assure the true disposition certainty and reality to the people of imān when they are in the verge of difficulties, hardships and trials as mentioned in order to remove their doubts, strength their position and istiqamah as mentioned:

قَالُواْ بَشَّرْنَاكَ بِالْحَقِّ فَلاَ تَكُن مِّنَ الْقَانِطِينَ 814 {الحجر/55}

وَأَتَيْنَاكَ بَالْحَقِّ وَإِنَّا لَصَادِقُونَ 815 {الحجر/64}

One can see that the certainty of the reality from Allah ﷻ destroys all these diseases of skepticisms, doubts, fears, uncertainties. Then, the heart of the person has a healing effect with the Qurān, the absolute truth reality from Allah ﷻ as mentioned وَقُلْ جَاء الْحَقُّ وَزَهَقَ الْبَاطِلُ إِنَّ الْبَاطِلَ

---

808. Say, "Are there of your 'partners' any who guides to the truth?" Say, "Allah guides to the truth. So is He who guides to the truth more worthy to be followed or he who guides not unless he is guided? Then what is [wrong] with you—how do you judge?"

809. And most of them follow not except assumption. Indeed, assumption avails not against the truth at all. Indeed, Allah is Knowing of what they do.

810. And Allah will establish the truth by His words, even if the criminals dislike it."

811. By His words.

812. And Satan will say when the matter has been concluded, "Indeed, Allah had promised you the promise of truth. And I promised you, but I betrayed you. But I had no authority over you except that I invited you, and you responded to me. So do not blame me; but blame yourselves. I cannot be called to your aid, nor can you be called to my aid. Indeed, I deny your association of me [with Allah] before. Indeed, for the wrongdoers is a painful punishment."

813. Angels

814. They said, "We have given you good tidings in truth, so do not be of the despairing."

815. And we have come to you with truth, and indeed, we are truthful.

كَانَ زَهُوقًا816 {الإسراء/81} وَنُنَزِّلُ مِنَ الْقُرْآنِ مَا هُوَ شِفَاء وَرَحْمَةٌ لِّلْمُؤْمِنِينَ وَلَا يَزِيدُ الظَّالِمِينَ إَلاَّ خَسَارًا817 {الإسراء/82}

One of the important points is that the people of knowledge is expected to recognize these realities, and certainties as mentioned وَلِيَعْلَمَ الَّذِينَ أُوتُوا الْعِلْمَ أَنَّهُ الْحَقُّ مِن رَّبِّكَ فَيُؤْمِنُوا بِهِ فَتُخْبِتَ لَهُ قُلُوبُهُمْ وَإِنَّ اللَّهَ لَهَادِ الَّذِينَ آمَنُوا إِلَى صِرَاطٍ مُّسْتَقِيمٍ818 {الحج/54}

Rasulullahﷺ gave assurances to the person. In a tahajjud dua, when the person wakes up in the middle of the night with fears, concerns, and self-accountability of checks and balances of their personal lives, these feelings and thoughts especially in the middle of of the night while being alone can be scary, depressive, and fearing.

At this time, when the mind and heart are fresh with silence and solitude, either the person can try to suppress all these mental and emotional states with depressant drug and sleeping aid. Or, he or she may read the tahajjud dua of Rasulullah ﷺ transforming the person from these depressive states into the fruitful opening states of certainty with this word819 الْحَقُّ as constantly repeated to assure the person about the reality, the truth, the unseen, the purpose and meanings in life. So that the person is not fearful depressive or panicking but now in certain states of assurance.

Yet, humans constantly forget as the word al-insan can require, then these routine practices become key in the form of 'ibadah and regularity. Rasulullah ﷺ as the applier of the Qurān shows us the meanings of الْحَقُّ, by applying it in our practice and dua to be the people of yaqin, certain and الْحَقُّ.

اللهم اجعلنا من المتهاجين. امين820.

One of the Names and Attributes of Allah ﷻ is al-Haqq. In the cases of doubt, uncertainty, depression and waswasa821, one can repeat this

---

816. And say, "Truth has come, and falsehood has departed. Indeed is falsehood, [by nature], ever bound to depart."

817. And We send down of the Qurān that which is healing and mercy for the believers, but it does not increase the wrongdoers except in loss.

818. And so those who were given knowledge may know that it is the truth from your Lord and [therefore] believe in it, and their hearts humbly submit to it. And indeed is Allah the Guide of those who have believed to a straight path.

819. The truth.

820. Oh Allah, make us from among those who pray tahajjud. Ameen.

821. Whispers in the heart. {From shaytaan}.

Name of Allah ﷻ with its number (108) of abjad to transform oneself to
the light trainquil and sakina states of certainty.

When a person goes against the social norms of their society, he or
she frequently becomes an outcast. This is because the person takes a
position against everyone. The flow of social norms can be similar to the
water flowing with a strong speed in Niagara Falls. Therefore, a person
should be very strong to be able to live, stand, and try to flow against this
strong flow. Furthermore, to change the flow of this speedy and strong
water in Niagara Falls is impossible unless there is a miracle. Similarly,
changing the flow of social norms in another direction indicates and
proves the prophethood of Rasulullah ﷺ. It is a miracle that Allah ﷻ
enables this social change through the prophethood of Rasulullah ﷺ.
Today, there are close to two billion followers of Islam. This miracle
itself shows the prophethood of Rasulullah ﷺ is haqq, truth, real and
authentic from Allah ﷻ.

When Rasulullah ﷺ brought the new teachings of Islam, as time
passed the number of Muslims increased. Islam has become a natural
and adaptable religion for humanity.

One can consider Rasulullah ﷺ was an ummi and that he did not
have a power in the society through wealth or position. He ﷺ did not
have any interest and inclination for power and wealth.

With the prophethood, he ﷺ took a very sober duty challenging the
existing norms and teachings. He overpowered all different ideologies,
and norms. Everyone loved him ﷺ. He ﷺ overpowered all established
behaviors and mannerisms. He ﷺ removed all the wild and evil customs
from the hearts. He ﷺ removed all the ugly and evil values and replaced
it with noble and beautiful norms and moral values.

He ﷺ removed wildness of darkness and harshness from the hearts
in the deserts and replaced with sensitive, genuine, merciful and caring
traits in the same hearts. The real and true reality of humanity reverted
to itself with his teachings ﷺ. Rasulullah ﷺ took them from the corners
of wilderness to the upper corners of civilization by making them
teachers of their time and their countries.

One can think about the injustices that are happening today.
Although we much popularize the words discrimination, justice,
fairness, equality and others in order to establish some fair social norms
and policies, there are a lot of oppressions happening in different parts
of the world.

In this regard, although there are some personal good traits and some good social norms in tribal systems, one was not able to even pronounce and popularize the phrases of discrimination, justice, fairness, and equality in that society. When we compare the pre-Islamic society with ours possibly we can say that we can be viewed as more civilized in some manners.

After Islam, one can review the focused and dense therapeutic and meditative individual changes in Makkah. These changes continue in Madinah after the migration. Yet, in Madinah, one can witness policy level changes with social structure and order in a Muslim community as the Muslims were trying to establish their first communal society.

In this perspective, one can analyze the movement started by Rasulullah 靉 against the injustices, unfairness, discrimination and oppression with the teachings of the Qurān and sunnah. Then, there is an establishment of a society with these social norms, beliefs and values.

Then, in further stages, during the time of Rasulullah 靉 and after his demise 靉, there has been the spread of these teachings, changing the entire social norms, beliefs, and values in different countries, regions and continents. The gist of these teachings is to upgrade the lost human dignity by reminding them about these lost teachings of fairness, justice, equality, and non-discriminatory policies.

This is similar to someone thirsty who is seeking water. Once he or she finds it, they drink it without hesitation. In this regard, the message of Islam was delivered to different societies, communities, regions, and people with different means. Our focus here is not the means of delivery but it is aftermath of acceptance, adaptation, permanency, durability, and continuity of these teachings. Similar to the thirsty man looking for water, he accepted the water because he needed it. The societies accepted teachings of Islam because they needed them. If there was no need the message would not be permanent. After its initial affects, it could have been lost. The teachings of Islām have stayed and became permanent in different continents.All of this acceptance, full and radical personal and communal changes in short periods can emphasize and dictate the truth, al-haqq, about the message of the Qurān and Rasulullah 靉. They all indicate the authenticity of the Prophet 靉.

In this perspective, one can review the Islamic history that once the message of Islam is delivered and accepted then, there has been no rejection at a full society level of the message of Islām. Yes, there is always the problem of practice among Muslims and then accordingly, there has been emerging apparent conflicts. Yet, almost no one has challenged and rejected the core values as presented by the Qurān and Rasulullah ﷺ in Islamic history. We are not mentioning a few possible individual cases due to their statistical insignificance among approximately two billion Muslims today and many more in the past.

There are definite and clear reasons for the absence of opposing cases to the core theology brought by the Qurān and Rasulullah ﷺ. There are definite and clear reason for the increasing number of Muslims. These reasons are the authenticity, plausibility, universality, objectivity, fairness, applicability, practicality, precision, harmony, and correctness of the teachings of the Qurān and Rasulullah ﷺ. This increase of Muslims was not due to missionary efforts of spreading these teachings.

One could have expected the opposite today due to negative representation of Islam in media and efforts of eliminating Islamic teachings through colonialism and post colonialism engagements in the recent history. One could have expected decreasing number of Muslims. Finally, one could have expected the fading off Islām due to both mental, psychological and power related efforts of renderings to demonize and abolish it.

Yet, once there is a reasonable and plausible teaching, it stays there as universals donot disappear. Similarly, the teachings of the Qurān and Rasulullah ﷺ are all universals. No one can eliminate them once they are in our realms of human reality.

Therefore, the increase of Muslims is due to natural acceptance of the reasonability of the Qurān and sunnah of Rasulullah ﷺ and following their universal teachings.

Middle Way in Understanding of Prophethood-Rasulullah ﷺ

When we consider different people in history, he or she can be polymath in a few subjects or fields. When we talk about today's field of expertise, people focus on one discipline or subjects, then they are called experts in that field. If they have the skills and means to excel in that field.

When one analyzes the life of Rasulullah ﷺ, one can witness the field of expertise in every field of life. It is as if Rasulullah ﷺ and other prophets of Allah ﷻ mention the guiding principles in each field and science that humanity can reach. This cannot be possible unless this expertise and perfection in all different lives are present with the enablement, Fadl and Tawfik of Allah ﷻ.

One can consider the balance and middleway of understanding in the approach of Prophethood. Prophets are people and humans. Yet, their actions are all guided by Allah ﷻ. They don't talk from their own ego as mentioned for Rasulullah {النجم/3} وَمَا يَنطِقُ عَنِ الْهَوَى [822]. Therefore, another form of revelation is gayru-matluw which are the practices of Rasulullah ﷺ. Since, Rasulullah ﷺ does not converse or practice from himself and everything is guided by Allah ﷻ, then his actions and all statements becomes another source of Divine teaching called as sunnah and hadith as mentioned: إِنْ {النجم/3}[823] وَمَا يَنطِقُ عَنِ الْهَوَى هُوَ إِلَّا وَحْيٌ يُوحَى [824]{النجم/4}

According to most of the muffasirûn[825],[826] مَا يَنطِقُ عَنِ الْهَوَى refers to the Qurān. The mufassir such as salabi and makki (rh), they mention that the ayah refers to Rasulullah ﷺ.

In understanding of the Prophethood, there are two different extremes. One is referring them as simple humans who do not know anything but they are claiming prophethood but they have alternative motives such as calling them sāhir[827], position seekers or other assertions as mentioned:

كَذَّبَتْ قَبْلَهُمْ قَوْمُ نُوحٍ فَكَذَّبُوا عَبْدَنَا وَقَالُوا مَجْنُونٌ وَازْدُجِرَ [828]{القمر/9}

قَالَ الْمَلَأُ مِن قَوْمِ فِرْعَوْنَ إِنَّ هَذَا لَسَاحِرٌ عَلِيمٌ [829]{الأعراف/109}

فَقَالَ الْمَلَأُ الَّذِينَ كَفَرُوا مِن قَوْمِهِ مَا هَذَا إِلَّا بَشَرٌ مِّثْلُكُمْ يُرِيدُ أَن يَتَفَضَّلَ عَلَيْكُمْ وَلَوْ شَاء اللَّهُ لَأَنزَلَ مَلَائِكَةً مَّا سَمِعْنَا بِهَذَا فِي آبَائِنَا الْأَوَّلِينَ [830]{المؤمنون/24}

---

822. Nor does he speak from [his own] inclination.
823. Nor does he speak from [his own] inclination.
824. It is not but a revelation revealed,
825. People who explain the Qurān.
826. Nor does he speak from [his own] inclination.
827. A person who practices magic.
828. The people of Noah denied before them, and they denied Our servant and said, "A madman," and he was repelled.
829. Said the eminent among the people of Pharaoh, "Indeed, this is a learned magician.
830. But the eminent among those who disbelieved from his people said, "This is not but a man like yourselves who wishes to take precedence over you; and if Allah had willed [to send a messenger], He would have sent down angels. We have not heard of this among our forefathers.

Another extreme is divinizing them due to their miracles and truthful engagements and overseeing their human features as mentioned:

وَقَالُوا اتَّخَذَ الرَّحْمَنُ وَلَدًا سُبْحَانَهُ بَلْ عِبَادٌ مُكْرَمُونَ {الأنبياء/26}[831] لَا يَسْبِقُونَهُ بِالْقَوْلِ وَهُم بِأَمْرِهِ يَعْمَلُونَ {الأنبياء/27}[832]

وَإِذْ قَالَ اللهُ يَا عِيسَى ابْنَ مَرْيَمَ أَأَنتَ قُلْتَ لِلنَّاسِ اتَّخِذُونِي وَأُمِّيَ إِلَهَيْنِ مِن دُونِ اللهِ قَالَ سُبْحَانَكَ مَا يَكُونُ لِي أَنْ أَقُولَ مَا لَيْسَ لِي بِحَقٍّ إِن كُنتُ قُلْتُهُ فَقَدْ عَلِمْتَهُ تَعْلَمُ مَا فِي نَفْسِي وَلَا أَعْلَمُ مَا فِي نَفْسِكَ إِنَّكَ أَنتَ عَلَّامُ الْغُيُوبِ {المائدة/116}[833]

Both above cases are extremes. The balance and middleway of Islam in understanding the prophethood is that prophets are humans and Rasulullah ﷺ was a human being:

وَمَا أَرْسَلْنَا قَبْلَكَ إِلَّا رِجَالًا نُّوحِي إِلَيْهِمْ فَاسْأَلُوا أَهْلَ الذِّكْرِ إِن كُنتُمْ لَا تَعْلَمُونَ[834] {الأنبياء/7} وَمَا جَعَلْنَاهُمْ جَسَدًا لَّا يَأْكُلُونَ الطَّعَامَ وَمَا كَانُوا خَالِدِينَ[835] {الأنبياء/8}

But, they, Rasulullah ﷺ and the prophets of Allah ﷻ, were not ordinary people but they were إِنَّا أَخْلَصْنَاهُم بِخَالِصَةٍ ذِكْرَى الدَّارِ {ص/46}[836] وَإِنَّهُمْ عِندَنَا لَمِنَ الْمُصْطَفَيْنَ الْأَخْيَارِ {ص/47}[837]. Rasulullah ﷺ is the messenger of Allah ﷻ. He was enabled by Allah ﷻ to deliver the message of the Qurān. He was enabled to show us the teachings of the Qurān in his life with the sahabah (ranhum) referred as sunnah or hadith. This is the balanced and middle way of two approaches when one reviews the responsibility of prophethood in Islam.

When there is a statement from a person, one can judge the profundity and complexity of this statement. A statement, a sentence, or a phrase can indicate the ignorance of a person. Yet, at the same time a

---

831. And they say, "The Most Merciful has taken a son." Exalted is He! Rather, they are [but] honored servants.

832. They cannot precede Him in word, and they act by His command.

833. By which Allah guides those who pursue His pleasure to the ways of peace and brings them out from darknesses into the light, by His permission, and guides them to a straight path.

834. And We sent not before you, [O Muhammad], except men to whom We revealed [the message], so ask the people of the message [i.e., former scriptures] if you do not know.

835. And We did not make them [i.e., the prophets] forms not eating food, nor were they immortal [on earth].

836. Indeed, We chose them for an exclusive quality: remembrance of the home [of the Hereafter].

837. And indeed they are, to Us, among the chosen and outstanding.

sentence, a phrase or a statement can indicate wisdom, intelligence, and profundity of another person.

When one reviews and analyzes the Qurān, there is a striking unusual obvious and clear distinction of the style of the Qurān from ordinary human speech. The style of the Qurān has the siyāq and sibāq, pre and post, inclusion of meanings, the wholistic approach of the overall meaning, the literature charging the emotions, senses and spiritual states and at the same time comforting the mind and intellect with sometimes simple, sometimes dense, and sometimes counterpart and symmetric meanings and varieties.

When one reviews and analyzes the Hadith, there is a noticeable excellence of the style of the hadith from ordinary human speech. It has short but dense meanings. There is the relevancy of the speech according to the audience, time, and addressing different level of learners.

With above considerations, one can realize that the Prophethood of Rasulullah ﷺ is al-Haqq, the truth. A man who is known to be illiterate in the society cannot claim the above speeches, statements or texts unless there is the miraculous enablement, Tawfîq, of Allah ﷻ, similar to prior true prophets of Allah ﷻ.

Freshness of Teachings

If there is a teaching, its value can change depending on the time and era. One can consider advances and applications of technology today. For example, a simple smartphone today can be used by a child. This is a very ordinary practice today.If we assume the presence of this same simple smartphone a few hundred years ago, then it would have been considered as a miracle and as something very extraordinary.

In another words, past's miracle today can become ordinary today. Similarly, if one reviews the ayahs of the Qurān and teachings of the Rasulullah ﷺ, these teachings are always fresh, new and inspiring. All the new discoveries through natural and social sciences support and strength this fresh disposition of the Qurān and sunnah of Rasulullah ﷺ.

This itself can show that both the Qurān and Rasulullah ﷺ is al-haqq, the truth.

Audience Based Instruction

When a person is teaching a subject to an audience, the target audience affects the presentation of the subject matter according to their understanding level. Due to this simple looking principle, current world education system of both K-12 and higher education are based on molding the same knowledge with detail with their content and then, accordingly presenting this knowledge to the different target audience.

K at the kindergarten level is the first schooling age around six to seven years old age starting to receive basic tools of learning such as reading, writing and identifying objects through texts. Then, with incrementation of levels through 1, 2, up to 12 with the growth and aging, the knowledge is increased with the increase in content. In this incrementation through grades and aging, the analysis, deductions, critical thinking, forming opinions and conclusions are embedded. Then, at the levels of higher education, specialization and expertise are expected. This is due to the limited human capacity of the need to focus. This is due to the increasing trends of the need for the people in the markets for specialized individuals in different fields.

In the above cases, one can find billions of books written for different age groups and for different fields of expertise to address different target audience with their age, understanding, expertise and background.

When we review the Qurān, the Qurān is the one book from Rabbul A'lamin , the Creator of all universes, galaxies, everything and everyone.

In this sense, according to Imam Ghazali and Ibn Abbas [27], each of the ayahs of the Qurān has more than sixty thousand meanings. This perspective can emphasize and correspond to the audience-based instruction depending on the time, context and emerging fields until the end of days with emerging inventions and discoveries.

In a more specific sense, the differentiation of the Qurān between muhkam[838] and mutashabih[839] can allude to the audience based teaching as explicitly mentioned:

هُوَ الَّذِيَ أَنزَلَ عَلَيْكَ الْكِتَابَ مِنْهُ آيَاتٌ مُحْكَمَاتٌ هُنَّ أُمُّ الْكِتَابِ وَأُخَرُ مُتَشَابِهَاتٌ فَأَمَّا الَّذِينَ فِي قُلُوبِهِمْ زَيْغٌ فَيَتَّبِعُونَ مَا تَشَابَهَ مِنْهُ ابْتِغَاء الْفِتْنَةِ وَابْتِغَاء تَأْوِيلِهِ وَمَا يَعْلَمُ تَأْوِيلَهُ

---

838. Precise.
839. Unspecific.

إِلاَّ اللّهُ وَالرَّاسِخُونَ فِي الْعِلْمِ يَقُولُونَ آمَنَّا بِهِ كُلٌّ مِّنْ عِندِ رَبِّنَا وَمَا يَذَّكَّرُ إِلاَّ أُوْلُواْ الأَلْبَابِ
{آل عمران/7}[840].

This ayah specifically indicates the classification of the ayahs as muhkam which have more clear, explicit and inclusive general guidelines and principles for all levels of learners with the approximation of the human language as mentioned مِنْهُ آيَاتٌ مُّحْكَمَاتٌ هُنَّ أُمُّ الْكِتَابِ[841]. Yet, the ayahs classified as mutashabih can require more expertise understanding and explanation as mentioned وَمَا يَعْلَمُ تَأْوِيلَهُ إِلاَّ اللّهُ وَالرَّاسِخُونَ فِي الْعِلْمِ يَقُولُونَ آمَنَّا بِهِ كُلٌّ مِّنْ عِندِ رَبِّنَا وَمَا يَذَّكَّرُ إِلاَّ أُوْلُواْ الأَلْبَابِ[842] {آل عمران/7}, especially when they are presented to the public.

In addition, the ayahs that seem to repeat with some differences and additions in the Qurān can indicate today's differentiated instruction, similar to different grade levels in education as mentioned اللّهُ نَزَّلَ أَحْسَنَ الْحَدِيثِ كِتَابًا مُّتَشَابِهًا مَّثَانِيَ تَقْشَعِرُّ مِنْهُ جُلُودُ الَّذِينَ يَخْشَوْنَ رَبَّهُمْ ثُمَّ تَلِينُ جُلُودُهُمْ وَقُلُوبُهُمْ إِلَى ذِكْرِ اللّهِ ذَلِكَ هُدَى اللّهِ يَهْدِي بِهِ مَن يَشَاء وَمَن يُضْلِلْ اللّهُ فَمَا لَهُ مِنْ هَادٍ[843] {الزمر/23}. There are some additions and expansions of knowledge in each grade levels in current and traditional systems of the education.

Similarly, the words مُّتَشَابِهًا مَّثَانِيَ[844] can indicate this repetition,[845] مَّثَانِيَ, in similar looking ayahs. Yet, there can be some incremental learning by few changes in the similar looking ayahs,[846] مُّتَشَابِهًا. Yet, these are all miraculous and excellent teaching methods of the Qurān. Today's

---

840. It is He who has sent down to you, [O Muhammad], the Book; in it are verses [that are] precise—they are the foundation of the Book—and others unspecific. As for those in whose hearts is deviation [from truth], they will follow that of it which is unspecific, seeking discord and seeking an interpretation [suitable to them]. And no one knows its [true] interpretation except Allah. But those firm in knowledge say, "We believe in it. All [of it] is from our Lord." And no one will be reminded except those of understanding.
841. In it are verses [that are] precise—they are the foundation of the Book
842. It is He who has sent down to you, [O Muhammad], the Book; in it are verses [that are] precise—they are the foundation of the Book—and others unspecific. As for those in whose hearts is deviation [from truth], they will follow that of it which is unspecific, seeking discord and seeking an interpretation [suitable to them]. And no one knows its [true] interpretation except Allah. But those firm in knowledge say, "We believe in it. All [of it] is from our Lord." And no one will be reminded except those of understanding.
843. Allah has sent down the best statement: a consistent Book wherein is reiteration. The skins shiver therefrom of those who fear their Lord; then their skins and their hearts relax at the remembrance [i.e., mention] of Allah. That is the guidance of Allah by which He guides whom He wills. And one whom Allah leaves astray—for him there is no guide.
844. Consistent book wherein is reiteration.
845. Consistent.
846. Wherein is reiteration.

educational systems finally adapt and use methodologies in the state wide secular mandated grade level curriculums.

This incremental learning and context and audience-based teaching is embedded in the piece by piece revelation of the Qurān in 23 years. It is interesting to note that the current ayah number is 23 in this discussion as another billion miracles of the Qurān as اللَّهُ نَزَّلَ أَحْسَنَ الْحَدِيثِ كِتَابًا مُتَشَابِهًا مَّثَانِيَ تَقْشَعِرُّ مِنْهُ جُلُودُ الَّذِينَ يَخْشَوْنَ رَبَّهُمْ ثُمَّ تَلِينُ جُلُودُهُمْ وَقُلُوبُهُمْ إِلَى ذِكْرِ اللَّهِ ذَٰلِكَ هُدَى اللَّهِ يَهْدِي بِهِ مَنْ يَشَاءُ وَمَن يُضْلِلِ اللَّهُ فَمَا لَهُ مِنْ هَادٍ [847]{الزمر/23}.

As a side note, miracles are nothing more than the revealing of the true realities by removing the possible barriers with seen and unseen realities. In this regard, the person reaches to a certain yaqin that if there are more miracles, the person can say "it is not going to increase my imān because I am already there. I am at hundred percent." One can call this as the state of a'ynal yaqin in dunya before akhirah. Ali (ra) mentions a similar statement.

At this level, the person enters to the world of amazements. He or she is now in constant world of amazements. Everything completes the jigsaw puzzle with their meanings. Everything in life makes sense, comprehensive and matching. Life and death now become and have absoluteness in its true meaning and purpose. Death and life have a harmony together but they don't conflict.

For some people, who have the true ihsān, life and death really may not mean much because, they continue their ihsān in this world, in their grave and afterlife. Even, for some, they may have their experience with ihsān before this life such as in qawlu bala that there is no gap or hole. For this exceptional people of Allah SWT, the namings or experiences death and life does not have much meaning. They are the same linear function without any gap or breaking points.

Then, these states naturally puts the person in verbal and heart embodiment of the dhikr, "[848]سبحان الله[849]، الله اكبر[850]، لا اله الا الله" as mentioned [851] تَقْشَعِرُّ مِنْهُ جُلُودُ الَّذِينَ يَخْشَوْنَ رَبَّهُمْ ثُمَّ تَلِينُ جُلُودُهُمْ وَقُلُوبُهُمْ إِلَى ذِكْرِ اللَّهِ.

---

847. Allah has sent down the best statement: a consistent Book wherein is reiteration. The skins shiver therefrom of those who fear their Lord; then their skins and their hearts relax at the remembrance [i.e., mention] of Allah. That is the guidance of Allah by which He guides whom He wills. And one whom Allah leaves astray—for him there is no guide.

848. Theres no God except Allah.

849. Glory be to Allah.

850. Allah is the greatest.

851. The skins shiver therefrom of those who fear their Lord; then their skins and their hearts relax at the remembrance [i.e., mention] of Allah.

Then, due to this Fadl[852] of Allah ﷻ as mentioned بِهِ يَهْدِي اللَّهُ هُدَى ذَلِكَ[853] تَقْشَعِرُّ مِنْهُ جُلُودُ الَّذِينَ يَخْشَوْنَ رَبَّهُمْ ثُمَّ تَلِينُ جُلُودُهُمْ وَقُلُوبُهُمْ إِلَى ذِكْرِ مَنْ يَشَاء in the ayah .اللَّهِ ذَلِكَ هُدَى اللَّهِ يَهْدِي بِهِ مَنْ يَشَاءُ وَمَنْ يُضْلِلِ اللَّهُ فَمَا لَهُ مِنْ هَادٍ[854] {الزمر/23}

Then, the person lives a life of Jannah in this world before death and continues this life after death as well. But, all these require the dhikr of thankfulness, gratitude and appreciation for Allah ﷻ with hamd as mentioned[855] وَقَالُوا الْحَمْدُ لِلَّهِ in the ayah وَقَالُوا الْحَمْدُ لِلَّهِ الَّذِي صَدَقَنَا وَعْدَهُ وَأَوْرَثَنَا .الْأَرْضَ نَتَبَوَّأُ مِنَ الْجَنَّةِ حَيْثُ نَشَاءُ فَنِعْمَ أَجْرُ الْعَامِلِينَ[856]{الزمر/74}

The cases of nasikh[857] and mansûkh[858] can indicate this target audience-based instruction. Allah ﷻ teaches us this human reality of learning, and development like the incremental steps of cognitive behavioral therapy (CBT). In this sense, this change to a better and higher state is in the educational systems through the differentiation of knowledge with great levels, age and discipline. Similarly, the notion of nasikh, and mansûkh in the Qurān has the same purpose of teaching us this delivery method of instruction as mentioned مَا نَنسَخْ مِنْ آيَةٍ أَوْ نُنسِهَا نَأْتِ .بِخَيْرٍ مِّنْهَا أَوْ مِثْلِهَا أَلَمْ تَعْلَمْ أَنَّ اللَّهَ عَلَىٰ كُلِّ شَيْءٍ قَدِيرٌ[859] {البقرة/106}

It is normal to have different people with different understanding levels due to their differences in age, education and accessibility to critical thinking and tools of learning due to their resources, time and interest.

Therefore, the Qurān, with the differentiated learning methodology for different levels of learners, present these core principles in different styles.

Therefore, when one reviews and analyzes the Qurān, the Qurān is the ocean of the source of all true knowledge with their delivery

---

852. Favor.

853. That is the guidance of Allah by which He guides whom He wills.

854. That is the guidance of Allah by which He guides whom He wills. And one whom Allah leaves astray—for him there is no guide.

855. And they will say, "Praise to Allah.

856. And they will say, "Praise to Allah, who has fulfilled for us His promise and made us inherit the earth [so] we may settle in Paradise wherever we will. And excellent is the reward of [righteous] workers."

857. Transcriber.

858. Transcription.

859. We do not abrogate a verse or cause it to be forgotten except that We bring forth [one] better than it or similar to it. Do you not know that Allah is over all things competent?

قُل لَّوْ كَانَ الْبَحْرُ مِدَادًا لِّكَلِمَاتِ رَبِّي لَنَفِدَ الْبَحْرُ قَبْلَ أَن تَنفَدَ:methods as mentioned
كَلِمَاتُ رَبِّي وَلَوْ جِئْنَا بِمِثْلِهِ مَدَدًا ⁸⁶⁰ {الكهف/109}
وَلَوْ أَنَّمَا فِي الْأَرْضِ مِن شَجَرَةٍ أَقْلَامٌ وَالْبَحْرُ يَمُدُّهُ مِن بَعْدِهِ سَبْعَةُ أَبْحُرٍ مَّا نَفِدَتْ
كَلِمَاتُ اللَّهِ إِنَّ اللَّهَ عَزِيزٌ حَكِيمٌ ⁸⁶¹ {لقمان/27}

Popular Language for Majority

Qurān is a teacher for all level of learners. As most of the people may not have expertise but their education level and intellectual sophistication can be average, the Qurān may seem to address this general audience initially and primarily with its style. Yet at the same time, the experts of each field receive its true and authentic openings for their disciplines.

Popular culture of each region and time has a popular language. In this regard, popular language can refer to the language of the majority of people in that society. In this sense, the language of intellectuals, poets, artists, scholars or philosophers may not be considered as the popular language.

In this regard, the popular language can have a limited capacity of the words, phrases and expressions. If one expresses a teaching or a core principal in their bare form, the majority may not understand them effectively. In this perspective, using the elements of the popular language can connect this majority population to the content.

Poetry & Literature

If one reviews the style of the poetry and literature, the starting point of these expressions is to express the content with multiple meanings with their emotional renderings.

In a style of poetry and literature, one can find a lot of similes, metaphors and allegories to emphasize and give strength to the convoluted meanings with their primary and secondary indications.

---

860. Say, "If the oceans were ink for [writing] the words of my Lord, the oceans would be exhausted before the words of my Lord were exhausted, even if We brought the like of it as a supplement."
861. And if whatever trees upon the earth were pens and the sea [was ink], replenished thereafter by seven [more] seas, the words of Allah would not be exhausted. Indeed, Allah is Exalted in Might and Wise.

One of the usages of poetry and literature is expressing intrinsic fine meanings that cannot be understood with plain language of narratives especially in popular ordinary language referred as prose.

In this sense, a metrical structure of writing, composed in poetic meter compared to a prose can induce the intended emotions by the writer for the audience. At the same time, the intended nonfictional realities and truths can be delivered with this writing.

Yet, there can be a lot of poetry and literature that can aim to excite the emotions of people but may not be careful its content with their truthfulness. This category can be called today as fictional, not real but written in a lyric form to excite and induce emotions.

Arabic is an enormously powerful mathematical, metrical, and at the same time lyrical language. If one asserts that Arabic has the highest categories of complexities, rationality, convolutions, and lyrical stance of metrical structure among all languages, this claim can have a basis.

In this regard, pure and classical Arabic can be traced to societies and tribes that are not affected with external import of the words from other languages.

Now, let's imagine and virtually visit a time, where there is a place in the middle of a desert keeping and using the original language of intricacies of the classical Arabic language. In this culture and society, literature is the highest asset for the people. People start or stop tribal wars due to implied explicit or implicit meanings in a poem. People take extreme actions with the renderings of poetry and literature.

Then, a Book, the Qurān is revealed through a messenger ﷺ who is not a poet, but ummi, translated as illiterate. This Book challenges all the literature and poetry of these people with factual content. The people who are challenged are at the highest level in literature and poetry.

An expert or a specialist knows the value of something in that field more than the average person. If these experts, scholars or specialists are ethical and honest, they state, affirm, and confirm the real value of this piece. They don't deny its value. Therefore, it is interesting to review the reactions of different audiences in their initial encounters with the Qurān.

.وَقَالُوا إِنْ هَذَا إِلَّا سِحْرٌ مُبِينٌ {الصافات/15} [862] One of the common reactions is This group of people understand the value of the Qurān with its different styles and meanings and they use the

expression[863] سِحْرٌ مُبِينٌ when they had initially encountered with the Qurān. This can indicate that there is the disabling and humbling effect of the Qurān on them as the people were experts, who had really understood the value of the language.

The word سِحْر [864] is something miraculous beyond the usual. The word مُبِينٌ [865] is that it is not illusionary but real. In this sense, if one looks at the effects of magicians on people, they are mostly based on illusionary engagements of the eye. Therefore, the Qurān makes them utter the words of disablement with the word[866] سِحْر, but at the same time, their real and affirming position is emerged that the Qurān is not illusionary with the word مُبِينٌ. In other words, if magic is illusionary, then it cannot be obvious. In their expression, they were really exclaiming as that this Qurān is not a ordinary and illsionary like magic but the Qurān is above all of them. Their implied meaning can indicate that the Qurān is[867] الْحَقُّ, the truth, but they don't accept it although they know it.

In another ayah, they accept the High and Noble position of the Qurān with the word سِحْر [868] again but they explain the covering of their stance as mentioned

وَلَمَّا جَاءهُمُ الْحَقُّ قَالُوا هَذَا سِحْرٌ وَإِنَّا بِهِ كَافِرُونَ [869] {الزخرف/30} وَقَالُوا لَوْلاَ نُزِّلَ هَذَا الْقُرْآنُ عَلَى رَجُلٍ مِّنَ الْقَرْيَتَيْنِ عَظِيمٍ [870] {الزخرف/31}.

Their objection is due to their diseases of the heart, such as jealousy or arrogance. They are not happy with the qadar of Allah ﷻ and with Divine Masihiyyah as mentioned.

---

862. And say, "This is not but obvious magic.
863. Obvious magic.
864. Magic.
865. Obvious.
866. Magic
867. The truth.
868. Magic.
869. But when the truth came to them, they said, "This is magic, and indeed we are, concerning it, disbelievers."
870. And they said, "Why was this Qurān not sent down upon a great man from [one of] the two cities?"

In that sense the word [871] سِحْر becomes a cover for all different disabling and humbling signs of Allah ﷻ when some of the people encounter as mentioned اقْتَرَبَتِ السَّاعَةُ وَانشَقَّ الْقَمَرُ [872] {القمر/1} وَإِن يَرَوْا آيَةً يُعْرِضُوا وَيَقُولُوا سِحْرٌ مُّسْتَمِرٌّ [873] {القمر/2}.

Today, one can replace this word سِحْر[874] with other words such as science. When there is a sign of amazement from Allah ﷻ, people tend to tag it with science or nature.

Today, one can consider these renderings of covering or kufr especially disguised with the terms or expressions such as "critical thinking" as mentioned إِنَّهُ فَكَّرَ وَقَدَّرَ [875] {المدثر/18} فَقُتِلَ كَيْفَ قَدَّرَ [876] {المدثر/19} ثُمَّ قُتِلَ كَيْفَ قَدَّرَ [877] {المدثر/20} ثُمَّ نَظَرَ [878] {المدثر/21} ثُمَّ عَبَسَ وَبَسَرَ [879] {المدثر/22} ثُمَّ أَدْبَرَ وَاسْتَكْبَرَ [880] {المدثر/23} فَقَالَ إِنْ هَذَا إِلاَّ سِحْرٌ يُؤْثَرُ [881] {المدثر/24}. One can see in this ayah this process of critical thinking when one encounters an authentic knowledge. This can be great.

Yet, the correct steps of analysis with critical thinking should lead to the correct, true and objective results but not wrong results due to bias. One can make an analysis with the following example:

Fruits are good for your health.

Apple is a fruit.

Therefore, apple is not good for your health.

Then, if one says "apple is not good for your health", then a reasonable person doesn't find this as the correct analysis and conclusion with the above premises for critical thinking. The logic and analysis should be

Fruits are good for your health.

Apple is a fruit.

Therefore, apple is good for your health.

Yet, the person can have an unimplied bias as "I don't like apples. Therefore, apple is not good for your health."

---

871. Magic
872. The Hour has come near, and the moon has split [in two].
873. And if they see a sign [i.e., miracle], they turn away and say, "Passing magic."
874. Magic.
875. Indeed, he thought and deliberated.
876. So may he be destroyed [for] how he deliberated.
877. Then may he be destroyed [for] how he deliberated.
878. Then he considered [again];
879. Then he frowned and scowled;
880. Then he turned back and was arrogant.
881. And said, "This is not but magic imitated [from others]."

Similarly, after the critical thinking of the person, source of his bias is mentioned in the above ayah as {المدثر/23} وَاسْتَكْبَرَ[882], arrogance as a core spiritual disease of the heart. All the biases stem from the spiritual diseases of the heart.

Another word that is used is شَاعِر for the Messenger (as):

وَيَقُولُونَ أَئِنَّا لَتَارِكُوا آلِهَتِنَا لِشَاعِرٍ مَّجْنُونٍ[883]{الصافات/36}.

فَذَكِّرْ فَمَا أَنتَ بِنِعْمَتِ رَبِّكَ بِكَاهِنٍ وَلَا مَجْنُونٍ[884]{الطور/29} أَمْ يَقُولُونَ شَاعِرٌ نَّتَرَبَّصُ بِهِ رَيْبَ الْمَنُونِ[885] {الطور/30}

This indicates the powerful effect of the style of the Qurān at another level. The ones who do not want to accept the teachings of the Qurān use tags or titles to accept the power of the Qurān and Rasulullah ﷺ as the Messenger. Yet, they do not follow these teachings.

The ayah {الحاقة/41} وَمَا هُوَ بِقَوْلِ شَاعِرٍ قَلِيلًا مَّا تُؤْمِنُونَ[886] strongly refutes their claim as poets شَاعِر. The poets, شَاعِر, generally tend to focus on the metrical structure of the writings exiting the emotions but they may not be careful about the truthfulness of the content. The poets can claim and assert fictional meanings to increase awe, and emotions victimizing and sacrificing the truths and realities. They may claim things that are false and they themselves don't necessarily do وَالشُّعَرَاء يَتَّبِعُهُمُ الْغَاوُونَ[887] {الشعراء/224} أَلَمْ تَرَ أَنَّهُمْ فِي كُلِّ وَادٍ يَهِيمُونَ[888] {الشعراء/225} وَأَنَّهُمْ يَقُولُونَ مَا لَا يَفْعَلُونَ[889]{الشعراء/226}

Yet, a person of imān can use the poetry for a good purpose without making false claims as mentioned إِلَّا الَّذِينَ آمَنُوا وَعَمِلُوا الصَّالِحَاتِ وَذَكَرُوا اللَّهَ كَثِيرًا وَانتَصَرُوا مِن بَعْدِ مَا ظُلِمُوا وَسَيَعْلَمُ الَّذِينَ ظَلَمُوا أَيَّ مُنقَلَبٍ يَنقَلِبُونَ[890] {الشعراء/227}. اللہ اعلم[891]

---

882. And was arrogant.
883. And were saying, "Are we to leave our gods for a mad poet?"
884. So remind, [O Muhammad], for you are not, by the favor of your Lord, a soothsayer or a madman.
885. Or do they say [of you], "A poet for whom we await a misfortune of time"?
886. And it is not the word of a poet; little do you believe.
887. And the poets—[only] the deviators follow them;
888. Do you not see that in every valley they roam.
889. And that they say what they do not do?
890. Except those [poets] who believe and do righteous deeds and remember Allah often and defend [the Muslims] after they were wronged. And those who have wronged are going to know to what [kind of] return they will be returned.
891. Allah knows the best.

Tanāzullāt-u ilāhiyyah, Re-Building the Lost Adab[892] with Allah

Yet, it is important to emphasize even with most of the average population that these are analogies (similes) and examples in the encounters of Transcendent Reality of Allah ﷻ with the limited humans in their expressions called language.

When a person is talking to a child, they may need to simplify the language and use words that would be understandable to a child. For the child, the most important objects could be his or her toys. A good teacher may generate examples from these toys. Yet, an outsider observing this and who may not truly understand the purpose of this dialogue between the child and the person can have wrong impression that the person does not have much knowledge and this person is wrong in their teaching.

Similarly, Allah ﷻ gives examples and uses a language in the Qurān through the socially constructed world that we live in to address most of the general population. One can call this reductionism of the meanings from Transcendent Infinite Reality to our limited realm of humans. This is called in its technical term as tanazullāt-u ilāhiyyah[893].

As in the case of above smile of a person teaching to a child, there is an imbedded genuineness displayed as the reductionism of the language to a child language. Tanazullāt-u ilāhiyyah is not a mere reductionism of meanings but it entails the Rahmah[894], and Fadl[895] of Allah ﷻ on humans. In other words, Allah ﷻ gives examples to increase understandability, relevance and connectivity of the person with Rabbul Alamin.

Yet, in our world of child and adult or parent interactions, when there is a proper adab of the child, then the child can utter words and express bodily movements such as hugging or kissing to display this increased love, affection, and adoration towards this person or a parent. Or, when there is no proper adab with the child, the child can misuse this niceness, kindness and childish language of the parent to transgress their limits by displaying in the manners such as acting up, being belligerent and even sometimes rude to the parent or adult. This is an abuse on the part of the child. In reality, the child does not have physical

---

892. Respect.
893. Reductionism of the realities by Allah (ﷻ) as a mercy and care for the limited realms of creation, humans.
894. Mercy.
895. Favor.

power, mind, and capacity to oppress or abuse the parent. Yet, this child in reality humiliates and opresseses their ownselves.

In the above case, the problem arises due to child's wrong interpretation or abuse of this proximity, and genuineness with the parent or this adult. In our classical terms, we call these boundaries of proximity as adab.

Adab is a technical term and thousands of books had been written about it historically. It is the appropriate etiquette of the physical, verbal, intellectual and emotional dispositions of the person depending on the context, the time, interaction, and individuals. This appropriateness is primarily determined by Allah ﷻ referred as halal, (Fardh, Sunnah & Mubāh) and haram (incld. Makrûh).

Adab is the application of the defining boundaries of halal as required and permissible, makrûh and harām as the prohibited and disliked items as designated by Allah ﷻ. Rasulullah ﷺ embodied showed us the application of this notion of adab at its zenith with Allah SWT and with all other creation. In this regard, one can consider and name all the sunnah of Rasulullah ﷺ as adab.

Adab are all protective manners, mental and emotional boundaries in order not to transgress the limits of halal and harām. The below diagram can visualize adab as:

In this regard, proximity, reductionism or tanazullāt-u ilāhiyyah[896] should not be misunderstood. A human should not abuse the privilege given by Allah ﷻ with the proximity and accessibility of Divine Breezes.

In this regard, the abuse of the proximity and making the individual more belligerent and ruder instead of appreciation can be observed in the case of Shaytān. Iblis as mentioned for the proper name of Shaytān was given allowance to be in the gatherings of angels. This was an extra privilege for him. Yet, instead of increasing appreciation and adoration to Rabbul Alamin with this privileged proximity, Shaytān abused it, oppressed himself and became rude and belligerent as mentioned: وَإِذْ قُلْنَا لِلْمَلَائِكَةِ اسْجُدُواْ لآدَمَ فَسَجَدُواْ إِلاَّ إِبْلِيسَ أَبَى وَاسْتَكْبَرَ وَكَانَ مِنَ الْكَافِرِينَ[897] {البقرة/34}

---

896. Reductionism of the realities by Allah as a mercy and care for the limited realms of creation, humans.
897. And [mention] when We said to the angels, "Prostrate before Adam"; so they prostrated, except for Iblees. He refused and was arrogant and became of the disbelievers.

Shaytān lost his adab with Rabbul alamin. Yet, with the Divine Masihiyyah, qadar of Allah ﷻ, Allah ﷻ did not respite him with punishment but gave time as Shaytān asked more time as mentioned قَالَ رَبِّ فَأَنظِرْنِي إِلَى يَوْمِ يُبْعَثُونَ [898] {ص/79}.

In this case, the individuals or groups of having no adab with Allah ﷻ and getting more time or allowance from Allah ﷻ and still maintaining their not respectful attitudes with Allah ﷻ without adab does not mean that their actions are approved by Allah ﷻ. Yet as it is mentioned:

فَلَمَّا نَسُواْ مَا ذُكِّرُواْ بِهِ فَتَحْنَا عَلَيْهِمْ أَبْوَابَ كُلِّ شَيْءٍ حَتَّى إِذَا فَرِحُواْ بِمَا أُوتُواْ أَخَذْنَاهُم بَغْتَةً فَإِذَا هُم مُّبْلِسُونَ [899] {الأنعام/44}

وَالَّذِينَ كَذَّبُواْ بِآيَاتِنَا سَنَسْتَدْرِجُهُم مِّنْ حَيْثُ لاَ يَعْلَمُونَ [900] {الأعراف/182} وَأُمْلِي لَهُمْ إِنَّ كَيْدِي مَتِينٌ [901] {الأعراف/183}

فَذَرْنِي وَمَن يُكَذِّبُ بِهَذَا الْحَدِيثِ سَنَسْتَدْرِجُهُم مِّنْ حَيْثُ لَا يَعْلَمُونَ [902] {القلم/44} وَأُمْلِي لَهُمْ إِنَّ كَيْدِي مَتِينٌ [903] {القلم/45}

Istidraj is the allowance of Allah ﷻ with their action but it is not a negligence. It is the extension of their times. The requested extensions make the cases against the requesters stronger. In the case of Shaytān, the requested extension for him makes the case against him stronger. In the case of the followers of Shaytān from humans and jinn, their innate desire to live a long life with oppression of worldly means as istidrāj,[904] make the case against them stronger. May Allah ﷻ protect all of us from istidrāj, Ameen.

---

898. He said, "My Lord, then reprieve me until the Day they are resurrected."
899. So when they forgot that by which they had been reminded, We opened to them the doors of every [good] thing until, when they rejoiced in that which they were given, We seized them suddenly, and they were [then] in despair.
900. But those who deny Our signs—We will progressively lead them [to destruction] from where they do not know.
901. And I will give them time. Indeed, My plan is firm.
902. So leave Me, [O Muhammad], with [the matter of] whoever denies this statement [i.e., the Qurān]. We will progressively lead them [to punishment] from where they do not know.
903. And I will give them time. Indeed, My plan is firm.
904. Desire of the wordly life.

As in the case of humans with their relationship with Allah ﷻ, some also followed the steps of Shaytān and lost their adab as mentioned:

أَوَلَمْ يَرَ الْإِنْسَانُ أَنَّا خَلَقْنَاهُ مِن نُّطْفَةٍ فَإِذَا هُوَ خَصِيمٌ مُّبِينٌ 905 {يس/77} وَضَرَبَ لَنَا مَثَلاً وَنَسِيَ خَلْقَهُ قَالَ مَنْ يُحْيِي الْعِظَامَ وَهِيَ رَمِيمٌ 906 {يس/78}

Therefore, one must know that tanazullāt-u ilāhiyyah through the smiles and languages and Divine Breezes from Rabbul Alamin should increase the indebtedness, appreciation, and adoration for Allah ﷻ. This adoration can be translated as 'abd of Allah ﷻ, being the true adorer of Allah ﷻ.

Muhkam & Mutashābih

One should remember that the primary and initial audience of the language increases the accessibility, relevance and connectivity of the majority of the people with the Qurān. These can be called muhkam.

Yet, since the Qurān is from Rabbul-Alamìn, there are teachings and verses of the Qurān that primarily can require expertise approach. These can be called mutashābih.

Yet, in each case of muhkam[907] and mutashābih[908] ayahs there are thousands of convoluted other meanings openings depending on the person, time, and advancement of the science. These can be accessible to scholars as mentioned as well as the A'rifin[909], Gnostics who may not have formal/intellectual training.

For example, one can try to understand Full Control, Full Authority and Full Enforcement of Allah ﷻ similar to a king in a country in human popular language of similitudes. Therefore, one can view the ayah الرَّحْمَنُ عَلَى الْعَرْشِ اسْتَوَى 910 {طه/5} accordingly.

---

905. Does man not consider that We created him from a [mere] sperm-drop—then at once he is a clear adversary?
906. And he presents for Us an example and forgets his [own] creation. He says, "Who will give life to bones while they are disintegrated?"
907. Precise.
908. Un-specific.
909. The ones who know and understand.
910. The Most Merciful [who is] above the Throne established.

Yet, one can and should see these perspectives in the ayahs classified as mutashabihāt[911] in the Qurānic ayahs are identified as muhkam[912] and mutashābihāt. This is mentioned in هُوَ الَّذِيَ أَنزَلَ عَلَيْكَ الْكِتَابَ مِنْهُ آيَاتٌ مُّحْكَمَاتٌ هُنَّ أُمُّ الْكِتَابِ وَأُخَرُ مُتَشَابِهَاتٌ فَأَمَّا الَّذِينَ في قُلُوبِهِمْ زَيْغٌ فَيَتَّبِعُونَ مَا تَشَابَهَ مِنْهُ ابْتِغَاء الْفِتْنَةِ وَابْتِغَاء تَأْوِيلِهِ وَمَا يَعْلَمُ تَأْوِيلَهُ إِلاَّ اللّهُ وَالرَّاسِخُونَ فِي الْعِلْمِ يَقُولُونَ آمَنَّا بِهِ كُلٌّ مِّنْ عِندِ رَبِّنَا وَمَا يَذَّكَّرُ إِلاَّ أُوْلُواْ الأَلْبَابِ[913] {آل عمران/7}.

Therefore, expertise in interpretation with caution and adab is needed in the understanding of these ayahs of mutashabihāt as mentioned وَتِلْكَ الأَمْثَالُ نَضْرِبُهَا لِلنَّاسِ وَمَا يَعْقِلُهَا إِلَّا الْعَالِمُونَ[914] {العنكبوت/43} compared to the bare literal understandings as the common people without expertise with popular language can initially prefer.

The ayahs of mutashabihat[915] have a style of cover and path like the transit roads. It helps the person to walk on a transit road in order to reach the real highway.

In another analogy, the ayahs of mutashabihat are similar to the eyeglasses with different numbers addressing different sight issues of a person.

Some of these ayahs address the issue of myopia or nearsightedness which the person may not able to see things clearly unless they are relatively close to the eyes [2]. With appropriate examples of the mutashabihāt, the proper lenses similar to eyeglasses can increase the number of visibility, recognition, and understanding by giving smiles and analogies in human language of social constructions. In this type of sight issue or basirah, the person may have lack of recognition and realization of something that is remarkably close. An example of this can be

إِنَّ رَبِّي قَرِيبٌ مُّجِيبٌ[916] {هود/61}

---

911. Un-specific.

912. Precise.

913. It is He who has sent down to you, [O Muhammad], the Book; in it are verses [that are] precise—they are the foundation of the Book—and others unspecific. As for those in whose hearts is deviation [from truth], they will follow that of it which is unspecific, seeking discord and seeking an interpretation [suitable to them]. And no one knows its [true] interpretation except Allah. But those firm in knowledge say, "We believe in it. All [of it] is from our Lord." And no one will be reminded except those of understanding.

914. And these examples We present to the people, but none will understand them except those of knowledge.

915. Un-specific.

916. Indeed, my Lord is near and responsive."

قُلْ إِن ضَلَلْتُ فَإِنَّمَا أَضِلُّ عَلَى نَفْسِي وَإِنِ اهْتَدَيْتُ فَبِمَا يُوحِي إِلَيَّ رَبِّي إِنَّهُ سَمِيعٌ قَرِيبٌ[917]
{سبأ/50}

وَنَحْنُ أَقْرَبُ إِلَيْهِ مِنْ حَبْلِ الْوَرِيدِ[918] {ق/16}

Some of these ayahs can address the issue of hyperopia or farsightedness. With appropriate examples of the mutashabihāt, the proper lenses similar to an eye glass can increase the number of visibility, recognition, and understanding by giving smiles and analogies in human language of social constructions. A person with this sight issue or lack of basira may not recognize if they are farsighted. In other words, they have may difficulties to understand some of these examples with human realities. An example of this can be

مِّنَ اللَّهِ ذِي الْمَعَارِجِ {المعارج/3}[919] تَعْرُجُ الْمَلَائِكَةُ وَالرُّوحُ إِلَيْهِ فِي يَوْمٍ كَانَ مِقْدَارُهُ خَمْسِينَ أَلْفَ سَنَةٍ[920] {المعارج/4}

يُدَبِّرُ الْأَمْرَ مِنَ السَّمَاءِ إِلَى الْأَرْضِ ثُمَّ يَعْرُجُ إِلَيْهِ فِي يَوْمٍ كَانَ مِقْدَارُهُ أَلْفَ سَنَةٍ مِّمَّا تَعُدُّونَ[921] {السجدة/5}

In both cases of mutashabihāt, one should always remember that we are humans and we try to construct with our human constructions of limitations. In this human eyesight construction, this limitation can be like astigmatism which is a defect in the eye or in a lens caused by a deviation from spherical curvature that results in distorted images [2].

In other words, our creation with a spherical shaped eyesight have limitations as humans. Similarly, our understandings are limited and have defects when try to make one-to-one literal correspondence of these examples in the Qurān. In this sense, with appropriate examples of the muhkam[922] ayahs, like the proper lenses in eyeglasses, can correct the distorted images due to human renderings or limitations of astigmatism

---

917. Say, "If I should err, I would only err against myself. But if I am guided, it is by what my Lord reveals to me. Indeed, He is Hearing and near."
918. And We are closer to him than [his] jugular vein.
919. [It is] from Allah, owner of the ways of ascent.
920. The angels and the Spirit [i.e., Gabriel] will ascend to Him during a Day the extent of which is fifty thousand years.
921. He arranges [each] matter from the heaven to the earth; then it will ascend to Him in a Day, the extent of which is a thousand years of those which you count.
922. Precise.

stemming from our own constructions and mutashabihāt ayahs. An example of this can be

{الشورى/11} ... [923]شَيْءٌ لَيْسَ كَمِثْلِهِ

{محمد/19} [924]... فَاعْلَمْ أَنَّهُ لَا إِلَهَ إِلَّا اللَّهُ

قُلْ هُوَ اللَّهُ أَحَدٌ [925]{الإخلاص/1} اللَّهُ الصَّمَدُ [926]{الإخلاص/2} لَمْ يَلِدْ وَلَمْ يُولَدْ [927]{الإخلاص/3} وَلَمْ يَكُنْ لَّهُ كُفُوًا أَحَدٌ [928]{الإخلاص/4}

Muhkam eyes in this sense serve as the core, guidelines and pillar setting dispositions in the encounters of limited humans with the Transcendent Knowledge present in the Qurān.

In this sense, Hadith is another form of Rahmah[929] and Fadl[930] of Allah ﷻ to teach us how to put in human practice correctly these Noble Contents. In this sense, hadith and sunnah of Rasulullah ﷺ have more muhkam[931] and core role of guidance for us compared to the required expertise and scholarly approaches of mutashābih[932] ayahs in the Qurān.

This does not mean that hadith does not need scholarly approach. There is the science of studying the hadith and expertise especially in authentication, contextualizing the purpose, and implementation in the methodology, usûl. Yet, Rasulullah ﷺ shows us how to implement the Qurān with the practices of sunnah and hadith. As one of his titles are "walking Qurān" [11].

Core Principles for Different Disciplines

Teachings of the Qurān and Rasulullah ﷺ are all based on the principles of the logic. Yet we follow and submit ourselves because these are wahiy, revelation. We don't do it because it is logical but it is from Allah ﷻ. Yet, Allah ﷻ does not order and reveal anything that is not beneficial for

---

923. There is nothing like unto Him.
924. So know, [O Muhammad], that there is no deity except Allah.
925. Say, "He is Allah, [who is] One.
926. Allah, the Eternal Refuge.
927. He neither begets nor is born.
928. Nor is there to Him any equivalent."
929. Mercy.
930. Favor.
931. Precise.
932. Un-specific.

humans. Therefore, regardless of the logic behind it, there is a benefit for it. Yet, teachings of the Qurān and Rasulullah ﷺ are all based on the principles of logic. Depending on the need, the detailing follows.

The principles and guidelines set by the Qurān and Rasulullah ﷺ can indicate the gist and essence of different disciplines accumulated over time with collective minds, efforts and findings of the experts in these fields over centuries. These disciplines can be referred as natural, social or other sciences or studies. In each field, over the years of findings, accumulation of literature and analysis, the scholars of each field and dicipline set the guidelines and principles through detailed theories for generalizations.

Yet, it is impossible for a person to set central unchanging permanent guidelines and core principles of each field unless it is a revelation from Allah ﷻ.

Therefore, the non-conflicting feature of the Qurān with new true scientific discoveries and social theories can indicate that the Qurān is al-haqq, and Rasulullah ﷺ is al-haqq.

To summarize above discussions, here are a few points: A person cannot be a real expert in many fields. They can be in a few but not many. We can call these exceptional people today as polymaths.

When there is the same statement from two different people, one can consider the value of this statement like a gold and the other can consider it like a value of silver.

Scientific knowledge occurs with the accumulation of knowledge and literature in that field. The guidelines and details of this discipline in science is updated overtime to approximate the most correct, perfect, and generalizable principles.

There are a lot of abstract theories in the past which have become applied theories today due to the new discoveries in technology and science with the change of time.

There is difference in the context of past, present and future.

The unsophisticated people such as the people of desert cannot hide or conceal their real dispositions like the sophisticated people of today with different implicit and explicit or internal and external stances referred as diplomacy, politics, or terms. In that perspective, these unsophisticated people can be more straightforward, open and honest compared to the ones who can have multiple consciousnesses.

There are a lot of disciplines of science that form and develop through the fulfilment of the need by collective efforts of people, time, and values of the society.

It is very unlikely and impossible for humans to fully foresee future events.

The rules and laws established by humans has an expiration date like the products produced by humans.

Time and space have huge impact on the real character traits and dispositions of humans.

There are a lot of things that used to be considered miraculous in the past became ordinary and insignificant today with the advancing tools of science and technology.

The origination, formation, maturation, and perfection of the discipline of a science cannot be achieved immediately, abruptly, and instantly only by one person. They need a collective effort with a gradual change of maturation overtime like a growing child.

Now, considering all the above core guidelines and principles, one can assume oneself at the time of Rasulullah ﷺ. There is a person who does not have any kingdom, wealth, or help from people. This person is challenging all the world. There is a huge and serious responsibility of prophethood on his shoulders. He has the guidelines and principles that is not like guidelines and principles of humans as mentioned فَأْتُوا[933] بِسُورَةٍ مِّن مِّثْلِهِ. Then, if one asks "where did these teachings come from and where are they going? What is their purpose?"

They would response as "We are the Words of Allah ﷻ, Kalāmullah[934]. We are with people. Even after the death of humans, and End of day, we will continue as the Kalāmullah. We will leave humans on earth, yet our companionship and friendship will continue to feed the souls of humans," as mentioned لَهُمُ الْبُشْرَى فِي الْحَيَاةِ الدُّنْيَا وَفِي الآخِرَةِ لاَ تَبْدِيلَ لِكَلِمَاتِ اللهِ ذَلِكَ هُوَ الْفَوْزُ الْعَظِيمُ[935] {يونس/64}.

In this sense, the critical expression لاَ تَبْدِيلَ لِكَلِمَاتِ اللهِ[936] can indicate the permanent attribute of Kalām[937] of Allah ﷻ compared to the temporary,

---

933. Then produce a Sûrah the like thereof.
934. The words of Allah.
935. For them are good tidings in the worldly life and in the Hereafter. No change is there in the words [i.e., decrees] of Allah. That is what is the great attainment.
936. No change is there in the words [i.e., decrees] of Allah.
937. Words.

transient and changing features of humans' kalam or principles or theories as outlined with science.

According to Imams Maturidi, Samarkandi, Wahidi, Thalabi and Baqhawi [7] in their tafāsir for the part of the ayah as لَا تَبْدِيلَ لِخَلْقِ اللهِ in فَأَقِمْ وَجْهَكَ لِلدِّينِ حَنِيفًا فِطْرَةَ اللهِ الَّتِي فَطَرَ النَّاسَ عَلَيْهَا لَا تَبْدِيلَ لِخَلْقِ اللهِ ذَلِكَ الدِّينُ الْقَيِّمُ وَلَكِنَّ أَكْثَرَ النَّاسِ لَا يَعْلَمُونَ ٩٣٨ {الروم/30} indicates that there is no change in the religion of Allah ﷻ.

One can again witness this core difference between the humans' teachings through methodology of trial and errors compared to the perfect teachings of Allah ﷻ as indicated in the ayah as: سُنَّةَ اللهِ فِي الَّذِينَ خَلَوْا مِن قَبْلُ وَلَن تَجِدَ لِسُنَّةِ اللهِ تَبْدِيلًا ٩٣٩ {الأحزاب/62}

اسْتِكْبَارًا فِي الْأَرْضِ وَمَكْرَ السَّيِّئِ وَلَا يَحِيقُ الْمَكْرُ السَّيِّئُ إِلَّا بِأَهْلِهِ فَهَلْ يَنظُرُونَ إِلَّا سُنَّتَ الْأَوَّلِينَ فَلَن تَجِدَ لِسُنَّتِ اللهِ تَبْدِيلًا وَلَن تَجِدَ لِسُنَّتِ اللهِ تَحْوِيلًا ٩٤٠ {فاطر/43}

سُنَّةَ اللهِ الَّتِي قَدْ خَلَتْ مِن قَبْلُ وَلَن تَجِدَ لِسُنَّةِ اللهِ تَبْدِيلًا ٩٤١ {الفتح/23}

Intricacies, Complexities and Convolutions of the Qurān and Hadith/Sunnah

One should remember that the Qurān is not a normal book. Rasulullah ﷺ is not a normal human and a messenger. The Qurān is from Rabbul Alamìn, the Creator, Maintainer and Upholder of the all the universes, systems, and galaxies, everything and anything known and unknown to us. One can visit the first volume of this book in the introduction as "What is the Qurān?"

Rasulullah ﷺ is the messenger delivering the message of the Qurān to us. In that sense, Rasulullah ﷺ representing the Qurān is chosen and sent to us by Rabbul Alamìn, Allah ﷻ. The reality of the Qurān being from Rabbul Alamîn and Rasulullah ﷺ chosen by Allah SWT naturally,

---

938. So direct your face [i.e., self] toward the religion, inclining to truth. [Adhere to] the fitrah of Allah upon which He has created [all] people. No change should there be in the creation of Allah. That is the correct religion, but most of the people do not know.

939. [This is] the established way of Allah with those who passed on before; and you will not find in the way of Allah any change.

940. [Due to] arrogance in the land and plotting of evil; but the evil plot does not encompass except its own people. Then do they await except the way [i.e., fate] of the former peoples? But you will never find in the way [i.e., established method] of Allah any change, and you will never find in the way of Allah any alteration.

941. [This is] the established way of Allah which has occurred before. And never will you find in the way of Allah any change.

realistically, and expectedly necessitates intricacies, complexities, and convolutions and other renderings in the Qurān and the Hadith, Sunnah, and the practices of Rasulullah 鐕.At another level, the Qurān is the final and last and all inclusive, perfect, complementary and protected scripture with Divine Assurance compared to prior scriptures from Allah 鐕. Relatedly, Rasulullah 鐕 as the source of Hadith and Sunnah is the final and last messenger and prophet sent by Allah 鐕 in the realm of humans. This reality of the Qurān as the final scripture naturally, realistically, and expectedly necessitates intricacies, complexities, and convolutions and other renderings in the Qurān and in the Hadith and Sunnah of Rasulullah 鐕 as the final messenger and prophet sent by Allah 鐕.

When we analyze the three words intricacy, complexity and convolution, the below table can help our understandings better with the words as indicated in English language as below [2]:

intricacy	convolution	complexity
design	logic	system
pattern	discourses	issue
detail	story	structure
web	explanation	interaction
network	extrapolation	relationship
carving	reasoning	trait
embroidery	scheme	mixture
melody		

If we analyze the Qurān within the above embedded meanings of intricacy with the styles of poetry, literature and euphony, one can realize different designs, patterns, detailing, web and networking, and showing different styles of carving, embroidery and melody through meanings, metric structures of poetry and literature, and recitational sciences of tajwîd.

Then, one can realize the convolution within the contextual and intended meanings through the renderings of logic, discourses, stories, explanation, extrapolations, reasonings and schemes within the ayahs and sûrahs.

In all cases, one can constantly realize and be amazed by the complexity of the Qurān with a holistic view of the systems, structures, interactions, relationships, traits, and mixtures of time and space and sometimes beyond time and space, with visible and invisible participants of humans, jinn, animals, stones, trees, birds, stars through the psychological and emotional states of joy, fear, panic, terror, tranquility and serenity around the presented issues or problems and goals.

Yet, in all above three categories complexities can increase when each unit of each category interacts with other units in different categories. For example, what happens when "logic" in "convolution" interacts with "melody" in "intricacy" if we just analyze a word in an ayah? Here is an example of this interaction of the word سَوَاء for the ayah قُلْ يَا أَهْلَ الْكِتَابِ تَعَالَوْاْ إِلَى كَلَمَةٍ سَوَاء بَيْنَنَا وَبَيْنَكُمْ أَلاَّ نَعْبُدَ إِلاَّ اللهَ وَلاَ نُشْرِكَ بِهِ شَيْئًا وَلاَ يَتَّخِذَ بَعْضُنَا بَعْضاً أَرْبَابًا مِّن دُونِ اللهِ فَإِن تَوَلَّوْاْ فَقُولُواْ اشْهَدُواْ بِأَنَّا مُسْلِمُونَ [942] {آل عمران/64} in an excerpt as:

Through the recitational interpretation of the Qurān, the Qurānic words have internal rhythm (i.e., Musiki, Turk.) among the words. The letters that compose the word, the words that compose the sentences (verses), and the sentences that compose the chapters all have an internal rhythm and beat that either paint or echo (or both) the contextual meaning in the Qurān. Even, the sound of elongated words in the grammatical context is another point of emphasis. In Arabic, not all the words have elongation. Sawāin (سَوَاء) has an elongation (mad) in its recitation on the vowels of ā or "aa" according to recitation (tajwid) rules of the Qurān. In this verse, sawāin, "common," with the elongation in ā or "aa" suggests that there are a lot of commonalities. As an example, if we elongate the word a "lot" as if it reads in English as a "Loooot" of commonalities as does sawaaaain in its proper Arabic tajwid. Elongation could imply the numerous or extended or many common values of Islam, Christianity, and Judaism. [8]

In the excerpt above, one can realize how can one letter and sound such as سَوَاء can have a complementary meaning within the meanings of the word, ayah (verse), chapter and all relationshipal analysis of the Qurān as indicated the category of complexity in the above table.

---

942. Say, "O People of the Scripture, come to a word that is equitable between us and you— that we will not worship except Allah and not associate anything with Him and not take one another as lords instead of Allah." But if they turn away, then say, "Bear witness that we are Muslims [submitting to Him]."

Yet, this excellence is normal because the Qurān is from Rabbul Alamin as the final and all inclusive and upholding scripture of prior scriptures. The Qurān is present strongly, authentically and realistically among humans.

One can realize similar disposition with the hadith and sunnah of Rasulullah ﷺ as Rasulullah ﷺ is the one who delivered the Qurān to us.

Yet, within all these complexities everything is harmonious directing to [943] "لا اله الا الله."

At another note, it is normal, expected and real when there are statements or aphorisms from the salaf as "If I lose something, I go back to Qurān to find it." This statement is a true and real statement to indicate that the Qurān has all minute, fine, detailed solutions for all the minute and complex problems of each individual and groups, and societies.

Yes, the Qurān and sunnah of Rasulullah ﷺ has individualized openings for each person. Technically, this leads to the embodiment of

[944]"حسبي الله لا اله الا انت عليك توكلت و انت رب العرش العظيم"

If you have the Qurān and Rasulullah ﷺ in your life, you really don't need any friend and support. If you don't have, then even if all world can be your supporter and friend, but really you don't have any true Friend.

[35]

اللهم تولنا من من توليت

وَقُلْنَا يَا آدَمُ اسْكُنْ أَنتَ وَزَوْجُكَ الْجَنَّةَ وَكُلاَ مِنْهَا رَغَداً حَيْثُ شِئْتُمَا وَلاَ تَقْرَبَا هَذِهِ الشَّجَرَةَ فَتَكُونَا مِنَ الْظَّالِمِينَ[945] {البقرة/35}

وَيَا آدَمُ اسْكُنْ أَنتَ وَزَوْجُكَ الْجَنَّةَ فَكُلاَ مِنْ حَيْثُ شِئْتُمَا وَلاَ تَقْرَبَا هَذِهِ الشَّجَرَةَ فَتَكُونَا مِنَ الْظَّالِمِينَ[946] {الأعراف/19}

---

943. Theres no god except Allah.
944. God suffices me, theres no god but you, I trust in you and you are the lord of the great throne.
945. And We said, "O Adam, dwell, you and your wife, in Paradise and eat therefrom in [ease and] abundance from wherever you will. But do not approach this tree, lest you be among the wrongdoers."
946. And "O Adam, dwell, you and your wife, in Paradise and eat from wherever you will but do not approach this tree, lest you be among the wrongdoers."

Disliked Items, Taqwa (Distancing) and Humans Tendencies

As we analyze the case of Adam as, there is a clear instruction as mentioned [947] وَلَا تَقْرَبَا هَذِهِ الشَّجَرَةَ فَتَكُونَا مِنَ الظَّالِمِين not to do an action. This can be called distancing oneself from a disliked item. This can be called Taqwa.

Yet, our human tendencies of nafs make us do things that are stated to be prohibitions by Allah ﷻ. The external effects such as Shaytān, as a clear enemy, try to approach us with different legitimizations of these prohibitions as

فَأَزَلَّهُمَا الشَّيْطَانُ [948]فَأَزَلَّهُمَا الشَّيْطَانُ عَنْهَا فَأَخْرَجَهُمَا مِمَّا كَانَا فِيهِ in the ayah [949] عَنْهَا فَأَخْرَجَهُمَا مِمَّا كَانَا فِيهِ وَقُلْنَا اهْبِطُواْ بَعْضُكُمْ لِبَعْضٍ عَدُوٌّ وَلَكُمْ فِي الأَرْضِ مُسْتَقَرٌّ وَمَتَاعٌ إِلَى حِينٍ {البقرة/36} in order to go against the guidelines set by Allah ﷻ.

Yet, in these cases, sometimes mind can be a poison to rationalize the things to do something wrong when assigned by Allah ﷻ. Or, it can be one of our weak points that we may forget or lose our control using our mind for ourselves to justify our mistakes as instigated by Shaytān as mentioned مَا نَهَاكُمَا رَبُّكُمَا عَنْ هَذِهِ الشَّجَرَةِ إِلاَّ أَن تَكُونَا مَلَكَيْنِ أَوْ تَكُونَا مِنَ الْخَالِدِينَ [950].{الأعراف/20}

In all these cases, the person makes Dhulm[951], transgressing over the legitimate boundaries. In this case, the consequential effect of this as the Dhulm is faced by the person.

In all these cases, as long as the person recognizes their position with this Dhulm as mentioned قَالاَ رَبَّنَا ظَلَمْنَا أَنفُسَنَا وَإِن لَّمْ تَغْفِرْ لَنَا وَتَرْحَمْنَا لَنَكُونَنَّ مِنَ الْخَاسِرِينَ[952] {الأعراف/23} and goes back to Allah ﷻ constantly as

---

947. But do not approach this tree, lest you be among the wrongdoers.
948. But Satan caused them to slip out of it and removed them from that [condition] in which they had been.
949. But Satan caused them to slip out of it and removed them from that [condition] in which they had been. And We said, "Go down, [all of you], as enemies to one another, and you will have upon the earth a place of settlement and provision for a time."
950. But Satan whispered to them to make apparent to them that which was concealed from them of their private parts. He said, "Your Lord did not forbid you this tree except that you become angels or become of the immortal."
951. Opression.
952. They said, "Our Lord, we have wronged ourselves, and if You do not forgive us and have mercy upon us, we will surely be among the losers."

the words tawbah, or inabah[953] can indicate then, Allah ﷻ can forgive the person as mentioned [954] فَتَلَقَّى آدَمُ مِن رَّبِّهِ كَلِمَاتٍ فَتَابَ عَلَيْهِ إِنَّهُ هُوَ التَّوَّابُ الرَّحِيمُ {البقرة/37}.

The avoidance from the harām referred as taqwa is critical. In this sense, balance of humanity is established by following the guidelines as established by Rasulullah ﷺ. Yes, we are humans and we have tendencies to do a lot of things in life. These human tendencies permitted by Allah SWT referred as halal. The practice of them is shown to us by Rasulullah ﷺ. In this regard, the detailing of the terms as fardh, wajib, sunnah, mustahab, or mubah are all different categorizations as structured by the legal schools as a Rahmah and Fadl from Allah ﷻ.

The purpose of prophethood is to show us the approved legitimizations of humans referred as halal.

In this sense, one can find a lot of examples.

There are human tendencies to eat and drink. Yet, there are few exceptions as a restriction as set by Allah ﷻ. This restriction can be the unclean animals and unhealthy drinks such as alcohol.

There are the human tendencies for different bodily senses. Yet, there are few exceptions as a restriction as set by Allah ﷻ. This restriction can be same gender relations.

There are the human tendencies to gain, earn and accumulate wealth. Yet, there are a few exceptions as a restriction as set by Allah ﷻ. This restriction can be interest.

Depending on the levels of taqwa, the sensitivities of people implementing can vary. Yet there is a minimum assigned as harām as a prohibited item.

In all above, almost everything is halal with few restrictions. This is also mentioned as

وَقُلْنَا يَا آدَمُ اسْكُنْ أَنتَ وَزَوْجُكَ الْجَنَّةَ وَكُلاَ مِنْهَا رَغَداً حَيْثُ شِئْتُمَا وَلاَ تَقْرَبَا هَذِهِ الشَّجَرَةَ فَتَكُونَا مِنَ الْظَّالِمِينَ [955] {البقرة/35}.

---

953. Turning to Allah.

954. Then Adam received from his Lord [some] words, and He accepted his repentance. Indeed, it is He who is the Accepting of repentance, the Merciful.

955. And We said, "O Adam, dwell, you and your wife, in Paradise and eat therefrom in [ease and] abundance from wherever you will. But do not approach this tree, lest you be among the wrongdoers."

وَيَا آدَمُ اسْكُنْ أَنتَ وَزَوْجُكَ الْجَنَّةَ فَكُلاَ مِنْ حَيْثُ شِئْتُمَا وَلاَ تَقْرَبَا هَذِهِ الشَّجَرَةَ فَتَكُونَا مِنَ الظَّالِمِينَ 956{الأعراف/19}

The key expression of حَيْثُ شِئْتُمَا 957 indicates majority of the items were set as halal for Adam as similar to us. Only one thing was impermissible as mentioned هَذِهِ الشَّجَرَةَ 958. One can imagine a vast forest or jungle like amazon and only one tree is prohibited among millions of trees.

One can analyze the below ayahs around the key word حَيْثُ 959 or with its similar meanings with other words.

Allah ﷻ gives all different types of food and drink to be halal to eat and drink as mentioned:

وَإِذْ قُلْنَا ادْخُلُواْ هَذِهِ الْقَرْيَةَ فَكُلُواْ مِنْهَا حَيْثُ شِئْتُمْ رَغَداً وَادْخُلُواْ الْبَابَ سُجَّداً وَقُولُواْ حِطَّةٌ نَّغْفِرْ لَكُمْ خَطَايَاكُمْ وَسَنَزِيدُ الْمُحْسِنِينَ 960{البقرة/58}

In one's relation with their spouse this accessibility is mentioned with أَنَّى نِسَآؤُكُمْ حَرْثٌ لَّكُمْ فَأْتُواْ حَرْثَكُمْ أَنَّى شِئْتُمْ وَقَدِّمُواْ لأَنفُسِكُمْ وَاتَّقُواْ اللهَ وَاعْلَمُواْ أَنَّكُم مُّلاَقُوهُ وَبَشِّرِ الْمُؤْمِنِينَ 962{البقرة/223} in شِئْتُمْ 961

In all above renderings, the efforts of a person looking into legal rulings as set by our pious salaf are valuable efforts in order not to engage with harām to displease Allah ﷻ. Even though the person may be seeking a way to do something permissible, and some people may view this as a way of abuse, yet this effort of the person shows at least the concern in front of Allah ﷻ compared to the ones who are in the valleys of "I don't care."

On the other hand, ignoring any type of ruling and viewing the legal rulings or the efforts of a person something backwards, religious abuse, and useless can be worse than the people of "I don't care." A person

---

956. And "O Adam, dwell, you and your wife, in Paradise and eat from wherever you will but do not approach this tree, lest you be among the wrongdoers."

957. From wherever you will.

958. This tree.

959. Wherever.

960. And [recall] when We said, "Enter this city [i.e., Jerusalem] and eat from it wherever you will in [ease and] abundance, and enter the gate bowing humbly and say, 'Relieve us of our burdens [i.e., sins].' We will [then] forgive your sins for you, and We will increase the doers of good [in goodness and reward]."

961. However you wish.

962. Your wives are a place of cultivation [i.e., sowing of seed] for you, so come to your place of cultivation however you wish and put forth [righteousness] for yourselves. And fear Allah and know that you will meet Him. And give good tidings to the believers.

of "I don't care" may not properly understand the importance of these legal rulings. Yet the other group's rationalization for considering "legal rulings" as backwards, abuse or useless can indicate arrogance of self-sufficiency, or overlooking about the guidelines set by Allah ﷻ.

Therefore, one should really investigate their real dispositions in our changing time of mental, social and spiritual problems.

In all of the above cases, one can ask "is the human nature or nafs who wants to oppose? or is it Shaytān that makes the person focus on the prohibited items in order to rebel like in this ayah?

From the sound logic point of view, one should really expect to say "Allah ﷻ made everything halal for me. Allah ﷻ advised not to engage with a few items for my own benefit." This should put the person in an appreciative state of shukr and hamd in their relationship with Allah ﷻ.

Yet, one should remember that Shaytān has a mission to direct humans and make them focus on the items that they were prohibited by Allah ﷻ as mentioned: أَلَمْ أَعْهَدْ إِلَيْكُمْ يَا بَنِي آدَمَ أَن لَّا تَعْبُدُوا الشَّيْطَانَ إِنَّهُ لَكُمْ عَدُوٌّ مُّبِينٌ [963] {يس/60} and {ص/82} [964] قَالَ فَبِعِزَّتِكَ لَأُغْوِيَنَّهُمْ أَجْمَعِينَ.

This means that humans illogically become possessed and obsessed by the few items that they were prohibited by Allah ﷻ. This obsession of the humans is instigated by the external effects of Shaytān by sending signals to the internal diseased parts of heart with arrogance, and jealousy and others.

Today's fake liberal approaches of open-mindedness making everything possible without any restrictions is outcome of this root disease of arrogance of self-sufficiency. That is "we don't want anyone or anything to tell us what is right or wrong, what to do." Yet, these same people of fake liberal trends need to enslave themselves in an institution or a job following all the guidelines, policies of what is right or wrong.

True open-mindedness, tolerance and acceptance are all virtuous traits. These good traits are more popularized as a positive outcome of our civilizations. Yet, we have increasing number of social problems.

In this perspective, a person should be open to hear the positions of scriptures if we really stand behind for true liberalism. In this sense, everyone is our brother and sister as the descendent of Adam as. Yet, everyhone has a free choice and has accountability with Allah ﷻ.

---

963. Did I not enjoin upon you, O children of Adam, that you not worship Satan—[for] indeed, he is to you a clear enemy—
964. [Iblees] said, "By Your might, I will surely mislead them all

True liberalism recognizes the choice as well the options presented with the religion. Yet, option is with the person in their personal choice.

One should really consider why the person is taking a position against these few restricted items as outlined by Allah ﷻ although Allah ﷻ as our Creator made almost everything halal and permissible? What does the person gain by engaging oneself with these prohibitions? Is the person following the popular trends of fake discourses of freedom or liberalism? Yet, our existence is based on our own free-will, free choice and accountability in front of Allah ﷻ.

[41]

وَآمِنُوا بِمَا أَنزَلْتُ مُصَدِّقاً لِّمَا مَعَكُمْ وَلاَ تَكُونُوا أَوَّلَ كَافِرٍ بِهِ وَلاَ تَشْتَرُوا بِآيَاتِي ثَمَناً قَلِيلاً
وَإِيَّايَ فَاتَّقُونِ 965 {البقرة/41}

It is interesting to analyze the expression ثَمَناً قَلِيلاً in the above ayah. This expression also comes in the below ayahs as:

فَوَيْلٌ لِّلَّذِينَ يَكْتُبُونَ الْكِتَابَ بِأَيْدِيهِمْ ثُمَّ يَقُولُونَ هَذَا مِنْ عِندِ اللّهِ لِيَشْتَرُوا بِهِ ثَمَناً قَلِيلاً فَوَيْلٌ
لَّهُم مِّمَّا كَتَبَتْ أَيْدِيهِمْ وَوَيْلٌ لَّهُمْ مِّمَّا يَكْسِبُونَ 966 {البقرة/79}

وَإِذَ أَخَذَ اللّهُ مِيثَاقَ الَّذِينَ أُوتُوا الْكِتَابَ لَتُبَيِّنُنَّهُ لِلنَّاسِ وَلاَ تَكْتُمُونَهُ فَنَبَذُوهُ وَرَاء ظُهُورِهِمْ
وَاشْتَرَوْا بِهِ ثَمَناً قَلِيلاً فَبِئْسَ مَا يَشْتَرُونَ 967 {آل عمران/187}

In all above cases, the context is related with the ayahs or scriptures revealed from Allah ﷻ. There are detailed explanations in the tafāsir about the renderings of ahlul-kitāb with their problematic renderings.

When one analyzes the expression ثَمَناً قَلِيلاً 968 in the context of revelation, there is the clear indication of nobility of all revelations as

---

965. And believe in what I have sent down confirming that which is [already] with you, and be not the first to disbelieve in it. And do not exchange My signs for a small price, and fear [only] Me.
966. And when they meet those who believe, they say, "We have believed"; but when they are alone with one another, they say, "Do you talk to them about what Allah has revealed to you so they can argue with you about it before your Lord?" Then will you not reason?
967. And [mention, O Muhammad], when Allah took a covenant from those who were given the Scripture, [saying], "You must make it clear [i.e., explain it] to the people and not conceal it." But they threw it away behind their backs and exchanged it for a small price. And wretched is that which they purchased.
968. Small price.

revealed from Allah ﷻ. In other words, the books of Allah ﷻ require respect, nobility, superiority and dignity.

In this regard, the people of the book gain their dignity or nobility due to association or relating themselves with the books of Allah ﷻ. When people detach themselves from the original revelation, then they distance themselves from the dignity, nobility, and honor due given to them originally by following original scriptures of Allah ﷻ.

Therefore, the religious scholars gain respect or dignity when they are associated with the original revelations, the scriptures, and teachings of Allah ﷻ and all the Prophets, and Rasulullah ﷺ.

In this regard, a religious scholar should ask him or herself, how and why can a disrespect lower the dignity? Accordingly, one can involve oneself in both their personal and social engagements with this intention.

Therefore, a person of the people of the book can maintain his or her true dignity by also recognizing and accepting that the Qurān is from Allah ﷻ. This is mentioned as [969] وَآمِنُواْ بِمَا أَنزَلْتُ مُصَدِّقاً لِّمَا مَعَكُمْ. The Qurān is original and source of full and pure dignity, nobility and establishing closeness to God.

[67]

Adab with Allah ﷻ, Adab with the Qurān, and Adab with the Sunnah

وَإِذْ قَالَ مُوسَى لِقَوْمِهِ إِنَّ اللهَ يَأْمُرُكُم أَنْ تَذْبَحُواْ بَقَرَةً قَالُواْ أَتَتَّخِذُنَا هُزُوءاً قَالَ أَعُوذُ بِاللهِ أَنْ أَكُونَ مِنَ الْجَاهِلِينَ [970] {البقرة/67}

When Allah ﷻ reveals ayahs and sends the prophets to deliver the message of Allah ﷻ, if we don't maintain the proper adab due to jahalah[971], ignorance, then there can be consequences. These ayahs of the Qurān and the instructions can come to us at different levels. In all different levels of the engagements of the ayahs, one of the expected dispositions from a true believer and a'bd of Allah ﷻ is to follow and submit oneself to the orders of Allah ﷻ. Allah ﷻ does not order anything irrational and

---

969. And believe in what I have sent down confirming that which is [already] with you.
970. And [recall] when Moses said to his people, "Indeed, Allah commands you to slaughter a cow." They said, "Do you take us in ridicule?" He said, "I seek refuge in Allah from being among the ignorant."
971. Ignorance.

without any wisdom and benefit. Yet, our true disposition with Allah ﷻ requires to follow and submit and before rationalizing it. This is due to being the a'bd of Allah ﷻ This dispotions should precede before all. If this order is switched, then a critical problem arises. A believer of Allah ﷻ cannot first start rationalizing everything then following it. This attitude can imply arrogance.

In this discussion, the people who are not Muslims should and can first rationalize before they follow and submit. On the other hand, the people who are Muslims should have adab with the teachings of Allah ﷻ if they call themselves as Muslims. They should at least display the verbal disposition that "whatever Allah ﷻ orders us we follow." At the same time, it is encouraged to try to humbly understand the hikmah and wisdom behind it.

One can review above dispositions with the cases Shaytān compared to angels.

Yet, Shaytān did not have adab with Allah ﷻ that arrogance and jealousy covered with reasoning. Angel's reasoning preceded with humility covered with following and submission.

Shaytān received the order of Allah SWT, understood it well, and put his reason before submission and following. This stance is embedded in arrogance, jealousy, and kufr leading to unappreciation as: قَالَ مَا مَنَعَكَ أَلاَّ تَسْجُدَ إِذْ أَمَرْتُكَ قَالَ أَنَاْ خَيْرٌ مِّنْهُ ﴿972﴾{الأعراف/12}

Angels did not understand the hikmah of creation of Adam as in the beginning but yet, they preceded with humility with following and submission as: قَالُواْ سُبْحَانَكَ لاَ عِلْمَ لَنَا إِلاَّ مَا عَلَّمْتَنَا إِنَّكَ أَنتَ الْعَلِيمُ الْحَكِيمُ ﴿973﴾ {البقرة/32}

The above two cases occurred both around the reason and intellect. One of the display of the reason is embedded in arrogance and jealousy as in the case of Shaytān. The reason as displayed as خَلَقْتَنِي مِن نَّارٍ وَخَلَقْتَهُ ﴿974﴾ مِن طِينٍ was only the cover for the real inner disposition of arrogance and jealousy as ﴿975﴾ أَنَاْ خَيْرٌ مِّنْهُ. Therefore, grammatically speaking, أَنَاْ خَيْرٌ مِّنْهُ is muqaddam as the essence and primary in the sentence structure compared the possibility of being presented later in the ayah.

---

972. [Allah] said, "What prevented you from prostrating when I commanded you?" [Satan] said, "I am better than him.

973. They said, "Exalted are You; we have no knowledge except what You have taught us. Indeed, it is You who is the Knowing, the Wise."

974. You created me from fire and created him from clay [i.e., earth]."

975. I am better than him.

In the second case of angels, humility and humbleness precedes [976] سُبْحَانَكَ لَا عِلْمَ لَنَا before the reason as إِلاَّ مَا عَلَّمْتَنَا[977]. This is the true tawhid of La ilaha illa Allah. In this sense, i'lm can be like an ilāh, deity, as one can compare two expressions below:

لَا عِلْمَ لَنَا إِلاَّ مَا عَلَّمْتَنَا[978]

لا إله الا الله[979]

Today's secular, philosophy, social science and other reason renderings of humans can be similar if they don't use the reason with humbleness and humility as إِلاَّ مَا عَلَّمْتَنَا[980]. In other words, the person can only know and understand with their capacity as a creation created by Allah ﷻ. Claiming otherwise is all arrogance and signals of the path of Shaytān.

If we analyze the above ayah around the word هُزُواً[981], the similar ayahs of the Qurān can be:

وَإِذَا طَلَّقْتُمُ النِّسَاء فَبَلَغْنَ أَجَلَهُنَّ فَأَمْسِكُوهُنَّ بِمَعْرُوفٍ أَوْ سَرِّحُوهُنَّ بِمَعْرُوفٍ وَلاَ تُمْسِكُوهُنَّ ضِرَارًا لَّتَعْتَدُواْ وَمَن يَفْعَلْ ذَلِكَ فَقَدْ ظَلَمَ نَفْسَهُ وَلاَ تَتَّخِذُواْ آيَاتِ اللّهِ هُزُوًا وَاذْكُرُواْ نِعْمَتَ اللّهِ عَلَيْكُمْ وَمَا أَنزَلَ عَلَيْكُمْ مِّنَ الْكِتَابِ وَالْحِكْمَةِ يَعِظُكُم بِهِ وَاتَّقُواْ اللّهَ وَاعْلَمُواْ أَنَّ اللّهَ بِكُلِّ شَيْءٍ عَلِيمٌ[982] {البقرة/231}

Sometimes, this attitude can display in the engagements of reason covered with arrogance in the cases of legal rulings as mentioned in the Qurān. These teachings aim to bring to justice in the potential chaotic nature of human societies and relationships. Yet, some can put their reason as the cover of their arrogance as mentioned with the word[983] هُزُوًا in the above ayah.

---

976. "Exalted are You; we have no knowledge.
977. Except what You have taught us.
978. we have no knowledge, except what You have taught us.
979. There is no god except Allah.
980. Except what You have taught us.
981. Ridicule.
982. And when you divorce women and they have [nearly] fulfilled their term, either retain them according to acceptable terms or release them according to acceptable terms, and do not keep them, intending harm, to transgress [against them]. And whoever does that has certainly wronged himself. And do not take the verses of Allah in jest. And remember the favor of Allah upon you and what has been revealed to you of the Book [i.e., the Qurān] and wisdom [i.e., the Prophet's sunnah] by which He instructs you. And fear Allah and know that Allah is Knowing of all things.
983. In jest.

يَا أَيُّهَا الَّذِينَ آمَنُوا لاَ تَتَّخِذُوا الَّذِينَ اتَّخَذُوا دِينَكُمْ هُزُوًا وَلَعِبًا مِّنَ الَّذِينَ أُوتُوا الْكِتَابَ مِن قَبْلِكُمْ وَالْكُفَّارَ أَوْلِيَاء وَاتَّقُوا اللَّهَ إِن كُنتُم مُّؤْمِنِينَ 984 {المائدة/57}

وَإِذَا نَادَيْتُمْ إِلَى الصَّلاَةِ اتَّخَذُوهَا هُزُوًا وَلَعِبًا ذَلِكَ بِأَنَّهُمْ قَوْمٌ لاَّ يَعْقِلُونَ 985 {المائدة/58}

One of the main purposes of Islam is to re-establish this lost adab with Allah ۞ and related shi'ar of Allah among ahlu-kitāb. Therefore, the person should not compromise from this core attitude of adab with Allah ۞, the Qurān and sunnah and with pious salaf due to popular trends of religion among Westerners. This adab is one of the main differences of Islam with others.

Another level of lost adab is related with the established prayers as986 وَإِذَا نَادَيْتُمْ إِلَى الصَّلاَةِ اتَّخَذُوهَا هُزُوًا وَلَعِبًا. Then, the terms of religious, religiosity, or fundamentalist develop from this lost adab when non-Muslims look at the Muslims praying five times a day. In this sense, they may implicitly or explicitly write and engage with the concepts that praying five times is being too religious. This piety or religiosity is not needed and difficult as part of their mockery mentioned as هُزُوًا وَلَعِبًا987. They think that this is a burden, astagfirullah. Therefore, Muslims don't realize this that they are stupid, not intelligent, and fundamentalist with different approaches of mockery, هُزُوًا وَلَعِبًا.

وَمَا نُرْسِلُ الْمُرْسَلِينَ إِلَّا مُبَشِّرِينَ وَمُنذِرِينَ وَيُجَادِلُ الَّذِينَ كَفَرُوا بِالْبَاطِلِ لِيُدْحِضُوا بِهِ الْحَقَّ وَاتَّخَذُوا آيَاتِي وَمَا أُنذِرُوا هُزُوًا988 {الكهف/56}

The concepts of argumentation as mentioned وَيُجَادِلُ الَّذِينَ كَفَرُوا989 covered with arrogance as mentioned بِالْبَاطِلِ لِيُدْحِضُوا بِهِ الْحَقَّ وَاتَّخَذُوا آيَاتِي وَمَا أُنذِرُوا هُزُوًا990 {الكهف/56} is always there. Yet, if these people even do some

---

984. O you who have believed, take not those who have taken your religion in ridicule and amusement among the ones who were given the Scripture before you nor the disbelievers as allies. And fear Allah, if you should [truly] be believers.

985. And when you call to prayer, they take it in ridicule and amusement. That is because they are a people who do not use reason.

986. And when you call to prayer, they take it in ridicule and amusement.

987. Ridicule and amusement.

988. And We send not the messengers except as bringers of good tidings and warners. And those who disbelieve dispute by [using] falsehood to [attempt to] invalidate thereby the truth and have taken My verses, and that of which they are warned, in ridicule.

989. And those who disbelieve dispute by [using] falsehood to [attempt to] invalidate thereby the truth.

990. And have taken My verses, and that of which they are warned, in ridicule.

virtuous and ethical acts, these may not have much value due to their inner disposition of arrogance, as mentioned in وَاتَّخَذُوا آيَاتِي وَرُسُلِي هُزُوًا!

الَّذِينَ ضَلَّ سَعْيُهُمْ فِي الْحَيَاةِ الدُّنْيَا وَهُمْ يَحْسَبُونَ أَنَّهُمْ يُحْسِنُونَ صُنْعًا 991{الكهف/104} أُولَئِكَ الَّذِينَ كَفَرُوا بِآيَاتِ رَبِّهِمْ وَلِقَائِهِ فَحَبِطَتْ أَعْمَالُهُمْ فَلَا نُقِيمُ لَهُمْ يَوْمَ الْقِيَامَةِ وَزْنًا 992{الكهف/105}

ذَلِكَ جَزَاؤُهُمْ جَهَنَّمُ بِمَا كَفَرُوا وَاتَّخَذُوا آيَاتِي وَرُسُلِي هُزُوًا! 993{الكهف/106}

Some of the below ayahs remind us this unchanging case of people not having adab with Allah ﷻ, with the ayahs of Allah ﷻ and with the shi'ar of Allah ﷻ as mentioned:

وَإِذَا رَآكَ الَّذِينَ كَفَرُوا إِن يَتَّخِذُونَكَ إِلَّا هُزُوًا! أَهَذَا الَّذِي يَذْكُرُ آلِهَتَكُمْ وَهُم بِذِكْرِ الرَّحْمَنِ هُمْ كَافِرُونَ 994{الأنبياء/36}

وَإِذَا رَأَوْكَ إِن يَتَّخِذُونَكَ إِلَّا هُزُوًا! أَهَذَا الَّذِي بَعَثَ اللَّهُ رَسُولًا 995{الفرقان/41}

وَمِنَ النَّاسِ مَن يَشْتَرِي لَهْوَ الْحَدِيثِ لِيُضِلَّ عَن سَبِيلِ اللَّهِ بِغَيْرِ عِلْمٍ وَيَتَّخِذَهَا هُزُوًا! أُولَئِكَ لَهُمْ عَذَابٌ مُهِينٌ 996{لقمان/6}

وَإِذَا عَلِمَ مِنْ آيَاتِنَا شَيْئًا اتَّخَذَهَا هُزُوًا! أُولَئِكَ لَهُمْ عَذَابٌ مُهِينٌ 997{الجاثية/9}

ذَلِكُم بِأَنَّكُمُ اتَّخَذْتُمْ آيَاتِ اللَّهِ هُزُوًا وَغَرَّتْكُمُ الْحَيَاةُ الدُّنْيَا فَالْيَوْمَ لَا يُخْرَجُونَ مِنْهَا وَلَا هُمْ يُسْتَعْتَبُونَ 998{الجاثية/35}

---

991. [They are] those whose effort is lost in worldly life, while they think that they are doing well in work."

992. Those are the ones who disbelieve in the verses of their Lord and in [their] meeting Him, so their deeds have become worthless; and We will not assign to them on the Day of Resurrection any weight [i.e., importance].

993. That is their recompense—Hell—for what they denied and [because] they took My signs and My messengers in ridicule.

994. And when those who disbelieve see you, [O Muhammad], they take you not except in ridicule, [saying], "Is this the one who mentions [i.e., insults] your gods?" And they are, at the mention of the Most Merciful, disbelievers.

995. And when they see you, [O Muhammad], they take you not except in ridicule, [saying], "Is this the one whom Allah has sent as a messenger?

996. And of the people is he who buys the amusement of speech to mislead [others] from the way of Allah without knowledge and who takes it [i.e., His way] in ridicule. Those will have a humiliating punishment.

997. And when he knows anything of Our verses, he takes them in ridicule. Those will have a humiliating punishment.

998. That is because you took the verses of Allah in ridicule, and worldly life deluded you." So that Day they will not be removed from it, nor will they be asked to appease [Allah].

[111]

وَقَالُواْ لَن يَدْخُلَ الْجَنَّةَ إِلاَّ مَن كَانَ هُوداً أَوْ نَصَارَى تِلْكَ أَمَانِيُّهُمْ قُلْ هَاتُواْ بُرْهَانَكُمْ إِن
كُنتُمْ صَادِقِينَ ⁹⁹⁹ {البقرة/111}

It is interesting to analyze the word بُرْهَان¹⁰⁰⁰. We as humans engage in
our unclear renderings which can be called suppositions, presumptions
and assumptions. Yet, these suppositions or assumptions cannot be
turned into an authentic valid theory, principle or reality unless it is
supported by an evidence in its totality of logical methodology. The
above ayah mention's some assumption of some people as لَن يَدْخُلَ الْجَنَّةَ ¹⁰⁰¹
إِلاَّ مَن كَانَ هُوداً أَوْ نَصَارَى Yet, when this assumption is not supported by a ¹⁰⁰²
بُرْهَان, evidence, then it turns to be a false supposition as expressed with
the word أَمَانِيُّهُمْ¹⁰⁰³.

One can review the ayahs with the word بُرْهَان in different parts of
the Qurān as:

يَا أَيُّهَا النَّاسُ قَدْ جَاءكُم بُرْهَانٌ مِّن رَّبِّكُمْ وَأَنزَلْنَا إِلَيْكُمْ نُورًا مُّبِينًا ¹⁰⁰⁴ {النساء/174}

In the above ayah, the traditional approaches for the word Burhan
can be the Qurān and/or Rasulullah ﷺ. In both cases, there is a clear
evidence. The Qurān is clearly stating from beginning to end, this book
is from Allah ﷻ. This is a Burhan, clear evidence not only because due to
all different miraculous features of the Qurān, but there are numerous
clear direct explicit indications that this book is sent by Allah ﷻ.

If there is a book that claims in all its places clearly that it is from the
Creator, then it deserves right to be reviewed, analyzed and one should
be investigated if that is really the case. In this sense, this explicit stance
of the Qurān as the Book of Allah ﷻ immediately from beginning to
end, elevates the Qurān at the highest level of evidence present today
and in all times among humans.

---

999. And they say, "None will enter Paradise except one who is a Jew or a Christian." That is
[merely] their wishful thinking. Say, "Produce your proof, if you should be truthful."
1000. Conclusive proof.
1001. None will enter Paradise except one who is a Jew or a Christian
1002. Conclusive proof.
1003. Their wishful thinking.
1004. O mankind, there has come to you a conclusive proof from your Lord, and We have sent
down to you a clear light.

Similarly, when there is a person who claims to be sent by Allah
🙵, and then this is a clear Burhan. It is a separate approach to check if
this person is authentic, true or not. Therefore, there were people who
expected a prophet at the time of Rasulullah 🙵 and wanted to check if
he 🙵 was the authentic prophet or not. This was a correct and natural
approach. Most peple accepted when they witnessed thousands of
clear evidence. Few did not accept due to their jealousy, arrogance, and
overwhelming negative group identities.

Therefore, if there is no clear evidence of something, then following
it foolheartedly can be a major mistake as mentioned

أَمِ اتَّخَذُوا مِن دُونِهِ آلِهَةً قُلْ هَاتُوا بُرْهَانَكُمْ هَذَا ذِكْرُ مَن مَّعِيَ وَذِكْرُ مَن قَبْلِي بَلْ أَكْثَرُهُمْ
لَا يَعْلَمُونَ الْحَقَّ فَهُم مُّعْرِضُونَ1005 {الأنبياء/24}

.وَمَا أَرْسَلْنَا مِن قَبْلِكَ مِن رَّسُولٍ إِلَّا نُوحِي إِلَيْهِ أَنَّهُ لَا إِلَهَ إِلَّا أَنَا فَاعْبُدُونِ1006 {الأنبياء/25}

So, in this case, it is always Rahmah, Adl, and Fadl of Allah 🙵 that
Allah 🙵 always sends clear evidence as mentioned وَمَا أَرْسَلْنَا مِن قَبْلِكَ مِن
.رَّسُولٍ إِلَّا نُوحِي إِلَيْهِ أَنَّهُ لَا إِلَهَ إِلَّا أَنَا فَاعْبُدُونِ1007 {الأنبياء/25}

The following ayah also supports, repeats, and emphasize this above
notion of Burhan as the clear evident as:

أَمَّن يَبْدَأُ الْخَلْقَ ثُمَّ يُعِيدُهُ وَمَن يَرْزُقُكُم مِّنَ السَّمَاء وَالْأَرْضِ أَإِلَهٌ مَّعَ اللَّهِ قُلْ هَاتُوا بُرْهَانَكُمْ
إِن كُنتُمْ صَادِقِينَ1008 {النمل/64}

In another case such as,

وَلَقَدْ هَمَّتْ بِهِ وَهَمَّ بِهَا لَوْلَا أَن رَّأَى بُرْهَانَ رَبِّهِ كَذَلِكَ لِنَصْرِفَ عَنْهُ السُّوءَ وَالْفَحْشَاء إِنَّهُ
مِنْ عِبَادِنَا الْمُخْلَصِينَ1009 {يوسف/24}

1005. Or have they taken gods besides Him? Say, [O Muhammad], "Produce your proof. This
[Qurān] is the message for those with me and the message of those before me." But most of
them do not know the truth, so they are turning away.

1006. And We sent not before you any messenger except that We revealed to him that, "There
is no deity except Me, so worship Me."

1007. And We sent not before you any messenger except that We revealed to him that, "There
is no deity except Me, so worship Me."

1008. Is He [not best] who begins creation and then repeats it and who provides for you from
the heaven and earth? Is there a

1009. And she certainly determined [to seduce] him, and he would have inclined to her had
he not seen the proof [i.e., sign] of his Lord. And thus [it was] that We should avert from him
evil and immorality. Indeed, he was of Our chosen servants.

Allah 🕮 can send clear signs to a person to guide the person and protect the person from displeasure of Allah 🕮. 1010 اللهم جعلنا منهم آمين

Depending on the level and close relation of the person with Allah 🕮, the person can sometimes immediately recognize these evident guiding points and take a heed from it. Or, sometimes if he did not recognize it, he or she may look in the past and tell oneself as "Allah 🕮 sent me this sign but I didn't recognize and take heed it from it." At this point, the person still can make istigfar and ask protection from the evil engagements of oneself with the dua of Rasulullah as "اللهم قني شر ما (قضيت1011)".In some cases, such as1012

اسْلُكْ يَدَكَ فِي جَيْبِكَ تَخْرُجْ بَيْضَاء مِنْ غَيْرِ سُوءٍ وَاضْمُمْ إِلَيْكَ جَنَاحَكَ مِنَ الرَّهْبِ فَذَانِكَ بُرْهَانَانِ مِن رَّبِّكَ إِلَى فِرْعَوْنَ وَمَلَئِهِ إِنَّهُمْ كَانُوا قَوْمًا فَاسِقِينَ {القصص/32}

these clear evidences presented in such a way to shock and to break the norms abruptly. This breaking can be through the means of things beyond the physical norms, customs and scientific theories and human engagements. These can be called miracles in its explicit, apparent, and obvious manifestation as clear evidences.

Therefore, since the veil of camouflaging is fully removed in such engagements of miracles, if the person still does not accept this reality and Burhan sent by Allah 🕮, then the person deems to be punished due to their now apparent, obvious jealousy and arrogance. This notion is expressed with the expression وَإِن يَرَوْاْ كُلَّ آيَةٍ1013 in the Qurān as mentioned:

وَإِن يَرَوْاْ كُلَّ آيَةٍ لاَّ يُؤْمِنُواْ بِهَا حَتَّى إِذَا جَآؤُوكَ يُجَادِلُونَكَ يَقُولُ الَّذِينَ كَفَرُواْ إِنْ هَذَآ إِلاَّ أَسَاطِيرُ الأَوَّلِينَ 1014 {الأنعام/25}

1010. O Allah, make us from them. Ameen.
1011. Oh Allah, protect me from the evil I did.
1012. Insert your hand into the opening of your garment; it will come out white, without disease. And draw in your arm close to you [as prevention] from fear, for those are two proofs from your Lord to Pharaoh and his establishment. Indeed, they have been a people defiantly disobedient."
1013. And if they should see every sign.
1014. And if they should see every sign, they will not believe in it. Even when they come to you arguing with you, those who disbelieve say, "This is not but legends of the former peoples."

سَأَصْرِفُ عَنْ آيَاتِيَ الَّذِينَ يَتَكَبَّرُونَ فِي الأَرْضِ بِغَيْرِ الْحَقِّ وَإِن يَرَوْاْ كُلَّ آيَةٍ لاَّ يُؤْمِنُواْ بِهَا وَإِن يَرَوْاْ سَبِيلَ الرُّشْدِ لاَ يَتَّخِذُوهُ سَبِيلاً وَإِن يَرَوْاْ سَبِيلَ الْغَيِّ يَتَّخِذُوهُ سَبِيلاً ذَلِكَ بِأَنَّهُمْ كَذَّبُواْ بِآيَاتِنَا وَكَانُواْ عَنْهَا غَافِلِينَ 1015 {146/الأعراف} وَالَّذِينَ كَذَّبُواْ بِآيَاتِنَا وَلِقَاء الآخِرَةِ حَبِطَتْ أَعْمَالُهُمْ هَلْ يُجْزَوْنَ إِلاَّ مَا كَانُواْ يَعمَلُونَ 1016 {147/الأعراف}

Therefore, one should recognize that in the afterlife, akhirah, there will be evidence-based judgments as mentioned وَنَزَعْنَا مِن كُلِّ أُمَّةٍ شَهِيدًا فَقُلْنَا هَاتُوا بُرْهَانَكُمْ فَعَلِمُوا أَنَّ الْحَقَّ لِلَّهِ وَضَلَّ عَنْهُم مَّا كَانُوا يَفْتَرُونَ 1017 {75/القصص}. In other words, the people who did not recognize Allah ﷻ in the true sense will be asked to bring their evidence why it was not the case. اللهم احفظنا من هذا، امين

[109]

Hasad

وَدَّ كَثِيرٌ مِّنْ أَهْلِ الْكِتَابِ لَوْ يَرُدُّونَكُم مِّن بَعْدِ إِيمَانِكُمْ كُفَّاراً حَسَدًا مِّنْ عِندِ أَنفُسِهِم مِّن بَعْدِ مَا تَبَيَّنَ لَهُمُ الْحَقُّ فَاعْفُواْ وَاصْفَحُواْ حَتَّى يَأْتِيَ اللَّهُ بِأَمْرِهِ إِنَّ اللَّهَ عَلَى كُلِّ شَيْءٍ قَدِيرٌ 1018 {109/البقرة}

أَمْ يَحْسُدُونَ النَّاسَ عَلَى مَا آتَاهُمُ اللّهُ مِن فَضْلِهِ فَقَدْ آتَيْنَآ آلَ إِبْرَاهِيمَ الْكِتَابَ وَالْحِكْمَةَ وَآتَيْنَاهُم مُّلْكًا عَظِيمًا 1019 {54/النساء}

وَمِن شَرِّ حَاسِدٍ إِذَا حَسَدَ 1020 {5/الفلق}

1015. I will turn away from My signs those who are arrogant upon the earth without right; and if they should see every sign, they will not believe in it. And if they see the way of consciousness, they will not adopt it as a way; but if they see the way of error, they will adopt it as a way. That is because they have denied Our signs and they were heedless of them.

1016. Those who denied Our signs and the meeting of the Hereafter—their deeds have become worthless. Are they recompensed except for what they used to do?

1017. And We will extract from every nation a witness and say, "Produce your proof," and they will know that the truth belongs to Allah, and lost from them is that which they used to invent.

1018. Many of the People of the Scripture wish they could turn you back to disbelief after you have believed, out of envy from themselves [even] after the truth has become clear to them. So pardon and overlook until Allah delivers His command. Indeed, Allah is over all things competent.

1019. Or do they envy people for what Allah has given them of His bounty? But We had already given the family of Abraham the Scripture and wisdom and conferred upon them a great kingdom.

1020. And from the evil of an envier when he envies."

Hasad & Kibir

There is the discussion among the salaf about the root of the spiritual diseases. According to some it is hasad, jealousy and according to some it is kibir, arrogance [28]. Not going too much into this discussion of what comes first, and the other is secondary, both are explicit and very dangerous roots related with the essence of the creation of the humans and jinn.

In other words, the realms of tests and trials apply to the lives of humans and jinn. The essence of these trials and tests are rooted with the manifestations hasad and kibir. They are both related. For the sake of the focus, we will try to focus here on the disease of hasad but one can also replace it and see similar approximations with the disease of kibir in these discussions.

In the discussions of the salaf, the dominant opinion of seems that kibir[1021] is the main source of this disease [28]. Hasad[1022] is the immediate manifestation and its practical application that can be more evident and leading force of it is destruction. It can be similar to that, if Fir'awn is the kibir, then Hamān is the hasad[1023]. One is the root and foundation as the kibir and the other is the application and its manifestation of it as hasad.

The manifestation of kufr in the belief of Allah ﷻ is related with hasad and kibir.

The manifestation of unappreciation behavior is related to parents is related and product of kibir and hasad.

The manifestation of killing another person is the product of hasad and kibir.

As we are focusing on the disease of hasad, hasad is the disease that is related with the person's strong self and group identity. This identity can blind the person when something that is factual is presented to this person. Yet, the person still maintains the denial in the search and disposition of protecting this identity. In this case, denial, lies, and false oaths are all the product and outcome of this effort of protecting this identity.

Self, ego, or nafs has the free will and choice. This ability of choice can induce kibir in the person. This free will and free choice of self

---

1021. Arrogance.
1022. Jealousy.
1023. Jealousy.

induces an identity in the person. Therefore, self identity of recognition can be either the first case of manifestation of kibir or manifestation of being a'bd of Allah ﷻ although the person has a choice and free will.

In other words, the person with this identity of self with the ability of making free choice and will can either take the route of the kibir with arrogance of self-sufficiency and confidence leading ultimately to individual ilāhs, deities as mentioned:

أَرَأَيْتَ مَنِ اتَّخَذَ إِلَهَهُ هَوَاهُ أَفَأَنتَ تَكُونُ عَلَيْهِ وَكِيلًا 1024{الفرقان/43}

أَفَرَأَيْتَ مَنِ اتَّخَذَ إِلَهَهُ هَوَاهُ وَأَضَلَّهُ اللَّهُ عَلَى عِلْمٍ وَخَتَمَ عَلَى سَمْعِهِ وَقَلْبِهِ وَجَعَلَ عَلَى بَصَرِهِ غِشَاوَةً فَمَن يَهْدِيهِ مِن بَعْدِ اللَّهِ أَفَلَا تَذَكَّرُونَ 1025{الجاثية/23}

وَمَن يَقُلْ مِنْهُمْ إِنِّي إِلَهٌ مِّن دُونِهِ فَذَلِكَ نَجْزِيهِ جَهَنَّمَ كَذَلِكَ نَجْزِي الظَّالِمِينَ 1026 {الأنبياء/29}

Or, the person with with this identity of self, with the ability of making free choice and executing their will can take the route of being a'bd of the Real Source of Kibriya, Allah ﷻ, with humbleness, humility and dependency on Rabbul A'lamìn leading ultimately to be a real and true a'bd of Allah ﷻ as mentioned:

وَمَا أَرْسَلْنَا مِن قَبْلِكَ مِن رَّسُولٍ إِلَّا نُوحِي إِلَيْهِ أَنَّهُ لَا إِلَهَ إِلَّا أَنَا فَاعْبُدُونِ 1027{الأنبياء/25}

} إِن كُلُّ مَن فِي السَّمَاوَاتِ وَالْأَرْضِ إِلَّا آتِي الرَّحْمَنِ عَبْدًا1028 {مريم/93}

Yet, this is a very fine line. Its detection, struggle or training and removal is very but very difficult. Rasulullah ﷺ mentions if there is a tiny bit of kibr in one's heart then, they won't be able to enter Jannah [8] [4] [9]. Therefore, one can understand the ayah of إِنَّا عَرَضْنَا الْأَمَانَةَ عَلَى السَّمَاوَاتِ

1024. Have you seen the one who takes as his god his own desire? Then would you be responsible for him?

1025. Have you seen he who has taken as his god his [own] desire, and Allah has sent him astray due to knowledge and has set a seal upon his hearing and his heart and put over his vision a veil? So who will guide him after Allah? Then will you not be reminded?

1026. And whoever of them should say, "Indeed, I am a god besides Him"—that one We would recompense with Hell. Thus do We recompense the wrongdoers.

1027. And We sent not before you any messenger except that We revealed to him that, "There is no deity except Me, so worship Me."

1028. There is no one in the heavens and earth but that he comes to the Most Merciful as a servant.

وَالْأَرْضِ وَالْجِبَالِ فَأَبَيْنَ أَن يَحْمِلْنَهَا وَأَشْفَقْنَ مِنْهَا وَحَمَلَهَا الْإِنسَانُ إِنَّهُ كَانَ ظَلُومًا جَهُولًا1029
{72/الأحزاب}with this understanding.

The amanah is the free will or choice. That has natural tendency to indulge in kibir like an animal who wants to wander without a leash. Holding this animal with the leash and directing to the allowed and permissible path requires effort, struggle and constant engagement with the animal.

Similarly, our own selves with free will and choice is like that animal that needs to have the leash not to go to impermissible lawns of kibir. That is not our lawn. Allah ﷻ mentions Al-Kibriyau Azamaatu [11] [4] whoever wants to share or comes to this impermissible field they are doomed. May Allah ﷻ protect us, Amìn.

In this regard if kibir is not detected and trained, then the second immediate soldier of kibir who is hasad who waiting to attack, transfuse, and in emotions, thoughts and ideas. Then, the next step is displaying these actions with evil.

In this regard, every hasad can be due to arrogance. Arrogance is difficult to detect. Hasad is easier to detect because hasad is the manifestation of the arrogance in the person's thoughts and emotions leading to actions.

Yes, we have different tendencies, emotions and thoughts. The main goal of our test is to constantly but constantly gauge them in a halal and permissible fields, lawns and areas of engagement. If someone feels hasad then, he or she immediately should ask forgiveness from Allah ﷻ due to the seed of arrogance. Hasad is the trunk and branches of the root of the arrogance.

Removing the root of the arrogance is the lifelong struggle and gist of the secrecy of life.

Hasad is the trunk and branch of the root of arrogance. The person may not see the invisible root under the ground but they can see the trunk and branches above the ground. An example of this can be وَمَثَلُ .كَلِمَةٍ خَبِيثَةٍ كَشَجَرَةٍ خَبِيثَةٍ اجْتُثَّتْ مِن فَوْقِ الْأَرْضِ مَا لَهَا مِن قَرَارٍ1030{26/إبراهيم}

An example of the self and nafs struggling in the removal of these diseases as the 'abd of Allah ﷻ can be similar to a good tree displaying

---

1029. Indeed, We offered the Trust to the heavens and the earth and the mountains, and they declined to bear it and feared it; but man [undertook to] bear it. Indeed, he was unjust and ignorant.
1030. And the example of a bad word is like a bad tree, uprooted from the surface of the earth, not having any stability.

good with a healthy root as mentioned أَلَمْ تَرَ كَيْفَ ضَرَبَ اللّٰهُ مَثَلاً كَلِمَةً طَيِّبَةً كَشَجَرَةٍ طَيِّبَةٍ أَصْلُهَا ثَابِتٌ وَفَرْعُهَا فِي السَّمَاءِ 1031 {إبراهيم/24}

Hasad & Identities

Arrogance as a disease can make the person blind and deaf when there is a reality, fact, reasonable and logical case presented. Yet, the arrogant does not hear or see any of them although the presenter may be constantly talking and showing different presentations to prove his or her factual and reasonable point as mentioned وَإِن تَدْعُوهُمْ إِلَى الْهُدَى لَا يَسْمَعُواْ وَتَرَاهُمْ يَنظُرُونَ إِلَيْكَ وَهُم لاَ يُبْصِرُونَ 1032 {الأعراف/198}.

When this self with arrogance situates him or herself in a group, this attitude of arrogance embedded in self-identity transforms itself to the attitude of arrogance embedded in a group identity. Yet, although one can see a group as a unit together with this ingenuine motivation of arrogance in reality, the self matters and the self as an individual is in shattered states as mentioned 1033 بَأْسُهُمْ بَيْنَهُمْ شَدِيدٌ تَحْسَبُهُمْ جَمِيعًا وَقُلُوبُهُمْ شَتَّى ذَلِكَ بِأَنَّهُمْ قَوْمٌ لَا يَعْقِلُونَ {الحشر/14}In this regard, these diseased individuals with arrogance carrying these group identities do not accept anything or anyone unless they have the ID card of their group. As mentioned, being in that group is just a vehicle or tool of the manifestation of this diseased self in the group.

Yet, in the same group, not all the individuals or selves may be similar carrying this similar approach of self with arrogance. There can be genuine, and sincere ones as mentioned:

رَبَّنَا آمَنَّا بِمَا أَنزَلَتْ وَاتَّبَعْنَا الرَّسُولَ فَاكْتُبْنَا مَعَ الشَّاهِدِينَ {آل عمران/53}1034

وَإِذَا سَمِعُواْ مَا أُنزِلَ إِلَى الرَّسُولِ تَرَى أَعْيُنَهُمْ تَفِيضُ مِنَ الدَّمْعِ مِمَّا عَرَفُواْ مِنَ الْحَقِّ يَقُولُونَ رَبَّنَا آمَنَّا فَاكْتُبْنَا مَعَ الشَّاهِدِينَ {المائدة/83}1035

1031. It produces its fruit all the time, by permission of its Lord. And Allah presents examples for the people that perhaps they will be reminded.
1032. And if you invite them to guidance, they do not hear; and you see them looking at you while they do not see.
1033. Their enmity among themselves is severe. You think that they are together, but their hearts are diverse. That is because they are people who do not reason.
1034. Our Lord, we have believed in what You revealed and have followed the messenger, so register us among the witnesses [to truth]."
1035. And when they hear what has been revealed to the Messenger, you see their eyes overflowing with tears because of what they have recognized of the truth. They say, "Our Lord, we have believed, so register us among the witnesses.

These genuine ones are the people when they are presented some factual data, logical and plausible approaches, they don't deny. They immediately go back to their real self as individuals beyond their group identities to decode who they are with humbleness and humility.

With humbleness and humility as the a'bd[1036] of Allah ﷻ or God, they immediately transform into the cautious states of vigilance in order to think, evaluate, and ponder in these presetantations, facts and realities. After this process, they exclaim this true, logical, and genuine approach of "[1037]ربنا فاكتبنا مع الشاهدين or و من نزل بحق[1038]" Here, al-Haqq is the all the truths and meanings with certainties as assigned by Allah ﷻ and Rasulullah ﷺ and all other authentic prophets and scriptures as sent by Allah ﷻ.

Today, one can call this as true open-mindedness, acceptance, tolerance and scientific and civilized societies.

The approach of the Qurãn is not telling the person or individuals to change identities, fans, clubs, or group associations. The Qurãn is simply, clearly and genuinely advising to consider logical, plausible and reasonable approaches with fairness and justice.

Hasad goes further. It desires the person to lose what they have, suffer and be in pain as mentioned أَمْ يَحْسُدُونَ النَّاسَ عَلَى مَا آتَاهُمُ اللّهُ مِن فَضْلِهِ فَقَدْ آتَيْنَا آلَ إِبْرَاهِيمَ الْكِتَابَ وَالْحِكْمَةَ وَآتَيْنَاهُم مُّلْكًا عَظِيمًا[1039] {النساء/54}

The people of hasad does not agree, accept or act to be open-minded unless the person or individual leave their group and go to another group as mentioned:

وَدَّ كَثِيرٌ مِّنْ أَهْلِ الْكِتَابِ لَوْ يَرُدُّونَكُم مِّن بَعْدِ إِيمَانِكُمْ كُفَّارًا حَسَدًا مِّنْ عِندِ أَنفُسِهِم مِّن بَعْدِ مَا تَبَيَّنَ لَهُمُ الْحَقُّ فَاعْفُوا وَاصْفَحُوا حَتَّى يَأْتِيَ اللّهُ بِأَمْرِهِ إِنَّ اللّهَ عَلَى كُلِّ شَيْءٍ قَدِيرٌ [1040]{البقرة/109}

1036. Servants,
1037. And he who came down with the truth.
1038. Oh Allah, write us among the witnesses.
1039. Or do they envy people for what Allah has given them of His bounty? But We had already given the family of Abraham the Scripture and wisdom167 and conferred upon them a great kingdom.
1040. Many of the People of the Scripture wish they could turn you back to disbelief after you have believed, out of envy from themselves [even] after the truth has become clear to them. So pardon and overlook until Allah delivers His command. Indeed, Allah is over all things competent.

The Qurān therefore strictly warns the people whose group identities go beyond their content identities as:

وَقَالُواْ لَن يَدْخُلَ الْجَنَّةَ إِلاَّ مَن كَانَ هُوداً أَوْ نَصَارَى تِلْكَ أَمَانِيُّهُمْ قُلْ هَاتُواْ بُرْهَانَكُمْ إِن كُنتُمْ صَادِقِينَ {111/البقرة} [1041]

وَقَالَتِ الْيَهُودُ وَالنَّصَارَى نَحْنُ أَبْنَاء اللهِ وَأَحِبَّاؤُهُ قُلْ فَلِمَ يُعَذِّبُكُم بِذُنُوبِكُم بَلْ أَنتُم بَشَرٌ مِّمَّنْ خَلَقَ يَغْفِرُ لِمَن يَشَاء وَيُعَذِّبُ مَن يَشَاء وَلِلّهِ مُلْكُ السَّمَاوَاتِ وَالأَرْضِ وَمَا بَيْنَهُمَا وَإِلَيْهِ الْمَصِيرُ {18/المائدة} [1042]

In other words, sometimes our group identities fueled by our individual self-related arrogant identities make us forget the principles and purpose of being in that group.

Therefore, healthy groups are formed by healthy individuals. The person who is in a group should constantly go always back to their healthy individual state to check if the person is in line with the group principles or guidelines compared to the people who are practicing these teachings.

The Qurān and sunnah of Rasulullah ﷺ are perfect, pure and complete. Yet, if a person is in a group of Muslims, and if some Muslims who practice them have some issues of alignment with the core principles, then a genuine Muslim should check the balance not according to the contemporary practice but according to the original source.

Yes, there may be some changing and updates as details of fiqh adapted by scholars can indicate. Yet, these are details as agreed as the usul of ijma of the scholars of the ummah in those emerging problems with their solutions.

Similarly, one can find the similar dispositions in different religions.

When a case is presented the person can do this self-check or alignment according to their healthy self using their mind, without arrogance.

May Allah ﷻ guide us, Amîn.

1041. And they say, "None will enter Paradise except one who is a Jew or a Christian." That is [merely] their wishful thinking. Say, "Produce your proof, if you should be truthful."

1042. But the Jews and the Christians say, "We are the children of Allah and His beloved." Say, "Then why does He punish you for your sins?" Rather, you are human beings from among those He has created. He forgives whom He wills, and He punishes whom He wills. And to Allah belongs the dominion of the heavens and the earth and whatever is between them, and to Him is the [final] destination.

Hasad & Its Display

وَمِن شَرِّ حَاسِدٍ إِذَا حَسَدَ 1043 {الفلق/5}

One can review hasad as display of arrogance in our actions. If arrogance is the intention, the hasad is its action.

The true healthy person has imān, islam, and ihsān [13].

The diseased person has arrogance, hasad and embodiment of shaytān.

The display one's imān is through islam. The display of one's arrogance is true hasad.

In the Qurān, Sûrah ikhlas

قُلْ هُوَ اللهُ أَحَدٌ 1044 {الإخلاص/1} اللهُ الصَّمَدُ 1045 {الإخلاص/2} لَمْ يَلِدْ وَلَمْ يُولَدْ 1046 {الإخلاص/3} وَلَمْ يَكُن لَّهُ كُفُوًا أَحَدٌ 1047 {الإخلاص/4} can indicate the true tawhid with imān, islam and ihsān for a healthy person. The sûrahs falaq and nas can indicate the possible diseases of arrogance with its display of hasad as

قُلْ أَعُوذُ بِرَبِّ الْفَلَقِ 1048 {الفلق/1} مِن شَرِّ مَا خَلَقَ 1049 {الفلق/2} وَمِن شَرِّ غَاسِقٍ إِذَا وَقَبَ 1050 {الفلق/3} وَمِن شَرِّ النَّفَّاثَاتِ فِي الْعُقَدِ 1051 {الفلق/4} وَمِن شَرِّ حَاسِدٍ إِذَا حَسَدَ 1052 {الفلق/5}

قُلْ أَعُوذُ بِرَبِّ النَّاسِ 1053 {الناس/1} مَلِكِ النَّاسِ 1054 {الناس/2} إِلَهِ النَّاسِ 1055 {الناس/3} مِن شَرِّ الْوَسْوَاسِ الْخَنَّاسِ 1056 {الناس/4} الَّذِي يُوَسْوِسُ فِي صُدُورِ النَّاسِ 1057 {الناس/5} مِنَ الْجِنَّةِ وَ النَّاسِ 1058 {الناس/6}

1043. And from the evil of an envier when he envies."
1044. Say, "He is Allah, [who is] One,
1045. Allah, the Eternal Refuge.
1046. He neither begets nor is born,
1047. Nor is there to Him any equivalent."
1048. Say, "I seek refuge in the Lord of day break.
1049. From the evil of that which He create.
1050. And from the evil of darkness when it settles.
1051. And from the evil of the blowers in knots.
1052. And from the evil of an envier when he envies."
1053. Say, "I seek refuge in the Lord of mankind,
1054. The Sovereign of mankind,
1055. The God of mankind,
1056. From the evil of the retreating whisperer.
1057. Who whispers [evil] into the breasts of mankind-
1058. From among the jinn and mankind."

In this regard, Sûrah falaq explicitly states this disease as وَمِن شَرِّ حَاسِدٍ
إِذَا حَسَدَ{الفلق/5}[1059], as when and how the process of hasad can occur وَمِن
شَرِّ غَاسِقٍ إِذَا وَقَبَ{الفلق/3}[1060] وَمِن شَرِّ النَّفَّاثَاتِ فِي الْعُقَدِ{الفلق/4}[1061]

Sûrah nãs explicitly states about the beings who are in the realms of
free choice and free will. These are humans and jinn. They can be either
in the valleys of imãn as stated with Sûrah ikhlas. Or, with their free
choice and free will, they can be in the valleys of kufr with arrogance,
kufr and sharr, evil as mentioned: مِن شَرِّ الْوَسْوَاسِ الْخَنَّاسِ{الناس/4}[1062] الَّذِي
يُوَسْوِسُ فِي صُدُورِ النَّاسِ{الناس/5}[1063] مِنَ الْجِنَّةِ وَ النَّاسِ{الناس/6}[1064]

In both cases, Allah ﷻ shows us the way of protection from others
about their evil as[1065] قُلْ أَعُوذُ and قُلْ أَعُوذُ بِرَبِّ الْفَلَقِ{الفلق/1}[1066] مِن شَرِّ مَا خَلَقَ
بِرَبِّ النَّاسِ{الناس/1}[1067] مَلِكِ النَّاسِ{الناس/2}[1068] إِلَهِ النَّاسِ{الناس/3}[1069]. Both the
disease and cure are there, الله اعلم[1070]

May Allah ﷻ protect us from our own selves and others.

[144-150]

اللهم اني اعوذ بك من شر نفسي و من شر الشيطان و شركه[1071]

قَدْ نَرَى تَقَلُّبَ وَجْهِكَ فِي السَّمَاء فَلَنُوَلِّيَنَّكَ قِبْلَةً تَرْضَاهَا فَوَلِّ وَجْهَكَ شَطْرَ الْمَسْجِدِ
الْحَرَامِ وَحَيْثُ مَا كُنتُمْ فَوَلُّواْ وُجُوهَكُمْ شَطْرَهُ وَإِنَّ الَّذِينَ أُوتُواْ الْكِتَابَ لَيَعْلَمُونَ أَنَّهُ الْحَقُّ
مِن رَّبِّهِمْ وَمَا اللّهُ بِغَافِلٍ عَمَّا يَعْمَلُونَ{البقرة/144}[1072] وَلَئِنْ أَتَيْتَ الَّذِينَ أُوتُواْ الْكِتَابَ

1059. And from the evil of an envier when he envies."
1060. And from the evil of darkness when it settles
1061. And from the evil of the blowers in knots
1062. From the evil of the retreating whisperer.
1063. Who whispers [evil] into the breasts of mankind–
1064. From among the jinn and mankind."
1065. From the evil of that which He create.
1066. Say, "I seek refuge in the Lord of day break.
1067. Say, "I seek refuge in the Lord of mankind,
1068. The Sovereign of mankind,
1069. The God of mankind,
1070. Allah knows best.
1071. Oh Allah, I seek refuge in you from the evil of myself. And from the evil of Shaytaan and his company.
1072. We have certainly seen the turning of your face, [O Muhammad], toward the heaven, and We will surely turn you to a Qiblah with which you will be pleased. So turn your face [i.e., yourself] toward al-Masjid al-haram. And wherever you [believers] are, turn your faces [i.e., yourselves] toward it [in prayer]. Indeed, those who have been given the Scripture [i.e., the Jews and the Christians] well know that it is the truth from their Lord. And Allah is not unaware of what they do.

بِكُلِّ آيَةٍ مَّا تَبِعُواْ قِبْلَتَكَ وَمَا أَنتَ بِتَابِعٍ قِبْلَتَهُمْ وَمَا بَعْضُهُم بِتَابِعٍ قِبْلَةَ بَعْضٍ وَلَئِنِ اتَّبَعْتَ
أَهْوَاءهُم مِّن بَعْدِ مَا جَاءكَ مِنَ الْعِلْمِ إِنَّكَ إِذاً لَّمِنَ الظَّالِمِينَ 1073 {البقرة/145}

الَّذِينَ آتَيْنَاهُمُ الْكِتَابَ يَعْرِفُونَهُ كَمَا يَعْرِفُونَ أَبْنَاءهُمْ وَإِنَّ فَرِيقاً مِّنْهُمْ لَيَكْتُمُونَ الْحَقَّ وَهُمْ
يَعْلَمُونَ 1074 {البقرة/146} الْحَقُّ مِن رَّبِّكَ فَلاَ تَكُونَنَّ مِنَ الْمُمْتَرِينَ 1075
وَلِكُلٍّ وِجْهَةٌ هُوَ مُوَلِّيهَا فَاسْتَبِقُواْ الْخَيْرَاتِ أَيْنَ مَا تَكُونُواْ يَأْتِ بِكُمُ اللّهُ جَمِيعًا إِنَّ اللّهَ عَلَى
كُلِّ شَيْءٍ قَدِيرٌ 1076 {البقرة/148} وَمِنْ حَيْثُ خَرَجْتَ فَوَلِّ وَجْهَكَ شَطْرَ الْمَسْجِدِ الْحَرَامِ
وَإِنَّهُ لَلْحَقُّ مِن رَّبِّكَ وَمَا اللّهُ بِغَافِلٍ عَمَّا تَعْمَلُونَ 1077 {البقرة/149} وَمِنْ حَيْثُ خَرَجْتَ
فَوَلِّ وَجْهَكَ شَطْرَ الْمَسْجِدِ الْحَرَامِ وَحَيْثُ مَا كُنتُمْ فَوَلُّواْ وُجُوهَكُمْ شَطْرَهُ لِئَلاَّ يَكُونَ لِلنَّاسِ
عَلَيْكُمْ حُجَّةٌ إِلاَّ الَّذِينَ ظَلَمُواْ مِنْهُمْ فَلاَ تَخْشَوْهُمْ وَاخْشَوْنِي وَلأُتِمَّ نِعْمَتِي عَلَيْكُمْ وَلَعَلَّكُمْ
تَهْتَدُونَ 1078 {البقرة/150}

Identities and Direction-Shatrah

These set of ayahs are remarkably interesting similar to others that project very critical points to analyze in today's social problems.

These ayahs are another proof for perfectness, generalizability, and universality of the Qurãn, Rasulullah ﷺ, and Islam as the final complete and unchangeable religion until the Day of Qiyamah.

Ibrahim as is the pillar and symbol of tawhid. He as also was accepted anonymously by people of the Book, ahlu-kitãb. He (as) built the Kabah. This universality of common tawhid in the belief of Allah ﷻ is embedded in Kabah as built by Ibrahim as. The Kabah as the unifying body of direction, shiar, commonality and universality of tawhid as the

---

1073. And if you brought to those who were given the Scripture every sign, they would not follow your qiblah. Nor will you be a follower of their qiblah. Nor would they be followers of one another's qiblah. So if you were to follow their desires after what has come to you of knowledge, indeed, you would then be among the wrongdoers.
1074. Those to whom We gave the Scripture know him [i.e., Prophet Muhammad (PBUH)] as they know their own sons. But indeed, a party of them conceal the truth while they know [it].
1075. The truth is from your Lord, so never be among the doubters.
1076. For each [religious following] is a [prayer] direction toward which it faces. So race to [all that is] good. Wherever you may be, Allah will bring you forth [for judgement] all together. Indeed, Allah is over all things competent.
1077. So from wherever you go out [for prayer, O Muhammad], turn your face toward al-Masjid al-haram, and indeed, it is the truth from your Lord. And Allah is not unaware of what you do.
1078. And from wherever you go out [for prayer], turn your face toward al-Masjid al-haram. And wherever you [believers] may be, turn your faces toward it in order that the people will not have any argument against you, except for those of them who commit wrong; so fear them not but fear Me. And [it is] so I may complete My favor upon you and that you may be guided.

perfect and universal religion of Islam again fits this excellent qadar[1079] and qada[1080] of Allah ﷻ.

A human or any limited being cannot plan human history, contexts or places. Allah ﷻ is al-Hakîm. Everything has the most perfect and beautiful in the qada[1081] and qadar[1082] of Allah ﷻ if one evalualates everything with hikmah, wisdom and understanding. There is the perfectness in Islam in all its teachings. Then, how should be the relationship of ahlu-kitab in their recognition of this perfectness? The following ayahs present extremely critical points to analyze in the above ayahs as الَّذِينَ آتَيْنَاهُمُ الْكِتَابَ[1084] or وَإِنَّ الَّذِينَ أُوتُواْ الْكِتَابَ لَيَعْلَمُونَ أَنَّهُ الْحَقُّ مِن رَّبِّهِمْ[1083] يَعْرِفُونَهُ كَمَا يَعْرِفُونَ أَبْنَاءهُمْ.

These ayahs can be seen in two perspectives with the forms[1085] لَيَعْلَمُونَ and يَعْرِفُونَهُ[1086]. When ahlu-kitab realize about the teachings of Islam, they will indeed, for sure, and certainly will know and understand is that Islam, the Qurān, and Rasulullah ﷺ are all the truth as mentioned الْحَقُّ[1087].

Even, this knowing will be such in such a certainty either by all or some of them, such as their scholars who study religions, scriptures and theology as mentioned يَعْرِفُونَهُ كَمَا يَعْرِفُونَ أَبْنَاءهُمْ[1088].

Then, one can ask, if this is so obvious, and if Islam is like a sun to them, so obvious and clear, and if they know it, then why don't they accept it?

First, the expression وَلَئِنْ أَتَيْتَ الَّذِينَ أُوتُواْ الْكِتَابَ بِكُلِّ آيَةٍ مَّا تَبِعُواْ قِبْلَتَكَ[1089] can indicate that even if you increase and show them obvious, clear, noticeable, flawless and perfect teachings of Islam, some will still not accept or follow it. This is a reality. Why?

1079. Destiny.
1080. Fate.
1081. Fate.
1082. Destiny.
1083. Indeed, those who have been given the Scripture [i.e., the Jews and the Christians] well know that it is the truth from their Lord.
1084. Those to whom We gave the Scripture know him [i.e., Prophet Muhammad (PBUH)] as they know their own sons.
1085. They know.
1086. Know him.
1087. The truth.
1088. Know him [i.e., Prophet Muhammad (PBUH)] as they know their own sons.
1089. And if you brought to those who were given the Scripture every sign, they would not follow your qiblah.

The answer is easy but sometimes difficult to rationalize although humans are advancing with critical thinking which requires humbleness in learning and applying them. The answer is[1090] وَمَا بَعْضُهُم بِتَابِعٍ قِبْلَةَ بَعْضٍ. In other words, today we call this hindrance as the blocking, obstructing, and preventing problems of individual or group "identities" when something right or truth presents itself.

With an understanding of tolerance or dialogue in the discussions of relevance, people still can hold to their identities but also accept something besides if there is a teaching of truth, fairness, honesty, actuality, and reality presented to them.

Therefore, when something so clear, and the person sees it, but others may not see it, the person becomes astonished and can become speechless. Some people can have these feelings of doubt of their own stance or disposition due to this clarity. He or she may ask himself why the person sees but others don't see. Then, the ayah directly forwards as الْحَقُّ مِن رَّبِّكَ فَلَا تَكُونَنَّ مِنَ الْمُمْتَرِينَ[1091] that this the truth, reality, and actuality and keep your certainty.

The word الْحَقُّ[1092] is repeated constantly to assure the person for example لَيَعْلَمُونَ أَنَّهُ الْحَقُّ[1093], and الْحَقُّ مِن رَّبِّكَ[1094], وَإِنَّهُ لَلْحَقُّ مِن رَّبِّكَ[1095]. Yet, the person should apply all the means of effort to have dialogue with them for them know about the true teachings of Islam. The only boundary is وَلَئِنِ اتَّبَعْتَ أَهْوَاءهُم مِّن بَعْدِ مَا جَاءكَ مِنَ الْعِلْمِ إِنَّكَ إِذاً لَّمِنَ الظَّالِمِينَ[1096]. This can show us encouragement to reach out to them and holding this precious, perfect, final, comprehensive and universal truth of Islam.

In all these contexts, everyone can be with the struggle of being on the path of Allah ﷻ by following the means of doing good deeds and competing about them as mentioned وَلِكُلٍّ وِجْهَةٌ هُوَ مُوَلِّيهَا فَاسْتَبِقُوا[1097] الْخَيْرَاتِ. Yet, Allah ﷻ will reveal everyone's truth disposition soon in their struggle as mentioned يَأْتِ بِكُمُ اللَّهُ جَمِيعًا[1098].

1090. Nor would they be followers of one another's qiblah.
1091. The truth is from your Lord, so never be among the doubters.
1092. The truth.
1093. They know that it is the truth.
1094. The truth from your lord.
1095. Indeed it is the truth from your lord.
1096. So if you were to follow their desires after what has come to you of knowledge, indeed, you would then be among the wrongdoers.
1097. For each [religious following] is a [prayer] direction toward which it faces. So race to [all that is] good.
1098. Allah will bring you forth [for judgement] all together.

Shatrah as a Span of Direction

On a side note, one of the important points to mention especially for the Muslims in the West is the word شَطْرَ[1099] to minimize or eliminate some of the arguments related with a ruling.

Muslims as immigrants in these countries purchase unused religious buildings such as churches in order to use them for their worship spaces. When they establish the qiblah, they try to optimize the space and usage of the space by considering the rulings with the word شَطْرَ.

In this sense, the word شَطْرَ can indicate a span of angle compared to the point as displayed by the phone or computer applications of digital compass devices. With the considerations of optimization of space, these buildings can have a direction within the angle set by the word شَطْرَ. Yet, the people who may have these phone applications can cause unnecessary argumentation if they don't know this ruling and Rahmah of Allah ﷻ as indicated with the word شَطْرَ.

If Muslims are building mosques from land, then it may be preferred to establish as much accuracy as possible with the current digital compass devices. Yet, the word شَطْرَ gives us the allowance of a span of angle in an accepted interval. Allah ﷻ knows the best.

Adab of Dua

When we analyze the ayah قَدْ نَرَى تَقَلُّبَ وَجْهِكَ فِي السَّمَاء فَلَنُوَلِّيَنَّكَ قِبْلَةً تَرْضَاهَا فَوَلِّ وَجْهَكَ شَطْرَ الْمَسْجِدِ الْحَرَامِ وَحَيْثُ مَا كُنتُمْ فَوَلُّواْ وُجُوهَكُمْ شَطْرَهُ وَإِنَّ الَّذِينَ أُوتُواْ الْكِتَابَ لَيَعْلَمُونَ أَنَّهُ الْحَقُّ مِن رَّبِّهِمْ وَمَا اللّهُ بِغَافِلٍ عَمَّا يَعْمَلُونَ[1100] {البقرة/144}, one can realize about adab of Rasulullah ﷺ his relationship with Allah ﷻ.

Sometimes, we want something, and we ask from Allah ﷻ. In this asking or dua, the adab of the person can be displayed depending on the way of making the dua, and its content with the dispositions of the heart and mind.

1099. Toward.
1100. We have certainly seen the turning of your face, [O Muhammad], toward the heaven, and We will surely turn you to a Qiblah with which you will be pleased. So turn your face [i.e., yourself] toward al-Masjid al-haram. And wherever you [believers] are, turn your faces [i.e., yourselves] toward it [in prayer]. Indeed, those who have been given the Scripture [i.e., the Jews and the Christians] well know that it is the truth from their Lord. And Allah is not unaware of what they do.

According to different levels of tawakkul[1101], taslîm[1102] and tawfidh[1103], people can have different levels of adab with Allah ﷻ through their engagements of dua.

According to our best free-will engagements and choices, we can desire to have something in a certain way. This desire can be related in a conversation to Allah ﷻ. This conversation can be referred as dua. This ayah normalizes this disposition through the example of Rasulullah ﷺ.

Yet, for the higher levels when they are in the valleys of tawakkul, taslîm and tawfidh, Allah ﷻ reveals and displays their inclination or desire قَدْ نَرَى تَقَلُّبَ وَجْهِكَ فِي السَّمَاءِ فَلَنُوَلِّيَنَّكَ قِبْلَةً تَرْضَاهَا[1104]. In this proximity and close relationship with Rabbul Alamin, Allah ﷻ becomes the hand and feet of the person as mentioned in the hadith [11] representing in a metaphorical language of this closeness and promixity of the person with Rabbul Alamin.

At this level, the thoughts and inclinations of the person can be transformed into reality by Allah ﷻ. The person can have an inclination to a certain choice. Yet, due to their adab he or she, may say 'al-khayru ma akhtarak, ya Allah[1105]" الخير ما اخترك،يا الله

Mujizah of the Qurān

As a side note, one of the mujizah of the Qurān besides many in these sets of ayahs is that the word شَطْرَ[1106] is mentioned five times. As there are five daily prayers, the person turns as mentioned شَطْرَ five times, subhanAllah!

[257]

اللّهُ وَلِيُّ الَّذِينَ آمَنُواْ يُخْرِجُهُم مِّنَ الظُّلُمَاتِ إِلَى النُّورِ وَالَّذِينَ كَفَرُواْ أَوْلِيَآؤُهُمُ الطَّاغُوتُ يُخْرِجُونَهُم مِّنَ النُّورِ إِلَى الظُّلُمَاتِ أُوْلَـئِكَ أَصْحَابُ النَّارِ هُمْ فِيهَا خَالِدُونَ[1107] {البقرة/257}

1101. Trust in Allah SWT
1102. Reliance in Allah SWT
1103. Full Trust and Reliance in Allah SWT
1104. We have certainly seen the turning of your face, [O Muhammad], toward the heaven, and We will surely turn you to a Qiblah with which you will be pleased.
1105. The good is what you choose, oh Allah!
1106. Toward.
1107. Allah is the ally of those who believe. He brings them out from darknesses into the light. And those who disbelieve—their allies are taghut. They take them out of the light into darknesses. Those are the companions of the Fire; they will abide eternally therein.

If we focus on the above ayah around the key word of الظُّلُمَاتِ[1108], we can review some other ayahs of the Qurān with the similar lexical and contextual meanings. For example:

يَا أَهْلَ الْكِتَابِ قَدْ جَاءكُمْ رَسُولُنَا يُبَيِّنُ لَكُمْ كَثِيرًا مِّمَّا كُنتُمْ تُخْفُونَ مِنَ الْكِتَابِ وَيَعْفُو عَن كَثِيرٍ قَدْ جَاءكُم مِّنَ اللّهِ نُورٌ وَكِتَابٌ مُّبِينٌ[1109] {المائدة/15} يَهْدِي بِهِ اللّهُ مَنِ اتَّبَعَ رِضْوَانَهُ سُبُلَ السَّلاَمِ وَيُخْرِجُهُم مِّنِ الظُّلُمَاتِ إِلَى النُّورِ بِإِذْنِهِ وَيَهْدِيهِمْ إِلَى صِرَاطٍ مُّسْتَقِيمٍ {المائدة/16}[1110]

وَالَّذِينَ كَذَّبُواْ بِآيَاتِنَا صُمٌّ وَبُكْمٌ فِي الظُّلُمَاتِ مَن يَشَإِ اللّهُ يُضْلِلْهُ وَمَن يَشَأْ يَجْعَلْهُ عَلَى صِرَاطٍ مُّسْتَقِيمٍ {الأنعام/39}[1111]

أَوَ مَن كَانَ مَيْتًا فَأَحْيَيْنَاهُ وَجَعَلْنَا لَهُ نُورًا يَمْشِي بِهِ فِي النَّاسِ كَمَن مَّثَلُهُ فِي الظُّلُمَاتِ لَيْسَ بِخَارِجٍ مِّنْهَا كَذَلِكَ زُيِّنَ لِلْكَافِرِينَ مَا كَانُواْ يَعْمَلُونَ {الأنعام/122}[1112]

قُلْ مَن رَّبُّ السَّمَاوَاتِ وَالأَرْضِ قُلِ اللّهُ قُلْ أَفَاتَّخَذْتُم مِّن دُونِهِ أَوْلِيَاء لاَ يَمْلِكُونَ لِأَنفُسِهِمْ نَفْعًا وَلاَ ضَرًّا قُلْ هَلْ يَسْتَوِي الأَعْمَى وَالْبَصِيرُ أَمْ هَلْ تَسْتَوِي الظُّلُمَاتُ وَالنُّورُ أَمْ جَعَلُواْ لِلّهِ شُرَكَاء خَلَقُواْ كَخَلْقِهِ فَتَشَابَهَ الْخَلْقُ عَلَيْهِمْ قُلِ اللّهُ خَالِقُ كُلِّ شَيْءٍ وَهُوَ الْوَاحِدُ الْقَهَّارُ[1113] {الرعد/16}

الَر كِتَابٌ أَنزَلْنَاهُ إِلَيْكَ لِتُخْرِجَ النَّاسَ مِنَ الظُّلُمَاتِ إِلَى النُّورِ بِإِذْنِ رَبِّهِمْ إِلَى صِرَاطِ الْعَزِيزِ الْحَمِيدِ[1114] {إبراهيم/1}

1108. Darknesses.

1109. O People of the Scripture, there has come to you Our Messenger making clear to you much of what you used to conceal of the Scripture and overlooking much. There has come to you from Allah a light and a clear Book [i.e., the Qurān]

1110. By which Allah guides those who pursue His pleasure to the ways of peace and brings them out from darknesses into the light, by His permission, and guides them to a straight path.

1111. But those who deny Our verses are deaf and dumb within darknesses. Whomever Allah wills—He leaves astray; and whomever He wills—He puts him on a straight path.

1112. And is one who was dead and We gave him life and made for him light by which to walk among the people like one who is in darkness, never to emerge therefrom? Thus it has been made pleasing to the disbelievers that which they were doing.

1113. Say, "Who is Lord of the heavens and earth?" Say, "Allah." Say, "Have you then taken besides Him allies not possessing [even] for themselves any benefit or any harm?" Say, "Is the blind equivalent to the seeing? Or is darkness equivalent to light? Or have they attributed to Allah partners who created like His creation so that the creation [of each] seemed similar to them?" Say, "Allah is the Creator of all things, and He is the One, the Prevailing."

1114. Alif, Lam, Raa. [This is] a Book which We have revealed to you, [O Muhammad], that you might bring mankind out of darknesses into the light by permission of their Lord—to the path of the Exalted in Might, the Praiseworthy—

وَلَقَدْ أَرْسَلْنَا مُوسَى بِآيَاتِنَا أَنْ أَخْرِجْ قَوْمَكَ مِنَ الظُّلُمَاتِ إِلَى النُّورِ وَذَكِّرْهُمْ بِأَيَّامِ اللهِ إِنَّ فِي ذَلِكَ لَآيَاتٍ لِّكُلِّ صَبَّارٍ شَكُورٍ [1115] {إبراهيم/5}

هُوَ الَّذِي يُصَلِّي عَلَيْكُمْ وَمَلَائِكَتُهُ لِيُخْرِجَكُم مِّنَ الظُّلُمَاتِ إِلَى النُّورِ وَكَانَ بِالْمُؤْمِنِينَ رَحِيمًا [1116] {الأحزاب/43}

وَمَا يَسْتَوِي الْأَعْمَى وَالْبَصِيرُ [1117] {فاطر/19} وَلَا الظُّلُمَاتُ وَلَا النُّورُ [1118] {فاطر/20}

هُوَ الَّذِي يُنَزِّلُ عَلَى عَبْدِهِ آيَاتٍ بَيِّنَاتٍ لِيُخْرِجَكُم مِّنَ الظُّلُمَاتِ إِلَى النُّورِ وَإِنَّ اللهَ بِكُمْ لَرَؤُوفٌ رَّحِيمٌ [1119] {الحديد/9}

أَعَدَّ اللهُ لَهُمْ عَذَابًا شَدِيدًا فَاتَّقُوا اللهَ يَا أُولِي الْأَلْبَابِ الَّذِينَ آمَنُوا قَدْ أَنزَلَ اللهُ إِلَيْكُمْ ذِكْرًا [1120] {الطلاق/10} رَّسُولًا يَتْلُو عَلَيْكُمْ آيَاتِ اللهِ مُبَيِّنَاتٍ لِيُخْرِجَ الَّذِينَ آمَنُوا وَعَمِلُوا الصَّالِحَاتِ مِنَ الظُّلُمَاتِ إِلَى النُّورِ وَمَن يُؤْمِن بِاللهِ وَيَعْمَلْ صَالِحًا يُدْخِلْهُ جَنَّاتٍ تَجْرِي مِن تَحْتِهَا الْأَنْهَارُ خَالِدِينَ فِيهَا أَبَدًا قَدْ أَحْسَنَ اللهُ لَهُ رِزْقًا [1121] {الطلاق/11}

One of the common themes in all above ayahs is that we are and can be potentially in zulumat of spiritual darkness, gloominess, depression, anxiety, fear, uneasiness, worry, sadness, disturbance, agitation, anger, stress, nervousness and all other types of qualitative and quantitative measures of spiritual pain. To eliminate and minimize them or to transform oneself from these spiritual painful states to the light and vastness of expansion of the heart and soul with true sakìna, tranquility, and calmness is through tawhid, imān, the Qurān and Sunnah of Rasulullah ﷺ.

1115. And We certainly sent Moses with Our signs, [saying], "Bring out your people from darknesses into the light and remind them of the days of Allah." Indeed in that are signs for everyone patient and grateful.

1116. It is He who confers blessing upon you, and His angels [ask Him to do so] that He may bring you out from darknesses into the light. And ever is He, to the believers, Merciful.

1117. Not equal are the blind and the seeing,

1118. Nor are the darknesses and the light.

1119. It is He who sends down upon His Servant [Muhammad (PBUH)] verses of clear evidence that He may bring you out from darknesses into the light. And indeed, Allah is to you Kind and Merciful.

1120. Allah has prepared for them a severe punishment; so fear Allah, O you of understanding who have believed. Allah has sent down to you a message [i.e., the Qurān].

1121. [He sent] a Messenger [i.e., Muhammad (PBUH)] reciting to you the distinct verses of Allah that He may bring out those who believe and do righteous deeds from darknesses into the light. And whoever believes in Allah and does righteousness—He will admit him into gardens beneath which rivers flow to abide therein forever. Allah will have perfected for him a provision.

In the practical sense, one can immediately rush to read and engage oneself with the Qurān and hadith if one has the feelings of anxieties and stress of painful gloominess of the heart and the soul. Yet, it can be very vital for daily regular engagements with the Qurān and hadith as a wird, as one's regular spiritual practices, besides the fard, required prayers.

[259]

أَوْ كَالَّذِي مَرَّ عَلَى قَرْيَةٍ وَهِيَ خَاوِيَةٌ عَلَى عُرُوشِهَا قَالَ أَنَّى يُحْيِي هَذِهِ اللهُ بَعْدَ مَوْتِهَا فَأَمَاتَهُ اللهُ مِئَةَ عَامٍ ثُمَّ بَعَثَهُ قَالَ كَمْ لَبِثْتَ قَالَ لَبِثْتُ يَوْمًا أَوْ بَعْضَ يَوْمٍ قَالَ بَل لَّبِثْتَ مِئَةَ عَامٍ فَانظُرْ إِلَى طَعَامِكَ وَشَرَابِكَ لَمْ يَتَسَنَّهْ وَانظُرْ إِلَى حِمَارِكَ وَلِنَجْعَلَكَ آيَةً لِّلنَّاسِ وَانظُرْ إِلَىَ الْعِظَامِ كَيْفَ نُنشِزُهَا ثُمَّ نَكْسُوهَا لَحْمًا فَلَمَّا تَبَيَّنَ لَهُ قَالَ أَعْلَمُ أَنَّ اللهَ عَلَى كُلِّ شَيْءٍ قَدِيرٌ [1122] {البقرة/259}

If we analyze this ayah around the expression[1123] كَمْ لَبِثْتَ, the similar ayahs can be:

وَكَذَلِكَ بَعَثْنَاهُمْ لِيَتَسَاءلُوا بَيْنَهُمْ قَالَ قَائِلٌ مِّنْهُمْ كَم لَبِثْتُمْ قَالُوا لَبِثْنَا يَوْمًا أَوْ بَعْضَ يَوْمٍ قَالُوا رَبُّكُمْ أَعْلَمُ بِمَا لَبِثْتُمْ فَابْعَثُوا أَحَدَكُم بِوَرِقِكُمْ هَذِهِ إِلَى الْمَدِينَةِ فَلْيَنظُرْ أَيُّهَا أَزْكَى طَعَامًا فَلْيَأْتِكُم بِرِزْقٍ مِّنْهُ وَلْيَتَلَطَّفْ وَلَا يُشْعِرَنَّ بِكُمْ أَحَدًا [1124] {الكهف/19}

قَالَ كَمْ لَبِثْتُمْ فِي الْأَرْضِ عَدَدَ سِنِينَ [1125] {المؤمنون/112} قَالُوا لَبِثْنَا يَوْمًا أَوْ بَعْضَ يَوْمٍ فَاسْأَلْ الْعَادِّينَ [1126] {المؤمنون/113}

1122. Or [consider such an example] as the one who passed by a township which had fallen into ruin. He said, "How will Allah bring this to life after its death?" So Allah caused him to die for a hundred years; then He revived him. He said, "How long have you remained?" He [the man] said, "I have remained a day or part of a day." He said, "Rather, you have remained one hundred years. Look at your food and your drink; it has not changed with time. And look at your donkey; and We will make you a sign for the people. And look at the bones [of this donkey]—how We raise them and then We cover them with flesh." And when it became clear to him, he said, "I know that Allah is over all things competent."
1123. How long have you remained?
1124. And similarly, We awakened them that they might question one another. Said a speaker from among them, "How long have you remained [here]?" They said, "We have remained a day or part of a day." They said, "Your Lord is most knowing of how long you remained. So send one of you with this silver coin of yours to the city and let him look to which is the best of food and bring you provision from it and let him be cautious. And let no one be aware of you."
1125. [Allah] will say, "How long did you remain on earth in number of years?"
1126. They will say, "We remained a day or part of a day; ask those who enumerate."

The meanings center around the word لَبِثْتَ [1127] in the Qurān emphasizes the perception about the time. When the reality is hundred years then, the person thinks it was a few hours or days, then it can show the lowliness of the time of dunya without much barakah[1128]. Yet, one considers the time in relation to having no barakah with its opposite of ocean of barakah, then a day can be equivalent to thousands of days of expansion as mentioned:

يُدَبِّرُ الْأَمْرَ مِنَ السَّمَاءِ إِلَى الْأَرْضِ ثُمَّ يَعْرُجُ إِلَيْهِ فِي يَوْمٍ كَانَ مِقْدَارُهُ أَلْفَ سَنَةٍ مِّمَّا تَعُدُّونَ [1129]{السجدة/5}

وَيَسْتَعْجِلُونَكَ بِالْعَذَابِ وَلَن يُخْلِفَ اللهُ وَعْدَهُ وَإِنَّ يَوْمًا عِندَ رَبِّكَ كَأَلْفِ سَنَةٍ مِّمَّا تَعُدُّونَ[1130] {الحج/47}

In other words, when a person relates him or herself with Allah ﷻ, Allah ﷻ expands the time and outcomes for that person, with barakah[1131], Ameenاللهم اجعلنا منهم [1132].

On the other, if the person relates themselves with Shaytān, then there is no barakah with their time. The disposition of this difference is mentioned as وَيَوْمَ تَقُومُ السَّاعَةُ يُقْسِمُ الْمُجْرِمُونَ مَا لَبِثُوا غَيْرَ سَاعَةٍ كَذَلِكَ كَانُوا يُؤْفَكُونَ [1133]{الروم/55} وَقَالَ الَّذِينَ أُوتُوا الْعِلْمَ وَالْإِيمَانَ لَقَدْ لَبِثْتُمْ فِي كِتَابِ اللهَ إِلَى يَوْمِ الْبَعْثِ فَهَذَا يَوْمُ الْبَعْثِ وَلَكِنَّكُمْ كُنتُمْ لَا تَعْلَمُونَ[1134] {الروم/56}

Also, sometimes expansion and contradiction of time can be a blessing for the person from Allah ﷻ.

1127. Stayed, lived.
1128. Blessings.
1129. He arranges [each] matter from the heaven to the earth; then it will ascend to Him in a Day, the extent of which is a thousand years of those which you count.
1130. And they urge you to hasten the punishment. But Allah will never fail in His promise. And indeed, a day with your Lord is like a thousand years of those which you count.
1131. Blessings.
1132. Oh Allah, make us from among them.
1133. And the Day the Hour appears the criminals will swear they had remained but an hour. Thus they were deluded.
1134. But those who were given knowledge and faith will say, "You remained the extent of Allah's decree until the Day of Resurrection, and this is the Day of Resurrection, but you did not used to know."

Juz 4

Sûrah 3—āli 'Imrān

[144]

وَمَا مُحَمَّدٌ إِلَّا رَسُولٌ قَدْ خَلَتْ مِن قَبْلِهِ الرُّسُلُ أَفَإِن مَّاتَ أَوْ قُتِلَ انقَلَبْتُمْ عَلَى أَعْقَابِكُمْ وَمَن يَنقَلِبْ عَلَى عَقِبَيْهِ فَلَن يَضُرَّ اللَّهَ شَيْئًا وَسَيَجْزِي اللَّهُ الشَّاكِرِينَ 1135 {آل عمران/144}

مَّا كَانَ مُحَمَّدٌ أَبَا أَحَدٍ مِّن رِّجَالِكُمْ وَلَكِن رَّسُولَ اللَّهِ وَخَاتَمَ النَّبِيِّينَ وَكَانَ اللَّهُ بِكُلِّ شَيْءٍ عَلِيمًا 1136 {الأحزاب/40}

وَالَّذِينَ آمَنُوا وَعَمِلُوا الصَّالِحَاتِ وَآمَنُوا بِمَا نُزِّلَ عَلَى مُحَمَّدٍ وَهُوَ الْحَقُّ مِن رَّبِّهِمْ كَفَّرَ عَنْهُمْ سَيِّئَاتِهِمْ وَأَصْلَحَ بَالَهُمْ 1137 {محمد/2}

مُحَمَّدٌ رَّسُولُ اللَّهِ وَالَّذِينَ مَعَهُ أَشِدَّاء عَلَى الْكُفَّارِ رُحَمَاء بَيْنَهُمْ تَرَاهُمْ رُكَّعًا سُجَّدًا يَبْتَغُونَ فَضْلًا مِّنَ اللَّهِ وَرِضْوَانًا سِيمَاهُمْ فِي وُجُوهِهِم مِّنْ أَثَرِ السُّجُودِ ذَلِكَ مَثَلُهُمْ فِي التَّوْرَاةِ وَمَثَلُهُمْ فِي الْإِنجِيلِ كَزَرْعٍ أَخْرَجَ شَطْأَهُ فَآزَرَهُ فَاسْتَغْلَظَ فَاسْتَوَى عَلَى سُوقِهِ يُعْجِبُ الزُّرَّاعَ لِيَغِيظَ بِهِمُ الْكُفَّارَ وَعَدَ اللَّهُ الَّذِينَ آمَنُوا وَعَمِلُوا الصَّالِحَاتِ مِنهُم مَّغْفِرَةً وَأَجْرًا عَظِيمًا 1138 {الفتح/29}

When we review the names of Rasulullah ﷺ as مُحَمَّدٌ[1139] in the above ayahs, one can try to analyze the role of Rasulullah ﷺ at our times and with our relationship with Rasulullah ﷺ. There are different names of Rasulullah ﷺ, yet one can focus مُحَمَّدٌ as mentioned in these ayahs.

1135. Muhammad is not but a messenger. [Other] messengers have passed on before him. So if he was to die or be killed, would you turn back on your heels [to unbelief]? And he who turns back on his heels will never harm Allah at all; but Allah will reward the grateful.

1136. Muhammad is not the father of [any] one of your men, but [he is] the Messenger of Allah and seal [i.e., last] of the prophets. And ever is Allah, of all things, Knowing.

1137. And those who believe and do righteous deeds and believe in what has been sent down upon Muhammad—and it is the truth from their Lord—He will remove from them their misdeeds and amend their condition.

1138. Muhammad is the Messenger of Allah; and those with him are forceful against the disbelievers, merciful among themselves. You see them bowing and prostrating [in prayer], seeking bounty from Allah and [His] pleasure. Their mark [i.e., sign] is on their faces [i.e., foreheads] from the trace of prostration. That is their description in the Torah. And their description in the Gospel is as a plant which produces its offshoots and strengthens them so they grow firm and stand upon their stalks, delighting the sowers—so that He [i.e., Allah] may enrage by them the disbelievers. Allah has promised those who believe and do righteous deeds among them forgiveness and a great reward.

1139. Muhammed (PBBUH).

The expression as Muhammad ﷺ as the Rasulullah ﷺ is explicitly mentioned as مُحَمَّدٌ رَّسُولُ اللَّهِ. Then, Allah ﷻ mentions as: لَقَدْ جَاءكُمْ رَسُولٌ مِّنْ أَنفُسِكُمْ عَزِيزٌ عَلَيْهِ مَا عَنِتُّمْ حَرِيصٌ عَلَيْكُم بِالْمُؤْمِنِينَ رَؤُوفٌ رَّحِيمٌ [1140]{التوبة/128}

One of the parts, we are missing today is to refresh ourselves in our connection with Rasulullah ﷺ. Rasulullah ﷺ as a human and as the messenger of Allah ﷻ showed us an applicable life with good and moral character induced with the piety and taqwa of the person with Allah ﷻ.

He ﷺ embodied all the utmost peak levels of virtue in all humanly engagements. In our personal lives, sometimes we forget to analyze and apply the teachings of sunnah. At the same time, we sometimes forget to extend a hand for the ones who may need our help from Muslims or non-Muslims by embodying the teachings of Rasulullah ﷺ. Since, we don't know much about Rasulullah ﷺ we don't practice the sunnah of Rasulullah ﷺ much. Since, we don't know and practice much, we can't naturally tell and transfer this knowledge.

It is important study the all the behavioral, emotional and other perspectives of Rasulullah ﷺ in our times of conflict.

1140. There has certainly come to you a Messenger from among yourselves. Grievous to him is what you suffer; [he is] concerned over you [i.e., your guidance] and to the believers is kind and merciful.

Juz 6

Sûrah 4—an-Nisã

[128]

Shuh—The World of Filthy Self

وَإِنِ امْرَأَةٌ خَافَتْ مِن بَعْلِهَا نُشُوزًا أَوْ إِعْرَاضًا فَلاَ جُنَاحَ عَلَيْهِمَا أَن يُصْلِحَا بَيْنَهُمَا صُلْحًا وَالصُّلْحُ خَيْرٌ وَأُحْضِرَتِ الأَنْفُسُ الشُّحَّ.وَإِن تُحْسِنُواْ وَتَتَّقُواْ فَإِنَّ اللهَ كَانَ بِمَا تَعْمَلُونَ خَبِيرًا 1141﴿النساء/128﴾

وَالَّذِينَ تَبَوَّؤُوا الدَّارَ وَالْإِيمَانَ مِن قَبْلِهِمْ يُحِبُّونَ مَنْ هَاجَرَ إِلَيْهِمْ وَلَا يَجِدُونَ فِي صُدُورِهِمْ حَاجَةً مِّمَّا أُوتُوا وَيُؤْثِرُونَ عَلَى أَنفُسِهِمْ وَلَوْ كَانَ بِهِمْ خَصَاصَةٌ وَمَن يُوقَ شُحَّ نَفْسِهِ فَأُوْلَئِكَ هُمُ الْمُفْلِحُونَ 1142﴿الحشر/9﴾

One should remember that the purpose of achievement, jihad and struggle is tazkiyatul nafs. Nafs is filled with diseases. For example أَلَمْ تَرَ إِلَى الَّذِينَ نُهُوا عَنِ النَّجْوَى ثُمَّ يَعُودُونَ لِمَا نُهُوا عَنْهُ وَيَتَنَاجَوْنَ بِالْإِثْمِ وَالْعُدْوَانِ وَمَعْصِيَتِ الرَّسُولِ وَإِذَا جَاؤُوكَ حَيَّوْكَ بِمَا لَمْ يُحَيِّكَ بِهِ اللهُ وَيَقُولُونَ فِي أَنفُسِهِمْ لَوْلَا يُعَذِّبُنَا اللهُ بِمَا نَقُولُ حَسْبُهُمْ جَهَنَّمُ يَصْلَوْنَهَا فَبِئْسَ الْمَصِيرُ 1143﴿المجادلة/8﴾

One can see in this ayah a person has an external interaction as nice and kind as 1144 وَإِذَا جَاؤُوكَ حَيَّوْكَ بِمَا لَمْ يُحَيِّكَ بِهِ اللهَ. In this externality, everything seems so normal, nice and in line with the teachings of Allah ﷻ.

1141. And if a woman fears from her husband contempt or evasion, there is no sin upon them if they make terms of settlement between them—and settlement is best. And present in [human] souls is stinginess. But if you do good and fear Allah—then indeed Allah is ever, with what you do, Acquainted.

1142. And [also for] those who were settled in the Home [i.e., al-Madinah] and [adopted] the faith before them. They love those who emigrated to them and find not any want in their breasts of what they [i.e., the emigrants] were given but give [them] preference over themselves, even though they are in privation. And whoever is protected from the stinginess of his soul—it is those who will be the successful.

1143. Have you not considered those who were forbidden from private conversation [i.e., ridicule and conspiracy] and then return to that which they were forbidden and converse among themselves about sin and aggression and disobedience to the Messenger? And when they come to you, they greet you with that [word] by which Allah does not greet you and say among themselves, "Why does Allah not punish us for what we say?" Sufficient for them is Hell, which they will [enter to] burn, and wretched is the destination.

1144. And when they come to you, they greet you with that [word] by which Allah.

Yet, in the internality of the essence as worded as nafs and the word أَنْفُسِهِمْ[1145] expressed in the plural form of addressing. In this sense, every nafs has its own world filled with filth, garbage, urine, disgusting and lowly engagements for the soul, rûh.

This filth is so much disgusting that Allah ﷻ, al-Sattār[1146], as a mercy gave humans the cover of externality with the physical body. No one knows the reality, essence and internal core of this world of the person.

Yes, every person's internal world is a world bigger than the earth that we are living in. This internal world smells, is repulsive, and disgusting. Therefore, Allah ﷻ protects us entering these worlds of others.

This filthy state of the world of the person can be called as شُحَّ as mentioned in وَالَّذِينَ تَبَوَّؤُوا الدَّارَ وَالْإِيمَانَ مِن قَبْلِهِمْ يُحِبُّونَ مَنْ هَاجَرَ إِلَيْهِمْ وَلَا يَجِدُونَ فِي صُدُورِهِمْ حَاجَةً مِّمَّا أُوتُوا وَيُؤْثِرُونَ عَلَى أَنفُسِهِمْ وَلَوْ كَانَ بِهِمْ خَصَاصَةٌ وَمَن يُوقَ شُحَّ نَفْسِهِ فَأُولَٰئِكَ هُمُ الْمُفْلِحُونَ[1147] {الحشر/9}

This world of شُحَّ[1148] has the elements in the dark air with selfishness, egotism and arrogance, poisonus plants of jealousy, fruits of greed, anger and vanity with the path ways of lies. This world is always dark as mentioned in the Qurān as كَانُوا أَنفُسَهُمْ يَظْلِمُونَ[1149]. There is no daylight. The atmosphere is always dark without any sky but with dark depressive and scary fogs.

Yet, our world or my world is not different than others unless there is the process of constant cleaning through first acceptance, or realization. Then, cleaning with istigfar and tawbah relating oneself with the Pure, al-Quddus, Allah ﷻ. This process is the essence of life and living. This process is the essence of the struggle of the life as mentioned by Rasulah ﷺ as the bigger jihad.

Yet, the process of the cleansing of this filth first starts with stopping once inentionaly, purposefully due to the fear of Allah ﷻ as can be called taqwa as mentioned[1150] in وَالَّذِينَ تَبَوَّؤُوا الدَّارَ وَالْإِيمَانَ مِن قَبْلِهِمْ يُحِبُّونَ وَمَن يُوقَ مَنْ هَاجَرَ إِلَيْهِمْ وَلَا يَجِدُونَ فِي صُدُورِهِمْ حَاجَةً مِّمَّا أُوتُوا وَيُؤْثِرُونَ عَلَى أَنفُسِهِمْ وَلَوْ كَانَ

1145. Themselves.
1146. The One who covers.
1147. And [also for] those who were settled in the Home [i.e., al-Madinah] and [adopted] the faith before them. They love those who emigrated to them and find not any want in their breasts of what they [i.e., the emigrants] were given but give [them] preference over themselves, even though they are in privation. And whoever is protected from the stinginess of his soul—it is those who will be the successful.
1148. Stinginess.
1149. They themselves were wronged.
1150. And whoever is protected.

بِهِمْ خَصَاصَةٌ وَمَن يُوقَ شُحَّ نَفْسِهِ فَأُوْلَئِكَ هُمُ الْمُفْلِحُونَ {الحشر/9}1151. Also, this is mentioned as وَأُحْضِرَتِ الأَنفُسُ الشُّحَّ. وَإِن تُحْسِنُواْ وَتَتَّقُواْ فَإِنَّ اللّهَ كَانَ بِمَا 1152 in تَعْمَلُونَ خَبِيرًا {النساء/128}1153.

With the initial stage and practices of taqwa one can go to the higher stages of pleasure of Allah ﷻ.

[150–152]

إِنَّ الَّذِينَ يَكْفُرُونَ بِاللّهِ وَرُسُلِهِ وَيُرِيدُونَ أَن يُفَرِّقُواْ بَيْنَ اللّهِ وَرُسُلِهِ وَيَقُولُونَ نُؤْمِنُ بِبَعْضٍ وَنَكْفُرُ بِبَعْضٍ وَيُرِيدُونَ أَن يَتَّخِذُواْ بَيْنَ ذَلِكَ سَبِيلاً {النساء/150}1154 أُوْلَئِكَ هُمُ الْكَافِرُونَ حَقًّا وَأَعْتَدْنَا لِلْكَافِرِينَ عَذَابًا مُّهِينًا {النساء/151}1155 وَالَّذِينَ آمَنُواْ بِاللّهِ وَرُسُلِهِ وَلَمْ يُفَرِّقُواْ بَيْنَ أَحَدٍ مِّنْهُمْ أُوْلَئِكَ سَوْفَ يُؤْتِيهِمْ أُجُورَهُمْ وَكَانَ اللّهُ غَفُورًا رَّحِيمًا {النساء/152}1156

The above ayahs are scary when one considers the historical and today's attitudes towards the sunnah of Rasulullah ﷺ as mentioned with إِنَّ الَّذِينَ يَكْفُرُونَ بِاللّهِ وَرُسُلِهِ وَيُرِيدُونَ أَن يُفَرِّقُواْ بَيْنَ اللّهِ وَرُسُلِهِ وَيَقُولُونَ نُؤْمِنُ بِبَعْضٍ وَنَكْفُرُ بِبَعْضٍ. وَيُرِيدُونَ أَن يَتَّخِذُواْ بَيْنَ ذَلِكَ سَبِيلاً {النساء/150}1157. Especially, a genuine and humble person really may not tend to incline towards this disposition when one realizes this waid with the ayah أُوْلَئِكَ هُمُ الْكَافِرُونَ حَقًّا وَأَعْتَدْنَا لِلْكَافِرِينَ عَذَابًا مُّهِينًا {النساء/151}1158. Then, Allah ﷻ mentions the people of haqq and

---

1151. And [also for] those who were settled in the Home [i.e., al-Madinah] and [adopted] the faith before them. They love those who emigrated to them and find not any want in their breasts of what they [i.e., the emigrants] were given but give [them] preference over themselves, even though they are in privation. And whoever is protected from the stinginess of his soul—it is those who will be the successful.
1152. And fear {Allah}.
1153. And if a woman fears from her husband contempt or evasion, there is no sin upon them if they make terms of settlement between them—and settlement is best. And present in [human] souls is stinginess. But if you do good and fear Allah—then indeed Allah is ever, with what you do, Acquainted.
1154. Indeed, those who disbelieve in Allah and His messengers and wish to discriminate between Allah and His messengers and say, "We believe in some and disbelieve in others," and wish to adopt a way in between.
1155. Those are the disbelievers, truly. And We have prepared for the disbelievers a humiliating punishment.
1156. But they who believe in Allah and His messengers and do not discriminate between any of them—to those He is going to give their rewards. And ever is Allah Forgiving and Merciful.
1157. Indeed, those who disbelieve in Allah and His messengers and wish to discriminate between Allah and His messengers and say, "We believe in some and disbelieve in others," and wish to adopt a way in between.
1158. Those are the disbelievers, truly. And We have prepared for the disbelievers a humiliating punishment.

what we call today as ahlu sunnah wal jamaàh[1159] as can be indicated with وَالَّذِينَ آمَنُواْ بِاللّهِ وَرُسُلِهِ وَلَمْ يُفَرِّقُواْ بَيْنَ أَحَدٍ مِّنْهُمْ أُوْلَـئِكَ سَوْفَ يُؤْتِيهِمْ أُجُورَهُمْ وَكَانَ اللّهُ غَفُورًا رَّحِيمًا[1160] {النساء/152}.

Juz 9

Sûrah 7—al-A'râf

[150]

وَلَمَّا رَجَعَ مُوسَى إِلَى قَوْمِهِ غَضْبَانَ أَسِفًا قَالَ بِئْسَمَا خَلَفْتُمُونِي مِن بَعْدِيَ أَعَجِلْتُمْ أَمْرَ رَبِّكُمْ وَأَلْقَى الأَلْوَاحَ وَأَخَذَ بِرَأْسِ أَخِيهِ يَجُرُّهُ إِلَيْهِ قَالَ ابْنَ أُمَّ إِنَّ الْقَوْمَ اسْتَضْعَفُونِي وَكَادُواْ يَقْتُلُونَنِي فَلاَ تُشْمِتْ بِيَ الأَعْدَاء وَلاَ تَجْعَلْنِي مَعَ الْقَوْمِ الظَّالِمِينَ[1161] {الأعراف/150}

Group Associations

The expression {الأعراف/150}[1162] وَلاَ تَجْعَلْنِي مَعَ الْقَوْمِ الظَّالِمِينَ is important to analyze in the Qurân. It is important to detach oneself from dhulm, oppression in group associations. In other words, if there is a group as mentioned with the word الْقَوْمُ[1163] who is in the position of making dhulm, oppression as mentioned with the word الظَّالِمِينَ[1164], then it is important to disconnect, isolate, detach and disengage oneself with this group. In this case, this detachment is verbalized and declared by the brother of Musa as, Harun as. Yet, in another ayah, Allah ﷻ instructs Rasulullah ﷺ and us about this important rule as is mentioned in قُل رَّبِّ إِمَّا تُرِيَنِّي مَا يُوعَدُونَ[1165] {المؤمنون/93} رَبِّ فَلَا تَجْعَلْنِي فِي الْقَوْمِ الظَّالِمِينَ[1166] {المؤمنون/94}.

Most of the time due to fear, people tend to support and side with the oppressor although they may not really agree with the zulm, oppression that these groups are doing. Then, the person ends up as one of the supporters of this group making dhulm, oppression due to mainly fear and conflict of interest engagements. Yet, Rasulullah ﷺ mentions that the lowest level of imān in the encounters of evil is to detach oneself from this evil and not to support the oppressor at least in their real sincere disposition of their heart and emotions. The next higher step is to say something to stop the evil. The highest step is to do something to stop the evil [11]. Yet, in the times of fitnah as the signs of last time as mentioned by Rasulullah ﷺ, it is very difficult to separate lies from the truth [11].

One can analyze the other parts of the Qurān about this expression:

وَإِذَا رَأَيْتَ الَّذِينَ يَخُوضُونَ فِي آيَاتِنَا فَأَعْرِضْ عَنْهُمْ حَتَّى يَخُوضُوا فِي حَدِيثٍ غَيْرِهِ وَإِمَّا يُنسِيَنَّكَ الشَّيْطَانُ فَلاَ تَقْعُدْ بَعْدَ الذِّكْرَى مَعَ الْقَوْمِ الظَّالِمِينَ 1167 {الأنعام/68}

When there is a group of people involved in verbal conversations of topics displeasing Allah ﷻ, sitting there and listening them can indicate a group association with them. Therefore, Allah ﷻ teaches us the action to take if the person cannot be in a position of counter arguing about these topics. Yet, if the person sits with them without a proper and correct intention, then the displeasure of Allah ﷻ can be on this person as well due to among this type of group or gathering.

Oppositely, as it is indicated in a different hadith, angels report about a person who did not have a good intention but he was in a good gathering that Allah ﷻ is pleased with. Allah ﷻ then forgave him due to his presence with the good people [11]. One can consider the opposite case of this hadith. It can indicate that if a good person associates him or herself in the engagements of evil or bad people, then he can be judged accordingly his group associations as mentioned in the above ayah. الله اعلم1168

1167. And when you see those who engage in [offensive] discourse concerning Our verses, then turn away from them until they enter into another conversation. And if Satan should cause you to forget, then do not remain after the reminder with the wrongdoing people.
1168. Allah knows best.

When one reviews the below in the case of people of A'raf as:

الظَّالِمِينَ [1169]{الأعراف/44} الَّذِينَ يَصُدُّونَ عَن سَبِيلِ اللَّه وَيَبْغُونَهَا عِوَجًا وَهُم بِالآخِرَة كَافِرُونَ [1170]{الأعراف/45} وَبَيْنَهُمَا حِجَابٌ وَعَلَى الأَعْرَافِ رِجَالٌ يَعْرِفُونَ كُلًّا بِسِيمَاهُمْ وَنَادَوْاْ أَصْحَابَ الْجَنَّةِ أَن سَلاَمٌ عَلَيْكُمْ لَمْ يَدْخُلُوهَا وَهُمْ يَطْمَعُونَ [1171]{الأعراف/46} وَإِذَا صُرِفَتْ أَبْصَارُهُمْ تِلْقَاء أَصْحَابِ النَّارِ قَالُواْ رَبَّنَا لاَ تَجْعَلْنَا مَعَ الْقَوْمِ الظَّالِمِينَ [1172]{الأعراف/47} وَنَادَى أَصْحَابُ الأَعْرَافِ رِجَالًا يَعْرِفُونَهُمْ بِسِيمَاهُمْ قَالُواْ مَا أَغْنَى عَنكُمْ جَمْعُكُمْ وَمَا كُنتُمْ تَسْتَكْبِرُونَ [1173]{الأعراف/48}

In the context of above ayahs, الظَّالِمِينَ[1174] can be the ones الَّذِينَ يَصُدُّونَ عَن سَبِيلِ اللَّهِ وَيَبْغُونَهَا عِوَجًا وَهُم بِالآخِرَةِ كَافِرُونَ[1175]{الأعراف/45}. There is a group of people that people of A'raf can know as

mentioned وَنَادَى أَصْحَابُ الأَعْرَافِ رِجَالًا يَعْرِفُونَهُمْ بِسِيمَاهُمْ[1176]. In the previous ayah, they make dua to Allah ﷻ as رَبَّنَا لاَ تَجْعَلْنَا مَعَ الْقَوْمِ الظَّالِمِينَ[1177]{الأعراف/47}. The question may arise as did they separate themselves in the dunya or are they asking this separation only in the akhirah?

1169. And the companions of Paradise will call out to the companions of the Fire, "We have already found what our Lord promised us to be true. Have you found what your Lord promised to be true?" They will say, "Yes." Then an announcer will announce among them, "The curse of Allah shall be upon the wrongdoers

1170. Who averted [people] from the way of Allah and sought to make it [seem] deviant while they were, concerning the Hereafter, disbelievers."

1171. And between them will be a partition [i.e., wall], and on [its] elevations are men who recognize all by their mark. And they call out to the companions of Paradise, "Peace be upon you." They have not [yet] entered it, but they long intensely.

1172. And when their eyes are turned toward the companions of the Fire, they say, "Our Lord, do not place us with the wrongdoing people."

1173. And the companions of the Elevations will call to men [within Hell] whom they recognize by their mark, saying, "Of no avail to you was your gathering and [the fact] that you were arrogant."

1174. Wrongdoers

1175. Who averted [people] from the way of Allah and sought to make it [seem] deviant while they were, concerning the Hereafter, disbelievers."

1176. And the companions of the Elevations will call to men [within Hell] whom they recognize by their mark,

1177. "Our Lord, do not place us with the wrongdoing people."

Juz 11

Sûrah 9—at-Tawbah

[64]

يَحْذَرُ الْمُنَافِقُونَ أَن تُنَزَّلَ عَلَيْهِمْ سُورَةٌ تُنَبِّئُهُم بِمَا فِي قُلُوبِهِم قُلِ اسْتَهْزِؤُواْ إِنَّ اللّهَ مُخْرِجٌ مَّا تَحْذَرُونَ ¹¹⁷⁸ {التوبة/64}

Qurān is for everyone for all the times as each ayah can have specific sababi nuzûl. In this perspective, analyzing this ayah with our personal encounters, sometimes we are afraid when we have a problem or we did an oppression to others, there can be an ayah of the Qurān or hadith of the Rasulullah ﷺ that we may read, hear or encounter that could be addressing to this problem. As the person gets more conscious of this reality, in a possible case of oppression by this person, he or she may be afraid to hear an ayah directly not approving the position of the person. Yet, if the person did an oppression or wrong to others, instead of running away from this reality, one should ask forgiveness from Allah ﷻ as well as from the people that this person had hurt, والله اعلم¹¹⁷⁹

[97]

الأَعْرَابُ أَشَدُّ كُفْرًا وَنِفَاقًا وَأَجْدَرُ أَلاَّ يَعْلَمُواْ حُدُودَ مَا أَنزَلَ اللّهُ عَلَى رَسُولِهِ وَاللّهُ عَلِيمٌ حَكِيمٌ ¹¹⁸⁰ {التوبة/97}

The essence of the religion is ikhlas. The essence of ikhlas is adab. Adab requires having respect to the shi'ar and hudud, guidelines as prescribed by Allah ﷻ. The whole purpose of four mazhabs is to remind these shi'ar and hudûd of Allah ﷻ in a structured and understandable way so that people can follow.

Yet, there were people in the past and there are people today who may not know these etiquettes or adab of following these guidelines. If then, they humbly follow what is established with the Qurān and

---

1178. The hypocrites are apprehensive lest a Sûrah be revealed about them, informing them of what is in their hearts. Say, "Mock [as you wish]; indeed, Allah will expose that which you fear."

1179. Allah knows best.

1180. The bedouins are stronger in disbelief and hypocrisy and more likely not to know the limits of what [laws] Allah has revealed to His Messenger. And Allah is Knowing and Wise.

sunnah through these legal schools then, inshAllah, they will be in a safer position. Yet, if they decide to assert without any basis of usûl, methodology following the Qurān and sunnah, then their destruction can be more harmful as mentioned أَشَدُّ كُفْرًا وَنِفَاقًا[1181] than others.

Because, they come as a Muslim. Then, they assert something strongly. Due to their strong assertion and presenting themselves as a Muslim can confuse the naïve ones. Therefore, their harm in the destruction of the social unity can be worse than others as mentioned أَشَدُّ كُفْرًا وَنِفَاقًا. This is due to not knowing their limits or knowing the adab corresponding to the true guidelines of Allah ﷻ and Rasulullah ﷺ as mentioned أَلَّا يَعْلَمُواْ حُدُودَ مَا أَنزَلَ اللهُ عَلَى رَسُولِهِ[1182].

One can see the many examples of these as a group movement today and in the past.

Sûrah 10—Yûnus

أَلَا إِنَّ أَوْلِيَاءَ اللهِ لَا خَوْفٌ عَلَيْهِمْ وَلَا هُمْ يَحْزَنُونَ[1183]{يونس/62} الَّذِينَ آمَنُواْ وَكَانُواْ يَتَّقُونَ[1184] {يونس/63} لَهُمُ الْبُشْرَى فِي الْحَيَاةِ الدُّنْيَا وَفِي الْآخِرَةِ لَا تَبْدِيلَ لِكَلِمَاتِ اللهِ ذَلِكَ هُوَ الْفَوْزُ الْعَظِيمُ[1185] {يونس/64}

[62–64]

This ayah is very critical in the changing life conditions of the person. If the person only takes Allah ﷻ as the One who can only attach, then there will not be any display of grief, worry and stress for this person in this dunya and afterlife. Yet, imān and goal of taqwa are the key to achieve this. As mentioned in the ayah وَلَا يَحْزُنكَ قَوْلُهُمْ إِنَّ الْعِزَّةَ لِلَّهِ جَمِيعًا هُوَ السَّمِيعُ الْعَلِيمُ[1186] {يونس/65}, the izzah[1187], recognition, and respect only can come for the person when he or she associates themselves with Allah ﷻ through the means of 'ibadah leading to taqwa.

1181. Stronger in disbelief and hypocrisy.
1182. More likely not to know the limits of what [laws] Allah has revealed.
1183. Unquestionably, [for] the allies of Allah there will be no fear concerning them, nor will they grieve—
1184. Those who believed and were fearing Allah.
1185. For them are good tidings in the worldly life and in the Hereafter. No change is there in the words [i.e., decrees] of Allah. That is what is the great attainment.
1186. And let not their speech grieve you. Indeed, honor [due to power] belongs to Allah entirely. He is the Hearing, the Knowing.
1187. Respect/ honor.

Juz 12

Sûrah 12—Yûsuf

[36–40]

وَدَخَلَ مَعَهُ السِّجْنَ فَتَيَانَ قَالَ أَحَدُهُمَآ إِنِّي أَرَانِي أَعْصِرُ خَمْرًا وَقَالَ الآخَرُ إِنِّي أَرَانِي أَحْمِلُ
فَوْقَ رَأْسِي خُبْزًا تَأْكُلُ الطَّيْرُ مِنْهُ نَبِّئْنَا بِتَأْوِيلِهِ إِنَّا نَرَاكَ مِنَ الْمُحْسِنِينَ 1188 {يوسف/36}
قَالَ لاَ يَأْتِيكُمَا طَعَامٌ تُرْزَقَانِهِ إِلاَّ نَبَّأْتُكُمَا بِتَأْوِيلِهِ قَبْلَ أَن يَأْتِيكُمَا ذَلِكُمَا مِمَّا عَلَّمَنِي رَبِّي إِنِّي
تَرَكْتُ مِلَّةَ قَوْمٍ لاَّ يُؤْمِنُونَ بِاللّهِ وَهُم بِالآخِرَةِ هُمْ كَافِرُونَ 1189 {يوسف/37}

وَاتَّبَعْتُ مِلَّةَ آبَآئِي إِبْرَاهِيمَ وَإِسْحَقَ وَيَعْقُوبَ مَا كَانَ لَنَا أَن نُّشْرِكَ بِاللّهِ مِن شَيْءٍ ذَلِكَ مِن
فَضْلِ اللّهِ عَلَيْنَا وَعَلَى النَّاسِ وَلَكِنَّ أَكْثَرَ النَّاسِ لاَ يَشْكُرُونَ 1190 {يوسف/38} يَا صَاحِبَيِ
السِّجْنِ أَأَرْبَابٌ مُّتَفَرِّقُونَ خَيْرٌ أَمِ اللّهُ الْوَاحِدُ الْقَهَّارُ 1191 {يوسف/39}

مَا تَعْبُدُونَ مِن دُونِهِ إِلاَّ أَسْمَاء سَمَّيْتُمُوهَا أَنتُمْ وَآبَآؤُكُم مَّا أَنزَلَ اللّهُ بِهَا مِن سُلْطَانٍ
إِنِ الْحُكْمُ إِلاَّ لِلّهِ أَمَرَ أَلاَّ تَعْبُدُواْ إِلاَّ إِيَّاهُ ذَلِكَ الدِّينُ الْقَيِّمُ وَلَكِنَّ أَكْثَرَ النَّاسِ لاَ يَعْلَمُونَ 1192
{يوسف/40}

One can analyze the above ayahs in the context of tabligh or dawah.
When people have tawajjuh[1193], some type of liking and adoring for us
as mentioned {يوسف/36}إِنَّا نَرَاكَ مِنَ الْمُحْسِنِينَ[1194], it is important gauge this

---

1188. And there entered the prison with him two young men. One of them said, "Indeed,
I have seen myself [in a dream] pressing wine." The other said, "Indeed, I have seen myself
carrying upon my head [some] bread, from which the birds were eating. Inform us of its
interpretation; indeed, we see you to be of those who do good."
1189. He said, "You will not receive food that is provided to you except that I will inform you
of its interpretation before it comes to you. That is from what my Lord has taught me. Indeed,
I have left the religion of a people who do not believe in Allah, and they, in the Hereafter, are
disbelievers.
1190. And I have followed the religion of my fathers, Abraham, Isaac and Jacob. And it was
not for us to associate anything with Allah. That is from the favor of Allah upon us and upon
the people, but most of the people are not grateful.
1191. O [my] two companions of prison, are separate lords better or Allah, the One, the
Prevailing?
1192. You worship not besides Him except [mere] names you have named them, you and
your fathers, for which Allah has sent down no authority. Legislation is not but for Allah. He
has commanded that you worship not except Him. That is the correct religion, but most of the
people do not know.
1193. To go/ turn to { Allah}.
1194. We see you to be of those who do good."

type of people's like or love for us to the true love, imān and tawhid for Allah ﷻ.

Also, in the above renderings of the ayahs, Yusuf as does not immediately give the answer of what they are looking for. He (as) first prepares the context of tawhid for their own benefit. Then, after this preparation, Yusuf as gives the possible interpretation related with the qadah and qadar of Allah ﷻ. This is more beneficial and less destructive for them because most of the people today and in the past were alienated from religion due to problems of theodicy [8] [9].

Juz 16

Sûrah 18—al-Kahf

[78 & 82]

Evil Seeming Incidents & Theodicy

قَالَ هَذَا فِرَاقُ بَيْنِي وَبَيْنِكَ سَأُنَبِّئُكَ بِتَأْوِيلِ مَا لَمْ تَسْتَطِع عَّلَيْهِ صَبْرًا ¹¹⁹⁵ {الكهف/78}

رَحْمَةً مِّن رَّبِّكَ وَمَا فَعَلْتُهُ عَنْ أَمْرِي ذَلِكَ تَأْوِيلُ مَا لَمْ تَسْطِع عَّلَيْهِ صَبْرًا ¹¹⁹⁶ {الكهف/82}

Sometimes, evil-seeming incidents push our limits of understanding, the hikmah and reason behind them.

A great prophet of Allah ﷻ, Musa as, tries to understand these evil-incidents in his journey with Khidr as by questioning the reasons behind the incidents. The word¹¹⁹⁷ تَسْتَطِع can indicate this difficult struggle understanding of the person with their limited abilities against the evil-seeming incidents.

Then, the word تَسْطِع indicates the relief of the person by the relief or drop of one ت in the initial case of تَسْتَطِع.

Yet, even the person knows the reasons, our human judgements call an evil-seeming incident as evil. Therefore, even if there is a relief by knowing the reasons, yet, there may not be full relief as the word تَسْطِع can indicate.

1195. [Al-Khidhr] said, "This is parting between me and you. I will inform you of the interpretation of that about which you could not have patience.
1196. As a mercy from your Lord. And I did it not of my own accord. That is the interpretation of that about which you could not have patience."
1197. Ability

In our human valuation system of assigning meanings, such as assigning something or someone being in pain, suffering and happiness is due to our social and human constructions of meanings.

Allah ﷻ knows everything beyond their time with their apparent and hidden manifestations in their true realities of purpose, value and assignment.

With this comprehensive ihāta, surrounding and inclusivity with power and knowledge, the creation purpose, goal, the existence in the world, the lives and the positions of all creation in this life, afterlife and more are all and fully known by Allah ﷻ as mentioned:

يَعْلَمُ مَا بَيْنَ أَيْدِيهِمْ وَمَا خَلْفَهُمْ وَلَا يُحِيطُونَ بِشَيْءٍ مِّنْ عِلْمِهِ إِلَّا بِمَا شَاءَ وَسِعَ كُرْسِيُّهُ السَّمَاوَاتِ وَالْأَرْضَ وَلَا يَؤُودُهُ حِفْظُهُمَا وَهُوَ الْعَلِيُّ الْعَظِيمُ [1198]{البقرة/255}

يَعْلَمُ مَا بَيْنَ أَيْدِيهِمْ وَمَا خَلْفَهُمْ وَلَا يَشْفَعُونَ إِلَّا لِمَنِ ارْتَضَى وَهُم مِّنْ خَشْيَتِهِ مُشْفِقُونَ [1199]{الأنبياء/28}

The very critical phrase of يَعْلَمُ مَا بَيْنَ أَيْدِيهِمْ وَمَا خَلْفَهُمْ[1200] can indicate this comprehensive ihāta of Allah ﷻ as mentioned وَلَا يُحِيطُونَ بِشَيْءٍ مِّنْ عِلْمِهِ[1201]. One can ask why this is so important?

Because, our judgement calls and valuations, and assignment of meanings on things, events, or people all based on our knowledge. If we don't have the comprehensive knowledge of something, then there will be naturally and normally wrong and false deductions, interferences and analysis.

Therefore, all evil seeming incidents is not evil unless it is assigned and classified by Allah ﷻ as an evil.

1198. Allah—there is no deity except Him, the Ever-Living, the Sustainer of [all] existence. Neither drowsiness overtakes Him nor sleep. To Him belongs whatever is in the heavens and whatever is on the earth. Who is it that can intercede with Him except by His permission? He knows what is [presently] before them and what will be after them, and they encompass not a thing of His knowledge except for what He wills. His Kursi extends over the heavens and the earth, and their preservation tires Him not. And He is the Most High, the Most Great.
1199. He knows what is [presently] before them and what will be after them, and they cannot intercede except on behalf of one whom He approves. And they, from fear of Him, are apprehensive.
1200. He knows what is [presently] before them and what will be after them,
1201. And they encompass not a thing of His knowledge

Therefore, in a broader perspective, all the deductive reasonings can be possible wrong unless it is checked with the inductive guidelines given by Allah ﷻ through the teachings of the Qurān and Rasulullah ﷺ.

The Absolute Comprehensive Knowledge can be indicated with the critical phrase يَعْلَمُ مَا بَيْنَ أَيْدِيهِمْ وَمَا خَلْفَهُمْ وَلَا يُحِيطُونَ بِشَيْءٍ مِّنْ عِلْمِهِ[1202].

The absolute comprehensive knowledge are the true inductive guidelines, valuations and assignments as set by Allah ﷻ

Humans effort are to try to approximate the true 'ilm of inductive guidelines as set by the Qurān and Rasulullah ﷺ through the incremental steps and struggles of deductive reasonings in lifelong journeys.

For example, an evil-seeming incident can happen to someone. He or she may die or be killed due to oppression of people for this person's ethical and true stance on the path of Allah ﷻ with their imān. Then, everyone around this person can interpret this with different explanations. Media or outside observers can amplify the effects of this evil-seeming incident. Then, people or public start developing fear in their inner selves. Then, people may alienate from religion due to this evil-seeming incident as if the religion was not able to help this person and the religion was the cause of this. Then, they blame God in these evil seeming incidents called as theodicy as a technical term.

Yet, in all these renderings, one should remember by constantly reciting ayatal kursi with the emphasis of the part يَعْلَمُ مَا بَيْنَ أَيْدِيهِمْ وَمَا[1203] خَلْفَهُمْ وَلَا يُحِيطُونَ بِشَيْءٍ مِّنْ عِلْمِهِ. Then, in this case of evil seeming incident, one can remember the ayah of the Qurān as

وَلاَ تَقُولُواْ لِمَنْ يُقْتَلُ فِي سَبِيلِ اللهِ أَمْوَاتٌ بَلْ أَحْيَاء وَلَكِن لاَّ تَشْعُرُونَ[1204]{البقرة/154}

وَلاَ تَحْسَبَنَّ الَّذِينَ قُتِلُواْ فِي سَبِيلِ اللهِ أَمْوَاتًا بَلْ أَحْيَاء عِندَ رَبِّهِمْ يُرْزَقُونَ[1205]{آل عمران/169}

Similarly, one can think about the case of a slaughtering of animal for eating purposes. From externality of vegetarians, it seems to be a very

1202. He knows what is [presently] before them and what will be after them, and they encompass not a thing of His knowledge

1203. He knows what is [presently] before them and what will be after them, and they encompass not a thing of His knowledge.

1204. And do not say about those who are killed in the way of Allah, "They are dead." Rather, they are alive, but you perceive [it] not.

1205. And never think of those who have been killed in the cause of Allah as dead. Rather, they are alive with their Lord, receiving provision.

cruel act of killing something which has a life. Yet, we judge through our human observations which is normal. Yet, Allah ﷻ is Just, al-Aʿdl[1206] and al-Rahman[1207]. Allah ﷻ does not oppress anything and anyone even not smaller than a thin hair:

إِنَّ اللَّهَ لاَ يَظْلِمُ مِثْقَالَ ذَرَّةٍ وَإِن تَكُ حَسَنَةً يُضَاعِفْهَا وَيُؤْتِ مِن لَّدُنْهُ أَجْرًا عَظِيمًا[1208] {النساء/40}

أَلَمْ تَرَ إِلَى الَّذِينَ يُزَكُّونَ أَنفُسَهُمْ بَلِ اللَّهُ يُزَكِّي مَن يَشَاء وَلاَ يُظْلَمُونَ فَتِيلاً[1209] {النساء/49}

وَمَن يَعْمَلْ مِنَ الصَّالِحَاتَ مِن ذَكَرٍ أَوْ أُنثَى وَهُوَ مُؤْمِنٌ فَأُوْلَئِكَ يَدْخُلُونَ الْجَنَّةَ وَلاَ يُظْلَمُونَ نَقِيرًا[1210]{النساء/124}

إِلَّا مَن تَابَ وَآمَنَ وَعَمِلَ صَالِحًا فَأُوْلَئِكَ يَدْخُلُونَ الْجَنَّةَ وَلاَ يُظْلَمُونَ شَيْئًا[1211] {مريم/60}

مَن جَاء بِالْحَسَنَةِ فَلَهُ عَشْرُ أَمْثَالِهَا وَمَن جَاء بِالسَّيِّئَةِ فَلاَ يُجْزَى إِلاَّ مِثْلَهَا وَهُمْ لاَ يُظْلَمُونَ[1212]{الأنعام/160}

إِنَّ اللَّهَ لاَ يَظْلِمُ النَّاسَ شَيْئًا وَلَكِنَّ النَّاسَ أَنفُسَهُمْ يَظْلِمُونَ[1213] {يونس/44}

وَعَلَى الَّذِينَ هَادُواْ حَرَّمْنَا مَا قَصَصْنَا عَلَيْكَ مِن قَبْلُ وَمَا ظَلَمْنَاهُمْ وَلَكِن كَانُواْ أَنفُسَهُمْ يَظْلِمُونَ[1214] {النحل/118}

1206. The Utterly Just.

1207. The Most Merciful.

1208. Indeed, Allah does not do injustice, [even] as much as an atom's weight; while if there is a good deed, He multiplies it and gives from Himself a great reward.

1209. Have you not seen those who claim themselves to be pure? Rather, Allah purifies whom He wills, and injustice is not done to them, [even] as much as a thread [inside a date seed].

1210. And whoever does righteous deeds, whether male or female, while being a believer—those will enter Paradise and will not be wronged, [even as much as] the speck on a date seed.

1211. Except those who repent, believe and do righteousness; for those will enter Paradise and will not be wronged at all.

1212. Whoever comes [on the Day of Judgement] with a good deed will have ten times the like thereof [to his credit], and whoever comes with an evil deed will not be recompensed except the like thereof; and they will not be wronged.

1213. Indeed, Allah does not wrong the people at all, but it is the people who are wronging themselves.

1214. And to those who are Jews We have prohibited that which We related to you before. And We did not wrong them [thereby], but they were wronging themselves.

فَكُلًّا أَخَذْنَا بِذَنبِهِ فَمِنْهُم مَّنْ أَرْسَلْنَا عَلَيْهِ حَاصِبًا وَمِنْهُم مَّنْ أَخَذَتْهُ الصَّيْحَةُ وَمِنْهُم مَّنْ خَسَفْنَا بِهِ الْأَرْضَ وَمِنْهُم مَّنْ أَغْرَقْنَا وَمَا كَانَ اللّه لِيَظْلِمَهُمْ وَلَكِن كَانُوا أَنفُسَهُمْ يَظْلِمُونَ {العنكبوت/40}[1215]

In the Qurãn, it is repetitively mentioned and emphasized in similar different forms that Allah ﷻ does not oppress such as [1216]إِنَّ اللّه لَا يَظْلِمُ, لَا يُظْلَمُونَ[1217] , وَمَا ظَلَمْنَاهُمْ[1218] ,وَمَا كَانَ اللّه لِيَظْلِمَهُمْ

We sometimes ask this question is this, what happened fair? Then, we question the qadar of Allah ﷻ. Yet, everything happens with fairness and justice even though we may not realize and see it as mentioned with the word [1219]بِالْقِسْطِ in وَلَوْ أَنَّ لِكُلِّ نَفْسٍ ظَلَمَتْ مَا فِي الْأَرْضِ لَافْتَدَتْ بِهِ وَأَسَرُّوا النَّدَامَةَ لَمَّا رَأَوُا الْعَذَابَ وَقُضِيَ بَيْنَهُم بِالْقِسْطِ وَهُمْ لاَ يُظْلَمُونَ[1220] {يونس/54}

وَلِكُلِّ أُمَّةٍ رَّسُولٌ فَإِذَا جَاء رَسُولُهُمْ قُضِيَ بَيْنَهُم بِالْقِسْطِ وَهُمْ لاَ يُظْلَمُونَ[1221] {يونس/47}

Nothing or no one is oppressed that everything and everyone is treated with justice underlined with the word [1222]أَحَدًا in وَوُضِعَ الْكِتَابُ فَتَرَى الْمُجْرِمِينَ مُشْفِقِينَ مِمَّا فِيهِ وَيَقُولُونَ يَا وَيْلَتَنَا مَالِ هَذَا الْكِتَابِ لَا يُغَادِرُ صَغِيرَةً وَلَا كَبِيرَةً إِلَّا أَحْصَاهَا وَوَجَدُوا مَا عَمِلُوا حَاضِرًا وَلَا يَظْلِمُ رَبُّكَ أَحَدًا[1223]{الكهف/49}

It is very interesting to note that Allah ﷻ emphasizes that even a small quantity with the words [1227]شَيْئًا, [1224]مِثْقَالَ ذَرَّةٍ, [1225]فَتِيلًا, [1226]نَقِيرًا in the above ayahs. This can show how everything is based on Adl and Justice

---

1215. So each We seized for his sin; and among them were those upon whom We sent a storm of stones, and among them were those who were seized by the blast [from the sky], and among them were those whom We caused the earth to swallow, and among them were those whom We drowned. And Allah would not have wronged them, but it was they who were wronging themselves.

1216. Indeed, Allah does not wrong {the people}.

1217. And We did not wrong them.

1218. And Allah would not have wronged them.

1219. In justice.

1220. And if each soul that wronged had everything on earth, it would offer it in ransom. And they will confide regret when they see the punishment; and they will be judged in justice, and they will not be wronged.

1221. And for every nation is a messenger. So when their messenger comes, it will be judged between them in justice, and they will not be wronged.

1222. Anyone.

1223. And the record [of deeds] will be placed [open], and you will see the criminals fearful of that within it, and they will say, "Oh, woe to us! What is this book that leaves nothing small or great except that it has enumerated it?" And they will find what they did present [before them]. And your Lord does injustice to no one.

1224. As much as an atom's weight.

1225. A thread.

1226. A date seed.

1227. At all.

وَالسَّمَاء رَفَعَهَا وَوَضَعَ الْمِيزَانَ {الرحمن/7} 1228 أَلَّا تَطْغَوْا of Allah ۞ as mentioned
فِي الْمِيزَانِ 1229{الرحمن/8} وَأَقِيمُوا الْوَزْنَ بِالْقِسْطِ وَلَا تُخْسِرُوا الْمِيزَانَ 1230{الرحمن/9}

But, yet, humans precede their own valuation over Allah ۞,
Astagfirullah. Then, they blame Allah ۞ , Astagfirullah, with evil,
injustice, and other reasons of alienation as one can see in Western
philosophy and religious though. May Allah ۞ protect us from this is
unjust attribution to Allah ۞, Amìn. Allah ۞ is the Rabbul A'lamìn gave
us so much and yet we, humans are ungrateful as mentioned:

إِنَّ الْإِنسَانَ لِرَبِّهِ لَكَنُودٌ 1231{العاديات/6}.

Adab with Allah ۞

One should remember that the whole purpose of religion is to instill the
adab with Allah ۞. Adab with Allah ۞ requires to have adab with what
Allah ۞ tells us to have adab. Having Adab with the Qurãn, Rasulullah
۞, and other parts of the adab all stems from the core adab with Allah
۞. This core adab with Allah ۞ stems from the tawhid. This core adab
stems from لَا اله الا الله1232As the person increases their ma'rifatullah, their
true knowledge about Allah ۞, then their adab with Allah ۞ should
increase. The effects of knowledge, I'lm, aging instilling the person
wisdom (hikmah), or increasing one's 'ibadah are all expected to increase
one's closeness and adab with Allah ۞. If not, then none of them has any
use. If it is not helping the person having more adab with Allah ۞ than
a previous day, then the person is in loss. Accordingly, one can increase
their adab in the reflections of the primary adab with Rasulullah ۞ and
other shi'ar of Islam.

Aging or getting older is another means through experience in order
to increase one's adab with Allah ۞. It is the another means to increase
respect for the shi'ar as Allah ۞ tells us to have adab with it.

In this sense, the realms and encounters of qadar as the manifestation
of the Divine Decree of Allah ۞ requires adab with it as the required
part of the adab with Allah ۞. In this sense, this adab regarding qadar

---

1228. And the heaven He raised and imposed the balance.
1229. That you not transgress within the balance.
1230. And establish weight in justice and do not make deficient the balance.
1231. Indeed mankind, to his Lord, is ungrateful.
1232. Theres no god except Allah.

and in its relation with Allah ﷻ can be entitled as tawakkul[1233], taslîm[1234], and tawfidh[1235].

Tawakkul can mean "I will come and listen to you." Taslim can mean "I will do what ever you tell me with no question." Tawfiz can mean "I am fully in submission to you."

Even at the most and difficult cases of evil-seeming incidents such as a bodily torture or at the time of death, sakaratul mawt, the pains of death, the person is still expected to keep this high standard of adab with Allah ﷻ. For example, when Ibrahim as was about to be thrown in a hot oven and grill of fire, he as did not complain a bit. Yet, his adab with Allah ﷻ manifested as only turning to Allah ﷻ with full tawakkul, taslim, and tawfiz. Therefore, the title of Khalîlullah, "Friend of Allah ﷻ," is given to Ibrahim as by Allah ﷻ.

When the person is afflicted with an evil, the adab requires them to admit the Qudrah and Masiyyah of Allah ﷻ and turn to Allah ﷻ for lutf. The person should be in the disposition that[1236] "يَا الله لَكَ المُلك وَلَا حَولَ وَلَا قُوَةَ إِلاَّ بِالله. اللهم أنت ربي لَا إله الا انت خَلَقتَنِى".

This disposition as taught by Rasulullah ﷺ reminds the person what their disposition should be with Allah ﷻ, our Creator, Rabbul A'lamìn. We are all creation, a'bd of Allah ﷻ. Then, asking lutf, easiness with[1237] "اللّهم إني أسألك العَفو فِي الدُنيَا وَ الاخِرة" is critical.

Actually, this disposition is taught to us in the Qurān directly as "رَبَّنا آتِنا فِي الدنيا حَسَنَة وَفِي الاخِرة حَسَنَة وَقِنَا عَذَابَ النّار"[1238]. In other words, we don't ask to be in difficulty in order to prove ourselves to Allah ﷻ.

Yet, when a difficulty hits we still try to hold with our teeth and hands tight in order not to slip and say or do something displeasing to Allah ﷻ. At the same time, asking constantly, easiness, lutf, afw and 'afiyah as we are weak is important in all states of this difficulty. The person should be always in the state of asking easiness from Allah ﷻ. We can lose at any time due to our weakness. Going back to Allah ﷻ and being in the embodiment of "La takilni nafsi tarfata a'yn" is critical.

1233. Trust and Reliance
1234. Submission
1235. Full Submission,Trust and Reliance
1236. Oh Allah, You own the all dominion, and there is no power or strength except in Allah. Oh Allah , you are my Lord, there is no god but you created me.
1237. Oh Allah, I ask you for forgiveness in this world and on the day of judgment.
1238. Our Lord, grant us in this world good, and in the hereafter good and save us from the hellfire.

Saying "I wish" is not having proper adab with qadar.

Sûrah 19—Maryam

[80 & 95]

وَنَرِثُهُ مَا يَقُولُ وَيَأْتِينَا فَرْدًا [1239] {مريم/80}

وَكُلُّهُمْ آتِيهِ يَوْمَ الْقِيَامَةِ فَرْدًا [1240] {مريم/95}

When we analyze the above ayahs around the word فَرْدًا[1241], there can be different meanings that can appeal at different times, places and conditions as the Qurān is from the One, al-Bāki, al-Hayy, al-Qayyum. Therefore, the Qurān is all fresh showing guidance for us. Our human understandings and interpretations are all limited and can expire as our bodies and life expires as mentioned وَمَا جَعَلْنَاهُمْ جَسَدًا لَّا يَأْكُلُونَ الطَّعَامَ وَمَا كَانُوا خَالِدِينَ[1242] {الأنبياء/8}.

One of the meanings that the word فَرْدًا[1243] can imply is the case of individual or personal accountability. The words personal or individual can imply customized approached for each person. This customized approach can imply privacy with the person and Allah ﷻ. Allah ﷻ is al-Zāhir and al-Bātin.

In this privacy with Allah ﷻ, if the person does not want to be embarrassed and ashamed of their real self, they need to have and desire to have privacy with Allah ﷻ in this dunya before it becomes too late in the akhirah. May Allah ﷻ protects us, Amìn.

The notions of seclusion in the mount of hira before prophethood and itiqāf and tahajjud after prophethood as our sunnah can indicate this desired privacy with Allah ﷻ as practiced and ordered us by the Habìb, (صلى الله عليه و سلم),

اللهم اني اسالك بحرمت حبيبك عندك، ان تغفرلنا و اجعلنا معهم في المقام المحمود[1244]

This privacy with Allah ﷻ is a required disposition of a true believer of Allah ﷻ. One of the embodiments of this privacy presented in this

---

1239. And We will inherit him [in] what he mentions, and he will come to Us alone.

1240. And all of them are coming to Him on the Day of Resurrection alone.

1241. Alone.

1242. And We did not make them [i.e., the prophets] forms not eating food, nor were they immortal [on earth].

1243. Alone.

1244. Oh Allah I ask you by your beloved one with you, to forgive us and make us with them in a commendable position.

Sûrah by our mother Maryam as and the name of this Sûrah is Maryam and the word افَرْدًا[1245] is indicated and repeated in this Sûrah.In this Sûrah again, the private relationship of Zakariyya as is mentioned especially with the word خَفِيًّا[1246] in {مريم/3}[1247] إِذْ نَادَى رَبَّهُ نِدَاء خَفِيًّا .

Sometimes, as we are distracted in life with especially all different tools of broadcasting and news through phones, computers, TV and internet, this privacy can become increasingly difficult.

One can view pandemic diseases such as Covid19 in the year of 2020 as the involuntary case of privacy with Allah ﷻ in the form of lockdowns in the houses almost in the entire world. Yet, if people still don't want to face their own real selves with these forced privacies as a Rahmah from Allah ﷻ in order to re-assess their relationship with Allah ﷻ, then the possibility of this privacy can be present in the afterlife in an undesired way as mentioned {مريم/95} وَكُلُّهُمْ آتِيهِ يَوْمَ الْقِيَامَةِ فَرْدًا[1248].

May Allah ﷻ protect us from al-aqibatu as-su'i[1249], Amìn.

Juz 17

Sûrah 21—al-Anbiyā'

[8]

وَمَا جَعَلْنَاهُمْ جَسَدًا لَّا يَأْكُلُونَ الطَّعَامَ وَمَا كَانُوا خَالِدِينَ[1250] {الأنبياء/8}

This ayah indicates one of the sunnatullah, the law of Allah ﷻ. Our bodies require physical nourishment with healthy and halal food and drink. Yet, the body frames that we have from flesh, water/blood and hard materials such as bones have an expiration date. They are not eternal.

Yet our rûh, soul is the essence as it has a relation with the Eternal, Allah ﷻ as mentioned {ص/72}[1251] فَإِذَا سَوَّيْتُهُ وَنَفَخْتُ فِيهِ مِن رُّوحِي فَقَعُوا لَهُ سَاجِدِينَ. The expression مِن رُّوحِي can indicate this relationship.Therefore, with

---

1245. Alone.

1246. Private.

1247. When he called to his Lord a private call [i.e., supplication].

1248. And all of them are coming to Him on the Day of Resurrection alone.

1249. A bad ending.

1250. And We did not make them [i.e., the prophets] forms not eating food, nor were they immortal [on earth].

1251. So when I have proportioned him and breathed into him of My [created] soul, then fall down to him in prostration."

the Divine Fadl and Rahmah, Allah ﷻ created and brought us from non-existence into existence.

We have all our identities called the real self with our souls but not with our bodies. Regardless of kāfir or mumin, everyone has this initial boost of advanced bounty of being in existence. This existence of our souls continues as the relation وَنَفَخْتُ فِيهِ مِن رُّوحِي[1252] can indicate.

The One, Allah ﷻ is the One Absolute True Real Existent as mentioned {البقرة/2/255}[1254] ... أللهُ and أللهُ لا إِلَهَ إِلاَّ هُوَ الْحَيُّ الْقَيُّومُ{آل عمران/2}[1253] لاَ إِلَهَ إِلاَّ هُوَ الْحَيُّ الْقَيُّوم.

Yet, with the Divine Fadl[1255] and Rahmah[1256], Allah ﷻ gives us life and keeps us existent and alive as وَنَفَخْتُ فِيهِ مِن رُّوحِي[1257] can indicate.

Anything that comes from Allah ﷻ has a non-ending blessing referred as barakah. In this regard, the pronoun ي in وَنَفَخْتُ فِيهِ مِن رُّوحِي can indicate our existence with our souls due to our unique blessed relationship due the Fadl and Rahmah of Allah ﷻ on us, الله اعلم [1258]with adab –Astagfirullah. Allah ﷻ is far beyond any type of human renderings of thoughts.

This existence is a nūr and a privileged assignment on us by Allah ﷻ.

In this regard, after being existent and created into existence, Allah ﷻ clearly states this second required disposition of nūr of imān with the full absolute true meaning and purpose as[1259] قَالُواْ بَلَى شَهِدْنَا and we all humans affirm it as أَلَسْتُ بِرَبِّكُمْ[1260] as mentioned:

وَإِذْ أَخَذَ رَبُّكَ مِن بَنِي آدَمَ مِن ظُهُورِهِمْ ذُرِّيَّتَهُمْ وَأَشْهَدَهُمْ عَلَى أَنفُسِهِمْ أَلَسْتُ بِرَبِّكُمْ قَالُواْ بَلَى شَهِدْنَا أَن تَقُولُواْ يَوْمَ الْقِيَامَةِ إِنَّا كُنَّا عَنْ هَذَا غَافِلِينَ[1261]{الأعراف/172}

Allah ﷻ is the Source of all absolute qualities and quantities as mentioned as أللهُ نُورُ السَّمَاوَاتِ وَالْأَرْضِ in نُورِهِ مَثَلُ نُورِهِ أللهُ نُورُ السَّمَاوَاتِ وَالْأَرْضِ

1252. And breathed into him of My [created] soul.
1253. Allah—there is no deity except Him, the Ever-Living, the Sustainer of [all] existence.
1254. Allah—there is no deity except Him, the Ever-Living, the Sustainer of [all] existence.
1255. Favor.
1256. Mercy.
1257. And breathed into him of My [created] soul.
1258. Allah knows best.
1259. Am I not your Lord?
1260. Yes, we have testified.
1261. And [mention] when your Lord took from the children of Adam—from their loins—their descendants and made them testify of themselves, [saying to them], "Am I not your Lord?" They said, "Yes, we have testified." [This]—lest you should say on the Day of Resurrection, "Indeed, we were of this unaware."

كَمِشْكَاةٍ فِيهَا مِصْبَاحٌ الْمِصْبَاحُ فِي زُجَاجَةٍ الزُّجَاجَةُ كَأَنَّهَا كَوْكَبٌ دُرِّيٌّ يُوقَدُ مِن شَجَرَةٍ مُّبَارَكَةٍ زَيْتُونِةٍ لَّا شَرْقِيَّةٍ وَلَا غَرْبِيَّةٍ يَكَادُ زَيْتُهَا يُضِيءُ وَلَوْ لَمْ تَمْسَسْهُ نَارٌ نُّورٌ عَلَى نُورٍ يَهْدِي اللَّهُ لِنُورِهِ مَن يَشَاءُ وَيَضْرِبُ اللَّهُ الْأَمْثَالَ لِلنَّاسِ وَاللَّهُ بِكُلِّ شَيْءٍ عَلِيمٌ [1262]{النور/35}.

Allah ﷻ is the Source of all and not dependent on anything or anyone as mentioned[1263] وَلَوْ لَمْ تَمْسَسْهُ نَارٌ.

All creation receive their nûr from Allah ﷻ.

The first nûr is the being in existence. After the first nûr of existence, an introduction of the second nûr, nûr of imãn and its acceptance in the realm of qawlu bala is present. Therefore, there is a double nûr for humans as can be indicated نُّورٌ عَلَى نُورٍ[1264]. The nûr of imãn comes with the hidãyah of Allah ﷻ as mentioned.

Then, the responsibility of free will with execution of decisions is given to humans with their bodily faculties until they die in this life. Some use their free will with arrogance of kasb in the engagements of heedless, covering and forgetting the initial disposition with the engagements of kufr. Some incline with humility and guided to imãn with the Fadl and Rahmah of Allah ﷻ as mentioned نُّورٌ عَلَى نُورٍ يَهْدِي[1265] اللَّهُ لِنُورِهِ مَن يَشَاءُ. The second group in this dunya continue the double nûr[1266] نُّورٌ عَلَى نُورٍ with both existence and imãn.

Their existence in the afterlife continues as they are created by the One Who is Eternal as mentioned[1267] وَنَفَخْتُ فِيهِ مِن رُّوحِي. Yet, in the case of other beings when Allah ﷻ gave other agents such as angels, Jibril as, Ruhul Qudus to give life such as to animals or plants, then their existence may be, [1268]والله اعلم بالادب, can be temporary.

In above cases, such as Jibril as or Isa as giving life with the permission and enablement of Allah ﷻ, can indicate the temporality of these lives in these beings because the life-giver is a created being. Yet, for the case humans, there is a direct attribution of their creation to Allah ﷻ.

1262. Allah is the Light of the heavens and the earth. The example of His light is like a niche within which is a lamp; the lamp is within glass, the glass as if it were a pearly [white] star lit from [the oil of] a blessed olive tree, neither of the east nor of the west, whose oil would almost glow even if untouched by fire. Light upon light. Allah guides to His light whom He wills. And Allah presents examples for the people, and Allah is Knowing of all things.

1263. Even if untouched by fire.

1264. Light upon light.

1265. Light upon light. Allah guides to His light whom He wills

1266. Light upon light.

1267. And breathed into him of My [created] soul.

1268. Allah knows best with respect.

In the case of humans, the direct attribution of ي is mentioned in
the part as وَنَفَخْتُ فِيهِ مِن رُّوحِي[1269].

The ability of giving temporary or transient life can be given by
Allah ﷻ to some of the agents or messengers such as Jibril as, Rûhul
Qudus[1270], وَرَسُولًا إِلَى بَنِي إِسْرَائِيلَ أَنِّي قَدْ جِئْتُكُم بِآيَةٍ مِّن, or Isa as as mentioned
رَّبِّكُمْ أَنِّي أَخْلُقُ لَكُم مِّنَ الطِّينِ كَهَيْئَةِ الطَّيْرِ فَأَنفُخُ فِيهِ فَيَكُونُ طَيْرًا بِإِذْنِ اللَّهِ وَأُبْرِىءُ الأَكْمَهَ
والأَبْرَصَ وَأُحْيِي الْمَوْتَى بِإِذْنِ اللَّهِ وَأُنَبِّئُكُم بِمَا تَأْكُلُونَ وَمَا تَدَّخِرُونَ فِي بُيُوتِكُمْ إِنَّ فِي ذَلِكَ لآيَةً
لَّكُمْ إِن كُنتُم مُّؤْمِنِينَ[1271] {آل عمران/49}.

One should realize that بِإِذْنِ اللَّه[1272] is constantly repeated to emphasize
that they are only agents. In this regard, it is reported by Rasulullah ﷺ
that Dajjāl or antichrist will claim deity by covering the reality of بِإِذْنِ اللَّه
as a test and trial for people.

May Allah ﷻ protect me, my family, my teachers, the brothers and
sisters, our jam'ah[1273], in this town, state, country and world, Amīn.

Today's electrical or programmed robots can also be similar to
giving life of the messengers of Allah ﷻ.

One should remember nothing happens without the permission of
Allah ﷻ, بِإِذْنِ اللَّه[1274].

In this sense, when one dies, or their bodily functions are terminated,
their soul is still alive in the qabir, grave. Yet, the responsibility with free
will is lifted but their existence continues.

Therefore, being a human regardless of having imān is the biggest
n'imah. Existence is the absolute light and good. The existence of the
person continues in the afterlife compared to non-existence of darkness.
Non-existence is the absolute darkness and evil. Therefore, kāfir is still
in a n'imah by being in existence.

After existence, in this life, the biggest ni'mah is imān. Imān is the
absolute light, nûr, and reality. The person of imān continues in nûr
immediately after creation, in this life and after life in Jannah. The

---

1269. And breathed into him of My [created] soul.
1270. The holy spirit {i.e. Jibreal (AS)}
1271. And [make him] a messenger to the Children of Israel, [who will say],'Indeed I have
come to you with a sign from your Lord in that I design for you from clay [that which is] like
the form of a bird, then I breathe into it and it becomes a bird by permission of Allah. And I
cure the blind [from birth] and the leper, and I give life to the dead—by permission of Allah.
And I inform you of what you eat and what you store in your houses. Indeed in that is a sign
for you, if you are believers.
1272. By permission of Allah.
1273. Congregation.
1274. By permission of Allah.

person of imān always maintains the state of being in Jannah, in this life, at their grave, and afterlife. One second of darkness of kufr or a tiny feeling of disconnect from Rabbul Alamìn can make this person feel the pain and anguish of Jahannam.

May Allah ﷻ don't disconnect us from imān and ihsān even less a than a second that we continuosulsy maintain the connection with Allah ﷻ without any gaps, Amìn!

Claims of kufr are attempts of covering existence and asserting the darkness of non-existence. Therefore, kufr or covering implies and indicates darkness. The person of kufr starts the journey with nûr of existence, then this nûr becomes faint or covered with kufr in this dunya. Then, the nûr of existence reveals itself when death comes as the responsibility period of free will is lifted. Yet, the kuffār continues their life with existence in the anguish and pains of regret in the afterlife. Yet, this is still existence.

اللهم توفنا مسلمين و الحقنا بالصالحين1275

[25–29]

وَمَا أَرْسَلْنَا مِن قَبْلِكَ مِن رَّسُولٍ إِلَّا نُوحِي إِلَيْهِ أَنَّهُ لَا إِلَهَ إِلَّا أَنَا فَاعْبُدُونِ 1276{الأنبياء/25} وَقَالُوا اتَّخَذَ الرَّحْمَنُ وَلَدًا سُبْحَانَهُ بَلْ عِبَادٌ مُّكْرَمُونَ 1277 {الأنبياء/26} لَا يَسْبِقُونَهُ بِالْقَوْلِ وَهُم بِأَمْرِهِ يَعْمَلُونَ1278 {الأنبياء/27} يَعْلَمُ مَا بَيْنَ أَيْدِيهِمْ وَمَا خَلْفَهُمْ وَلَا يَشْفَعُونَ إِلَّا لِمَنِ ارْتَضَى وَهُم مِّنْ خَشْيَتِهِ مُشْفِقُونَ1279 {الأنبياء/28} وَمَن يَقُلْ مِنْهُمْ إِنِّي إِلَهٌ مِّن دُونِهِ فَذَلِكَ نَجْزِيهِ جَهَنَّمَ كَذَلِكَ نَجْزِي الظَّالِمِينَ 1280{الأنبياء/29}

When one reviews above ayahs, one can realize the staging of shirk and kufr.

1275. Oh Allah, make us pass away as muslims, and be joined with the righteous.
1276. And We sent not before you any messenger except that We revealed to him that, "There is no deity except Me, so worship Me."
1277. And they say, "The Most Merciful has taken a son." Exalted is He! Rather, they are [but] honored servants.
1278. They cannot precede Him in word, and they act by His command.
1279. He knows what is [presently] before them and what will be after them, and they cannot intercede except on behalf of one whom He approves. And they, from fear of Him, are apprehensive.
1280. And whoever of them should say, "Indeed, I am a god besides Him"—that one We would recompense with Hell. Thus do We recompense the wrongdoers.

1281. وَقَالُوا اتَّخَذَ الرَّحْمَنُ وَلَدًا as Allah ﷻ with partnership claiming ,First. Then, open and explicit declaration of shirk and kufr as وَمَن يَقُلْ مِنْهُمْ إِنِّي1282 إِلَهٌ مِّن دُونِهِ. With these open and explicit renderings of shirk and kufr, the ayah {الأنبياء/25} 1283 وَمَا أَرْسَلْنَا مِن قَبْلِكَ مِن رَّسُولٍ إِلَّا نُوحِي إِلَيْهِ أَنَّهُ لَا إِلَهَ إِلَّا أَنَا فَاعْبُدُونِ, with the part لَا إِلَهَ إِلَّا أَنَا فَاعْبُدُونِ1284 can indicate this necessary emphasis with the pronoun أنا1285 instead of the Lafdh1286 Mubarak, Allah ﷻ.

Imbedded Shirk of Self with[1287] انا

Having a self as a human can indicate أنا1288. Yet, the existence of the self of the person and all the creation with their identities of self أنا are relative with the Real أَنَا, Allah ﷻ. In other words, our self-identities are given to us as a measurement tool to recognize the Source, the Real, Allah ﷻ but not claim uluhiyyah with any type of pseudo and false claims.

In other words, we may not genuinely appreciate Allah ﷻ as our Creator if we don't have أَنَا. With our existence of identity of self, we have a measure unit similar to an inch or millimeter to try to measure our distance, meaning as to recognize and approximate our understandings and appreciation for Transcendent Infinite Reality, Allah ﷻ.

To make above example clearer, if there is a table, measuring the size of this table with a measurestick can give us better understanding of its size compared to our estimations with our eyes. Similarly, the self or أَنَا given to us with a free-will by Allah ﷻ is a measurestick to understand our limits on the path of increasing our knowledge, ma'rifah about the One, Allah ﷻ Who does not have any limits.

Our أَنَا can have free will of decision making and executing. Yet, these are all limited and dependent on the Mashiyyah of Allah ﷻ, the Real أَنَا. When we understand the real disposition of our أَنَا as fully dependent on the Real أَنَا, Allah ﷻ, then we receive real power and barakah as we are now relying not on our weak أَنَا but on the Real أَنَا, Allah ﷻ.

1281. And they say, "The Most Merciful has taken a son."
1282. And whoever of them should say, "Indeed, I am a god besides Him"
1283. And We sent not before you any messenger except that We revealed to him that, "There is no deity except Me, so worship Me."
1284. There is no deity except Me, so worship Me.
1285. Me.
1286. Word.
1287. Me.
1288. Me

In this regard, the people of the heart, ahlu-tasawwuf systematize the purpose of life as dissolving this small minuscule of the ice of أَنَا in the ocean of the Real أَنَا, Allah ﷻ. Sayri ilā Allah is the struggle of this process. Sayri fillah or fanā fillah can be the achievement of this dissolvement of this ice which means truly embodying tawhid with La ilaha illa Allah.

Yet, for Muslims, our implicit fears, concerns, and expectations from others except from Allah ﷻ can be related to the first staging of shirk as mentioned وَقَالُوا اتَّخَذَ الرَّحْمَنُ وَلَدًا[1289]. The implicit expectation from others as a form of shirk can be expressed in other parts of the Qurān. True tawhid, embodiment of La ilaha illa Allah, entails expecting from Allah ﷻ and fully turning to Allah ﷻ.

The second staging of shirk for Muslims can imply arrogance, conceit, jealousy vanity and superiority as mentioned [1290] وَمَن يَقُلْ مِنْهُمْ إِنِّي إِلَٰهٌ مِّن دُونِه. This is a worse shirk and kufur than the first as one remember Shaytān that he has the tag of believing and knowing Allah ﷻ, yet the arrogance made him the epitome of the highest level of implicit shirk and kufr.

Explicit Shirk of Claims with[1291] انا for Others

Explicit shirk of claims in its first staging can indicate open verbal claims of this disposition compared the undetected dispositions of the previous cases. In this case, the part وَقَالُوا اتَّخَذَ الرَّحْمَنُ وَلَدًا[1292] can indicate groups such as Christians or other who explicitly pronounce this.

Similarly, the second staging of shirk and kufr can also indicate open verbal claims of this disposition compared the undetected dispositions of the previous cases. In this case, the part وَمَن يَقُلْ مِنْهُمْ إِنِّي إِلَٰهٌ مِّن دُونِه[1293] can indicate individuals such as Fira'wn as mentioned in the Qurān or Dajjāl in their open claims as mentioned in the hadith [11]. Yet, in the first case of shirk of partnership, it becomes a group movement adapting this position of expecting benefit from others such as the examples of Christians or idol worshippers who recognize Allah ﷻ but expect things

---

1289. And they say, "The Most Merciful has taken a son."
1290. And whoever of them should say, "Indeed, I am a god besides Him"
1291. Me.
1292. And they say, "The Most Merciful has taken a son."
1293. And whoever of them should say, "Indeed, I am a god besides Him"

from others. This can show general majority human trends of fear, panic and trying address their problems and concerns with wrong solutions of expecting things from others except from Allah ﷻ.

In the second case of shirk and kufr, it becomes a personal representation of this self-identity through arrogance, vanity and conceit such as the examples of Shaytān, Firawn or Dajjāl. This can show overconfidence and feelings of superiority in their self-identities as viewing themselves as deities and giving themselves uluhiyyah.

The interaction between two cases makes a collective identity. The ones with self-identity of arrogance and kibir[1294] lead the ones, the groups or masses who are weak and expecting benefits from the false overconfident benefactors. This is mentioned in:

وَقَالَ الَّذِينَ كَفَرُوا لَن نُّؤْمِنَ بِهَٰذَا الْقُرْآنِ وَلَا بِالَّذِي بَيْنَ يَدَيْهِ وَلَوْ تَرَى إِذِ الظَّالِمُونَ مَوْقُوفُونَ عِندَ رَبِّهِمْ يَرْجِعُ بَعْضُهُمْ إِلَىٰ بَعْضٍ الْقَوْلَ يَقُولُ الَّذِينَ اسْتُضْعِفُوا لِلَّذِينَ اسْتَكْبَرُوا لَوْلَا أَنتُمْ لَكُنَّا مُؤْمِنِينَ 1295 {سبأ/31}

قَالَ الَّذِينَ اسْتَكْبَرُوا لِلَّذِينَ اسْتُضْعِفُوا أَنَحْنُ صَدَدْنَاكُمْ عَنِ الْهُدَىٰ بَعْدَ إِذْ جَاءكُم بَلْ كُنتُم مُّجْرِمِينَ 1296 {سبأ/32} وَقَالَ الَّذِينَ اسْتُضْعِفُوا لِلَّذِينَ اسْتَكْبَرُوا بَلْ مَكْرُ اللَّيْلِ وَالنَّهَارِ إِذْ تَأْمُرُونَنَا أَن نَّكْفُرَ بِاللَّهِ وَنَجْعَلَ لَهُ أَندَادًا وَأَسَرُّوا النَّدَامَةَ لَمَّا رَأَوُا الْعَذَابَ وَجَعَلْنَا الْأَغْلَالَ فِي أَعْنَاقِ الَّذِينَ كَفَرُوا هَلْ يُجْزَوْنَ إِلَّا مَا كَانُوا يَعْمَلُونَ 1297 {سبأ/33}

Although everyone will understand their real case and disposition, but it will be a late realization in the akhirah, May Allah ﷻ protect us from inner and outer engagements of shirk and kufr, Amìn.

1294. Arrogance/ Pride.
1295. And those who disbelieve say, "We will never believe in this Qurān nor in that before it." But if you could see when the wrongdoers are made to stand before their Lord, refuting each others' words... Those who were oppressed will say to those who were arrogant, "If not for you, we would have been believers."
1296. Those who were arrogant will say to those who were oppressed, "Did we avert you from guidance after it had come to you? Rather, you were criminals."
1297. Those who were oppressed will say to those who were arrogant, "Rather, [it was your] conspiracy of night and day when you were ordering us to disbelieve in Allah and attribute to Him equals." But they will [all] confide regret when they see the punishment; and We will put shackles on the necks of those who disbelieved. Will they be recompensed except for what they used to do?

[42]

Fear, Panic and Virus

قُلْ مَن يَكْلَؤُكُم بِاللَّيْلِ وَالنَّهَارِ مِنَ الرَّحْمَنِ بَلْ هُمْ عَن ذِكْرِ رَبِّهِم مُّعْرِضُونَ[1298]
{الأنبياء/42}

Sometimes, our fears make us forget our purpose, meaning and goal in life. When there are trials and tests in one's personal life instilling fear, uncertainty and panic, the person is expected to turn to Allah ﷻ. These trials and tests are all reminders of turning back to Allah ﷻ. Yet, the person finds other means to turn to other than Allah ﷻ to seek protection, to sooth the person and ease from their fears with placebo effects.

Yet, when there is a social, communal and global fears of unknown tagged items such as terrorism, then people may tend to isolate themselves with these tagged items. If this tagged item is religion, then they isolate themselves from it. They may tend to isolate themselves from Islam or other religious affiliations. If this tagged item is a group such as Muslims or a race, then they try to isolate themselves with the pseudo effects of seeking protection and easing their fears.

Yet, when there is a social, communal and global fears of unknowns such as pandemic diseases spreading through virus, then there is no identifiable case or a tagged item that the person can find and isolate themselves from. This can be implied in this ayah as قُلْ مَن يَكْلَؤُكُم بِاللَّيْلِ وَالنَّهَارِ مِنَ الرَّحْمَنِ بَلْ هُمْ عَن ذِكْرِ رَبِّهِم مُّعْرِضُونَ[1299] {الأنبياء/42}.

Then, since there are no placebo effects of pseudo isolations, then this can build irreparable spiritual damages in a person if the person is not connected to Allah ﷻ with dhikrullah, remembrance of Allah ﷻ. When these means become weak, then the person is at least expected to use this as an opportunity to truly embody permanent stations of tawhid and remember and go back to Allah ﷻ as mentioned [1300] لَعَلَّهُمْ يَرْجِعُونَ {الروم/41} (they may go back)

1298. Say, "Who can protect you at night or by day from the Most Merciful?" But they are, from the remembrance of their Lord, turning away.
1299. Say, "Who can protect you at night or by day from the Most Merciful?" But they are, from the remembrance of their Lord, turning away.
1300. Perhaps they will return.

In its true sense, virus or other embedded fears are all means to remind us the reality that مَن يَكْلَؤُكُم بِاللَّيْلِ وَالنَّهَارِ مِنَ الرَّحْمَنِ [1301] (Who could protect you, by night or by day, from the Most Gracious, Ar-Rahman (Allah ﷻ)?) Yet, the point of all these fears are to remind the person dhikrullah, the true dhikr of our Rabb بَلْ هُمْ عَن ذِكْرِ رَبِّهِم مُّعْرِضُونَ [1302] (And yet, from a remembrance of their Rabb, Sustainer, do they stubbornly turn away).

In other words, all the difficulties, diseases, turmoil are fasad, mischief due to human renderings, kasb as mentioned[1303] ظَهَرَ الْفَسَادُ فِي الْبَرِّ وَالْبَحْرِ بِمَا كَسَبَتْ أَيْدِي النَّاسِ لِيُذِيقَهُم بَعْضَ الَّذِي عَمِلُوا لَعَلَّهُمْ يَرْجِعُونَ {الروم/41}. Yes, we make and cause the evil, turmoil and be the reason of different viruses and diseases. Yet, the Divine Mashiyyah[1304], allowance of Allah ﷻ for those things coming to humans' reality of existence is due to لَعَلَّهُمْ يَرْجِعُونَ [1305] {الروم/41} (they may go back) so that they can use these trials and tests to go back to Allah ﷻ, to remember Allah ﷻ as dhikrullah.

Yes, all different levels of means and pseudo effects can change with their apparent fake existence. Sometimes, there can be apparent means that the person can make a strong shirk with Allah ﷻ. These apparent means can prevail at the times of dajjalic era and at the end of times as science, and other cases. Then, when this apparent means do something to solve a problem as a test or trial, then the people can take these means as shirk with Allah ﷻ. As reported by Rasulullah 11] ﷺ], this is one of the expected features of Dajjāl as affecting or mesmerizing people and gaining followers. Yet, the people of true imān still knows the One Who gives and allows the reasons and effects is Allah ﷻ but not the apparent, implicit, weak or strong means or reasons.

In this sense, going back and reliance on Allah ﷻ can imply taking off all the burden of fears, and panic from our weak shoulders and being happy and relaxed with the remembrance of Allah ﷻ. Allah ﷻ can change anything at any time beyond the means and reasons for us as long as the person is in the full embodiment of dhikrullah.

1301. Who can protect you at night or by day from the Most Merciful?
1302. But they are, from the remembrance of their Lord, turning away.
1303. Calamities have appeared on land and sea because of what the hands of the people have earned, so that He (Allah) makes them taste some of what they did, in order that they may go back (to the right way/dhikrullah).
1304. Permission of Allah.
1305. Perhaps they will return.

[42–47]

قُلْ مَن يَكْلَؤُكُم بِاللَّيْلِ وَالنَّهَارِ مِنَ الرَّحْمَنِ بَلْ هُمْ عَن ذِكْرِ رَبِّهِم مُّعْرِضُونَ¹³⁰⁶
{الأنبياء/42} أَمْ لَهُمْ آلِهَةٌ تَمْنَعُهُم مِّن دُونِنَا لَا يَسْتَطِيعُونَ نَصْرَ أَنفُسِهِمْ وَلَا هُم مِّنَّا
يُصْحَبُونَ¹³⁰⁷ {الأنبياء/43} بَلْ مَتَّعْنَا هَؤُلَاءِ وَآبَاءهُمْ حَتَّى طَالَ عَلَيْهِمُ الْعُمُرُ أَفَلَا يَرَوْنَ
أَنَّا نَأْتِي الْأَرْضَ نَنقُصُهَا مِنْ أَطْرَافِهَا أَفَهُمُ الْغَالِبُونَ¹³⁰⁸ {الأنبياء/44}

قُلْ إِنَّمَا أُنذِرُكُم بِالْوَحْيِ وَلَا يَسْمَعُ الصُّمُّ الدُّعَاء إِذَا مَا يُنذَرُونَ¹³⁰⁹{الأنبياء/45} وَلَئِن
مَّسَّتْهُمْ نَفْحَةٌ مِّنْ عَذَابِ رَبِّكَ لَيَقُولُنَّ يَا وَيْلَنَا إِنَّا كُنَّا ظَالِمِينَ¹³¹⁰ {الأنبياء/46} وَنَضَعُ
الْمَوَازِينَ الْقِسْطَ لِيَوْمِ الْقِيَامَةِ فَلَا تُظْلَمُ نَفْسٌ شَيْئًا وَإِن كَانَ مِثْقَالَ حَبَّةٍ مِّنْ خَرْدَلٍ أَتَيْنَا بِهَا
وَكَفَى بِنَا حَاسِبِينَ¹³¹¹ {الأنبياء/47}

Gaflah

These ayahs are remarkably interesting to analyze. Besides their many meanings, one of the very intrinsic spiritual disease is mentioned. This is gaflah, heedlessness. To allude this spiritual disease, one of the key words is طَالَ in the ayah بَلْ مَتَّعْنَا هَؤُلَاءِ وَآبَاءهُمْ حَتَّى طَالَ عَلَيْهِمُ الْعُمُرُ أَفَلَا يَرَوْنَ أَنَّا نَأْتِي الْأَرْضَ نَنقُصُهَا مِنْ أَطْرَافِهَا أَفَهُمُ الْغَالِبُونَ¹³¹²{الأنبياء/44}.

When our life is long, when our engagements become routine, when we tend to ignore things, and this negligence become normalized, then this can form another type of very intrinsic deep layers of gaflah, heedlessness.

For example, a person being constantly warned about importance of praying tahajjud, then but still this person does not pray tahajjud and sleeps. In this type of engagement of sleep, the person normalizes

---

1306. Say, "Who can protect you at night or by day from the Most Merciful?" But they are, from the remembrance of their Lord, turning away.
1307. Or do they have gods to defend them other than Us? They are unable [even] to help themselves, nor can they be protected from Us.
1308. But, [on the contrary], We have provided good things for these [disbelievers] and their fathers until life was prolonged for them. Then do they not see that We set upon the land, reducing it from its borders? Is it they who will overcome?
1309. Say, "I only warn you by revelation." But the deaf do not hear the call when they are warned.
1310. And if [as much as] a whiff of the punishment of your Lord should touch them, they would surely say, "O woe to us! Indeed, we have been wrongdoers."
1311. And We place the scales of justice for the Day of Resurrection, so no soul will be treated unjustly at all. And if there is [even] the weight of a mustard seed, We will bring it forth. And sufficient are We as accountant.
1312. But, [on the contrary], We have provided good things for these [disbelievers] and their fathers until life was prolonged for them. Then do they not see that We set upon the land, reducing it from its borders? Is it they who will overcome?

all these warnings, possible punishments and normalizes the missed opportunities by missing tahajjud. Then, at this point, the breezes of this ayah come as قُلْ مَن يَكْلَؤُكُم بِاللَّيْلِ وَالنَّهَارِ مِنَ الرَّحْمَنِ بَلْ هُم عَن ذِكْرِ رَبِّهِم مُّعْرِضُونَ {الأنبياء/42}[1313]

This ayah indicates with an extraordinarily strong reminder with قُلْ مَن يَكْلَؤُكُم بِاللَّيْلِ وَالنَّهَارِ [1314] with genuineness as mentioned with مِنَ[1315] الرَّحْمَنِ but yet, emphasizing and underlining this devastating and heartbreaking point and reality as هُمْ عَن ذِكْرِ رَبِّهِم مُّعْرِضُونَ {الأنبياء/42}[1316]

Yes, the whole point of life is ذِكْرِ رَبِّهِم[1317] as the Qurān starts with الْحَمْدُ لِلَّهِ رَبِّ الْعَالَمِينَ {الفاتحة/2}. In this sense, dhikr is this constant awareness and consciousness of Rabbul Alamin, Allah ﷻ. The absence of dhikr any second harms the person but not anyone else.

Therefore, ghaflah[1318] is opposite of dhikrullah. The person is either in dhikrullah or in gaflah. There is no middle state. It is like the binary system of either one or zero as all the computer technology is built on. One can represent dhikrullah, La ilaha illa Allah. Zero can represent gaflah of nothingness without Allah ﷻ.

In the above ayah قُلْ مَن يَكْلَؤُكُم بِاللَّيْلِ وَالنَّهَارِ مِنَ الرَّحْمَنِ بَلْ هُم عَن ذِكْرِ رَبِّهِم مُّعْرِضُونَ {الأنبياء/42}[1319] مَن يَكْلَؤُكُم بِاللَّيْلِ وَالنَّهَارِ, the reality is mentioned as مِنَ الرَّحْمَنِ. This is reality but without any over or under estimation. Yet, this reality is warning that is expected to instill at least some fear in the person to go back to Dhikrullah. One's relationship with Allah ﷻ requires being ashamed. The reality requires the zeal and boost of appreciation and gratefulness for Allah ﷻ as mentioned ذِكْرِ رَبِّهِم[1320] through رَبِّ الْحَمْدُ لِلَّه الْعَالَمِينَ[1321] {الفاتحة/2}. There are two points to emphasize. One is that this is a reality. The other is warning and fear instilment is just a tool of means to help people break their gaflah.

It is a reality. In other words, the teachings of the Qurān are not mere logical or philosophical engagements of a person but is a reality, and real from Allah ﷻ as mentioned قُلْ إِنَّمَا أُنذِرُكُم بِالْوَحْي وَلَا يَسْمَعُ الصُّمُّ الدُّعَاءَ

1313. Say, "Who can protect you at night or by day from the Most Merciful?" But they are, from the remembrance of their Lord, turning away.

1314. Say, "Who can protect you at night or by day.

1315. From the Most Merciful?"

1316. But they are, from the remembrance of their Lord, turning away.

1317. Remembrance of their Lord.

1318. Heedlessness.

1319. "Who can protect you at night or by day from the Most Merciful?"

1320. Remembrance of their lord.

1321. All praise is due to Allah, the lord of the worlds.

إِذَا مَا يُنذَرُونَ [1322] {الأنبياء/45}. Yet, they continue with their heedlessness, gaflah as mentioned وَلَا يَسْمَعُ الصُّمُّ الدُّعَاء إِذَا مَا يُنذَرُونَ [1323] {الأنبياء/45}. One of the synonyms of heedless is the person being spiritually blind and deaf as the ayah explicitly states.

Fear or warning is a means to break the gaflah, heedlessness as mentioned وَلَئِن مَّسَّتْهُمْ نَفْحَةٌ مِّنْ عَذَابِ رَبِّكَ لَيَقُولُنَّ يَا وَيْلَنَا إِنَّا كُنَّا ظَالِمِينَ [1324] {الأنبياء/46}. As it is analyzed in Isharatul Ijãz [10], the repetition of the form nakrah indicating diminutive meanings, and the implied meanings from each word of this ayah can indicate the teeny and miniscule amount of trial or punishment that the person undergoes. In other words, as the ijãz of the Qurãn indicates that this tiny amount is a means to break the ghaflah[1325] but not really to punish the person. If Allah ﷻ wants, the person can be destroyed immediately.

The ayahs further analyze the possible reasons of this gaflah as أَمْ لَهُمْ آلِهَةٌ تَمْنَعُهُم مِّن دُونِنَا لَا يَسْتَطِيعُونَ نَصْرَ أَنفُسِهِمْ وَلَا هُم مِّنَّا يُصْحَبُونَ [1326] {الأنبياء/43}. In this sense, people may tend to ignore and don't give attention to something if they have some alternatives. In other words, we tend to prioritize our time, engagments and prefrences due to our limited time and focus. In this sense, we may deem something to be more important than somethingelse.

Allah ﷻ clearly mentions as أَمْ لَهُمْ آلِهَةٌ تَمْنَعُهُم مِّن دُونِنَا [1327]. If this is the case, whatever those implicit or explicit cases are, they cannot even help their own selves[1328] لَا يَسْتَطِيعُونَ نَصْرَ أَنفُسِهِمْ. They are themselves in need.

Another point is that people expect identity, group or click related ownership. People can have a strong social network that there is an expected protection by an individual or through this association. If this is the reason of preference, then this option is not possible in the case of one's relation with Allah ﷻ as mentioned[1329] وَلَا هُم مِّنَّا يُصْحَبُونَ {الأنبياء/43}. Then, this cannot be also a real disposition.

1322. Say, "I only warn you by revelation." But the deaf do not hear the call when they are warned.

1323. " But the deaf do not hear the call when they are warned.

1324. And if [as much as] a whiff of the punishment of your Lord should touch them, they would surely say, "O woe to us! Indeed, we have been wrongdoers."

1325. Headlessness.

1326. Or do they have gods to defend them other than Us? They are unable [even] to help themselves, nor can they be protected from Us.

1327. Or do they have gods to defend them other than Us?

1328. They are unable [even] to help themselves.

1329. Nor can they be protected from Us.

There are and can be people who can be motivated with these false choices of preferences.

The Core of Gaflah as the monotonous routines of normalization versus freshness of futuwaah

Yet, the core reason of gaflah can be indicated with the negation of other possibilities with the word بَلْ in [1330] بَلْ مَتَّعْنَا هَؤُلَاء وَآبَاءهُمْ حَتَّى طَالَ عَلَيْهِمُ الْعُمُرُ. [1331]

When our life is long, when our engagements become routine, when we tend to ignore things, and this negligence become normalized, then this can form another type of very intrinsic deep layers of ghaflah, heedlessness.

As mentioned before, one of the key words is طَالَ [1332] in the ayah بَلْ مَتَّعْنَا هَؤُلَاء وَآبَاءهُمْ حَتَّى طَالَ عَلَيْهِمُ الْعُمُرُ أَفَلَا يَرَوْنَ أَنَّا نَأْتِي الْأَرْضَ نَنقُصُهَا مِنْ أَطْرَافِهَا أَفَهُمُ الْغَالِبُونَ [1333] {الأنبياء/44}. We will analyze this word طَالَ in other contexts of the Qurān inshAllah. Here are some of the ayahs:

فَرَجَعَ مُوسَى إِلَى قَوْمِهِ غَضْبَانَ أَسِفًا قَالَ يَا قَوْمِ أَلَمْ يَعِدْكُمْ رَبُّكُمْ وَعْدًا حَسَنًا أَفَطَالَ عَلَيْكُمُ الْعَهْدُ أَمْ أَرَدتُّمْ أَن يَحِلَّ عَلَيْكُمْ غَضَبٌ مِّن رَّبِّكُمْ فَأَخْلَفْتُم مَّوْعِدِي [1334] {طه/86}

أَلَمْ يَأْنِ لِلَّذِينَ آمَنُوا أَن تَخْشَعَ قُلُوبُهُمْ لِذِكْرِ اللَّهِ وَمَا نَزَلَ مِنَ الْحَقِّ وَلَا يَكُونُوا كَالَّذِينَ أُوتُوا الْكِتَابَ مِن قَبْلُ فَطَالَ عَلَيْهِمُ الْأَمَدُ فَقَسَتْ قُلُوبُهُمْ وَكَثِيرٌ مِّنْهُمْ فَاسِقُونَ [1335] {الحديد/16}

وَإِذَا أُنزِلَتْ سُورَةٌ أَنْ آمِنُواْ بِاللّهِ وَجَاهِدُواْ مَعَ رَسُولِهِ اسْتَأْذَنَكَ أُوْلُواْ الطَّوْلِ مِنْهُمْ وَقَالُواْ ذَرْنَا نَكُن مَّعَ الْقَاعِدِينَ [1336] {التوبة/86}

1330. But.
1331. But, [on the contrary], We have provided good things for these [disbelievers] and their fathers until life was prolonged for them.
1332. Prolonged.
1333. But, [on the contrary], We have provided good things for these [disbelievers] and their fathers until life was prolonged for them. Then do they not see that We set upon the land, reducing it from its borders? Is it they who will overcome?
1334. So Moses returned to his people, angry and grieved. He said, "O my people, did your Lord not make you a good promise? Then, was the time [of its fulfillment] too long for you, or did you wish that wrath from your Lord descend upon you, so you broke your promise [of obedience] to me?"
1335. Has the time not come for those who have believed that their hearts should become humbly submissive at the remembrance of Allah and what has come down of the truth? And let them not be like those who were given the Scripture before, and a long period passed over them, so their hearts hardened; and many of them are defiantly disobedient.
1336. And when a Sûrah was revealed [enjoining them] to believe in Allah and to fight with His Messenger, those of wealth among them asked your permission [to stay back] and said, "Leave us to be with them who sit [at home]."

Our normalizations of the ni'mahs[1337] can be a poison for us. Then, these normalizations lead to the next step of unawareness, assumptions of being normal and adopt passivism as a way of life. Spiritual passivism is spiritual inertia. The person does not want to change and be excited to the higher levels through the constant dispositions of awareness and amazements of imãn. Yet, this spiritual inertia leads to spiritual laziness, heedless and gaflah. The time in that sense as expressed with طَالَ[1338] adds and increases this state of inertia through gravitational heedless of normalizations. This hardening happens at the spiritual level of heart. This spiritual soft and liquid states of heart and soul, rûh change phases into solid state overtime as mentioned فَطَالَ عَلَيْهِمُ الْأَمَدُ فَقَسَتْ قُلُوبُهُمْ[1339]. This can be true for ahlu-kitãb[1340].

From the perspective of mukhalif, the opposite of the meanings, is in mentioned[1341] فَرَجَعَ مُوسَى إِلَى قَوْمِهِ غَضْبَانَ أَسِفًا قَالَ يَا قَوْمِ أَلَمْ يَعِدْكُمْ رَبُّكُمْ وَعْدًا حَسَنًا أَفَطَالَ عَلَيْكُمُ الْعَهْدُ. In this specific case, although there is no long time of departure of Musa as from his people, there is gaflah of forgetting the constant and recent ni'mahs of Allah ﷻ. This was the original a'hd that consciousness, and regularity for the appreciation of Allah ﷻ.

In this sense, if the gaflah happens immediately, then this can indicate the quick changing of characters through breaking promises and lies. This unsettled character types with constant change, lies and breaking promises can indicate nifãq. Nifãq can induce the gadab of the prophets. Nifãq can lead to gadab of Allah ﷻ as mentioned فَرَجَعَ مُوسَى إِلَى قَوْمِهِ غَضْبَانَ أَسِفًا قَالَ يَا قَوْمِ أَلَمْ يَعِدْكُمْ رَبُّكُمْ وَعْدًا حَسَنًا أَفَطَالَ عَلَيْكُمُ الْعَهْدُ أَمْ أَرَدتُّمْ أَن يَحِلَّ عَلَيْكُمْ غَضَبٌ مِّن رَّبِّكُمْ فَأَخْلَفْتُم مَّوْعِدِي[1342] {طه/86}. In other perspective, gadab of the prophet for their people can induce gadab of Allah ﷻ on them.

On the other, if the gaflah happens over time in extended periods of time, then this can lead to dalalah. In this sense, وَلَا يَكُونُوا كَالَّذِينَ أُوتُوا[1343]

1337. Blessings.

1338. Prolonged.

1339. A long period passed over them, so their hearts hardened

1340. People of the book {i.e. jews amd Christians}.

1341. So Moses returned to his people, angry and grieved. He said, "O my people, did your Lord not make you a good promise? Then, was the time [of its fulfillment] too long for you.

1342. So Moses returned to his people, angry and grieved. He said, "O my people, did your Lord not make you a good promise? Then, was the time [of its fulfillment] too long for you, or did you wish that wrath from your Lord descend upon you, so you broke your promise [of obedience] to me?"

1343. And let them not be like those who were given the Scripture before, and a long period passed over them, so their hearts hardened.

الْكِتَابَ مِن قَبْلُ فَطَالَ عَلَيْهِمُ الْأَمَدُ فَقَسَتْ قُلُوبُهُم, can indicate an established gaflah leading to permanent states of hardening of the hearts.

Spiritual Passivism & Activism

One of the side results of ghaflah is spiritual passivism. Spiritual passivism is the disposition of not acting when there is al-haqq to be followed as mentioned[1344] أَلَمْ يَأْنِ لِلَّذِينَ آمَنُوا أَن تَخْشَعَ قُلُوبُهُمْ لِذِكْرِ اللَّهَ وَمَا نَزَلَ مِنَ الْحَقِّ. The sign of spiritual passivism is being heedless,and unchanging heart in the dispositions of dhikrullah, remembrance of Allah ﷻ.

Spiritual passivism is the disposition of not acting to change an evil. Spiritual passivism is the disposition of "I don't care about others as long as I am ok."

Yet, spiritual passivism is deadly. It kills the person before others.

The opposite of spiritual passivism is spiritual activism. Spiritual activism is the disposition of acceptance, open-mindedness and following when there is al-haqq to be followed as mentioned وَإِذَا سَمِعُوا مَا أُنزِلَ إِلَى الرَّسُولِ تَرَى أَعْيُنَهُمْ تَفِيضُ مِنَ الدَّمْعِ مِمَّا عَرَفُوا مِنَ الْحَقِّ يَقُولُونَ رَبَّنَا آمَنَّا فَاكْتُبْنَا مَعَ الشَّاهِدِينَ[1345] {المائدة/83}. The sign of spiritual activism is crying, and changing of the spirituality and heart in the engagements of dhikrullah, remembrance of Allah ﷻ.

Spiritiual activism is the disposition of acting to change an evil. Spiritual passivism is the disposition of the constant concern about others, all living beings and things.

Spiritual activism or pessimism is not related with age. There can be people who are 25 years old and they could be spiritual dead and passive. There can be people who are 85 years old who are spiritually fresh and active.

In this sense, spiritual activism is the futuwwah. Futuwwah is the spirit of embodiment of dhikrullah. Dhikrullah leads to full reliance in Allah ﷻ. Futuwwah is the spiritual activism who take their full power from Allah ﷻ, as mentioned إِذْ أَوَى الْفِتْيَةُ إِلَى الْكَهْفِ فَقَالُوا رَبَّنَا آتِنَا مِن لَّدُنكَ رَحْمَةً

1344. Has the time not come for those who have believed that their hearts should become humbly submissive at the remembrance of Allah and what has come down of the truth?

1345. And when they hear what has been revealed to the Messenger, you see their eyes overflowing with tears because of what they have recognized of the truth. They say, "Our Lord, we have believed, so register us among the witnesses.

وَهَيِّئْ لَنَا مِنْ أَمْرِنَا رَشَدًا[1346] {الكهف/10}. The worldly means of power, fear or pain can be all minute or trivial as long as the full power comes from Allah ﷻ through dua and dhikrullah as mentioned[1347] رَبَّنَا آتِنَا مِن لَّدُنكَ رَحْمَةً وَهَيِّئْ لَنَا مِنْ أَمْرِنَا رَشَدًا.

Juz 18

Sûrah 24- an-Nûr

[20–21]

وَلَوْلَا فَضْلُ اللَّهِ عَلَيْكُمْ وَرَحْمَتُهُ وَأَنَّ اللَّهَ رَؤُوفٌ رَحِيمٌ[1348] {النور/20}

يَا أَيُّهَا الَّذِينَ آمَنُوا لَا تَتَّبِعُوا خُطُوَاتِ الشَّيْطَانِ وَمَن يَتَّبِعْ خُطُوَاتِ الشَّيْطَانِ فَإِنَّهُ يَأْمُرُ بِالْفَحْشَاءِ وَالْمُنكَرِ وَلَوْلَا فَضْلُ اللَّهِ عَلَيْكُمْ وَرَحْمَتُهُ مَا زَكَا مِنكُم مِّنْ أَحَدٍ أَبَدًا وَلَٰكِنَّ اللَّهَ يُزَكِّي مَن يَشَاءُ وَاللَّهُ سَمِيعٌ عَلِيمٌ[1349] {النور/21}

One should embody that hidayah, and tazkiyatul nafs is from the Fadl and Rahmah of Allah ﷻ. This expression وَلَوْلَا فَضْلُ اللَّهِ عَلَيْكُمْ وَرَحْمَتُهُ[1350] is constantly repeated in this Sûrah. No one can claim a right or privilege in hidayah and tazkiya except it is the Fadl and Rahmah of Allah ﷻ.

Sometimes, in the engagements of mind, one can know and think that they understood something related with kalam. Yet, this understanding even can be a source of misguidance for the person if the person does not embody humbleness, humility and constant need for Allah ﷻ. This disposition of humility or humbleness inshAllah can attract the Fadl and Rahmah of Allah ﷻ. Yes, discourses of kalam, or renderings about the approximation of meanings about the Names and

---

1346. [Mention] when the youths retreated to the cave and said, "Our Lord, grant us from Yourself mercy and prepare for us from our affair right guidance."
1347. "Our Lord, grant us from Yourself mercy and prepare for us from our affair right guidance."
1348. And if it had not been for the favor of Allah upon you and His mercy...and because Allah is Kind and Merciful.
1349. O you who have believed, do not follow the footsteps of Satan. And whoever follows the footsteps of Satan—indeed, he enjoins immorality and wrongdoing. And if not for the favor of Allah upon you and His mercy, not one of you would have been pure, ever, but Allah purifies whom He wills, and Allah is Hearing and Knowing.
1350. And if it had not been for the favor of Allah upon you and His mercy

Attributes of Allah ﷻ can become useful, transformative and beneficial with the Fadl[1351] and Rahmah[1352] of Allah ﷻ.

If that is not the case, there have been numerous philosophers engaging their minds about cosmology and ontology, yet, intellectual death coupled with spiritual death is not uncommon if the person does not have guidance from Allah ﷻ with the Fadl and Rahmah of Allah ﷻ as mentioned [1353] وَمَن لَّمْ يَجْعَلِ اللَّهُ لَهُ نُورًا فَمَا لَهُ مِن نُورٍ One can analyze the meanings of the ayah [1354] أَوْ كَظُلُمَاتٍ فِي بَحْرٍ لُّجِّيٍّ يَغْشَاهُ مَوْجٌ مِّن فَوْقِهِ مَوْجٌ مِّن فَوْقِهِ سَحَابٌ ظُلُمَاتٌ بَعْضُهَا فَوْقَ بَعْضٍ إِذَا أَخْرَجَ يَدَهُ لَمْ يَكَدْ يَرَاهَا وَمَن لَّمْ يَجْعَلِ اللَّهُ لَهُ نُورًا فَمَا لَهُ مِن نُورٍ {النور/40}. In this ayah, one can realize the possibility of the spiritual dead engagements especially happening with the engagements of mind signified with the layers of كَظُلُمَاتٍ[1355]. In this case, there is an emphasis for the guidance of Allah ﷻ with the part وَمَن لَّمْ يَجْعَلِ اللَّهُ لَهُ[1356] نُورًا فَمَا لَهُ مِن نُورٍ.

Learning knowledge is important as long as it is beneficial. Sometimes, a specific knowledge for the hass, experts, can be deadly or harmful for the amm, general public. Kalam can be one of the possible examples for this. Especially, when the points of kalam are mixed with the frame work of Western philosophy, this can be harmful especially for the general who may not be aware of the diseases introduced by delusional philosophy. The general audience who may not be much aware of the delusional parts of the Western philosophy, then knowledge about kalam can have more harm than its benefits for the person of a'mm from these lectures and engagements.

In this sense, these lectures, or engagements can be very beneficial for the students and learners of Western discourses of philosophy, psychology, anthropology, or sociology. Even, an average natural scientist who may not be much interested in philosophy of science can possibly distracted with a knowledge if he or she does not feel the need for it.

1351. Favor.
1352. Mercy.
1353. And he to whom Allah has not granted light—for him there is no light.
1354. Or [they are] like darknesses within an unfathomable sea which is covered by waves, upon which are waves, over which are clouds—darknesses, some of them upon others. When one puts out his hand [therein], he can hardly see it. And he to whom Allah has not granted light—for him there is no light.
1355. Darknesses.
1356. And he to whom Allah has not granted light—for him there is no light.

If the general public, amm has this tendency for the kalam, one should try to learn and engage oneself with the immediate intersecting beneficial knowledges of kalam with tazkiya or tasawwuf. One of the possible readings to engage the person can be Ataullah Iskandari (rh)'s manual [29]. This work condenses the detail explanations of kalam into the forms of aphorisms with beneficial and immediate and easy accessible knowledge about Allah ﷻ. The works of Imam Ghazali can expand these condensed forms into more understandable language by general, amm Muslims.

[55]

وَعَدَ اللَّهُ الَّذِينَ آمَنُوا مِنكُمْ وَعَمِلُوا الصَّالِحَاتِ لَيَسْتَخْلِفَنَّهُم فِي الْأَرْضِ كَمَا اسْتَخْلَفَ الَّذِينَ
مِن قَبْلِهِمْ وَلَيُمَكِّنَنَّ لَهُمْ دِينَهُمُ الَّذِي ارْتَضَى لَهُمْ وَلَيُبَدِّلَنَّهُم مِّن بَعْدِ خَوْفِهِمْ أَمْنًا يَعْبُدُونَنِي لَا
يُشْرِكُونَ بِي شَيْئًا وَمَن كَفَرَ بَعْدَ ذَلِكَ فَأُولَئِكَ هُمُ الْفَاسِقُونَ 1357 {النور/55}

When we see people suffering, being tortured or imprisoned without any cause and we cannot do anything about it, we become spiritually paralyzed and question our religious identity, disposition, or piety.

Yet, due to this pessimistic spiritual states of hopelessness and feeling extremely down, Allah ﷻ mentions in this ayah with a very strong emphasis لَيَسْتَخْلِفَنَّهُمْ 1358, لَيُمَكِّنَنَّ 1359, and لَيُبَدِّلَنَّهُم 1360. If one analyzes these takids, they are considered as the highest level of tak'id, qasam, or emphasis with nun thakila and lām. This can be another Rahmah and Fadl of Allah ﷻ that at the times we cannot rationalize about the torture of the believers of Allah ﷻ. Then, Allah ﷻ mentions with a very strong ta'kid that this will and can change.

Regardless of the conditions, our goal is to establish an individual life to meet with Allah ﷻ with a clean and accountable free book as much as possible. We all hope this from the Fadl and Rahmah of Allah ﷻ that we are not questioned, Ameen.

1357. Allah has promised those who have believed among you and done righteous deeds that He will surely grant them succession [to authority] upon the earth just as He granted it to those before them and that He will surely establish for them [therein] their religion which He has preferred for them and that He will surely substitute for them, after their fear, security, [for] they worship Me, not associating anything with Me. But whoever disbelieves after that—then those are the defiantly disobedient.

1358. Grant them succession [to authority].

1359. Establish for them [therein].

1360. Substitute for them.

Juz 19

Sûrah 26—ash-Shuàrä'

[9]

{وَإِنَّ رَبَّكَ لَهُوَ الْعَزِيزُ الرَّحِيمُ 1361}{الشعراء/9}

One can analyze the Name and Attribute of Allah ﷻ الْعَزِيزُ [1362]in the Qurãn and with the lens of this ayah as repeated in this Sûrah. اعلم الله [1363], as this Name this Name and Attribute of Allah ﷻ الْعَزِيزُ is constructed from the first two letters of ع and ز, then there can have some relation with the word[1364] الْعِزَّةَ.

In this regard, i'zzah[1365], الْعِزَّةَ, recognition, and respect only can come for the person when he or she associates themselves with Allah ﷻ through the means of 'ibadah leading to taqwa: وَلاَ يَحْزُنكَ قَوْلُهُمْ إِنَّ الْعِزَّةَ لِلّهِ جَمِيعًا هُوَ السَّمِيعُ الْعَلِيمُ[1366] {يونس/65} .

In this sense, the true reflection of i'zzah only can come by associating oneself with only Allah ﷻ and taking Allah ﷻ as only the Waliyy as mentioned

أَلا إِنَّ أَوْلِيَاء اللّهِ لاَ خَوْفٌ عَلَيْهِمْ وَلاَ هُمْ يَحْزَنُونَ [1367]{يونس/62} الَّذِينَ آمَنُواْ وَكَانُواْ يَتَّقُونَ[1368] {يونس/63} لَهُمُ الْبُشْرَى فِي الْحَيَاةِ الدُّنْيَا وَفِي الآخِرَةِ لاَ تَبْدِيلَ لِكَلِمَاتِ اللّه ذَلِكَ هُوَ الْفَوْزُ الْعَظِيمُ[1369] {يونس/64} يَحْزُنكَ قَوْلُهُمْ إِنَّ الْعِزَّةَ لِلّه جَمِيعًا هُوَ السَّمِيعُ الْعَلِيمُ {يونس/65}[1370]

When we analyze the ayah[1371] {الشعراء/9} وَإِنَّ رَبَّكَ لَهُوَ الْعَزِيزُ الرَّحِيمُ, one can possibly understand the reflection of this true I'zzah as manifested

---

1361. And indeed, your Lord—He is the Exalted in Might, the Merciful.
1362. Exalted in Might,
1363. Allah knows best.
1364. Might.
1365. Honor.
1366. And let not their speech grieve you. Indeed, honor [due to power] belongs to Allah entirely. He is the Hearing, the Knowing.
1367. Unquestionably, [for] the allies of Allah there will be no fear concerning them, nor will they grieve.
1368. Those who believed and were fearing Allah.
1369. That is what is the great attainment.
1370. And let not their speech grieve you. Indeed, honor [due to power] belongs to Allah entirely. He is the Hearing, the Knowing.
1371. And indeed, your Lord—He is the Exalted in Might, the Merciful.

with the Name and Attribute of Allah ﷻ الْعَزِيزُ [1372]can be reflected on the awliya[1373] of Allah ﷻ with the Name and Attribute of Allah ﷻ as الرَّحِيمُ[1374]. One can remember the classical interpretation of the muffasirûn for the Name and Attribute of Allah ﷻ as الرَّحِيمُ to be the special manifestation, favors and n'imahs of Allah ﷻ for the mu'mins.

With the above approach if one can analyze the ayahs in this Sûrah as there is an initial introduction with وَإِنَّ رَبَّكَ لَهُوَ الْعَزِيزُ الرَّحِيمُ {الشعراء/9}[1375]. Then, there are multiple cases of humans, nations, and people at different times of the history, in different places and with different versions of seeking power, authority, recognition, fame, position and title. Yet, Allah ﷻ through their messengers reminds the reality of the holder of true authority and how they can transform their fake and false seeking of position and recognition by associating themselves only with Allah ﷻ. Yet, they insist and then, they don't want to leave their fake associations. Then, in the cases of below ayahs, there is the manifestation of this true authority of Allah ﷻ with their end results as indicated with the Name and Attribute of Allah ﷻ as[1376] الْعَزِيزُ. The manifestation of 'izzah can be on the believers with true and only association with Allah ﷻ as this can be indicated with the Name and Attribute of Allah ﷻ with الرَّحِيمُ[1377]:

وَإِنَّ رَبَّكَ لَهُوَ الْعَزِيزُ الرَّحِيمُ [1378]{الشعراء/68}

وَإِنَّ رَبَّكَ لَهُوَ الْعَزِيزُ الرَّحِيمُ {الشعراء/104}

وَإِنَّ رَبَّكَ لَهُوَ الْعَزِيزُ الرَّحِيمُ {الشعراء/122}

وَإِنَّ رَبَّكَ لَهُوَ الْعَزِيزُ الرَّحِيمُ {الشعراء/140}

وَإِنَّ رَبَّكَ لَهُوَ الْعَزِيزُ الرَّحِيمُ {الشعراء/159}

وَإِنَّ رَبَّكَ لَهُوَ الْعَزِيزُ الرَّحِيمُ {الشعراء/175}

وَإِنَّ رَبَّكَ لَهُوَ الْعَزِيزُ الرَّحِيمُ {الشعراء/191}

1372. Exalted in Might.
1373. Friends of Allah (ﷻ).
1374. The Merciful.
1375. And indeed, your Lord—He is the Exalted in Might, the Merciful.
1376. Exalted in Might.
1377. The Merciful.
1378. And indeed, your Lord—He is the Exalted in Might, the Merciful.

In all the above cases, the people are reversed with their expectations of seeking 'izzah behind wrong, fake, and false means, partners and associations rather than the true, absolute and permanent source of 'izzah[1379].

This concept of reversal of authority can be also understood with the a'yah قَالَتْ إِنَّ الْمُلُوكَ إِذَا دَخَلُوا قَرْيَةً أَفْسَدُوهَا وَجَعَلُوا أَعِزَّةَ أَهْلِهَا أَذِلَّةً وَكَذَلِكَ يَفْعَلُونَ {النمل/34}[1380]. When the person is not the true holder of the 'izzah except Allah ﷻ, then this pseudo or false 'izzah can be reversed at any time. If there is the true holder of 'izzah, this reversal cannot be outcome. The person can be turned into lowly and disrespected position at any time.

Therefore, one of the possible reasons of hidayah for Balkhis can be understanding this reality and accepting Islam instead of associating oneself with the false, fake and ingenuine power and authority holders. When Balkhis witnessed the kingdom of Sulayman as with the extend of the power, and Sulayman associated all this power to the Source of Power Allah ﷻ, then Balkhis accepted Islam. This also on her part displays intelligence of getting means through deductive and inductive reasoning.

Then, the Sûrah ends with this emphasis as a reminder for the believers that they should only truly take Allah ﷻ as their waliyy so that they can be elevated with I'zzah[1381] as mentioned [1382] وَتَوَكَّلْ عَلَى الْعَزِيزِ الرَّحِيمِ {الشعراء/217}.

[19–22]

The Successful Stance Against Challenges

قَالَ أَلَمْ نُرَبِّكَ فِينَا وَلِيدًا وَلَبِثْتَ فِينَا مِنْ عُمُرِكَ سِنِينَ 1383{الشعراء/18} وَفَعَلْتَ فَعْلَتَكَ الَّتِي فَعَلْتَ وَأَنتَ مِنَ الْكَافِرِينَ 1384{الشعراء/19}

1379. Honor.
1380. She said, "Indeed kings—when they enter a city, they ruin it and render the honored of its people humbled. And thus do they do.
1381. Honor.
1382. And rely upon the Exalted in Might, the Merciful.
1383. [Pharaoh] said, "Did we not raise you among us as a child, and you remained among us for years of your life?
1384. And [then] you did your deed which you did, and you were of the ungrateful."

قَالَ فَعَلْتُهَا إِذًا وَأَنَا مِنَ الضَّالِّينَ {الشعراء/20} ¹³⁸⁵ فَفَرَرْتُ مِنكُمْ لَمَّا خِفْتُكُمْ فَوَهَبَ لِي
رَبِّي حُكْمًا وَجَعَلَنِي مِنَ الْمُرْسَلِينَ {الشعراء/21} ¹³⁸⁶ وَتِلْكَ نِعْمَةٌ تَمُنُّهَا عَلَيَّ أَنْ عَبَّدتَّ
بَنِي إِسْرَائِيلَ {الشعراء/22} ¹³⁸⁷

When one analyzes the psychology patterns about the individuals or groups in the case of Musa as and his interaction with Fira'wn and his followers, some remarkably interesting consistent mind and emotion related dispositions display.

In the above set of ayahs, Fir'awn first starts with genuine seeming reminders to Musa as that for example, Fir'awn did so much for Musa as. There is a genuine seeming emotional rendering dialogue engaged by Fir'awn by using the phrases such as¹³⁸⁸ نُرَبِّكَ فِينَا وَلِيدً and then, وَلَبِثْتَ¹³⁸⁹ فِينَا مِنْ عُمُرِكَ سِنِينَ. Then, the following strong genuine and kind parent-children seeming relation or response is given by Fir'awn to Musa as وَفَعَلْتَ فَعْلَتَكَ الَّتِي فَعَلْتَ وَأَنتَ مِنَ الْكَافِرِينَ¹³⁹⁰. In our popular language of parent children relations, one can view this state moment of Firawn as "After all these that I did so much for you, are you going to do this to me? Don't you feel any type of indebtedness and gratitude?"

In the above strong position of Fira'wn, a person of imān is expected to be emotionally affected and if really the relation of indebtedness exists, a kind response can be expected as in the case of Ibrahim as with the repeated phrase of ¹³⁹¹ يَا أَبَتِ :

إِذْ قَالَ لِأَبِيهِ يَا أَبَتِ لِمَ تَعْبُدُ مَا لَا يَسْمَعُ وَلَا يُبْصِرُ وَلَا يُغْنِي عَنكَ شَيْئًا {مريم/42} ¹³⁹² يَا
أَبَتِ إِنِّي قَدْ جَاءنِي مِنَ الْعِلْمِ مَا لَمْ يَأْتِكَ فَاتَّبِعْنِي أَهْدِكَ صِرَاطًا سَوِيًّا {مريم/43} ¹³⁹³ يَا

1385. [Moses] said, "I did it, then, while I was of those astray [i.e., ignorant].

1386. So I fled from you when I feared you. Then my Lord granted me judgement [i.e., wisdom and prophethood] and appointed me [as one] of the messengers.

1387. And is this a favor of which you remind me—that you have enslaved the Children of Israel?"

1388. Did we not raise you among us as a child?

1389. And you remained among us for years of your life?

1390. And [then] you did your deed which you did, and you were of the ungrateful."

1391. O my father.

1392. [Mention] when he said to his father, "O my father, why do you worship that which does not hear and does not see and will not benefit you at all?

1393. O my father, indeed there has come to me of knowledge that which has not come to you, so follow me; I will guide you to an even path.

أَبَتِ لَا تَعْبُدِ الشَّيْطَانَ إِنَّ الشَّيْطَانَ كَانَ لِلرَّحْمَنِ عَصِيًّا¹³⁹⁴ {مريم/44} يَا أَبَتِ إِنِّي أَخَافُ
أَن يَمَسَّكَ عَذَابٌ مِّنَ الرَّحْمَنِ فَتَكُونَ لِلشَّيْطَانِ وَلِيًّا¹³⁹⁵ {مريم/45}

Both cases seem to be similar, fir'awn as the parent of Musa as and
Ibrahim as 's father or uncle according to some mufassirun [15]. They
are both kāfir. Yet, Ibrahim as still maintains this rational and thankful
gratitude to his father or uncle with the repetition of very genuine and
kind expression of يَا أَبَتِ. Ibrahim as recognizes this and maintains it in
his nature.

In this case, Musa as still maintains his rational stance and expresses
that this upbringing was not a genuine one as expressed قَالَ فَعَلْتُهَا إِذًا وَأَنَا
مِنَ الضَّالِّينَ¹³⁹⁶ {الشعراء/20} فَفَرَرْتُ مِنكُمْ لَمَّا خِفْتُكُمْ فَوَهَبَ لِي رَبِّي حُكْمًا وَجَعَلَنِي مِنَ
الْمُرْسَلِينَ¹³⁹⁷ {الشعراء/21} وَتِلْكَ نِعْمَةٌ تَمُنُّهَا عَلَيَّ أَنْ عَبَّدتَّ بَنِي إِسْرَائِيلَ¹³⁹⁸ {الشعراء/22}.
Musa as states that he does not have any type of upbringing loyalty for
Fir'awn similar to a father similar to the case of Ibrahim although he
was a kāfir.

[23–35]

The Successful Stance Against Challenges

قَالَ فِرْعَوْنُ وَمَا رَبُّ الْعَالَمِينَ¹³⁹⁹ {الشعراء/23} قَالَ رَبُّ السَّمَاوَاتِ وَالْأَرْضِ
وَمَا بَيْنَهُمَا إِن كُنتُم مُّوقِنِينَ¹⁴⁰⁰ {الشعراء/24} قَالَ لِمَنْ حَوْلَهُ أَلَا تَسْتَمِعُونَ
¹⁴⁰¹{الشعراء/25} قَالَ رَبُّكُمْ وَرَبُّ آبَائِكُمُ الْأَوَّلِينَ¹⁴⁰² {الشعراء/26} قَالَ إِنَّ رَسُولَكُمُ
الَّذِي أُرْسِلَ إِلَيْكُمْ لَمَجْنُونٌ¹⁴⁰³ {الشعراء/27} قَالَ رَبُّ الْمَشْرِقِ وَالْمَغْرِبِ وَمَا بَيْنَهُمَا إِن

1394. O my father, do not worship [i.e., obey] Satan. Indeed Satan has ever been, to the Most
Merciful, disobedient.
1395. O my father, indeed I fear that there will touch you a punishment from the Most
Merciful so you would be to Satan a companion [in Hellfire]."
1396. [Moses] said, "I did it, then, while I was of those astray [i.e., ignorant].
1397. So I fled from you when I feared you. Then my Lord granted me judgement [i.e., wisdom
and prophethood] and appointed me [as one] of the messengers.
1398. And is this a favor of which you remind me—that you have enslaved the Children of
Israel?"
1399. Said Pharaoh, "And what is the Lord of the worlds?"
1400. [Moses] said, "The Lord of the heavens and earth and that between them, if you should
be convinced."
1401. [Pharaoh] said to those around him, "Do you not hear?"
1402. [Moses] said, "Your Lord and the Lord of your first forefathers."
1403. [Pharaoh] said, "Indeed, your 'messenger' who has been sent to you is mad."

كُنتُمْ تَعْقِلُونَ 1404﴿الشعراء/28﴾ قَالَ لَئِنِ اتَّخَذْتَ إِلَـٰهًا غَيْرِي لَأَجْعَلَنَّكَ مِنَ الْمَسْجُونِينَ1405
﴿الشعراء/29﴾ قَالَ أَوَلَوْ جِئْتُكَ بِشَيْءٍ مُّبِينٍ 1406﴿الشعراء/30﴾ قَالَ فَأْتِ بِهِ إِن كُنتَ
مِنَ الصَّادِقِينَ 1407﴿الشعراء/31﴾ فَأَلْقَىٰ عَصَاهُ فَإِذَا هِيَ ثُعْبَانٌ مُّبِينٌ 1408﴿الشعراء/32﴾
وَنَزَعَ يَدَهُ فَإِذَا هِيَ بَيْضَاءُ لِلنَّاظِرِينَ 1409﴿الشعراء/33﴾ قَالَ لِلْمَلَإِ حَوْلَهُ إِنَّ هَـٰذَا
لَسَاحِرٌ عَلِيمٌ 1410﴿الشعراء/34﴾ يُرِيدُ أَن يُخْرِجَكُم مِّنْ أَرْضِكُم بِسِحْرِهِ فَمَاذَا تَأْمُرُونَ
1411﴿الشعراء/35﴾

Then, Fira'wn takes the position of being rational 1412قَالَ فِرْعَوْنُ وَمَا رَبُّ
الْعَالَمِينَ as a response to the stance and prior rational disposition of Musa
as. Yet, when Musa as is consistent with his rationality bringing different
logical and reasonable proofs to Fira'wn, the rationality of Fira'wn again
gets lost through emotions, irrationality, humiliation as mentioned قَالَ
قَالَ إِنَّ رَسُولَكُمُ الَّذِي أُرْسِلَ إِلَيْكُمْ لَمَجْنُونٌ 1414 and لِمَنْ حَوْلَهُ أَلَا تَسْتَمِعُونَ1413 ﴿الشعراء/25﴾
﴿الشعراء/27﴾.

Then this irrationality peaks with the threat as 1415قَالَ لَئِنِ اتَّخَذْتَ إِلَـٰهًا
غَيْرِي لَأَجْعَلَنَّكَ مِنَ الْمَسْجُونِينَ ﴿الشعراء/29﴾.

Yet, in this type of threat Musa as still maintains his rationality and
reason as قَالَ أَوَلَوْ جِئْتُكَ بِشَيْءٍ مُّبِينٍ 1416﴿الشعراء/30﴾.

As his threat is logically and reasonably suppressed by the miracle as
shown Musa as, Fira'wn cannot exit this argument unless he also renders
to logic in order not to seem as stupid as قَالَ لِلْمَلَإِ حَوْلَهُ إِنَّ هَـٰذَا لَسَاحِرٌ عَلِيمٌ
1417﴿الشعراء/34﴾. يُرِيدُ أَن يُخْرِجَكُم مِّنْ أَرْضِكُم بِسِحْرِهِ فَمَاذَا تَأْمُرُونَ 1418﴿الشعراء/35﴾

1404. [Moses] said, "Lord of the east and the west and that between them, if you were to reason."
1405. [Pharaoh] said, "If you take a god other than me, I will surely place you among those imprisoned."
1406. [Moses] said, "Even if I brought you something [i.e., proof] manifest?"
1407. [Pharaoh] said, "Then bring it, if you should be of the truthful."
1408. So [Moses] threw his staff, and suddenly it was a serpent manifest.
1409. And he drew out his hand; thereupon it was white for the observers.
1410. [Pharaoh] said to the eminent ones around him, "Indeed, this is a learned magician.
1411. He wants to drive you out of your land by his magic, so what do you advise?"
1412. Said Pharaoh, "And what is the Lord of the worlds?"
1413. [Pharaoh] said to those around him, "Do you not hear?"
1414. [Pharaoh] said, "Indeed, your 'messenger' who has been sent to you is mad."
1415. [Pharaoh] said, "If you take a god other than me, I will surely place you among those imprisoned."
1416. [Moses] said, "Even if I brought you something [i.e., proof] manifest?"
1417. [Pharaoh] said to the eminent ones around him, "Indeed, this is a learned magician.
1418. He wants to drive you out of your land by his magic, so what do you advise?"

This shows that it is important to maintain the logic although one is going through cycles of emotional abuse, reasonable seeming-listenings, threats and logical-seeming conclusions.

[41–51]

The Successful Stance Against Challenges

فَلَمَّا جَاءَ السَّحَرَةُ قَالُوا لِفِرْعَوْنَ أَئِنَّ لَنَا لَأَجْرًا إِن كُنَّا نَحْنُ الْغَالِبِينَ 1419 {الشعراء/41} قَالَ نَعَمْ وَإِنَّكُمْ إِذًا لَّمِنَ الْمُقَرَّبِينَ 1420 {الشعراء/42} قَالَ لَهُم مُّوسَىٰ أَلْقُوا مَا أَنتُم مُّلْقُونَ 1421 {الشعراء/43} فَأَلْقَوْا حِبَالَهُمْ وَعِصِيَّهُمْ وَقَالُوا بِعِزَّةِ فِرْعَوْنَ إِنَّا لَنَحْنُ الْغَالِبُونَ 1422 {الشعراء/44} فَأَلْقَىٰ مُوسَىٰ عَصَاهُ فَإِذَا هِيَ تَلْقَفُ مَا يَأْفِكُونَ 1423 {الشعراء/45} فَأُلْقِيَ السَّحَرَةُ سَاجِدِينَ 1424 {الشعراء/46} قَالُوا آمَنَّا بِرَبِّ الْعَالَمِينَ 1425 {الشعراء/47} رَبِّ مُوسَىٰ وَهَارُونَ 1426 {الشعراء/48} قَالَ آمَنتُمْ لَهُ قَبْلَ أَنْ آذَنَ لَكُمْ إِنَّهُ لَكَبِيرُكُمُ الَّذِي عَلَّمَكُمُ السِّحْرَ فَلَسَوْفَ تَعْلَمُونَ لَأُقَطِّعَنَّ أَيْدِيَكُمْ وَأَرْجُلَكُم مِّنْ خِلَافٍ وَلَأُصَلِّبَنَّكُمْ أَجْمَعِينَ 1427 {الشعراء/49} قَالُوا لَا ضَيْرَ إِنَّا إِلَىٰ رَبِّنَا مُنقَلِبُونَ 1428 {الشعراء/50} إِنَّا نَطْمَعُ أَن يَغْفِرَ لَنَا رَبُّنَا خَطَايَانَا أَن كُنَّا أَوَّلَ الْمُؤْمِنِينَ 1429 {الشعراء/51}

One can see a similar pattern between the Fira'wn and magicians in the above ayahs. The pattern of emotional abuse and reasonable-seeming listening is mentioned as فَلَمَّا جَاءَ السَّحَرَةُ قَالُوا لِفِرْعَوْنَ أَئِنَّ لَنَا لَأَجْرًا إِن كُنَّا نَحْنُ الْغَالِبِينَ 1430 {الشعراء/41} قَالَ نَعَمْ وَإِنَّكُمْ إِذًا لَّمِنَ الْمُقَرَّبِينَ 1431 {الشعراء/42}.

Yet when magicians change their stance as قَالُوا آمَنَّا بِرَبِّ الْعَالَمِينَ 1432 قَالَ آمَنتُمْ لَهُ قَبْلَ أَنْ آذَنَ لَكُمْ إِنَّهُ لَكَبِيرُكُمُ {الشعراء/47} , then the threats start as

---

1419. And when the magicians arrived, they said to Pharaoh, "Is there indeed for us a reward if we are the predominant?"

1420. He said, "Yes, and indeed, you will then be of those near [to me]."

1421. Moses said to them, "Throw whatever you will throw."

1422. So they threw their ropes and their staffs and said, "By the might of Pharaoh, indeed it is we who are predominant."

1423. Then Moses threw his staff, and at once it devoured what they falsified.

1424. So the magicians fell down in prostration [to Allah].

1425. They said, "We have believed in the Lord of the worlds,

1426. The Lord of Moses and Aaron."

1427. [Pharaoh] said, "You believed him [i.e., Moses] before I gave you permission. Indeed, he is your leader who has taught you magic, but you are going to know. I will surely cut off your hands and your feet on opposite sides, and I will surely crucify you all."

1428. They said " No harm, indeed to our lord we return".

1429. Indeed, we aspire that our Lord will forgive us our sins because we were the first of the believers."

1430. And when the magicians arrived, they said to Pharaoh, "Is there indeed for us a reward if we are the predominant?"

1431. He said, "Yes, and indeed, you will then be of those near [to me]."

1432. They said, "We have believed in the Lord of the worlds,

الَّذِي عَلَّمَكُمُ السِّحْرَ فَلَسَوْفَ تَعْلَمُونَ لَأُقَطِّعَنَّ أَيْدِيَكُمْ وَأَرْجُلَكُم مِّنْ خِلَافٍ وَلَأُصَلِّبَنَّكُمْ أَجْمَعِينَ[1433]
{الشعراء/49}.

Yet, again in these threats, magicians maintain their resoanability and logic similar to the dialogue of Musa as against the threats of Firaw'n. Magicians respond rationally as قَالُوا لَا ضَيْرَ إِنَّا إِلَى رَبِّنَا مُنقَلِبُونَ[1434] {الشعراء/50} إِنَّا نَطْمَعُ أَن يَغْفِرَ لَنَا رَبُّنَا خَطَايَانَا أَن كُنَّا أَوَّلَ الْمُؤْمِنِينَ[1435]{الشعراء/51}.

These above patterns in the ayahs indicate and emphasize the importance of maintaining our reason and rationality when we are facing challenges. It is extremely easy to lose oneself with emotions. Yet, it is very difficult to maintain logic and reasonability against the challenges, threats, vulgar treatment, abuse, bullying and oppression. The ones who maintain patience with a response embedded in logic and reason can be successful at the end of this battle. والله اعلم[1436]

Sûrah 27—an- Naml

[15, 19 & 40]

وَلَقَدْ آتَيْنَا دَاوُودَ وَسُلَيْمَانَ عِلْمًا وَقَالَا الْحَمْدُ لِلَّهِ الَّذِي فَضَّلَنَا عَلَى كَثِيرٍ مِّنْ عِبَادِهِ الْمُؤْمِنِينَ[1437] {النمل/15}

قَالَ الَّذِي عِندَهُ عِلْمٌ مِّنَ الْكِتَابِ أَنَا آتِيكَ بِهِ قَبْلَ أَن يَرْتَدَّ إِلَيْكَ طَرْفُكَ فَلَمَّا رَآهُ مُسْتَقِرًّا عِندَهُ قَالَ هَذَا مِن فَضْلِ رَبِّي لِيَبْلُوَنِي أَأَشْكُرُ أَمْ أَكْفُرُ وَمَن شَكَرَ فَإِنَّمَا يَشْكُرُ لِنَفْسِهِ وَمَن كَفَرَ فَإِنَّ رَبِّي غَنِيٌّ كَرِيمٌ[1438] {النمل/40}

1433. [Pharaoh] said, "You believed him [i.e., Moses] before I gave you permission. Indeed, he is your leader who has taught you magic, but you are going to know. I will surely cut off your hands and your feet on opposite sides, and I will surely crucify you all."
1434. They said " No harm, indeed to our lord we return".
1435. Indeed, we aspire that our Lord will forgive us our sins because we were the first of the believers."
1436. Allah knows best.
1437. And We had certainly given to David and Solomon knowledge, and they said, "Praise [is due] to Allah, who has favored us over many of His believing servants."
1438. Said one who had knowledge from the Scripture, "I will bring it to you before your glance returns to you." And when [Solomon] saw it placed before him, he said, "This is from the favor of my Lord to test me whether I will be grateful or ungrateful. And whoever is grateful—his gratitude is only for [the benefit of] himself. And whoever is ungrateful—then indeed, my Lord is Free of need and Generous."

فَتَبَسَّمَ ضَاحِكًا مِّن قَوْلِهَا وَقَالَ رَبِّ أَوْزِعْنِي أَنْ أَشْكُرَ نِعْمَتَكَ الَّتِي أَنْعَمْتَ عَلَيَّ وَعَلَى وَالِدَيَّ وَأَنْ أَعْمَلَ صَالِحًا تَرْضَاهُ وَأَدْخِلْنِي بِرَحْمَتِكَ فِي عِبَادِكَ الصَّالِحِينَ 1439 {النمل/19}

When we review the cases of each prophet, there can be an emerging prominent feature of each prophet. From each case, we can try to focus on their situation and try to relate ourselves to what and how we can adapt teachings in our lives that Allah ﷻ is pleased with us.

One of these cases is the case of bounties of nimahs either through wealth, knowledge and other means. In these cases, a mumin should know how to construct their internal disposition of heart and mind. As soon as the person tend to have a miniscule feeling or thought of giving credit or praise to their ownself instead of embodying Alhamdulillah, then the person can open the doors of shirk for themselves leading to the displeasure of Allah ﷻ with bad consequences, May Allah ﷻ protect us from this, Ameen.

So, what do we do?

Some Muslims prefer to negate everything and give everything to Allah ﷻ. Some are in constant inner dispositions of seeing themselves as fasiq and munāfiq and they can view those bounties as an istidraj.

As all can be valuable efforts, and struggles on the way of pleasing Allah ﷻ, the question can arise, what can be the easiest and safest way for the regular people like us when we are given a bounty, blessing and we can use it to please Allah ﷻ more but do not make shirk?

Again the examples in the lives of role models, as in this case Sulayman as embodying this position of ni'mah's[1440] and teaching us, how our inner disposition should be similar to his father Dawud as :

يَعْمَلُونَ لَهُ مَا يَشَاء مِن مَّحَارِيبَ وَتَمَاثِيلَ وَجِفَانٍ كَالْجَوَابِ وَقُدُورٍ رَّاسِيَاتٍ اعْمَلُوا آلَ دَاوُودَ شُكْرًا وَقَلِيلٌ مِّنْ عِبَادِيَ الشَّكُورُ 1441 {سبأ/13}

1439. So [Solomon] smiled, amused at her speech, and said, "My Lord, enable me to be grateful for Your favor which You have bestowed upon me and upon my parents and to do righteousness of which You approve. And admit me by Your mercy into [the ranks of] Your righteous servants."

1440. Blessings.

1441. They made for him what he willed of elevated chambers, statues, bowls like reservoirs, and stationary kettles. [We said], "Work, O family of David, in gratitude." And few of My servants are grateful.

For example, when we analyze the ayah وَقَالَا الْحَمْدُ لِلَّهِ الَّذِي فَضَّلَنَا عَلَى كَثِيرٍ مِّنْ عِبَادِهِ الْمُؤْمِنِينَ {النمل/15}[1442], the first part of acceptance of ni'mah and giving full and all credit to Allah ﷻ is critical as mentioned: وَقَالَا الْحَمْدُ[1443] لِلَّهِ. Then, making a self-realization in detailing of this full and all credit to Allah ﷻ by explaining further for their own selves through attributing this n'imah fully to Allah ﷻ but not taking any credit for it فَضَّلَنَا[1444]. That, this is the Fadl of Allah ﷻ. The Real Doer and Fa'il is Allah ﷻ in the verb فَضَّلَنَا from the nahw perspective.

One should realize that these are the inner side of their dispositions and duas. It is not public declaration or proclamation or a lecture of Sulayman as. Allah ﷻ is bringing us the critical sincere self-reflection and accountability moments of these role models such as Sulayman as in their private seclusive states with Allah ﷻ what they are verbalizing and embodying in their heart and mind.

Then, after these inner dispositions of giving full and all credit to Allah ﷻ, accepting the ni'mah comes forward as الَّذِي فَضَّلَنَا عَلَى كَثِيرٍ مِّنْ[1445] عِبَادِهِ الْمُؤْمِنِينَ. In other words, saying "Yes, that is true. Allah ﷻ with the Fadl[1446] gave us different means such as 'ilm[1447] or wealth that a lot of believers, mumins did not receive."

Although the other approaches can be valid such as seeing yourself as fasiq or munāfiq and viewing these bounties as a possible istidraj, if the person does not establish a balance in these inner struggles, the person can convince him or herself overtime through the waswasa, temptations of the nafs and/or Shaytān that whatever he or she does good with this bounty does not really have value for Allah ﷻ, therefore there is no point of doing it. After a point, if the person was trying to engage themselves with this nimah to do something good, then he or she stops doing it after a while due to the possible outcome of this disposition. In other words, there is no motivation for this person to continue to do amalu-salih due to overwhelmingly being in the states of viewing everything as a possible istidraj.

1442. And they said, "Praise [is due] to Allah, who has favored us over many of His believing servants."

1443. And they said, "Praise [is due] to Allah.

1444. Favored us.

1445. Who has favored us over many of His believing servants."

1446. Honor

1447. Knowlege.

The reason for the people of second group seeing themselves as a fasiq and munāfiq with the possibilities of istidraj is that it is in the beginning easier and safer to embody yourself as a fasiq and munāfiq while you are engaged with these bounties so that there is no arrogance or self-credit given to this person. Yet, in the possibilities of long-term waswasa with experienced Shaytān over thousands of years, there is the possibility of stopping doing something good or virtuous with aging, laziness.

For the first group as embodied by Sulayman as, it may feel a little bit uncomfortable to accept one having more bounties than others due to the possibilities of making shirk and at that time, heinous nafs can claim implicitly some share from them. Yet, making constant shukr of them by realizing and accepting it and trying to increase it to achieve more to please Allah ﷻ can be safer as embodied by Rasulullah الله اعلم[1448] In both cases, having ni'mah[1449] is not a sign of virtue that if someone has more or less bounty or n'imah that person is virtuous or not for Allah ﷻ. The point is to see as a test in order to reveal the real attitude of this person with these ni'mahs as mentioned: قَالَ هَذَا مِن فَضْلِ رَبِّي لِيَبْلُوَنِي أَأَشْكُرُ أَمْ أَكْفُرُ[1450].

In both cases of approach, the person accepts them as ni'mah. One sees these ni'mah as good and useful and tries to increase their shukr by giving full credit to Allah ﷻ.

The other can see them as useless with the fear of being istidraj when viewing themselves fully as fasiq and munāfiq and therefore, this person does not give value to this n'imah and does not care if there is this n'imah[1451] or not.

In the case of first group as in Sulayman as, he as uses remarkably interesting expression that we may take it as granted in وَمَن شَكَرَ[1452] لِ. فَإِنَّمَا يَشْكُرُ لِنَفْسِهِ. One can expect that وَمَن شَكَرَ فَإِنَّمَا يَشْكُرُ لله[1453]. Yet, if لِ is for sababiyah, when a person makes shukr to Allah ﷻ, they benefit their own selves by recognizing the n'imah. Allah does not need

---

1448. Allah knows best.
1449. Blessings.
1450. This is from the favor of my Lord to test me whether I will be grateful or ungrateful.
1451. Knowledge.
1452. And whoever is grateful—his gratitude is only for [the benefit of] himself
1453. And whoever is grateful—his gratitude is only for Allah.

humans' recognition and their recognition does not change anything as mentioned[1454] وَمَن كَفَرَ فَإِنَّ رَبِّي غَنِيٌّ كَرِيمٌ.

Then, here is the gist of this position of shukr and hamd mentioned in فَتَبَسَّمَ ضَاحِكًا مِّن قَوْلِهَا وَقَالَ رَبِّ أَوْزِعْنِي أَنْ أَشْكُرَ نِعْمَتَكَ الَّتِي أَنْعَمْتَ عَلَيَّ وَعَلَى وَالِدَيَّ وَأَنْ أَعْمَلَ صَالِحًا تَرْضَاهُ وَأَدْخِلْنِي بِرَحْمَتِكَ فِي عِبَادِكَ الصَّالِحِينَ[1455] {النمل/19}.

When we analyze this ayah, we can get further how the first groups engagement can expand as وَقَالَ رَبِّ أَوْزِعْنِي أَنْ أَشْكُرَ نِعْمَتَكَ الَّتِي أَنْعَمْتَ عَلَيَّ[1456]. This can mean that "Oh Allah, I am in constant states of making shukr[1457] and hamd receiving your ni'mahs on me. So, increase your ni'mahs more and more so that I can be in constant and continuous states of amazements of hamd[1458] and shukr[1459] to you." In other words, "I can be in constant amazements of your ni'mahs that my tongue, my heart and my mind are in continuous, innate, and automatic dhikrs and chants of الحمد لله، الشكر لله[1460] and my body is constant prostrations of shukr through salah and other 'ibadahs."

I also give thanks to the people who delivers for me starting with my parents as you ordered to my, Ya Allah ﷻ as mentioned وَعَلَى وَالِدَيَّ[1461].

"Oh Allah, increase your ni'mahs so that I can do amalu salih that can please You, Ya Allah" as mentioned وَأَنْ أَعْمَلَ صَالِحًا تَرْضَاهُ[1462]

In other words, one can be constantly in the position of dhikr and shukr constantly saying Alhamdulillah, al-shukru lillah being in the states of nafsul mutmainna and radiyah as mentioned يَا أَيَّتُهَا النَّفْسُ الْمُطْمَئِنَّةُ[1463] {الفجر/27} ارْجِعِي إِلَى رَبِّكِ رَاضِيَةً مَّرْضِيَّةً[1464] {الفجر/28}. Or the second group can be in the constant position of blaming their own nafs and cursing for their wrong renderings and in the engagements of displeasure of

---

1454. And whoever is ungrateful—then indeed, my Lord is Free of need and Generous."
1455. So [Solomon] smiled, amused at her speech, and said, "My Lord, enable me to be grateful for Your favor which You have bestowed upon me and upon my parents and to do righteousness of which You approve. And admit me by Your mercy into [the ranks of] Your righteous servants.
1456. "My Lord, enable me to be grateful for Your favor which You have bestowed upon me
1457. Gratitude.
1458. Praise.
1459. Gratitude.
1460. All praise is due to Allah, All thanks is to Allah.
1461. And upon my parents.
1462. And that I do righteousness of which You approve
1463. [To the righteous it will be said], "O reassured soul.
1464. Return to your Lord, well-pleased and pleasing [to Him],

Allah ﷻ with nafsul lawwamah as mentioned in 1465وَلَا أُقْسِمُ بِالنَّفْسِ اللَّوَّامَةِ {القيامة/2}.

Yet, after all these dhikrs, shukrs, 'ibadahs, recognitions, amazements with all your ni'mahs I do not deserve the Jannah and being with good people in the akhirah except it is with your Rahmah as mentioned وَأَدْخِلْنِي بِرَحْمَتِكَ فِي عِبَادِكَ الصَّالِحِينَ 1466{النمل/19}.

Yet, people in these ni'mahs1467 being in the position of shukr are not many as mentioned {سبأ/13} 1468وَقَلِيلٌ مِّنْ عِبَادِيَ الشَّكُورُ. May Allah ﷻ protect us and make us from the Shakirin, Amìn.

One can review that the word Fadl1469 of Allah for the ni'mahs of dunya and Rahmah can be for the n'imahs of Akhirah. When one reviews the ayahs

وَدَاوُودَ وَسُلَيْمَانَ إِذْ يَحْكُمَانِ فِي الْحَرْثِ إِذْ نَفَشَتْ فِيهِ غَنَمُ الْقَوْمِ وَكُنَّا لِحُكْمِهِمْ شَاهِدِينَ 1470{الأنبياء/78} فَفَهَّمْنَاهَا سُلَيْمَانَ وَكُلًّا آتَيْنَا حُكْمًا وَعِلْمًا وَسَخَّرْنَا مَعَ دَاوُودَ الْجِبَالَ يُسَبِّحْنَ وَالطَّيْرَ وَكُنَّا فَاعِلِينَ1471 {الأنبياء/79} وَعَلَّمْنَاهُ صَنْعَةَ لَبُوسٍ لَّكُمْ لِتُحْصِنَكُم مِّن بَأْسِكُمْ فَهَلْ أَنتُمْ شَاكِرُونَ1472 {الأنبياء/80}

The expression concludes the true and highest disposition to be expected from a believer is to be a person of constant trait and quality of making shukr as mentioned1473 {الأنبياء/80} فَهَلْ أَنتُمْ شَاكِرُونَ.

Yet, this very fine line in making shukr requires accepting all the bounties and nimahs but not denying and not giving any credit to oneself and giving all but all credit only to Allah ﷻ solely and sincerely to Allah ﷻ as mentioned1474 {الأنبياء/79} وَكُنَّا فَاعِلِينَ.

On a side note, the expression وَكُنَّا فَاعِلِينَ {الأنبياء/79} can also indicate that Allah ﷻ gives all these bounties to all humankind in their civilized

---

1465. And I swear by the reproaching soul [to the certainty of resurrection].
1466. And admit me by Your mercy into [the ranks of] Your righteous servants.
1467. Blessings.
1468. And few of My servants are grateful.
1469. Favor.
1470. And [mention] David and Solomon, when they judged concerning the field—when the sheep of a people overran it [at night], and We were witness to their judgment.
1471. And We gave understanding of it [i.e., the case] to Solomon, and to each [of them] We gave judgment and knowledge. And We subjected the mountains to exalt [Us], along with David and [also] the birds. And We were doing [that].
1472. And We taught him the fashioning of coats of armor to protect you from your [enemy in] battle. So will you then be grateful?
1473. So will you then be grateful?
1474. And We were doing [that].

developments. One can now relate this very critical point with some of today's discussions of "do we need religion or religious teachings for ethics or civilizations?" The answer is clear "Yes." Allah ﷻ already gave and taught humans through wahiy, revelation from the beginning of human history. Claiming this is another modern form of kufr besides many apparent forms of kufr that some of the humans are engaging themselves.

When we review the cases of the responsibility of prophethood given to other prophets, one can realize that Rasulullah ﷺ collects in his prophethood all the separate individual emerging prominent features of each prophet. Rasulullah was the epitome of hamd and shukr as Muhammad ﷺ is the person of[1475] "افلم أكون عبدا شكورا". Rasulullah ﷺ is called the lead prophet and human being. As all the prophets are role models for humans, the lead prophet necessitates to be the lead of all humans, sayyidul-bashar[1476].

In the ayah, فَتَبَسَّمَ ضَاحِكًا مِّن قَوْلِهَا وَقَالَ رَبِّ أَوْزِعْنِي أَنْ أَشْكُرَ نِعْمَتَكَ الَّتِي أَنْعَمْتَ عَلَيَّ وَعَلَى وَالِدَيَّ وَأَنْ أَعْمَلَ صَالِحًا تَرْضَاهُ وَأَدْخِلْنِي بِرَحْمَتِكَ فِي عِبَادِكَ الصَّالِحِينَ[1477] {النمل/19}, it mentions that the way to please Allah ﷻ with amalu-salih as mentioned[1478] أَعْمَلَ صَالِحًا تَرْضَاهُ.

In other words, one can ask ni'mah so that he or she can be in the full embodiment of shukr and hamd to Allah ﷻ رَبِّ أَوْزِعْنِي أَنْ أَشْكُرَ[1479] نِعْمَتَكَ الَّتِي أَنْعَمْتَ عَلَيَّ. At the same time, he or she can show gratitude to others to please Allah ﷻ as Allah ﷻ ordered as mentioned عَلَيَّ وَعَلَى[1480] وَالِدَيَّ.

Then, the means or vehicle of ni'mahs in order to make shukr and hamd to Allah ﷻ should be represented with amulu salih as mentioned أَعْمَلَ صَالِحًا[1481]. This can be the dhikrs of hamd[1482], salah, all the 'ibadah, as well as helping others, teaching them as instructed by Allah ﷻ in order

---

1475. Should I Not be a thankful sevant.
1476. The leader of mankind.
1477. So [Solomon] smiled, amused at her speech, and said, "My Lord, enable me to be grateful for Your favor which You have bestowed upon me and upon my parents and to do righteousness of which You approve. And admit me by Your mercy into [the ranks of] Your righteous servants.
1478. To do righteousness of which You approve.
1479. My Lord, enable me to be grateful for Your favor which You have bestowed upon me and upon my parents
1480. Upon me and upon my parents.
1481. I do righteousness.
1482. Praise.

to please Allah ﷺ as mentioned تَرْضَاه[1483]. It is not all the amal, actions the ones as instructed, outlined as virtuous by Allah ﷺ in the Qurān and Sunnah of Rasulullah ﷺ..

Then, after all this, still going to Jannah and being with good people in this dunya and akhirah is not due to one's kasb but with the Rahmah[1484] of Allah ﷺ as mentioned [1485]وَأَدْخِلْنِي بِرَحْمَتِكَ فِي عِبَادِكَ الصَّالِحِينَ.

Here, one can conclude that one should always ask the means to be amazed with shukr, hamd in order to increase one's imān. The amazement of this ni'mah with shukr and hamd to Allah ﷺ will please Allah ﷺ. The expression of this amazement with shukr and hamd will be through amalu-salih. Yet, in all these engagements one should constantly do self-accountability, check that they should not trust this amal. They all can be istidraj. They should always trust the Rahmah of Allah ﷺ.

In this balance of fear and hope being in the ni'mahs, if one is overwhelmed with the amazements of ni'mahs then, he or she should increase their hamd, shukr and gratitude for these amazements as Rasulullah ﷺ did as "11" [13] " افلم أكون عبدا شكورا[1486]].

If the person cannot support and transform the effect of these amazements with shukr and hamd to the Real Owner in its complete sense, if and when even a tiny bit of self-credibility, recognition, and arrogance tries to enter to the heart and mind with hawah of cynical engagements of nafs and Shaytān, then the person should immediately entertain the possibility of this being and istidraj or a test as practiced by Dawud as:

قَالَ لَقَدْ ظَلَمَكَ بِسُؤَالِ نَعْجَتِكَ إِلَى نِعَاجِهِ وَإِنَّ كَثِيرًا مِّنْ الْخُلَطَاء لَيَبْغِي بَعْضُهُمْ عَلَى بَعْضٍ إِلَّا الَّذِينَ آمَنُوا وَعَمِلُوا الصَّالِحَاتِ وَقَلِيلٌ مَّا هُمْ وَظَنَّ دَاوُودُ أَنَّمَا فَتَنَّاهُ فَاسْتَغْفَرَ رَبَّهُ وَخَرَّ رَاكِعًا وَأَنَابَ (سجدة مستحبة)[1487]{ص/24} فَغَفَرْنَا لَهُ ذَلِكَ وَإِنَّ لَهُ عِندَنَا لَزُلْفَى وَحُسْنَ مَآبٍ[1488] {ص/25}

1483. That which you approve.
1484. Mercy.
1485. And admit me by Your mercy into [the ranks of] Your righteous servants.
1486. Should I not be a thankful servant.
1487. [David] said, "He has certainly wronged you in demanding your ewe [in addition] to his ewes. And indeed, many associates oppress one another, except for those who believe and do righteous deeds—and few are they." And David became certain that We had tried him, and he asked forgiveness of his Lord and fell down bowing [in prostration] and turned in repentance [to Allah].
1488. So We forgave him that; and indeed, for him is nearness to Us and a good place of return.

In order to maintain this balance, the approach can be implemented at different times differently. When the person is in the hopeless states and stopping the amalu salih, then he should at these times should view their actions as amalu salih and increase hamd and shukr and continue for their amalu salih by increasing it but not stopping.

If the person is overwhelmed with the abundance of nima'hs, openings, and amalu salih, then he or she should entertain them still with shukr and hamd continuing the amalu-salih and increasing it but always including the possibility of istidraj as a safeguard in order not to fail on the path of achievement for the Pleasure of Allah ﷻ with the Fadl and Rahmah of Allah ﷻ.

Juz 21

Sûrah 29—al- 'Ankabût

فَآمَنَ لَهُ لُوطٌ وَقَالَ إِنِّي مُهَاجِرٌ إِلَى رَبِّي إِنَّهُ هُوَ الْعَزِيزُ الْحَكِيمُ[1489] {العنكبوت/26}

إِنَّ اللَّهَ يَعْلَمُ مَا يَدْعُونَ مِن دُونِهِ مِن شَيْءٍ وَهُوَ الْعَزِيزُ الْحَكِيمُ[1490] {العنكبوت/42}

وَهُوَ الَّذِي يَبْدَأُ الْخَلْقَ ثُمَّ يُعِيدُهُ وَهُوَ أَهْوَنُ عَلَيْهِ وَلَهُ الْمَثَلُ الْأَعْلَى فِي السَّمَاوَاتِ وَالْأَرْضِ وَهُوَ الْعَزِيزُ الْحَكِيمُ[1491] {الروم/27}

خَالِدِينَ فِيهَا وَعْدَ اللَّهِ حَقًّا وَهُوَ الْعَزِيزُ الْحَكِيمُ[1492] {لقمان/9}

وَلَوْ أَنَّمَا فِي الْأَرْضِ مِن شَجَرَةٍ أَقْلَامٌ وَالْبَحْرُ يَمُدُّهُ مِن بَعْدِهِ سَبْعَةُ أَبْحُرٍ مَّا نَفِدَتْ كَلِمَاتُ اللَّهِ إِنَّ اللَّهَ عَزِيزٌ حَكِيمٌ[1493] {لقمان/27}

1489. And Lot believed him. [Abraham] said, "Indeed, I will emigrate to [the service of] my Lord. Indeed, He is the Exalted in Might, the Wise."

1490. Indeed, Allah knows whatever thing they call upon other than Him. And He is the Exalted in Might, the Wise.

1491. 1065- And it is He who begins creation; then He repeats it, and that is [even] easier for Him. To Him belongs the highest description [i.e., attribute] in the heavens and earth. And He is the Exalted in Might, the Wise.

1492. 1066 Wherein they abide eternally; [it is] the promise of Allah [which is] truth. And He is the Exalted in Might, the Wise.

1493. And if whatever trees upon the earth were pens and the sea [was ink], replenished thereafter by seven [more] seas, the words of Allah would not be exhausted. Indeed, Allah is Exalted in Might and Wise.

One can review the Name and Attribute of Allah[1494] الْعَزِيزِ ﷺ as coming with another Name and Attribute of Allah ﷺ as الْحَكِيمُ[1495]. It is important to try to understand the combination of these two Names and Attributes of Allah ﷺ.

Sûrah 30- ar-Rûm

[1–8]

To emphasize a very critical point, this Sûrah starts with a case study as:

الم [1496]{الروم/1} غُلِبَتِ الرُّومُ[1497] {الروم/2} فِي أَدْنَى الْأَرْضِ وَهُم مِّن بَعْدِ غَلَبِهِمْ سَيَغْلِبُونَ[1498] {الروم/3} فِي بِضْعِ سِنِينَ لِلَّهَ الْأَمْرُ مِن قَبْلُ وَمِن بَعْدُ وَيَوْمَئِذٍ يَفْرَحُ الْمُؤْمِنُونَ[1499] {الروم/4}

In this case, in its apparent from the people of the Rûm or Rome as representing the believers at that time loses in the battle. In this loss, there were a lot of issues, speculations and conversations happening that would demoralize, dishearten, depress, and sadden the Muslims. Then, Allah ﷺ gives a future event about the same case that would hearten, boost, and uplift the Muslims. Yet, at the same time to remind us not to judge events in their apparent forms as mentioned in يَعْلَمُونَ ظَاهِرًا مِّنَ الْحَيَاةِ الدُّنْيَا وَهُمْ عَنِ الْآخِرَةِ هُمْ غَافِلُونَ[1500] {الروم/7}.

Most of the time, we cannot rationalize the evil-seeming incidents happening in the world. In this regard, depending on the religion, people seem to alienate from their religion and God. This also happens or can happen at different levels for Muslims depending on their embodiment of imãn.

In this regard of possible alienation, Allah ﷺ clearly mentions this problem as[1501] يَعْلَمُونَ ظَاهِرًا مِّنَ الْحَيَاةِ الدُّنْيَا. In others, an incident or occurrence may look evil-seeming, yet in its reality it may not be the

---

1494. Exalted in Might,
1495. The wise.
1496. 1044 Alif, Lam, Meem.
1497. Within three to nine years. To Allah belongs the command [i.e., decree] before and after. And that day the believers will rejoice
1498. In the nearest land. But they, after their defeat, will overcome
1499. Within three to nine years. To Allah belongs the command [i.e., decree] before and after. And that day the believers will rejoice
1500. They know what is apparent of the worldly life, but they, of the Hereafter, are unaware.
1501. They know what is apparent of the worldly life.

case. For example, وَلاَ تَقُولُواْ لِمَنْ يُقْتَلُ فِي سَبِيلِ اللهِ أَمْوَاتٌ بَلْ أَحْيَاء وَلَكِن لاَّ تَشْعُرُونَ {البقرة/154}[1502], as mentioned in this ayah, when a person dies in a seeming-catastrophe, we immediately break down with sorrow. Yet, this agony embedded with death as mentioned with أَمْوَاتٌ[1503] is replaced in their true reality only known by Allah ﷻ that they are not dead by they are alive as mentioned with بَلْ أَحْيَاء[1504].

Another example can be the people that we hear or watch in the news about people being tortured, imprisoned or suffering. The Qurān gives the prime example of this torture with burning and imprisonment in the fire for the case of Ibrahim as. Yet, the true reality of this case is revealed to us by Allah ﷻ as قُلْنَا يَا نَارُ كُونِي بَرْدًا وَسَلَامًا عَلَى إِبْرَاهِيمَ[1505] {الأنبياء/69}.

In all these cases and others, we always judge with zahir, the immediate apparent but not with the inner real and true meanings. This can be normal especially with the usul, methodology of fiqh as نحن نحكم بظاهر. Yet, as mentioned with the ayah يَعْلَمُونَ ظَاهِرًا مِّنَ الْحَيَاةِ الدُّنْيَا[1506] that there are true realities beyond what is apparent to humans.

Therefore, a mu'min should constantly run back to Allah ﷻ in all cases of evil or good seeming incidents. Sometimes, our nafs is embedded with fears, worries, and blame. Sometimes Shaytān can give us these ideas. Sometimes, our friends amplifying these problems or fears, or sometimes our purposeless engagements with people or media can amplify the effects of these evil-seeming incidents on the hearts, minds, and souls of the person. Then, the person with their weak spiritual shoulders become weaker and weaker, and then become spiritually paralyzed.

Yes, we are humans. Yes, when we hear a calamity we feel these shocking effects on our souls, heart and mind. As a human, we should feel concerned about others like our own selves. We carry fears, worries and anxieties. With all these realities, we should try to a get meaning as instructed by Allah ﷻ and use those as opportunities to excel and boost our relationship with Allah ﷻ.

1502. 1049- And do not say about those who are killed in the way of Allah, "They are dead." Rather, they are alive, but you perceive [it] not.
1503. They are dead.
1504. Rather they are alive.
1505. We [i.e., Allah] said, "O fire, be coolness and safety upon Abraham."
1506. They know what is apparent of the worldly life.

One should remember that whatever happens in the world, we are here for a short period of time. An evil or good seeming incident, world matters or current events, shocking news, and all our engagements have very short lives. Our goal is not to lose focus with a lot of distractions in this short life. Rasulullah ﷺ emphasizes the real focus as the big jihad compared to other struggles. Then, the ayah continues about the real focus that is expected from person as the big jihad. That is, focusing on one's self, nafs أَوَلَمْ يَتَفَكَّرُوا فِي أَنفُسِهِمْ[1507] as mentioned in the immediately following ayah:

أَوَلَمْ يَتَفَكَّرُوا فِي أَنفُسِهِم مَّا خَلَقَ اللَّهُ السَّمَاوَاتِ وَالْأَرْضَ وَمَا بَيْنَهُمَا إِلَّا بِالْحَقِّ وَأَجَلٍ مُّسَمًّى وَإِنَّ كَثِيرًا مِّنَ النَّاسِ بِلِقَاء رَبِّهِمْ لَكَافِرُونَ[1508] {الروم/8}

Yes, focus on your nafs. That is the reality that you need to face, train and better it. Focus on your nafs before it is too late when you will meet with Allah ﷻ as mentioned[1509] وَإِنَّ كَثِيرًا مِّنَ النَّاسِ بِلِقَاء رَبِّهِمْ لَكَافِرُونَ. Yes, insān as the word النَّاس can indicate about this feature of the nafs that tries to make the person heedless and forgetful of this Great Meeting with Allah ﷻ. Yet, focus on your nafs for your greatest jihad, struggle in order to constantly fight with it although this nafs tries to knock you down at each second. Ask help constantly from Allah ﷻ as "wa la takilni nafsan tarfata 'ayn", "Oh Allah, donot leave us with our own selves less than a second" [24] as Rasulullah ﷺ taught us.

Regarding big or smaller struggle, Jihad, one should remember that بِنَصْرِ اللَّهِ يَنصُرُ مَن يَشَاء وَهُوَ الْعَزِيزُ الرَّحِيمُ {الروم/5}[1510] وَعْدَ اللَّهِ لَا يُخْلِفُ اللَّهُ وَعْدَهُ وَلَكِنَّ أَكْثَرَ النَّاسِ لَا يَعْلَمُونَ {الروم/6}[1511]. Allah ﷻ can help the person and inshAllah will help the person or people if the people fulfil the means of their position with Allah ﷻ.

1507. 1054 Do they not contemplate within themselves?
1508. Do they not contemplate within themselves? Allah has not created the heavens and the earth and what is between them except in truth and for a specified term. And indeed, many of the people, in the meeting with their Lord, are disbelievers.
1509. And indeed, many of the people, in the meeting with their Lord, are disbelievers.
1510. 1057 the Exalted in Might, the Merciful.
1511. [It is] the promise of Allah. Allah does not fail in His promise, but most of the people do not know.

[22]

وَمِنْ آيَاتِهِ خَلْقُ السَّمَاوَاتِ وَالْأَرْضِ وَاخْتِلَافُ أَلْسِنَتِكُمْ وَأَلْوَانِكُمْ إِنَّ فِي ذَلِكَ لَآيَاتٍ لِّلْعَالِمِينَ [1512]{الروم/22/}

One asks the question that what is the hikmah of mentioning about galaxies with[1513] وَمِنْ آيَاتِهِ خَلْقُ السَّمَاوَاتِ وَالْأَرْضِ and in the same ayah immediately, the ayah mentions about the diversity of humans with their language and ethnic background with[1514] وَاخْتِلَافُ أَلْسِنَتِكُمْ وَأَلْوَانِكُمْ؟

All the ayahs of Allah ﷻ show different Names and Attributes of Allah ﷻ with the true tawhid as mentioned at the end of the ayah with إِنَّ فِي ذَلِكَ لَآيَاتٍ لِّلْعَالِمِينَ[1515]. In this sense, al-Wāhid is the Name of Allah ﷻ that one can realize about Oneness of Allah ﷻ in collective bodies of systems such as skies, galaxies, earth, human species and other collective bodies forming systems and groups.

As the Name of Allah ﷻ is al-Wāhid that can be seen in outer space. Sometimes, mind and heart can be in the heedless states of not recognizing if the accessibility of the sign or ayah always points to skies or galaxies. Then, when accessibility measures are changed to observable human realm to show this same collectiveness as a sign, ayah of Allah ﷻ emphasizing tawhid of Allah ﷻ, then the routine of gaflah can be broken. In other words, changing accessibility measures can break the negative states of routines and heedlessness as indicated with the Arabic word of gaflah.

If we take وَاخْتِلَافُ أَلْسِنَتِكُمْ وَأَلْوَانِكُمْ[1516] indicating the Name of Allah ﷻ as al-Ahad[1517], this can be another style of breaking the ghaflah. In other words, sometimes collective bodies can indicate distance, separation, isolation and defocus. A person may ask that is great but what does it do for me? This tendency of gaflah can be broken by focusing the person on individual cases with the Name of Allah ﷻ as al-Ahad. With this Name of Allah ﷻ, the person can induce more relevance, closeness and focus

---

1512. And of His signs is the creation of the heavens and the earth and the diversity of your languages and your colors. Indeed in that are signs for those of knowledge.

1513. And of His signs is the creation of the heavens and the earth

1514. The diversity of your languages and your colors.

1515. Indeed in that are signs for those of knowledge.

1516. The diversity of your languages and your colors.

1517. The unique.

to connect oneself to the true tawhid of Allah ﷻ as mentioned وَاخْتِلَافُ[1518]
أَلْسِنَتِكُمْ وَأَلْوَانِكُمْ.

In this case, the Name of Allah ﷻ as al-Ahad can require and indicate on the focus of one piece and self-focus like internal or greater Jihad as mentioned by Rasulullah ﷺ. The Name of Allah ﷻ as al-Wahid can indicate group and collective bodies as societies, communities, jama'ahs and social work or action-based form of Jihad as mentioned by Rasulullah ﷺ.

Yet, both are important. Al-Ahad can indicate the natural and expected and constant and continuous focus of the person on one-self as Sûrah Ikhlas repeats this Name Al-Ahad twice. Sûrah Ikhlas is the epitome of the Qurân. After the cases of social work, Rasulullah ﷺ reminds us this essence of self-focus as this Name of Allah ﷻ can indicate with the dua as:

"Aibuna, Taiubuuna, A'biduna, liRabbina Hamidun, We return, repent, worship and praise our Lord [13]." In all the engagements of physical and spiritual discourses, all the return, the end and the goal is Allah ﷻ. In this sense the word a'ibuna can signify this point. Yet, this turning to Allah ﷻ should be in the state of tawbah, asking forgiveness with since regret and apology. The way to express is in the form of 'ibadah verbally and physically at the highest level called sajdah. At the end of this return, we don't feel anything negative, unappreciative, unnatural, forced or evil, but we will be thankful and appreciate that we have Allah ﷻ. We have a home and the One who can shelter us is only Allah ﷻ. In all these states, we should have true disposition of Hamd for Allah ﷻ.

Juz 23

Sûrah 36—Yã sìn

و اضرب لنا مثلا و نسي خلقه[1519]

For this above ayah, one can just review dictionary explanations of only two organs in our body. One is brain as:

The human brain consists of three main parts. (i) The forebrain, greatly developed into the cerebrum, consists of two hemispheres joined

1518. The diversity of your languages and your colors.
1519. And he strikes out a likeness for us and forgets his own creation.

by a bridge of nerve fibers, and is responsible for thought and control of speech. (ii) The midbrain, the upper part of the tapering brainstem, contains cells involved in eye movements. (iii) The hindbrain, the lower part of the brainstem, contains cells responsible for breathing and for regulating heart action, the flow of digestive juices, and other unconscious actions and processes. The cerebellum, which lies behind the brain stem, plays an important role in the execution of highly skilled movements [1].

The other organ is heart as:

A hollow muscular organ that pumps the blood through the circulatory system by rhythmic contraction and dilation. In vertebrates there may be up to four chambers (as in humans), with two atria and two ventricles. Atrium is the each of the two upper cavities of the heart from which blood is passed to the ventricles. The right atrium receives deoxygenated blood from the veins of the body; the left atrium receives oxygenated blood from the pulmonary vein. Ventricles are the each of the two main chambers of the heart, left and right [1].

After just looking at the above two definitions and functions of two organs, one can ask: did we decide about their functions and existence? Do we control their functions? We have it and use it. After this, there is no word for the answer of the question of قَالَ مَن يُحْيِي الْعِظَامَ وَهِيَ رَمِيمٌ Qala man yuhyiyul izāma wa hiya ramim, except Allah ﷻ!, SubhanAllah!, Alhamdulillah!, La ilaha illa Allah! Allahu Akbar!

Sûrah 37—as—Sãffãt

Child—Father Relations

فَلَمَّا بَلَغَ مَعَهُ السَّعْيَ قَالَ يَا بُنَيَّ إِنِّي أَرَى فِي الْمَنَامِ أَنِّي أَذْبَحُكَ فَانظُرْ مَاذَا تَرَى قَالَ يَا أَبَتِ افْعَلْ مَا تُؤْمَرُ سَتَجِدُنِي إِن شَاءَ اللَّهُ مِنَ الصَّابِرِينَ 1520 {الصافات/102}

When one analyzes the expression يَا أَبَتِ in the above ayah with the ayahs below as

---

1520. And when he reached with him [the age of] exertion, he said, "O my son, indeed I have seen in a dream that I [must] sacrifice you, so see what you think." He said, "O my father, do as you are commanded. You will find me, if Allah wills, of the steadfast."

إِذْ قَالَ لِأَبِيهِ يَا أَبَتِ لِمَ تَعْبُدُ مَا لَا يَسْمَعُ وَلَا يُبْصِرُ وَلَا يُغْنِي عَنكَ شَيْئًا ¹⁵²¹{مريم/42} يَا أَبَتِ إِنِّي قَدْ جَاءَنِي مِنَ الْعِلْمِ مَا لَمْ يَأْتِكَ فَاتَّبِعْنِي أَهْدِكَ صِرَاطًا سَوِيًّا ¹⁵²²{مريم/43} يَا أَبَتِ لَا تَعْبُدِ الشَّيْطَانَ إِنَّ الشَّيْطَانَ كَانَ لِلرَّحْمَنِ عَصِيًّا¹⁵²³ {مريم/44} يَا أَبَتِ إِنِّي أَخَافُ أَن يَمَسَّكَ عَذَابٌ مِّنَ الرَّحْمَنِ فَتَكُونَ لِلشَّيْطَانِ وَلِيًّا ¹⁵²⁴{مريم/45}

then, one can realize that a person is treated in the same way as they treat their fathers and parents.

The exact genuine exclamation of يَا أَبَتِ¹⁵²⁵ is used by Ibrahim as for his father in the ayahs above. Then, his son Ismael as uses later the same respectful genuine expression of¹⁵²⁶ يَا أَبَتِ for this father as يَا أَبَتِ افْعَلْ مَا تُؤْمَرُ.

This can indicate one of the sunnatullah as whatever a person does for their parents, the same can be exacted for their treatment by their children subhanAllah!

On the other hand, the similar genuine child-father relation is emphasized with this critical word of يَا أَبَتِ¹⁵²⁷ between Yaqub as and Yusuf as in the ayah as وَرَفَعَ أَبَوَيْهِ عَلَى الْعَرْشِ وَخَرُّوا لَهُ سُجَّدًا وَقَالَ يَا أَبَتِ هَذَا تَأْوِيلُ رُؤْيَايَ مِن قَبْلُ قَدْ جَعَلَهَا رَبِّي حَقًّا وَقَدْ أَحْسَنَ بِي إِذْ أَخْرَجَنِي مِنَ السِّجْنِ وَجَاءَ بِكُم مِّنَ الْبَدْوِ مِن بَعْدِ أَن نَّزَغَ الشَّيْطَانُ بَيْنِي وَبَيْنَ إِخْوَتِي إِنَّ رَبِّي لَطِيفٌ لِّمَا يَشَاءُ إِنَّهُ هُوَ الْعَلِيمُ الْحَكِيمُ ¹⁵²⁸{يوسف/100}

Also, the gender of the child does not matter. It can be the boys as sons as indicated in the above cases. Or it can be girls as daughters as mentioned with this critical word يَا أَبَتِ as قَالَتْ إِحْدَاهُمَا يَا أَبَتِ اسْتَأْجِرْهُ إِنَّ خَيْرَ مَنِ اسْتَأْجَرْتَ الْقَوِيُّ الْأَمِينُ ¹⁵²⁹ {القصص/26}

1521. [Mention] when he said to his father, "O my father, why do you worship that which does not hear and does not see and will not benefit you at all?
1522. O my father, indeed there has come to me of knowledge that which has not come to you, so follow me; I will guide you to an even path.
1523. O my father, do not worship [i.e., obey] Satan. Indeed Satan has ever been, to the Most Merciful, disobedient.
1524. O my father, indeed I fear that there will touch you a punishment from the Most Merciful so you would be to Satan a companion [in Hellfire]."
1525. O my father.
1526. O my father, do as you are commanded.
1527. O my father.
1528. And he raised his parents upon the throne, and they bowed to him in prostration. And he said, "O my father, this is the explanation of my vision of before. My Lord has made it reality. And He was certainly good to me when He took me out of prison and brought you [here] from bedouin life after Satan had induced [estrangement] between me and my brothers. Indeed, my Lord is Subtle in what He wills. Indeed, it is He who is the Knowing, the Wise.
1529. One of the women said, "O my father, hire him. Indeed, the best one you can hire is the strong and the trustworthy."

Sûrah 38- Sâd

[24–25 & 34–35]

وَظَنَّ دَاوُودُ أَنَّمَا فَتَنَّاهُ فَاسْتَغْفَرَ رَبَّهُ وَخَرَّ رَاكِعًا وَأَنَابَ (سجدة مستحبة)1530{ص/24}
فَغَفَرْنَا لَهُ ذَلِكَ وَإِنَّ لَهُ عِندَنَا لَزُلْفَى وَحُسْنَ مَآبٍ1531 {ص/25}

وَلَقَدْ فَتَنَّا سُلَيْمَانَ وَأَلْقَيْنَا عَلَى كُرْسِيِّهِ جَسَدًا ثُمَّ أَنَابَ1532{ص/34} قَالَ رَبِّ اغْفِرْ لِي
وَهَبْ لِي مُلْكًا لَّا يَنبَغِي لِأَحَدٍ مِّنْ بَعْدِي إِنَّكَ أَنتَ الْوَهَّابُ1533 {ص/35}

It is important to realize the type of disposition one should take at the times of difficulties, trials, and tests. In the case of prophets of Allah ﷻ, these tests or trials can come to reveal their true high disposition. In the case of people like us, we attract difficulties or tests on ourselves due to our zulm, oppression and wrong renderings.

Yet, in both cases, the solution is the same as exemplified by the role models, prophets of Allah ﷻ. The first step is to run back to Allah ﷻ. Ask, beg and cry for forgiveness about our own zulm to our own nafs, our own selves. Yet, at the same time, always but always keeping the good opinion, zann about Allah ﷻ that Allah ﷻ is al-Kareem[1534], al-Gafur[1535], ar-Rahman[1536], Dhul Fadl wa Dhul Rahmah[1537], at-Tawwāb[1538], al-Wahhāb[1539], al-Mannān[1540].

Knowing and fully embodying that Allah ﷻ is not like human beings. Allah ﷻ does not render similar to humans such as delaying, holding or refraining from bestowing forgiveness. As soon as the person opens his or her hand with ikhlas, al-Wahhab immediately forgives this person. This person becomes close to Allah ﷻ. As soon as the person opens his or her hands, Allah ﷻ as al-Sattar, covers all the dirty, filthy

---

1530. And David became certain that We had tried him, and he asked forgiveness of his Lord and fell down bowing [in prostration] and turned in repentance [to Allah].

1531. So We forgave him that; and indeed, for him is nearness to Us and a good place of return.

1532. And We certainly tried Solomon and placed on his throne a body; then he returned.

1533. He said, "My Lord, forgive me and grant me a kingdom such as will not belong to anyone after me. Indeed, You are the Bestower."

1534. The generous.

1535. The forgiving.

1536. The most merciful.

1537. The one with merit and the one with mercy.

1538. The ever-Pardoning.

1539. The bestower.

1540. The giver of all benefits.

and disgusting feelings, emotions, thoughts, words, and actions of the person. Therefore, the person should not refrain from going back to Allah ﷻ but rush to it.

This concept of rushing for Allah ﷻ can be indicated in[1541] وَظَنَّ دَاوُودُ أَنَّمَا فَتَنَّاهُ فَاسْتَغْفَرَ رَبَّهُ وَخَرَّ رَاكِعًا وَأَنَابَ. As soon Dawud as had this thought or feeling, he immediately fell in sajdah for inabah[1542], tawbah[1543], forgiveness. Immediately, therefore, the forgiveness of Allah ﷻ immediately follows and is present as فَغَفَرْنَا لَهُ ذَلِكَ[1544].

Having and embodying always good thunn[1545] about Allah ﷻ is very critical. This is mentioned by another epitome role models, Ibrahim as, to his people about this problematic wrong rendering as فَمَا ظَنُّكُم بِرَبِّ الْعَالَمِينَ[1546] {الصافات/87}.

Always running back to Allah ﷻ is the key. The dua of Rasulullah ﷺ as[1547] "[اللهم انا نعوذ برضاك من سخطك و بمعافتك من عقوبتك....]". Rasulullah ﷺ had the revelation of these duas from Allah ﷻ how to make dua and connect to Allah ﷻ and establish our correct creed. If one started scholastically as a down-up or deductive approach, he or she possibly arrive or not to the gist of this dua after possibly many years of compilation of the mental incremental steps.

One should remember that the extension of duas made by the awliya of Allah ﷻ and salaf, always take the frame work of the revelation from Qurān and the Sunnah. The true salaf expand on the duas of the Rasulullah ﷺ, reward or present these teachings in different arrangements words or formats. In other words, the greatness or dense forms of the writings or duas of the pious salaf are due to their backbone or pillars raised on the teachings of the Qurān and sunnah of Rasulullah ﷺ.

1541. And David became certain that We had tried him, and he asked forgiveness of his Lord and fell down bowing [in prostration] and turned in repentance [to Allah].
1542. Turning to Allah (ﷻ).
1543. Repentance.
1544. So We forgave him of that.
1545. Thought.
1546. Then what is your thought about the Lord of the worlds?"
1547. Oh allah, we seek refuge in your pleasure from your wrath. And in your forgiveness from your punishment.

[82-84]

{ قَالَ فَبِعِزَّتِكَ لَأُغْوِيَنَّهُمْ أَجْمَعِينَ 1548{ص/82} إِلاَّ عِبَادَكَ مِنْهُمُ الْمُخْلَصِينَ 1549 {ص/83}

قَالَ فَالْحَقُّ وَالْحَقَّ أَقُولُ 1550 {ص/84}

The gist of the creation is ikhlas. As mentioned with the word الْمُخْلَصِينَ[1551], everyone will be destroyed except the ones with ikhlas. Ikhlas is very difficult to achieve and maintain. To achieve the state of ikhlas one should be aware of one's all inner renderings, engagements, feelings and thoughts and accordingly take necessary actions. To be in the station of ikhlas, one should maintain this constant and continuous self-inner check and take the necessary corrective actions.

When a feeling comes bothering the person and making him uncomfortable, the person should immediately indulge in muraqaba, self-inner check, to identify the source of the problem. Sometimes, identifying the problems can take a second, sometimes a minute, sometimes an hour, sometimes days, and years. Yet, it is possible that without proper identification, there won't be any proper action. Then, he or she may end up in a bad ending as mentioned in the rest of the ayah as {ص/85}[1552] لَأَمْلَأَنَّ جَهَنَّمَ مِنكَ وَمِمَّن تَبِعَكَ مِنْهُمْ أَجْمَعِينَ.

Sometimes, the source of the problem can be arrogance. Sometimes, it can be riya, showing-off. Sometimes it can be other diseases. Rasulullah ﷺ mentions that identifying and detecting this problem can be so difficult sometimes and similar to a black ant walking in a dark room [16].

One can possibly see, identify and detect this problem except with the Fadl, Rahmah, Mercy of Allah ﷻ as in all cases. Therefore, as one should do the self-check of muhasaba and muraqaba, and yet, one should also at the same time constantly make firar, run to Allah ﷻ with faqr and ajz of full poverty, weakness, and destitute. It is expected that this disposition of ajz and faqr can open the doors of Rahmah and Fadl inshAllah.

1548. [Iblees] said, "By Your might, I will surely mislead them all.
1549. Except, among them, Your chosen servants."
1550. [Allah] said, "The truth [is My oath], and the truth I say—
1551. Chosen/
1552. [That] I will surely fill Hell with you and those of them that follow you all together."

Imam Ghazali rh mentions this disposition in a dense and detailed statement. He indicates that everyone including the worshippers, and scholars are all in loss except the ones who have ikhlas, the real sincerity, who do everything for the pleasure of Allah 28] ﷻ].

Another difficulty can arise due the uncertainty of one's inner disposition. In other words, there were a lot of salaf such as Omar (RA) from the sahabah, and a lot from the tabi'in, were afraid to die as a munāfiq or kāfir. In other words, this uncertainty of being among[1553] الْمُخْلَصِينَ or not is real and it can deteriorate the person. No one knows their real and true inner intention and disposition. The person will not know their real position until one dies and meets with Allah ﷻ.

If the person has an inner safety, then this can bring and attract trials or tests as mentioned أَفَأَمِنُواْ مَكْرَ اللّهِ فَلاَ يَأْمَنُ مَكْرَ اللّهِ إِلاَّ الْقَوْمُ الْخَاسِرُونَ {الأعراف/99}[1554].

A person can be standing up all night praying and fasting all day. A scholar can be teaching the sacred knowledge and having thousands of students. A scholar can be writing volumes of books about the sacred knowledge. Yet, all can carry the pitfalls and dangerous black holes of vacuum as mentioned in the hadith of Rasulullah ﷺ the black ant walking in the dark room [16].

The constant awareness of muhasaba and murāqaba of inner self-check is critical in every second.

On the other hand, if there were no clear guidelines of the Qurān and sunnah as structuralized as in fiqh, the outer sciences, then it is possible that one can lose one's mind become majnun-lunatic. Yet, the purpose of fiqh in this perspective is to follow the guidelines of external sciences as the clear orders from Allah ﷻ in order to maintain adab with Allah ﷻ. This disposition of these external guidelines can set the balance of not losing oneself in the required disposition of self-check of muraqaba and muhasaba and not become majnun with the Fadl[1555], Rahmah[1556] and Grace of Allah ﷻ.

1553. The sincere {ones}.
1554. Then, did they feel secure from the plan of Allah? But no one feels secure from the plan of Allah except the losing people.
1555. Favor.
1556. Mercy.

At all these engagements accompanied with the tears of the person with abundant crying as the external signs of this faqr[1557] and a'jz[1558] in front of Allah ﷻ can be some of the true positive externalities if performed in solitude without anyone around to maximize the possibility of ikhlas, sincerity.May Allah ﷻ protect us, help us, maintain our inner and outer balance in our state and stations in order to be among the الْمُخْلَصِينَ[1559] with the Fadl, Rahmah and Tawfiq of Allah ﷻ, Amìn.

Juz 26

Sûrah 47—Muhammad

أَفَلَا يَتَدَبَّرُونَ الْقُرْآنَ أَمْ عَلَى قُلُوبٍ أَقْفَالُهَا [1560]{محمد/24}

The word tadabbur comes often in the Qurān. It can have the meanings of focusing and thinking on the ayahs of the Qurān leading to marifah of Allah ﷻ. Then, performing this circle of oscillation of thinking, anaylyzing, and deducing can be indicated with the root of the word دبر. The word tadabbur can indicate textual guidance of the Qurān or the Qurān guided thinking and analysis.

Another example is أَفَلَا يَتَدَبَّرُونَ الْقُرْآنَ وَلَوْ كَانَ مِنْ عِندِ غَيْرِ اللهِ لَوَجَدُواْ فِيهِ اخْتِلَافًا كَثِيرًا [1561]{النساء/82}

On the other hand, taffakur can be any focused thinking and analysis other than Qurān on social, natural and personal engagements leading to marifah of Allah ﷻ. For example, أَوَلَمْ يَتَفَكَّرُوا فِي أَنفُسِهِم مَّا خَلَقَ اللَّهُ السَّمَاوَاتِ وَالْأَرْضَ وَمَا بَيْنَهُمَا إِلَّا بِالْحَقِّ وَأَجَلٍ مُّسَمًّى وَإِنَّ كَثِيرًا مِّنَ النَّاسِ بِلِقَاء رَبِّهِمْ لَكَافِرُونَ [1562]{الروم/8}

أَوَلَمْ يَتَفَكَّرُوا مَا بِصَاحِبِهِم مِّن جِنَّةٍ إِنْ هُوَ إِلَّا نَذِيرٌ مُّبِينٌ [1563]{الأعراف/184}

1557. Poverty.

1558. Laziness.

1559. The chose {ones}.

1560. Then do they not reflect upon the Qurān, or are there locks upon [their] hearts?

1561. Then do they not reflect upon the Qurān? If it had been from [any] other than Allah, they would have found within it much contradiction.

1562. Do they not contemplate within themselves? Allah has not created the heavens and the earth and what is between them except in truth and for a specified term. And indeed, many of the people, in the meeting with their Lord, are disbelievers.

1563. Then do they not give thought? There is in their companion [i.e., Muhammad (PBUH)] no madness. He is not but a clear warner.

اللَّهُ يَتَوَفَّى الْأَنْفُسَ حِينَ مَوْتِهَا وَالَّتِي لَمْ تَمُتْ فِي مَنَامِهَا فَيُمْسِكُ الَّتِي قَضَى عَلَيْهَا الْمَوْتَ وَيُرْسِلُ الْأُخْرَى إِلَى أَجَلٍ مُسَمًّى إِنَّ فِي ذَلِكَ لَآيَاتٍ لِّقَوْمٍ يَتَفَكَّرُونَ 1564{الزمر/42}

Juz 28

Sûrah 59—al-Hashr

[10]

Ghill—The Stains of Heart & Chest

وَالَّذِينَ جَاؤُوا مِن بَعْدِهِمْ يَقُولُونَ رَبَّنَا اغْفِرْ لَنَا وَلِإِخْوَانِنَا الَّذِينَ سَبَقُونَا بِالْإِيمَانِ وَلَا تَجْعَلْ فِي قُلُوبِنَا غِلًّا لِّلَّذِينَ آمَنُوا رَبَّنَا إِنَّكَ رَؤُوفٌ رَّحِيمٌ 1565{الحشر/10}

وَنَزَعْنَا مَا فِي صُدُورِهِم مِّنْ غِلٍّ إِخْوَانًا عَلَى سُرُرٍ مُّتَقَابِلِينَ 1566{الحجر/47} لَا يَمَسُّهُمْ فِيهَا نَصَبٌ وَمَا هُم مِّنْهَا بِمُخْرَجِينَ 1567{الحجر/48}

وَنَزَعْنَا مَا فِي صُدُورِهِم مِّنْ غِلٍّ تَجْرِي مِن تَحْتِهِمُ الْأَنْهَارُ وَقَالُواْ الْحَمْدُ لِلَّهِ الَّذِي هَدَانَا لِهَذَا وَمَا كُنَّا لِنَهْتَدِيَ لَوْلَا أَنْ هَدَانَا اللَّهُ لَقَدْ جَاءتْ رُسُلُ رَبِّنَا بِالْحَقِّ وَنُودُواْ أَن تِلْكُمُ الْجَنَّةُ أُورِثْتُمُوهَا بِمَا كُنتُمْ تَعْمَلُونَ 1568{الأعراف/43}

The word غِلًّا is حقدا which can translate as grudge, rancor or animosity according to Imam Thalabi (rh) [30]. According to Imam Baqawi (rh) [31] and many other mufassirûn, this word can indicate غشاً وحسداً وبغضاً. This can mean hatred, jealousy and not being straight forward. In a hadith mentioned by Ibn Kathir (rh) reported by Baqawi (rh) [3] about the conflicts among Muslims especially after Rasulullah ﷺ.

1564. Allah takes the souls at the time of their death, and those that do not die [He takes] during their sleep. Then He keeps those for which He has decreed death and releases the others for a specified term. Indeed in that are signs for a people who give thought.

1565. And [there is a share for] those who came after them, saying, "Our Lord, forgive us and our brothers who preceded us in faith and put not in our hearts [any] resentment toward those who have believed. Our Lord, indeed You are Kind and Merciful."

1566. And We will remove whatever is in their breasts of resentment, [so they will be] brothers, on thrones facing each other.

1567. No fatigue will touch them therein, nor from it will they [ever] be removed.

1568. And We will have removed whatever is within their breasts of resentment, [while] flowing beneath them are rivers. And they will say, "Praise to Allah, who has guided us to this; and we would never have been guided if Allah had not guided us. Certainly the messengers of our Lord had come with the truth." And they will be called, "This is Paradise, which you have been made to inherit for what you used to do."

When we engage with others, we tend to have some feelings that may make us uncomfortable. The word غِلّ can indicate these negative feelings as the stains of a pure and clean heart. These negative feelings can emerge immediately in the person after the person remembers an incident or memory, talks or sees another individual. Sometimes, it can be related when the person hears something. Sometimes, it may reveal itself when the person passes from a place. The symptoms of these feelings can be discomfort, a feeling bothering from internal senses, uneasiness, or immediate change of state of sakina into some problematic disturbed internal states. Sometimes, these feelings last few seconds, sometimes hours and sometimes days.

It is always important to recognize one's shortcomings especially at these times and take refuge in Allah ﷻ with ta'awwuz, au'zu billahi min ashaytani rajìm. One can engage oneself more with dhikr, rememberance of Allah ﷻ especially through salah, recitation of the Qurãn, istigfar at these times. These engagements can give the stamina to the person with the Fadl and Grace of Allah ﷻ to maintain sabr, patience to unshackle oneself from the detrimental effects and results of these disturbing internal feelings.

Sometimes, the person can do a purposeful seclusion detaching oneself from people so that the person does not hurt others under the control of these negative feelings.

If these feelings emerge when the person interacts with another person, then the person should try to detect the problem why or how these negative feelings defined as غِلّ[1569] forms so that in the similar situations, the person can possibly train oneself.

As a starting point, making dua to Allah ﷻ to remove these feelings is always the key as[1570] رَبَّنَا اغْفِرْ لَنَا وَلِإِخْوَانِنَا الَّذِينَ سَبَقُونَا بِالْإِيمَانِ وَلَا تَجْعَلْ فِي قُلُوبِنَا غِلًّا لِّلَّذِينَ آمَنُوا رَبَّنَا إِنَّكَ رَؤُوفٌ رَّحِيمٌ.

Secondly, the person should look at his or her spiritual diseases and then, detect the specific problem in oneself as the detail or contextualized case of غِلّ[1571]. For example, while the person was in interaction with another individual, did the person feel that he did not receive much

---

1569. Resentment.
1570. "Our Lord, forgive us and our brothers who preceded us in faith and put not in our hearts [any] resentment toward those who have believed. Our Lord, indeed You are Kind and Merciful."
1571. Resentment.

or deserved respect while talking or communicating with this person? Did the person feel that the other person was arrogant or haughty? Did the person feel that the a trust was broken when the other individual exposed the secrets of this person? These questions with our assumtions, whether true or false, can go further.

Yet, if we analyze these questions with the principles of tasawwuf, then everything should be taken as a self-reflective point as a problem of spiritual disease in the person but not in the other person. For example, getting frustrated due to the feelings of undeserved or poor or low treatment can be a sickness of superiority in the person him or herself rather than on the other person. This can be the relevant and beneficial knowledge for the person to know and accordingly work on himself or herself. Rasulullah ﷺ did not have any feelings of غِلّ. Therefore, the narrators mention that Rasulullah ﷺ did not get upset in his personal treatments of disrespected encounters.

Sometimes, we may not understand the source of this comfort mentioned as غِلّ. Yet, this can be a problem or a disease that the person may need to identify its source and work on it and ask help from Allah ﷻ as mentioned in the dua form in this ayah. Yet, the person should immediately and always engage him or herself with istighfar, to remove these feelings.

Today, we may refer to them as judgment of others. The spiritual sickness of the problem of judgment as mentioned in tasawwuf can be branching out from jealousy, envy, and arrogance. Especially, when people are interacting with other Muslims, either it can be a gathering, lecture, a visit, or others, these feelings can immediately rush to the person if the person is not on the path of cleaning one's heart and mind with istighfar regularly and continuously.

In this perspective of غِلّ[1572] is the disease or stain of the heart. One can understand the effect and result of this disease in the afterlife from the ayahs as {الدخان/45}[1573] كَغَلْيِ الْحَمِيمِ [1574]{الدخان/46} كَالْمُهْلِ يَغْلِي فِي الْبُطُونِ.

1572. Resentment.
1573. Like murky oil, it boils within bellies
1574. Like the boiling of scalding water.

!اللهم اجرنا من ألنار، آمين **Allahumma Ajirna Min-an-nār, Amìn!**

[19]

وَلَا تَكُونُوا كَالَّذِينَ نَسُوا اللَّهَ فَأَنسَاهُمْ أَنفُسَهُمْ أُوْلَئِكَ هُمُ الْفَاسِقُونَ 1575 {الحشر/19}

أَوَلَمْ يَتَفَكَّرُوا فِي أَنفُسِهِم مَّا خَلَقَ اللَّهُ السَّمَاوَاتِ وَالْأَرْضَ وَمَا بَيْنَهُمَا إِلَّا بِالْحَقِّ وَأَجَلٍ مُّسَمًّى وَإِنَّ كَثِيرًا مِّنَ النَّاسِ بِلِقَاء رَبِّهِمْ لَكَافِرُونَ 1576 {الروم/8}

سَنُرِيهِمْ آيَاتِنَا فِي الْآفَاقِ وَفِي أَنفُسِهِمْ حَتَّى يَتَبَيَّنَ لَهُمْ أَنَّهُ الْحَقُّ أَوَلَمْ يَكْفِ بِرَبِّكَ أَنَّهُ عَلَى كُلِّ شَيْءٍ شَهِيدٌ 1577 {فصلت/53}

The gist of the creation is ikhlas. Ikhlas is very difficult to achieve and maintain. To achieve the state of ikhlas one should be aware of one's all inner renderings, engagements, feelings and thoughts as mentioned[1578] سَنُرِيهِمْ آيَاتِنَا فِي الْآفَاقِ وَفِي أَنفُسِهِمْ [1579] and , أَوَلَمْ يَتَفَكَّرُوا فِي أَنفُسِهِمْ.Accordingly, one can take necessary actions. To be in the station of ikhlas, one should maintain this constant and continuous self-inner check and take the necessary corrective actions.

When a feeling comes bothering the person and making him uncomfortable, the person should immediately indulge in muraqaba, self-inner check, to identify the source of the problem. Sometimes, identifying the problems can take a second, sometimes a minute, sometimes an hour, sometimes days, and years. Yet, it is possible that without proper identification, there won't be any proper action.

One should remember that the purpose of achievement, jihad and struggle is called tazkiyatul nafs. Nafs has filled with diseases as for example أَلَمْ تَرَ إِلَى الَّذِينَ نُهُوا عَنِ النَّجْوَى ثُمَّ يَعُودُونَ لِمَا نُهُوا عَنْهُ وَيَتَنَاجَوْنَ بِالْإِثْمِ

1575. And be not like those who forgot Allah, so He made them forget themselves. Those are the defiantly disobedient.
1576. Do they not contemplate within themselves? Allah has not created the heavens and the earth and what is between them except in truth and for a specified term. And indeed, many of the people, in the meeting with their Lord, are disbelievers.
1577. We will show them Our signs in the horizons and within themselves until it becomes clear to them that it is the truth. But is it not sufficient concerning your Lord that He is, over all things, a Witness?
1578. Do they not contemplate within themselves?
1579. We will show them Our signs in the horizons and within themselves

وَالْعُدْوَانِ وَمَعْصِيَتِ الرَّسُولِ وَإِذَا جَاؤُوكَ حَيَّوْكَ بِمَا لَمْ يُحَيِّكَ بِهِ اللَّهُ وَيَقُولُونَ فِي أَنفُسِهِمْ لَوْلَا

يُعَذِّبُنَا اللَّهُ بِمَا نَقُولُ حَسْبُهُمْ جَهَنَّمُ يَصْلَوْنَهَا فَبِئْسَ الْمَصِيرُ [1580] {المجادلة/8}

One can see in this ayah a person has an external interaction as nice and kind as[1581] وَإِذَا جَاؤُوكَ حَيَّوْكَ بِمَا لَمْ يُحَيِّكَ بِهِ اللَّهُ. In this externality, everything seems so normal, nice and in line with the teachings of Allah ﷻ.

Yet, in the internality of the essence as worded as nafs and the word أَنفُسِهِمْ[1582] expressed in the plural form of addressing. In this sense, every nafs has its own world filled with filth, garbage, spiritual urine which are disguisting and lowly engagements for the soul, rûh which aims for the high and the pleasure of Allah ﷻ. This filth is so disgusting that Allah ﷻ, al-Sattar, as a mercy gave humans the cover of externality with the physical body. No one knows the reality, essence and internal core of this inner world of the person. Most of the time, the person himself or herself may not even know their own inner world of the realities. If they don't do the steps of tazkayatul nafs in the guidance of the Qurãn and Sunna of Rasulullah ﷺ in this life before it is too late, then some may realize it in the afterlife in front of Rabbul Alamin. May Allah ﷻ protect us from this late realization and make us work on our selves with the pleasure of Allah ﷻ, Amìn.

Yes, every person has a spiritual world bigger than this physical earth that we are living in. This world smells, is repulsive, and disgusting. Therefore, Allah ﷻ protects us entering these worlds of others.

1580. Have you not considered those who were forbidden from private conversation [i.e., ridicule and conspiracy] and then return to that which they were forbidden and converse among themselves about sin and aggression and disobedience to the Messenger? And when they come to you, they greet you with that [word] by which Allah does not greet you and say among themselves, "Why does Allah not punish us for what we say?" Sufficient for them is Hell, which they will [enter to] burn, and wretched is the destination.
1581. And when they come to you, they greet you with that [word] by which Allah does not greet you.
1582. Themselves.

Shuh—The World of Filthy Self

This filthy state of the world of the person can be called as شُحّ[1583] as mentioned in وَالَّذِينَ تَبَوَّؤُوا الدَّارَ وَالْإِيمَانَ مِن قَبْلِهِمْ يُحِبُّونَ مَنْ هَاجَرَ إِلَيْهِمْ وَلَا يَجِدُونَ فِي صُدُورِهِمْ حَاجَةً مِّمَّا أُوتُوا وَيُؤْثِرُونَ عَلَى أَنفُسِهِمْ وَلَوْ كَانَ بِهِمْ خَصَاصَةٌ وَمَن يُوقَ شُحَّ نَفْسِهِ فَأُوْلَئِكَ هُمُ الْمُفْلِحُونَ[1584]{الحشر/9}

فَاتَّقُوا اللَّهَ مَا اسْتَطَعْتُمْ وَاسْمَعُوا وَأَطِيعُوا وَأَنفِقُوا خَيْرًا لِّأَنفُسِكُمْ وَمَن يُوقَ شُحَّ نَفْسِهِ فَأُوْلَئِكَ هُمُ الْمُفْلِحُونَ[1585]{التغابن/16}

وَإِنِ امْرَأَةٌ خَافَتْ مِن بَعْلِهَا نُشُوزًا أَوْ إِعْرَاضًا فَلاَ جُنَاحَ عَلَيْهِمَا أَن يُصْلِحَا بَيْنَهُمَا صُلْحًا وَالصُّلْحُ خَيْرٌ وَأُحْضِرَتِ الأَنفُسُ الشُّحَّ وَإِن تُحْسِنُواْ وَتَتَّقُواْ فَإِنَّ اللهَ كَانَ بِمَا تَعْمَلُونَ خَبِيرًا[1586]{النساء/128}

This world of شُحّ[1587] has the elements in the dark air with selfishness, egotism and arrogance, poisonous plants of jealousy, fruits of greed, anger and vanity with the path ways of lies. This world is always dark as mentioned in the Qurān as كَانُوا أَنفُسَهُمْ يَظْلِمُونَ[1588]. There is no daylight. The atmosphere is always dark without any sky but with dark depressive and scary fogs.

Yet, our world or my world is not different than others unless there is the process of constant cleaning through first acceptance, or realization. Then, cleaning with istigfar and tawbah relating oneself with the Pure, al-Qud-dus[1589]. This process is the essence of life and living. This process is the essence of the struggle of the life as mentioned by Rasullah ﷺ as the bigger jihad.

1583. Stinginess.
1584. And [also for] those who were settled in the Home [i.e., al-Madinah] and [adopted] the faith before them. They love those who emigrated to them and find not any want in their breasts of what they [i.e., the emigrants] were given but give [them] preference over themselves, even though they are in privation. And whoever is protected from the stinginess of his soul—it is those who will be the successful.
1585. So fear Allah as much as you are able and listen and obey and spend [in the way of Allah]; it is better for your selves. And whoever is protected from the stinginess of his soul—it is those who will be the successful.
1586. And if a woman fears from her husband contempt or evasion, there is no sin upon them if they make terms of settlement between them—and settlement is best. And present in [human] souls is stinginess. But if you do good and fear Allah—then indeed Allah is ever, with what you do, Acquainted.
1587. Stinginess.
1588. They themselves were wronged.
1589. The one who is free from all blemishes.

Yet, the process of cleansing of this filth first starts with stopping oneself intentionally, and purposely due to fear of Allah ﷻ as this can be called taqwa as mentioned [1590] in وَمَن يُوقَ وَالَّذِينَ تَبَوَّؤُوا الدَّارَ وَالْإِيمَانَ مِن قَبْلِهِمْ يُحِبُّونَ مَنْ هَاجَرَ إِلَيْهِمْ وَلَا يَجِدُونَ فِي صُدُورِهِمْ حَاجَةً مِّمَّا أُوتُوا وَيُؤْثِرُونَ عَلَىٰ أَنفُسِهِمْ وَلَوْ كَانَ بِهِمْ خَصَاصَةٌ ۚ وَمَن يُوقَ شُحَّ نَفْسِهِ فَأُولَٰئِكَ هُمُ الْمُفْلِحُونَ [1591] {الحشر/9}.

With the initial stage and practices of taqwa one can go to the higher stages of pleasure of Allah ﷻ as mentioned {27/الفجر} يَا أَيَّتُهَا النَّفْسُ الْمُطْمَئِنَّةُ ارْجِعِي إِلَىٰ رَبِّكِ رَاضِيَةً مَّرْضِيَّةً {28/الفجر}

In this perspective شُحّ is the world of the raw, unfiltered self that needs tazkiya.

Different Worlds of Nafs and Heart

The world of raw and unfiltered nafs is the world of شُحّ[1592] as mentioned in the expression شُحَّ نَفْسِهِ[1593]. In this world of the self, when there is tazkiya, the self starts realizing the intrinsic diseases of the heart referred as stains or diseases of the heart referred as غِلّ as mentioned in the expression فِي قُلُوبِنَا غِلٌّ[1594].

1590. And whoever is protected
1591. And [also for] those who were settled in the Home [i.e., al-Madinah] and [adopted] the faith before them. They love those who emigrated to them and find not any want in their breasts of what they [i.e., the emigrants] were given but give [them] preference over themselves, even though they are in privation. And whoever is protected from the stinginess of his soul—it is those who will be the successful.
1592. Stinginess.
1593. Stinginess of his soul.
1594. In our hearts [any] resentment.

Juz 30

Sûrah 106—Quraysh

لِإِيلَافِ قُرَيْشٍ 1595 {قريش/1} إِيلَافِهِمْ رِحْلَةَ الشِّتَاء وَالصَّيْفِ 1596 {قريش/2} فَلْيَعْبُدُوا رَبَّ هَذَا الْبَيْتِ 1597 {قريش/3} الَّذِي أَطْعَمَهُم مِّن جُوعٍ وَآمَنَهُم مِّنْ خَوْفٍ 1598 {قريش/4}

It is important to analyze the notion of خَوْفٍ, fear. In other parts of the Qurān, this word خَوْفٍ comes also as:

فَتَلَقَّى آدَمُ مِن رَّبِّهِ كَلِمَاتٍ فَتَابَ عَلَيْهِ إِنَّهُ هُوَ التَّوَّابُ الرَّحِيمُ 1599 {البقرة/37}

قُلْنَا اهْبِطُواْ مِنْهَا جَمِيعاً فَإِمَّا يَأْتِيَنَّكُم مِّنِّي هُدًى فَمَن تَبِعَ هُدَايَ فَلاَ خَوْفٌ عَلَيْهِمْ وَلاَ هُمْ يَحْزَنُونَ 1600 {البقرة/38}

It is interesting to analyze that the word[1601] خَوْف comes in the above ayah about Adam as and Hawwa as after they made tawbah and their tawbah were accepted. Then, they were assigned for their lives on the earth by Allah ﷻ. Being on the earth can indicate being in fear خَوْف. In this regard, the only way to cope with this fear is to follow the guidance, the Qurān and sunnah of Rasulullah ﷺ as mentioned[1602] يَأْتِيَنَّكُم مِّنِّي هُدًى فَمَن تَبِعَ هُدَايَ فَلاَ خَوْفٌ عَلَيْهِمْ. In some other parts of the Qurān the word خَوْف is mentioned as:

إِنَّ الَّذِينَ آمَنُواْ وَالَّذِينَ هَادُواْ وَالنَّصَارَى وَالصَّابِئِينَ مَنْ آمَنَ بِاللّهِ وَالْيَوْمِ الآخِرِ وَعَمِلَ صَالِحاً فَلَهُمْ أَجْرُهُمْ عِندَ رَبِّهِمْ وَلاَ خَوْفٌ عَلَيْهِمْ وَلاَ هُمْ يَحْزَنُونَ 1603 {البقرة/62}

1595. For the accustomed security of Quraish.
1596. Their accustomed security {in} the caravan of winter and summer.
1597. Let them worship the lord of this house.
1598. Who has fed then {saving them} from hunger and made them safe {saving them} from fear.
1599. Then Adam received from his Lord [some] words, and He accepted his repentance. Indeed, it is He who is the Accepting of repentance, the Merciful.
1600. We said, "Go down from it, all of you. And when guidance comes to you from Me, whoever follows My guidance—there will be no fear concerning them, nor will they grieve.
1601. Fear.
1602. When guidance comes to you from Me, whoever follows My guidance—there will be no fear concerning them.
1603. Indeed, those who believed and those who were Jews or Christians or Sabeans [before Prophet Muhammad (PBUH)]—those [among them] who believed in Allah and the Last Day and did righteousness—will have their reward with their Lord, and no fear will there be concerning them, nor will they grieve.

بَلَى مَنْ أَسْلَمَ وَجْهَهُ لِلَّهِ وَهُوَ مُحْسِنٌ فَلَهُ أَجْرُهُ عِندَ رَبِّهِ وَلاَ <u>خَوْفٌ عَلَيْهِمْ</u> وَلاَ هُمْ يَحْزَنُونَ¹⁶⁰⁴
{البقرة/112}

الَّذِينَ يُنفِقُونَ أَمْوَالَهُم بِاللَّيْلِ وَالنَّهَارِ سِرًّا وَعَلانِيَةً فَلَهُمْ أَجْرُهُمْ عِندَ رَبِّهِمْ وَلاَ <u>خَوْفٌ</u>
عَلَيْهِمْ وَلاَ هُمْ يَحْزَنُونَ¹⁶⁰⁵{البقرة/274}

إِنَّ الَّذِينَ آمَنُواْ وَعَمِلُواْ الصَّالِحَاتِ وَأَقَامُواْ الصَّلاَةَ وَآتَوُاْ الزَّكَاةَ لَهُمْ أَجْرُهُم عِندَ رَبِّهِمْ
وَلاَ <u>خَوْفٌ عَلَيْهِمْ</u> وَلاَ هُمْ يَحْزَنُونَ¹⁶⁰⁶ {البقرة/277}

فَرِحِينَ بِمَا آتَاهُمُ اللّهُ مِن فَضْلِهِ وَيَسْتَبْشِرُونَ بِالَّذِينَ لَمْ يَلْحَقُواْ بِهِم مِّنْ خَلْفِهِمْ أَلاَّ <u>خَوْفٌ</u>
عَلَيْهِمْ وَلاَ هُمْ يَحْزَنُونَ¹⁶⁰⁷ {آل عمران/170}

إِنَّ الَّذِينَ آمَنُواْ وَالَّذِينَ هَادُواْ وَالصَّابِؤُونَ وَالنَّصَارَى مَنْ آمَنَ بِاللّهِ وَالْيَوْمِ الآخِرِ وَعَمِلَ
صَالِحًا فَلاَ <u>خَوْفٌ عَلَيْهِمْ</u> وَلاَ هُمْ يَحْزَنُونَ¹⁶⁰⁸{المائدة/69}

وَمَا نُرْسِلُ الْمُرْسَلِينَ إِلاَّ مُبَشِّرِينَ وَمُنذِرِينَ فَمَنْ آمَنَ وَأَصْلَحَ فَلاَ <u>خَوْفٌ عَلَيْهِمْ</u> وَلاَ هُمْ
يَحْزَنُونَ¹⁶⁰⁹{الأنعام/48}

يَا بَنِي آدَمَ إِمَّا يَأْتِيَنَّكُمْ رُسُلٌ مِّنكُمْ يَقُصُّونَ عَلَيْكُمْ آيَاتِي فَمَنِ اتَّقَى وَأَصْلَحَ فَلاَ <u>خَوْفٌ</u>
عَلَيْهِمْ وَلاَ هُمْ يَحْزَنُونَ¹⁶¹⁰{الأعراف/35}

1604. Yes, [on the contrary], whoever submits his face [i.e., self] in Islam to Allah while being a doer of good will have his reward with his Lord. And no fear will there be concerning them, nor will they grieve.

1605. Those who spend their wealth [in Allah's way] by night and by day, secretly and publicly—they will have their reward with their Lord. And no fear will there be concerning them, nor will they grieve.

1606. Indeed, those who believe and do righteous deeds and establish prayer and give zakah will have their reward with their Lord, and there will be no fear concerning them, nor will they grieve.

1607. Rejoicing in what Allah has bestowed upon them of His bounty, and they receive good tidings about those [to be martyred] after them who have not yet joined them—that there will be no fear concerning them, nor will they grieve.

1608. Indeed, those who have believed [in Prophet Muhammad (PBUH)] and those [before him (PBUH)] who were Jews or Sabeans or Christians—those [among them] who believed in Allah and the Last Day and did righteousness—no fear will there be concerning them, nor will they grieve.

1609. And We send not the messengers except as bringers of good tidings and warners. So whoever believes and reforms—there will be no fear concerning them, nor will they grieve.

1610. O children of Adam, if there come to you messengers from among you relating to you My verses [i.e., scriptures and laws], then whoever fears Allah and reforms—there will be no fear concerning them, nor will they grieve.

أَلَا إِنَّ أَوْلِيَاءَ اللَّهِ لَا خَوْفٌ عَلَيْهِمْ وَلَا هُمْ يَحْزَنُونَ 1611 {يونس/62}

{ يَا عِبَادِ لَا خَوْفٌ عَلَيْكُمُ الْيَوْمَ وَلَا أَنتُمْ تَحْزَنُونَ 1612 {الزخرف/68}

إِنَّ الَّذِينَ قَالُوا رَبُّنَا اللَّهُ ثُمَّ اسْتَقَامُوا فَلَا خَوْفٌ عَلَيْهِمْ وَلَا هُمْ يَحْزَنُونَ 1613 {الأحقاف/13}

As one can realize the words خَوْفٌ[1614] and يَحْزَنُونَ[1615] come together. One can correlate with these meanings. People build up fear due to their engagements or what they did. In other words, the word hazan يَحْزَنُونَ can indicate the concerns related with the past. Our wrong doings that we did in the past, can leave us with the traces and emotions of fear.

In this sense, one should always check their real disposition with Allah ﷻ and ask protection from fear and worries of the past. Therefore, one should really think and make istikhara and mashwarah before they do or say anything, in order to eliminate or minimize worries or fears that can be induced by any engagements of the person. The word خَوْف[1616] comes in also as:

فَمَا آمَنَ لِمُوسَى إِلَّا ذُرِّيَّةٌ مِّن قَوْمِهِ عَلَى خَوْفٍ مِّن فِرْعَوْنَ وَمَلَئِهِمْ أَن يَفْتِنَهُمْ وَإِنَّ فِرْعَوْنَ لَعَالٍ فِي الْأَرْضِ وَإِنَّهُ لَمِنَ الْمُسْرِفِينَ 1617 {يونس/83}. In this case, one can realize how خَوْف, fear can be a factor in people's decision making and showing their disposition. There are people or entities threaten people and induce fear, to gauge or direct people's sound dispositions or decision makings into different stances. The word خَوْف comes in also as:

وَعَدَ اللَّهُ الَّذِينَ آمَنُوا مِنكُمْ وَعَمِلُوا الصَّالِحَاتِ لَيَسْتَخْلِفَنَّهُمْ فِي الْأَرْضِ كَمَا اسْتَخْلَفَ الَّذِينَ مِن قَبْلِهِمْ وَلَيُمَكِّنَنَّ لَهُمْ دِينَهُمُ الَّذِي ارْتَضَى لَهُمْ وَلَيُبَدِّلَنَّهُم مِّن بَعْدِ خَوْفِهِمْ أَمْنًا يَعْبُدُونَنِي

1611. Unquestionably, [for] the allies of Allah there will be no fear concerning them, nor will they grieve—

1612. [To whom Allah will say], "O My servants, no fear will there be concerning you this Day, nor will you grieve,

1613. Indeed, those who have said, "Our Lord is Allah," and then remained on a right course— there will be no fear concerning them, nor will they grieve.

1614. Fear.

1615. They grieve.

1616. Fear.

1617. But no one believed Moses, except [some] offspring [i.e., youths] among his people, for fear of Pharaoh and his establishment that they would persecute them. And indeed, Pharaoh was haughty within the land, and indeed, he was of the transgressors.

لَا يُشْرِكُونَ بِي شَيْئًا وَمَن كَفَرَ بَعْدَ ذَلِكَ فَأُوْلَئِكَ هُمُ الْفَاسِقُونَ ⁱ⁶¹⁸{النور/55} وَأَقِيمُوا
الصَّلَاةَ وَآتُوا الزَّكَاةَ وَأَطِيعُوا الرَّسُولَ لَعَلَّكُمْ تُرْحَمُونَ ⁱ⁶¹⁹ {النور/56}

One can realize that in different parts of the Qurān when the word خَوْف is
mentioned, it can be related our own renderings and actions that instill
and cause us these depressive states of fear. Yet, Allah ﷻ mentions that[1620]
وَلَيُبَدِّلَنَّهُم مِّن بَعْدِ خَوْفِهِمْ أَمْنًا, these states can change as long as the person or
people are in the engagement of the true remembrance of Allah ﷻ and
they are not making shirk or kufr as mentioned [1621]يَعْبُدُونَنِي لَا يُشْرِكُونَ بِي
شَيْئًا.Another perspective of fear is mentioned for the engagements of the
mass media as:

وَإِذَا جَاءهُمْ أَمْرٌ مِّنَ الأَمْنِ أَوِ الْخَوْفِ أَذَاعُواْ بِهِ وَلَوْ رَدُّوهُ إِلَى الرَّسُولِ وَإِلَى أُوْلِي الأَمْرِ
مِنْهُمْ لَعَلِمَهُ الَّذِينَ يَسْتَنبِطُونَهُ مِنْهُمْ وَلَوْلاَ فَضْلُ اللّهِ عَلَيْكُمْ وَرَحْمَتُهُ لاَتَّبَعْتُمُ الشَّيْطَانَ إِلاَّ
قَلِيلاً ⁱ⁶²²{النساء/83}

The above ayah especially underlines the concept of broadcasting
without any purpose. There can be news instilling fear or insecurity.
Yet, this should not be broadcasted or publicized immediately. This
unfiltered news can instill in public the emotions or worries of fear or
false security. Before this news is publicized, they should be analyzed by
the experts and scholars about their truth and their possible effects on
people.

　　As long as people are maintaining their true disposition of imān
and 'ibadah to Allah ﷻ then the factors of fear may not be there, as
mentioned فَلْيَعْبُدُوا رَبَّ هَذَا الْبَيْتِ ⁱ⁶²³{قريش/3} الَّذِي أَطْعَمَهُم مِّن جُوعٍ وَآمَنَهُم مِّنْ

1618. Allah has promised those who have believed among you and done righteous deeds
that He will surely grant them succession [to authority] upon the earth just as He granted it to
those before them and that He will surely establish for them [therein] their religion which He
has preferred for them and that He will surely substitute for them, after their fear, security, [for]
they worship Me, not associating anything with Me. But whoever disbelieves after that—then
those are the defiantly disobedient.

1619. And establish prayer and give zakah and obey the Messenger—that you may receive
mercy.

1620. Surely substitute for them, after their fear, security.

1621. They worship Me, not associating anything with Me.

1622. And when there comes to them something [i.e., information] about [public] security
or fear, they spread it around. But if they had referred it back to the Messenger or to those of
authority among them, then the ones who [can] draw correct conclusions from it would have
known about it. And if not for the favor of Allah upon you and His mercy, you would have
followed Satan, except for a few.

1623. Let them worship the Lord of this house.

خَوْفٍ1624{قريش/4}. If the people change their real, expected and true disposition with Allah ﷻ, then the factors of fear can come again as mentioned:

وَضَرَبَ اللَّهُ مَثَلاً قَرْيَةً كَانَتْ آمِنَةً مُطْمَئِنَّةً يَأْتِيهَا رِزْقُهَا رَغَدًا مِّن كُلِّ مَكَانٍ فَكَفَرَتْ بِأَنْعُمِ اللَّهِ فَأَذَاقَهَا اللَّهُ لِبَاسَ الْجُوعِ وَالْخَوْفِ بِمَا كَانُوا يَصْنَعُونَ1625{النحل/112}

In this regard, the person can pull or attract the trials or tests related with fear and other distresses and tribulations on themselves as mentioned:

وَلَنَبْلُوَنَّكُم بِشَيْءٍ مِّنَ الْخَوْفِ وَالْجُوعِ وَنَقْصٍ مِّنَ الأَمَوَالِ وَالأَنفُسِ وَالثَّمَرَاتِ وَبَشِّرِ الصَّابِرِينَ1626{البقرة/155}

May Allah ﷻ protect us from fear of everything except the fear of Allah ﷻ, Amìn.

Sûrah 112—al- Ikhlãs

قُلْ هُوَ اللَّهُ أَحَدٌ1627{الإخلاص/1} اللَّهُ الصَّمَدُ1628{الإخلاص/2} لَمْ يَلِدْ وَلَمْ يُولَدْ1629{الإخلاص/3} وَلَمْ يَكُن لَّهُ كُفُوًا أَحَدٌ1630{الإخلاص/4}

Inquiring about Allah ﷻ truly without any guidance is a full fallacy according to the social construction theory [1]. We derive meanings for everything according to the world we live in. Yet, Allah ﷻ is beyond from all these constructions, as mentioned1631 لَيْسَ كَمِثْلِهِ شَيْءٌ وَهُوَ السَّمِيعُ البَصِيرُ {الشورى/11}. The true knowledge about Allah ﷻ should be given and followed as instructed by the Qurãn and Sunnah.

One can witness the problems if people follow these constructed meanings solely with human mind without any guidance and proof

---

1624. Who has fed them {saving them} from hunger and made them safe { saving them} from fear.
1625. And Allah presents an example: a city [i.e., Makkah] which was safe and secure, its provision coming to it in abundance from every location, but it denied the favors of Allah. So Allah made it taste the envelopment of hunger and fear for what they had been doing.
1626. And We will surely test you with something of fear and hunger and a loss of wealth and lives and fruits, but give good tidings to the patient.
1627. Say "He is Allah, {who is} one.
1628. Allah, the Eternal Refuge.
1629. He neither begets nor is born.
1630. Nor is there to Him any equivalent.
1631. There is nothing like unto Him, and He is the Hearing, the Seeing.

from Allah ﷻ as in the case of trinity and other false renderings. The notions of children, son, father, etc. are all examples of this problem of assigning valuations and meanings according to our humanly social construction.

Thomas Edison invented our pear-shaped carbon filament lamp [2]. If we assume this lamp one day becomes alive and talks, one can ask this lamp about its inventor. Then, this lamp can possibly assume a being who is pear-shaped like this lamp. Yet, it is beyond this lamp's imagination to construct something or someone with eyes, ears, nose, hair, with arms, hands and a body.

Although this is just an imagination and example, here is the case where exactly the social constructions theories [1] fit in that we assign meanings to the things according to the world and habitat that we live in. We make comparisons and analysis according to what we see. Our imaginations and thinking, analysis, and conclusions of assignments are all according to these observations [1]. Yet, approaching to know Allah ﷻ fully without any guidance is a full fallacy according to the social construction theory.

One can approximate to the true marifah of Allah ﷻ only through the guidance of wahiy, the Qurān and Sunnah. In this sense, this Sûrah establishes these core pillars of tawhid about the ma'rifah[1632] of Allah ﷻ.

1632. Knowledge of Allah (ﷻ).

BIBLIOGRAPHY

[1] U. P. Oxford, "Oxford Dictionaries," 2016. [Online]. Available: http://www.oxforddictionaries.com/us/definition/american_english/. [Accessed 2016].

[2] A. Tahawi, SHARH AL KABIR 'ALA AL-'AQEEDAH AL-TAHAWI, Dar Al-Dhakha'ir, 2017.

[3] I. Kasir, Tafsir al-Qur'an al-Azim, Beirut: Dar al-Ilm, 1982.

[4] S. Abu-Dawud, Sunan Abu Dawud, Riyadh: Darussalam, 2008.

[5] A. An-Nasa'i, Sunan An-Nasai, Riyadh: Daraussalalm, 2007.

[6] A. B. Hanbal, Musnad Imam Ahmad Ibn Hanbal, Dar-Us-Salam Publications, 2012.

[7] M. al-Alusi., Ar-Rūh al-Ma'ānī fī Tafsīri-l-Qur'āni-l-'Aẓīm wa Sab'u-l-Mathānī, Dar Ihya Turath al-Arabi , 2000.

[8] M. Tirmizi, Jami At-Tirmizi, Dar-us-Salam, 2007.

[9] I. Majah, Sunan Ibn-i-Majah, Kitab Bhavan, 2000.

[10] N. C. Ring, Introduction to the Study of Religion, New York: Orbis, 2007.

[11] A. Muslim, Sahih Muslim (translated by Siddiqui, A.), Peace Vision, 1972.

[12] A. al-Bayhaqi, AL-SUNAN AL-KABIR, Dar 'Aalim al-Kutub, 2013.

[13] M. Al-Bukhari, The translation of the meanings of Sahih Al-Bukhari, Kazi Publications, 1986.

[14] L. Ridgeon, Jawanmardi: A Sufi Code of Honour, Edinburgh University Press, 2011.

[15] M. Razi, Mafatih al-Ghayb known as al-Tafsir al-Kabir, Cairo: Dar Ibya al-Kutub al-Bahiyya, 1172.

[16] I. Bukhari, Al-Adab Al-Mufrad, UK Islamic Academy, 2006.

[17] Critchley, The Book of Dead Philosophers, Australia: Melbourne University Publishing, 2008.

[18] A.-M. al-Daylamī, Musnad al-Firdaws (مخطوطة مسند الفردوس), Maktaba Ustadh Doctor Mohammad bin Torkey.

[19] I. Ishaq, The Life of Muhammad, Oxford University Press, 2002.

[20] S. Saadat, "Human Embryology and the Holy Quran: An Overview," *International Journal of Health Sciences,* vol. 3, no. 1, pp. 103–109, 2009.

[21] E. D. English, Christians, Muslims, and Jews in Medieval and Early Modern Spain Interaction and Cultural Change, University of Notre Dame Press, 2000.

[22] M. Hart, A Ranking of the Most Influential Persons in History, Carol Publishing Group, 1978.

[23] M. S. Bernstein, Stories of Joseph: Narrative Migrations Between Judaism and Islam, Wayne State University Press, 2009.

[24] M. i. A. Hakim, Al-Mustadrak: `ala al-sahihayn, Dar al-Kutub al-`Ilmiyyah, 1990, p. 1/612.

[25] J. W. C. J. S. R. Anthony M. Orum, Changing Societies Essential Sociology for Our Times, Rowman & Littlefield Publishers, 1999.

[26] J. Best, Social Problems, New York: W. W. Norton & Company, Inc., 2013.

[27] A. I. Abbas, Tafsir Ibn Abbas, Fons Vitae, 2008.

[28] M. Al-Ghazali, Ihya 'Ulum al-Din, Dar al-Fikr, 2004.

[29] I. Ata'illah, Book Of Aphorisms, Ibn Ata'illah's Kitabu al-Hikam, English, Islamic Book Trust, 2010.

[30] A. I. Thalabi, Al-Kashaf wal bayan, Beirut: DKI, 2004.

[31] H. Baghawi, Tafsir al-Baghawi al-musamma Ma'alim al-tanzil, Bayrut: Dar al-Ma'rifah, 1987.

[32] T. Y. Ozkan, A Muslim Response to Evil: S. N. on the Theodicy, Routledge, 2016.

[33] Sanders-Packard, The Air We Breathe: Sociology of Religion, Kendall Hunt, 2017.

[34] S. Vahide, The Collection of Light, ihlas nur publication, 2001.

[35] M. Asad, The message of the Quran: Translated and explained., Al-Andalus Gibraltar, 1980.

[36] T. Usmani, An Approach to the Qur'anic Sciences, Adam Publishers,, 2006.

[37] Y. Kumek, The Noble Quran: Selected Passages From Al-Quran Al-Kareem With Interpreted Meanings, Buffalo, New York: Medina House Publishing, 2020.

[38] I. Majah, Sunan Ibn Majah, Darus-Salam, 2007.

AUTHOR BIO

Dr. Kumek had classical training in Islamic sciences from the respected Shuyûqh/Teachers of Turkey, India, Egypt, Yemen, Somalia, Morocco, Sudan, and the United States. He stayed and studied classical Islamic sciences in Egypt and Turkey as well.

In his Western training, education and teaching experience, Dr. Kumek has acted as the religious studies coordinator at State University of New York (SUNY) Buffalo State and taught undergraduate and graduate courses in religious studies at SUNY at Buffalo State, Niagara University, Daemen College and Harvard Divinity School. Dr. Kumek also pursued doctorate degree in physics at SUNY at Buffalo published academic papers in the areas of quantum physics and medical physics. Then, he decided to engage with the world of social sciences through social anthropology, education, and cultural anthropology in his doctorate studies and subsequently, spent a few years as a research associate in the anthropology department of the same university and subsequently, completed a postdoctoral fellowship at Harvard Divinity school. Some of his book titles include sociology through religion, religious literacy through ethnography, selected passages from the Qurān, selected passages from the Hadith (titled as Rasulullah ﷺ) and selected prayers of the Prophet Muhammad ﷺ (titled as Pearls and Diamonds). Dr. M. Yunus Kumek is currently teaching on Muslim Ministry and Spiritual Care at Harvard Divinity School.

ACKNOWLEDGMENTS

I would like to thank all my unnamed teachers, friends, and students for their input, ideas, suggestions, help, and support during and before the preparation of this book.

I would like to thank Dr. David Banks, faculty of the Department of Anthropology, State University of New York (SUNY), Sister Toni Hajdaj, Sister Umm Aisha, Dr. AbdulAhad, Br. Ali Rifat and His wife Sister Yildiz at-Turki, Sheikh Dr. Omar of Maryland al-Hindi, Sheikh Tamer of Buffalo, and Sheikh Ali of Hartford Seminary, Sisters Asya Hamad, Amina Osman, and Fatima Samrodia of Darul-Ulum Madania of Buffalo for all their editing, suggestions and comments.

I want to also thank the team of Medina House Publishing in all their preparations and efforts at all stages of this book especially Br. Murat, Br. Khalid (Halit), Br. Mehmet (Matt) and Sister Karen.

Lastly, I would like to thank all of my family members for their patience with me during the preparation of this book.

We ask Allah ﷻ to accept all our efforts with the Divine Karam, Fadl, and Grace but not with our faulty and limited efforts deeming rejection.
اللَّهُمَّ صلِّ عَلى سَيِّدِناَ وَ حَبِيْبَنَا وَ مَوْلَانَا مُحَمَّد.

Index

www.ingramcontent.com/pod-product-compliance
Lightning Source LLC
Chambersburg PA
CBHW021136090426
42740CB00008B/805